B.C.

597

SCRIPTURE, TRADITION, AND INTERPRETATION

EVERETT F. HARRISON

SCRIPTURE, TRADITION, AND INTERPRETATION

*Essays Presented to Everett F. Harrison
by His Students and Colleagues
in Honor of His Seventy-fifth Birthday*

Edited by **W. Ward Gasque**

and **William Sanford LaSor**

William B. Eerdmans Publishing Company

Copyright © 1978 by Wm. B. Eerdmans Publishing Co.
255 Jefferson Ave. SE, Grand Rapids, MI 49503
All rights reserved
Printed in the United States of America

Library of Congress Cataloging in Publication Data
Main entry under title:

Scripture, tradition, and interpretation.

  Bibliography: p. 313.
  Includes index.
  1. Bible—Criticism, interpretation, etc.—Addresses,
essays, lectures. 2. Harrison, Everett Falconer,
1902– —Addresses, essays, lectures. 3. Harrison,
Everett Falconer, 1902– —Bibliography. I. Harrison,
Everett Falconer, 1902– II. Gasque, W. Ward.
III. LaSor, William Sanford.
BS540.S37   220.6   77-13335
ISBN 0-8028-3507-4

Contents

III. INTERPRETATION

Preface

The man in whose honor these essays are published has left a profound mark upon the lives of many colleagues, pupils, and friends. All of us have been deeply impressed by his careful scholarship, his unaffected piety, and his disciplined commitment to the ministry to which he has been called. In so many ways Everett F. Harrison, Emeritus Professor of New Testament at Fuller Theological Seminary, personifies the deepest aspirations of each of his students and associates who has contributed to this volume.

The nineteen essays gathered together in this *Festschrift* represent not only the high regard which many contemporary New Testament students, young and old, have for the recipient, but they also represent the theological and exegetical issues with which he has wrestled and upon which he has focused the attention of those who have sat at his feet. He has shared with us a love for the written Word of God which has been contagious, and he has constantly challenged us by example and by exhortation to resist the temptation to squeeze Scripture into a mold of our own creation.

Our hope is that by his written as well as spoken word, and by his quiet confidence, he will continue to be an inspiration to us and to others for many years to come.

The editors wish to acknowledge the assistance of Linda Hauch, Christine C. Jewett, Dallard Schindell, Elaine Schmitz, and Roger Stronstad, who have helped in a variety of ways with the copy-editing, proof-reading, indexing, and checking of bibliography.

W. WARD GASQUE
WILLIAM SANFORD LASOR

Abbreviations

Arndt	Arndt-Gingrich-Bauer, *A Greek-English Lexicon of the New Testament* (1957)
ASV	American Standard Version
BDPT	*Baker's Dictionary of Practical Theology* (1967)
Bibl	*Biblica*
BJRL	*Bulletin of John Rylands Library*
CmbF	*Cambridge Fish*
CBQ	*Catholic Biblical Quarterly*
CT	*Christianity Today*
CTM	*Concordia Theological Monthly*
Ectr	*Encounter*
Ety	*Eternity*
ETS	*Evangelical Theological Society*
Exp	*The Expositor*
EGT	*Expositor's Greek Testament*
ExpT	*The Expository Times*
GD	Bavinck, *Gereformeerde Dogmatiek* (1928)
HTR	*Harvard Theological Review*
HS	Berkouwer, *Holy Scripture* (1975)
IDB	*Interpreter's Dictionary of the Bible*
JAAR	*Journal of the American Academy of Religion*
JBL	*Journal of Biblical Literature*
JES	*Journal of Ecumenical Studies*
JETS	*Journal of the Evangelical Theological Society*
KJV	King James Version
Log	*Logos*
LXX	The Septuagint
MT	Masoretic Text
MM	*Moody Monthly*

NeoT	Neotestamentica
NBCR	New Bible Commentary Revised
NBD	New Bible Dictionary
NEB	New English Bible
NTS	New Testament Studies
NPNF	Nicene and Post Nicene Fathers
NovTest	Novum Testamentum
OthS	The Other Side
PA	Post American
PST	Kuyper, Principles of Sacred Theology (1968)
1QS	Manual of Discipline from Qumran 1
RefJ	The Reformed Journal
RevEx	Review and Expositor
RHPR	Revue d'Histoire et de Philosophie Religieuses
RSV	Revised Standard Version
Sem	Semitica
Soj	Sojourners
StudPat	Studia Patristica
StudEv	Studia Evangelica
StudTh	Studia Theologica
TDNT	Theological Dictionary of the New Testament
TSF	Theological Students Fellowship
ThStud	Theological Studies
ThLZ	Theologische Literaturzeitung
ThZ	Theologische Zeitschrift
TWNT	Theologisches Wörterbuch zum Neuen Testament (1932)
ThNN	Theology, News and Notes
TEV	Today's English Version
Vang	Vanguard
VoxEv	Vox Evangelica
ZNTW	Zeitschrift für die neutestamentliche Wissenschaft

Everett Falconer Harrison: A Tribute

DAVID ALLAN HUBBARD

Only one light was on in the row of faculty offices as I strolled down the hall. It was the afternoon of December 31, and the rest of Pasadena was girding itself for the Rose Parade and the Rose Bowl game. But not Everett Harrison. His lamp was on; his typewriter was busy. This would surprise no one who knows him. He has lived like that for the fifty years since his ordination as a Presbyterian minister in 1927.

Hard work and quiet enthusiasm have characterized Dr. Harrison's life from the beginning. The factors that account for this are many. His home was surely one. His father, Norman Baldwin Harrison, set a prodigious example of diligence for the whole family as missionary in Alaska (Everett was born at Skagway, July 2, 1902, during that period of missionary service), as pastor to Presbyterian churches in Seattle, Minneapolis, and St. Louis, and as an influential speaker and writer on Christian discipleship.

Everett's days at the University of Washington (A.B., 1923) gave him opportunity to establish his patterns of discipline. While majoring in Greek and minoring in history, he was active in numerous Christian organizations: University Presbyterian Church, Seattle, where he put his musical talents to work in the orchestra; Christian Endeavor; a Westminster Club which he helped to found for Presbyterian students; and especially the Student Volunteer Band, whose weekly 7:00 A.M. prayer meeting was a great source of spiritual fellowship and instruction in his life. In his last years in Washington, he preached in a small church in Manchester and then served as an assistant to Dr. W. A. Major of the Mt. Baker Park Presbyterian Church. Added to these assignments in ministry was a cluster of part-time jobs like postal clerk, longshoreman, traveling salesman (once for a book called *Farm Economy* and again for Wear-Ever aluminum cooking utensils), and foreman of a fruitpicking crew.

1

Everett Harrison continued his formal training for ministry at the Bible Institute of Los Angeles, Princeton Theological Seminary (Th.B., 1927), and Princeton University (M.A., 1927). His aptitude for languages was sharpened by extensive work in Semitics as well as in New Testament Greek. His classmates recall not only his diligence and his brilliance, but also his puckish humor. One story has it that Everett, who served as a teaching assistant to Robert Dick Wilson, was sent with orders to cancel a certain class that the professor could not meet. Instead, Harrison raffishly wrote a Hebrew quiz on the blackboard and chortled inwardly over the fact that he had captured for erudition an hour that might have been devoted to leisure!

Following a year in Canada as pastor of the River John Presbyterian Church in Nova Scotia, he began what was to be his lifetime service as a teacher. For nearly twenty years he taught at Dallas Theological Seminary, first in the area of Hebrew and Old Testament and later in the field of New Testament. Those years were enriched by two experiences which have contributed measurably to the impact of his ministry.

The first was a term of language study in Peking, China, followed by a year of teaching at the Hunan Bible Institute in Changsha, China (1930–32). There Everett and his bride (Arline Marie Prichard, whom he had married in St. Louis on June 30, 1930) were able to fulfill a call to mission overseas that had been sparked by the Student Volunteer Movement a decade earlier.

The second hiatus in his tenure at Dallas Seminary (Th.D., 1939), to which he returned from China in 1932, was an extensive term of pastoral activity and graduate study in the Philadelphia area from 1940 to 1944. Everett combined a fruitful pastorate at the Third Presbyterian Church of Chester, Pennsylvania, with graduate studies in Hellenistic Greek at the University of Pennsylvania (Ph.D., 1950). Both the mission station and the pulpit have cast their continuous shadow across his scholar's desk during the years of his ministry at Dallas and Fuller. Consequently neither his teaching nor his writing has been detached from the specific needs of his students. He has known firsthand what they will experience in struggling to communicate the gospel across cultural barriers and in troubled parishes.

It was in 1947 that Charles E. Fuller and Harold John Ockenga announced the founding of Fuller Theological Seminary in Pasadena, California. Integral to that announcement was the appointment of the four charter faculty members who were to work with President Ockenga: Wilbur M. Smith, Carl F. H. Henry, Harold Lindsell, and Everett F. Harrison. The move from Dallas was a substantial one— and for many reasons. Five in number, the Harrison children ranged in age from fifteen to five: Marjorie Estelle, Everett Falconer, Jr., James Prichard, Arline Marie, and Ruth Frances. The old black Cadillac sedan (complete with jumpseats) that ferried the family west became an institution from the day it lumbered into the driveway of Highgate, the original campus, and disgorged its passengers. Daniel P. Fuller, our founder's son and present colleague, and Carl F. H. Henry still witness with wide-eyed amazement to the Harrisons' sevenfold arrival.

From the days of the first class of thirty-seven to the present, when our student body has stretched to forty times that number, Harrison's name has been inextricably identified with Fuller. And for a host of reasons.

His wide knowledge and keen judgment have endeared him to each generation of students, many of whom have been inspired to follow the path of New Testament scholarship as their ministry. The tributes of some of them are offered in this book. I came to Fuller in its third class—1949. Since that time Everett Harrison has been one of my own heroes. Courses with him in the Septuagint and Paulinism rank among the finest academic experiences of my life. His dogged attention to detail and his sound analytical skill were models of careful scholarship. And no one could register firm disagreement with more gentleness when we apprentices tested our theories against his knowledge. So much respect did we have for him that it was a common saying among men of my vintage that, if we had to take all of our courses from one professor, Harrison would be the one.

Participation in the life of the Seminary at every level has been a constant contribution of his. The Monday morning faculty prayer meeting, the daily chapel, the routine committees, the social or recreational activities—all of these experiences have been blessed by his regular presence.

Two labors of love stand out in my memory. One is Everett's diligent engagement in the task of planning for our Graduate School of Psychology in the years before its founding in 1965. The other is his patient sharing in the discussions of a committee, first appointed by Harold Ockenga, to strengthen the Fuller Statement of Faith, which was finally approved in 1972. Years of arduous effort went into both of those—effort which Harrison expended with great good will, even though the quiet solitude of his study was a much more congenial environment to him than the rough-and-tumble deliberations of academic committees. Those, by the way, were the years when his scholar's lamp burned almost incessantly and his annual vacation periods averaged something like five days.

Though singularly dedicated to the work at Fuller, Dr. Harrison has always had an eye and a heart for the church worldwide. Much of what he has accomplished in writing and editing has had in view the needs of large sectors of Christ's body. The textbooks on New Testament introduction, the life of Christ, and the book of Acts are cases in point. The introduction has been translated into Italian and Chinese among other languages. The *Wycliffe Commentary,* the revision of *Alford's Greek New Testament,* and *Baker's Dictionary of Theology* have been widely used as reference sources throughout the English-speaking world. His clear eye for biblical interpretation and his keen ear for graceful English made him a valued member of the translation team that gave us the *New American Standard Bible* and the *New International Version.* And his sermons and pamphlets on suffering and other topics have circulated by the tens of thousands.

Whenever old grads gather from Dallas, Fuller, or Trinity Evangelical Divinity School, where Everett has taught from time to time in recent years, if the conversation turns to him, one phrase will surface quickly—his prayers. Tardiness has been more rare in Harrison's classes than anywhere else I know. Students simply do not want to miss the spiritual experience of hearing him pray. The lofty language, the biblical phrases, the unfeigned sincerity are only part of it. Most important is the sense of intimate awe of God and reverent friendship with him. Everett Harrison prays as one who knows God and who knows that such knowledge is life's highest treasure.

There is no accounting for such depth of faith apart from the suffering which has been his frequent companion. For years he battled the constant threat of iritis which hampered his reading and writing for days at a time. Ten years ago an attack of infectious arthritis confined him to bed and wheelchair for a couple of months. Painful beyond words was the loss of two of his children: Estelle in 1964 and Everett, Jr. in 1972. The firm and quiet trust that the Harrisons demonstrated in testing circumstances was more eloquent witness to God's sustaining grace than a shelf of sermons.

The ripeness that comes from suffering has room for humor. Puns as well as prayer are part of Everett's life. More than a few faculty deliberations have been enriched in their sanity by some subtle play on words which began as a twinkle in Harrison's eyes and ended in gales of rollicking laughter as his colleagues caught the nuances and clutched their sides.

In temperament, Arline Harrison seems ideally suited to live with Everett. At least she has been giving that impression for more than forty-five years. Her wit matches his. Her scholarly curiosity and teaching skills have given her a ministry alongside his. As a special teacher in the Pasadena public schools, Mrs. Harrison's list of courses looks like a whole curriculum—Spanish, French, German, English, Chinese, and Latin could be named for a start. As the grandmother of eight children and the great-grandmother of two, she continues to provide her special blend of love and wisdom to those for whom she cares. My own knowledge of Christian discipleship has been enhanced by thirty years of friendship with her.

Had I the power to give a substantial gift to each of our sister institutions—the Christian colleges and theological schools of our continent—it would be this: thirty years of service from a professor with the wit and wisdom, the piety and scholarship of Everett Harrison. This would be the highest kind of philanthropy. How many people are there who can discuss the various interpretations of an obscure New Testament *hapax legomenon* and the fine points of a Lakers' basketball game in the same conversation?

Ten years ago we noted Harrison's sixty-fifth birthday with a plaque and a promotion to a Senior Professorship. Five years ago we marked his seventieth milestone with the title Emeritus Professor and an oil portrait that hangs in the Weyerhaeuser Reading Room of our McAlister Library. Now we, his friends and admirers, present these essays as tokens of esteem to a beloved man who has enriched us all.

His schedule is so pressing, and his writing commitments so numerous, that it may take him some time to get to them all. We can assume, however, that anyone whose lamp blazes strong on New Year's Eve will crowd this bit of reading into his schedule along with the rest. As he does he will have a modest measure of our love and appreciation.

I. Scripture

1: Authority and Scripture

GEOFFREY W. BROMILEY

Most crises in the history of the Church have been crises of authority. The central question of past and present ecclesiastical conflicts has been that of identifying the locus of authority for the Church. The purpose of this essay is to give perspective to this debate, which continues to concern theologians and non-theologians, by examining the meaning of the term "authority" in the Scriptures, defining the limits of its biblical usage, setting forth the variety of interpretations historically applied to the term, and suggesting a model for interpreting authority to the Church today.

1. Definition

In biblical and Christian usage "authority" is predominantly the equivalent of the Greek *exousia* (from the verb *exestin*). "Power" in one of its senses can also be a rendering of the same Greek noun, although it more commonly represents the distinct, if materially related, *dynamis.* Other words that underlie the English "authority" are *epitagē*, "command" (Tit 2:15), *hyperochē* (1 Tim 2:2), *dynastēs* (Acts 8:27), and *authenteō* (1 Tim 2:12).

Primarily the verb *exestin* has two interconnected senses: "be free, unimpeded," and "have the right or permission," which may include moral as well as legal right. What is suggested is a possibility of doing (or not doing) something because there are no impediments and there is, positively, the necessary permission or authorization.

The noun expresses the same concepts as the verb. Hence the primary meaning of *exousia* is power to do something because nothing stands in the way. The difference from *dynamis* is that this is power based on extrinsic considerations, whereas *dynamis* is intrinsic ability. Nevertheless, the two terms obviously overlap in the power or capability itself.

The second meaning is naturally that of authorization. In this case the power has been conferred by a superior power, court, or norm, whether this be political (the king or ruler), judicial (the law), or something more general (e.g., custom). Authorized power, which may be conferred corporately as well as individually, constitutes a right. Within the political and social structure, for instance, this may be the right of officials, parents, property owners, or rulers, while in the cultural sphere it may be the right to act without question as custom allows.

Yet the right expressed by *exousia* is not abstract. It carries with it real power, even though this be extrinsically rather than intrinsically derived. The third nuance, then, brings once again a very close kinship to *dynamis.* In practice the real power based on authorization, or lack of obstacles, cannot easily be differentiated from the power that is innate. Negatively, potential obstacles might vary; but positively, the ability amounts to the same thing. Sometimes, of course, the source of power matters a great deal, as in a question whether the power of a ruler is innate or derived. In many practical instances, however, the source is of no account whatever. For this reason "power" can often be a better rendering of *exousia* than "authority" or "right," even though the latter might still be implied.

By a strange if not illogical development, *exousia* can come to stand in antithesis to law rather than dependence on it. This gives us the fourth sense, "freedom." At this point a tension between the first and second senses is resolved in favor of the first. What can authorize (e.g., custom), can also restrain or impede. Ability in the sense of freedom from external obstacle can thus mean freedom from external power, even though in another setting it might mean authorization by it.

A final important usage, however, rests on the second sense. This is the employment of *exousia* for "office," "office-bearer," "ruler," or, in the plural, "authorities." The main concept here is that of wielding a power conferred. The authorities are the offices— or, more properly, the officers—to whom power has been officially entrusted. It is perhaps worth noting that the term does not seem to be used for government as such.

2. Biblical Material

Two Hebrew words are translated "authority" in the Old Testament, but the examples are extraordinarily sparse and contribute little to the development of the concept. The first word, *rebôt*, occurs in Prov 29:2. The usual rendering is to the effect that the people rejoice when the righteous are "in authority" (participle of *rābâ*, "be great," "increase"). The second term, *tōqep*, is found in Esth 9:29. Here "full written authority" is given by Esther and Mordecai in confirmation of the second letter about Purim. A parallel statement in verse 32 says that the command of Queen Esther fixed these practices of Purim.

In the sphere of biblical and Judaic literature we find the normal uses of *exousia*. However, the LXX also made a distinctive application of the term, which from the standpoint of biblical and theological development was of almost incalculable significance. It found *exousia* the most suitable term to express the sovereignty of God (his complete freedom from all restraints) as distinct from his might or power. The Greek word thus acquired a new sense in which it came to stand not for authorization but for the absolute divine freedom that is also the source of all authorization. Even the regular meanings, then, were brought in the last analysis into a new theological relation.

In this regard the Greek word came to borrow in part from the Hebrew, which also seems to have shaped the LXX use of *exousia* for "sphere of power." Furthermore, *exousia* became virtually coextensive with the rabbinic *rešût*, which may well have made some contribution to the distinctive nuances of New Testament usage.

The most significant New Testament usage is the application of *exousia* to God as in the LXX. God has authority both in the sense that he has absolute possibility or freedom of action, being under neither necessity nor restraint, and also in the sense that he is the only ultimate source of all other authorization and power (cf. Luke 12:5; Acts 1:7; Jude 25). So complete is the authority of God that it may be compared with the power of the potter over the clay (Rom 9:21). In relation to the universe the authority of God is indeed that of creator as well as ruler. It is worked out in both nature and history. Thus God controls the natural and historical forces that fulfill his purposes (Rev 6:8; 9:3, 10, 19).

Thus far the New Testament does not differ substantially from the LXX in its use of *exousia*, or from rabbinic theology in its use of *rešût*. The same might be said when the term is specifically applied to subordinate powers or authorities (as in 1 Cor 15:24; 1 Pet 3:22; Eph 1:21), or to the civil authority exercised by kings, magistrates, priests, or stewards (as in Luke 7:8; Mark 13:34; Acts 9:14; Rom 13:1–3; Titus 3:1). Indeed, the same is still true when *exousia* is rather oddly used of Satan. In this connection "sphere of power" obviously comes into the picture, and yet also the sense of "authorization," or at least "permission," since neither the demonic nor the political world has the same kind of authority as God but can function only within or under the divine sovereignty. If in relation to evil or evil forces this creates a problem, it is plain that dualism would create a more serious problem. Hence the Bible makes it clear beyond question that all subsidiary forces, including Satan and his world, can have power only inasmuch as this is conferred by God. Even if antichrist seems to derive his authority from Satan (Rev 13:2), the final authority of God is always presupposed (cf. Luke 22:53).

If there is little new in all this, the situation changes radically when we come to the authority of Christ. To be sure, the power that Christ exercises within his earthly commission, for example, that of forgiving sins (Mark 2:10), or exorcism (3:15), or teaching (Matt 7:29), or judgment (John 5:27), is a power granted by the Father. The great truth brought to light in the New Testament, however, is that Christ is more than a man who is commissioned by God. He is himself God. This means that his authority, as divine authority, is also self-grounded.

The power he enjoys is thus the power of his own sovereignty in concert with that of the Father (John 10:18; Rev 12:10ff.). It is an absolute power free from all limitations (Matt 28:18). It is also a power that underlies all other authority, as in the charges of Christ to his disciples (Mark 6:7ff.) and to the apostles (John 20:22f.). The particular sphere of this power is the world of men (John 17:2), and it includes the right of final judgment (5:27). Recurrent references to the giving of this authority by the Father make it plain that no rivalry with God's power is intended. Absolute authority pertains to Christ, and indeed to the Holy Spirit too, because this authority is seen in fact to be one and the same as the authority of the Father; that is, it is the authority of the triune God.

Christ, however, is not alone. He is accompanied by the apostles whom he chose, associated with, and sent out with his own authorization. It is natural, then, that there should be an authority of the apostolate. This is supported by the practice of the apostles. It is also formulated expressly, not only in the charge of Mark 6:7, but also in the saying of Paul in 2 Cor 10:8 (cf. also Matt 10:1; Mark 3:15; 2 Thes 3:9).

This is not, of course, an absolute or inherent authority. It is an authority of commissioning by the Lord. Hence the elements of derivativeness and responsibility are prominent. The apostle is put in charge by his Lord, and it is essential that he make a proper use of his authority (cf. Mark 13:34). Nevertheless, the authority also carries with it certain rights, e.g., that of support by the churches (1

Cor 9:4ff.). More broadly, the teaching and guiding authority of the apostle is a mediation of the authority of Christ. His ministry is backed by Christ himself. This is what makes it possible. This is also what gives it incontestable validity in the Church.

If Christ is accompanied by the apostles, he is also accompanied by believers in general. It is not surprising, then, that the New Testament can also speak of the *exousia* of the Church and of individual Christians. What is surprising, however, is what is said about that authority. For Christians have the authority to become the children of God (John 1:12). The two primary senses of the word may both be seen here. On the one hand, they are given a new possibility that they could not have in themselves. On the other hand, they are granted a right or title. Inasmuch as they receive the one Son of God, they themselves have a legitimate sonship conferred upon them.

In addition, Christians are granted freedom in the sense of the right to do certain things (1 Cor 6:12). Now it is true that in the passages in 1 Corinthians Paul is more concerned about a right or wrong use of this "authority." We are to do what is appropriate and what is of service to edification. Nevertheless, even when faced by possible misuse, the apostle does not deny the authority as such. All things are indeed lawful even if all are not expedient and all do not edify. For this is a freedom, an authorization, a permission which Christ himself has conferred and which is received in faith: the freedom of the children of God. The true answer to misuse is not surrender but true and proper use. Although enigmatic, *exousia* in 1 Cor 7:37 might well be grouped in the same category.

3. Historical Survey

a. Early Church

The chief lesson of the New Testament—namely, that authority finally rests in God and that this authority is embodied in Jesus Christ—was learned well in the early Church. The Church grounded itself upon the fact that God in Jesus Christ stands behind both the faith that is believed and the faith that believes it. God in Jesus Christ is the authority that establishes the Christian life with its new possibilities; and God in Jesus Christ is Lord of the Church, exercising this lordship by the Holy Spirit, so that all decisions and actions, whether doctrinal or practical, must derive from him and take their validity from him. Whatever difficulties or ambiguities there might have been both in the first centuries and later, the authority of God was accepted and advocated as the fundamental principle.

A further lesson was also learned: that this authority is exercised through the apostles and the community. Even though serious divergence later arose, this common presupposition was always held. As God the Father sent Christ, so Christ commissioned, equipped, and sent the apostles. He gave them divine authority to preach the gospel, to instruct in Christian knowledge, and to exercise control over the churches. Apostolic right and privilege, of course, were not inherent power. The apostles had authority because they were authorized by God himself. Put another way, Christ exercised his own rule and authority through them.

Nevertheless, the death of the apostles posed a new question, one that received different answers, or at least an ambivalent answer, in the age of the fathers. The question was an obvious one: What is the locus of apostolic authority after the passing of the apostles themselves? How does God—Father, Son, and Spirit—exercise his own absolute authority in the post-apostolic Church? On whom or what does authorization come in succession to the apostles?

A single and straightforward answer to this question was difficult. For one thing, there seemed at the very outset to be two alternatives: (1) the apostolic writings, added to the existing and accepted canon of Old Testament Scripture, and (2) the ongoing authority of the Church, including the special authority vested in those who were set up apostolically as its pastors and teachers. Even if Scripture is adopted as the supreme and normative source, however, there are in the New Testament itself different forms and areas and levels of authority, and many issues—especially those of minor importance—will still have to be decided according to other criteria. On the other hand, if a greater function is ascribed to the Church, a variety of further alternatives opens up when the center of ecclesiastical authority is sought. Is it to be found in the community as such, in its bishops or ministers, in synods (local, provincial, or ecumenical), in creeds, in traditions, in the fathers, in a combination of these, or in one or the other according to the subject at issue?

As regards the fundamental choice between Scripture and the Church, it might seem that Scripture is a new factor that does not arise at all in what the New Testament itself has to say about *exousia.* In fact, however, the New Testament does recognize Scripture as the voice of God. As the Old Testament writers introduced their messages with the daring "Thus saith the Lord," so our Lord himself and the New Testament authors quote Old Testament statements as authoritative: "As Scripture says. . . ." It is natural and inevitable, then, that the immediate post-apostolic Christians should inherit the same approach to the Old Testament; and it is no less natural and inevitable that they should extend this approach to the works of the divinely commissioned and authorized apostles (works that later became the New Testament canon), finally introducing their copious quotations (as in *2 Clement* 2:4) with the time-honored formulas. In other words, all the holy writings came to be seen and accepted as an established form in which the authority of God, mediated through the biblical authors, should be permanently exercised in the Church.

In fact, the fathers are virtually unanimous in ascribing a normative role to Scripture as a primary source of revelation. In addition to the continuous appeal to Scripture in patristic writings, the care for a proper recognition of the New Testament canon, and the labor expended on exposition of the biblical books, one might quote the rejection of purely oral tradition in Irenaeus.[1] Athanasius also makes a distinction between the "holy and inspired writings," which are self-sufficient, and other works that are a commentary on them.[2] Origen states firmly: "We must needs call the holy scripture to witness; for our judgments and expositions without these witnesses are worthy no credit."[3] Basil asks that convincing and convicting words and deeds "be confirmed by the testimony of God's scriptures."[4] Augustine, referring to Cyprian's works, says that he "weighs them by the canonical writings."[5] John of Damascus, pointing to his basic authority, says: "All that was ever delivered by the law, the prophets, the apostles, and the evangelists, we receive, acknowledge, and give reverence unto them, searching nothing besides them."[6]

On the other hand, the fathers had a strong sense that authority resided also in the ongoing apostolic tradition as represented especially in the orderly ministry and the rule of faith. Irenaeus and Tertullian both found the appeal to this authority especially valuable in refutation of Gnosticism, for it provided an answer to Gnostics who would not accept Scripture but spoke of a secret tradition, a historico-geographical basis for the authenticity of orthodox teaching, and a useful hermeneutical principle in meeting Gnostic interpretations of Scripture. Tertullian can even complain that Scripture without tradition is ambiguous,[7] although both he and Irenaeus seem to view Scripture and tradition, or the rule of faith, as substantially the same thing, or at least as two different and complementary forms of the same thing.

The situation had changed, however, by the fourth century. If Basil of Caesarea demanded Scriptural confirmation, he also argued that the tradition preserved in Scripture is incomplete.[8] Jerome too, although he can speak strongly of the need for the authority and testimony of Scripture,[9] can refer at the same time to many things that are accepted on the basis of tradition alone.[10] Chrysostom even appeals to the Scriptures themselves (2 Thes 2:15) in support of the view that the apostles transmitted many things not put in writing.[11] Along different lines, Vincent of Lérins (d. before 450) finally subjects Scripture to the Church with his principle that, while Scripture is intrinsically adequate, a regulative interpretation is needed, this being supplied not by tradition alone but by the threefold criterion of what is held "everywhere, always, by all." As Barth observes,[12] the addition "by all" means, in effect, the enforcement of an official understanding; and this is the more dangerous in that Vincent's opposition to change does not rule out a progress controlled by the teaching office in its consensus. The significant point in all this is that not only has tradition emerged as supplementary to Scripture, but Scripture itself has been deprived of any effective authority through its hermeneutical subjection to the Church—or rather, in practice, to the Church's hierarchy.

b. Medieval West

The pattern set by Vincent of Lérins tended to dominate the understanding of authority throughout the Middle Ages. In the West it resulted in a tilting of the scales in favor of the authority of the Church. This may be seen at four points. First, a more or less general acceptance of the fourfold scheme of exegesis helped to shackle the Bible by making its exposition extremely complicated. Second, dogmatic definitions such as that of transubstantiation promoted development under alien norms beyond the limits of legitimate interpretation. Third, canon law codified ecclesiastical authority in an effective, practical form that enhanced the power of the hierarchy. Finally, the papacy, while challenged from time to time, as in the Conciliar Movement of the fourteenth century, focused ultimate authority on the bishop of Rome both as heir to the supreme apostolic authority of Peter and also, on this basis, as vicar of Christ himself, enjoying and exercising the plenitude of power that properly belongs to the Lord. Naturally, these developments met with opposition. The Eastern Churches provided some counterbalance with their stress on the authority of the ecumenical synods. The limits of allegorical exegesis were frequently recognized. On political as well as ecclesiastical and doctrinal grounds, challenges were issued again and again against the papal claims. The unfortunate thing, however, is that for many years these forces were not sufficient to put up effective resistance against the Church's exploitation of its own authority in all branches of ecclesiastical life in the West.

Thus the development of doctrine ineluctably led to changes, and even innovations, which Vincent of Lérins had neither anticipated nor desired. Medieval practice, while authorized and commanded by canon law, seemed in the event to produce a monstrous caricature of New Testament Christianity. The Church's authoritative exposition of Scripture turned out to be far from infallible when brought under the scrutiny of Renaissance scholarship, which also served to spotlight the vast difference between medieval practice and thinking on the one side, and that of the apostolic Church on the other.

c. Reformation

Once the issues began to come out into the open with Luther's theses of 1517 and the ensuing controversy, it quickly became apparent that the protest involved a drastic rethinking of the way in which Christ's authority is exercised and particularly of the relationship between Scripture and Church in the mediation of apostolic authority to and through the post-apostolic community. The reformers cannot deny, of course, that the Church and its various expressions (e.g. ministry, confessions, synods, and fathers) do have a lawful measure of authority. Their contention is, however, that it is in and through the prophetic and apostolic writings of Holy Scripture that God exercises supreme and ultimate authority in the Church, whether in doctrine or practice. Other authorities are subsidiary and derivative.

The Reformation confessions make this point and bring out its ramifications with a happy blend of force, comprehensiveness, and conciseness. Thus the French Confession (1559) states that "the Word contained in these books receives its authority from God alone" and that "all things should be examined, regulated, and reformed according to these books." The Belgic Confession (1561) approves the Scriptures "because the Holy Ghost witnesseth in our hearts that they are from God"; with them nothing can be compared, and "whatsoever doth not agree with this infallible rule" is to be rejected. The Westminster Confession (1647) concludes its more extended discussion with the notable statement (I, 10) that the supreme judge in controversies and in the examinations of Church decisions "can be no other but the Holy Ghost speaking in the scripture." This accords with the earlier teaching of Heinrich Bullinger in the Second Helvetic Confession (1566) that in matters of faith "we cannot admit any other judge than God himself, pronouncing by the holy scripture what is true. . . ." The Epitome of the Lutheran Formula of Concord (1576) advances a similar understanding: "We believe, confess, and teach that the only rule and norm according to which all dogmas and all doctors ought to be esteemed and judged is no other whatever than the prophetic and apostolic writings of both the Old and the New Testament. . . . Holy scripture alone is acknowledged as the judge, norm, and rule according to which, as by the (only) touchstone, all doctrines are to be examined and judged." As Quenstedt puts it, Holy Scripture is judge as the voice of the supreme and infallible Judge, the Holy Spirit.

As noted, a proper place can be found for secondary authorities. Both the Scots Confession (1560) and the Anglican Articles (1571) may be quoted in favor of the common view that the Church has authority to institute and reform traditions, "so that nothing be ordained against God's word." The Second Helvetic Confession, too, concedes that in the interpretation of Scripture the fathers and councils should be taken into account, so long as the duty of modest dissent is recognized when they set down things not in agreement with the Scriptures.

To summarize, three points are made here. First, absolute authority lies with God himself, exercised through Christ and the Holy Spirit. Second, the voice of God is heard primarily in Holy Scripture, not merely because this is historically the first and authentic deposit of the prophetic and apostolic record, but because God himself has raised it up to fulfill this purpose. Third, subsidiary authorities have a valid function, but discharge it properly only in submission to the divine authority expressed primarily in and through Scripture.

Unfortunately, Roman Catholicism did not accept—nor even perhaps understand—this position. It naturally did not dispute the supreme authority of Christ. It also gave to Scripture an eminent place. Yet even in the Reformation age it defended its doctrines and practices by invoking the complementary authorities of fathers and tradition. Thus, in the Leipzig Disputation (1519) Eck hurled not only texts but also the interpretations of the fathers against Luther and accused him of arrogance when, faced by the latter, "he contradicted them all without a blush, and said that he would stand alone against a thousand." As regards tradition, the Council of Trent took the decisive step in Session IV (1546) when it made the pronouncement: "This synod receives and venerates, with equal pious affection, all the books both of the New and the Old Testaments, since one God is the author of both, together with the said traditions, as well those pertaining to faith as those pertaining to morals. . . ." According to this dogma, traditions found in apostolic sees such as Rome can also claim to be of apostolic or even dominical origin, even though not preserved in the apostolic writings; and they may thus be accorded a status equal to that of written Scriptures.

In the post-Reformation era, however, the Roman understanding of authority has taken a different turn. Greater stress has been laid on the authority of the Church than on tradition. Already in Reformation days it was argued that Christians accept Scripture basically because it has been authored and authorized by the Church. For a time, indeed, the curious and self-destructive thesis was advanced in some circles, that by reason of its obvious fallibility Scripture would not be credited without the Church's backing. Later, attention shifted back again to the interpretative role of the Church, or of the Church's teaching office, and finally of the pope. The argument here is simple. Scripture is indeed the ultimate norm. Nevertheless, the Church, enlightened by the Holy Spirit, has the task of correctly expounding and applying Scripture. In this task it is guided and governed by its head. Its ultimate Head, of course, is Christ himself; but in terms of Christ's earthly representation the head is Peter's successor, the bishop of Rome. The infallibility decree of 1870 brings this understanding to its logical conclusion and climax: "The Roman Pontiff, when he speaks *ex cathedra* [i.e., when in fulfilling the office of Pastor and Teacher of all Christians on his supreme apostolical authority, he defines a doctrine concerning faith or morals to be held by the Universal Church], through the divine assistance promised him in blessed Peter, is endowed with that infallibility, with which the divine Redeemer has willed that His Church—in defining doctrine concerning faith or morals—should be equipped: and therefore, such definitions of the Roman Pontiff of themselves—and not by virtue of the consent of the Church—are irreformable." What is biblical is held to be authoritative. In the last resort, however, the pope expounds and declares what is biblical. Effective authority thus comes to be vested not in Scripture but in its hermeneutical master, whose decisions are final and irrevocable.

d. Liberal Protestantism

The modern age has brought different but no less radical challenges through the Liberal Protestantism that began to flourish in the latter part of the seventeenth century. In an early form this involved the exaltation of human reason to a highly authoritative role in doctrinal and moral teaching. On this view "reason is not less from God than revelation; 'tis the candle, the guide, the judge he has lodged within every man that cometh into the world."[13] To the dictates of reason, then, revelation itself must submit.[14] God himself maintains ultimate authority. Here, however, he exercises it in a completely different way, choosing reason rather than Church or Scripture as his primary instrument. A problem, of course, is that reason can just as easily exalt itself against God so that he himself comes under its dictates. This is precisely what happened in many circles in the rational subjectivism of the eighteenth century, which made autonomous man the ultimate arbiter of all truth.

As it turned out, the older rationalism proved much less than adequate when it came under the scrutiny of Hume's scepticism and the epistemological analysis of Kant. Other expressions of human domination thus arose to replace it in the form of the so-called religious *a priori* in man. Kant's moral imperative, Schleiermacher's sense of absolute dependence, and the consciousness of Hegel's religious philosophy all play this role. Common to all these self-contradictory reconstructions is the refusal to let God alone be the true authority even in the things of God and the committal of this authority to man, whether corporately or in the highly individualistic form in which each man fashions and chooses his own God—or even proclaims the total absence of God in the form of the secularization or humanization of the gospel.

e. New Alternatives

Between the extremes of Roman ecclesiasticism and Liberal subjectivism some great alternatives to the Reformation view have been attempted. Building on one aspect of the Reformation appeal, some movements have proposed the authority of an early Catholic consensus somewhat along the lines of Eastern Orthodoxy. Anglican groups have been leaders in this field. With their fears of the evils of private judgment, the Mercersburg theologians in North America, especially Nevin, worked along not dissimilar lines although with a stronger emphasis on the authority of Holy Scripture. The difficulty, of course, is that consensus among the fathers is hard to come by, and even if it is attained there is no reason to suppose that the early Church was any less fallible than the medieval or modern Church. On many occasions, even in early days, the minority has been right and the majority tragically wrong. Such attempts to achieve consensus might even result in the absurdity that the expert in church history becomes the new pope.

Pietism, on the other hand, has tended at some points to seek authority in evangelical experience. This canon might be applied apologetically: Christianity is true because I have found it so in my own life. It might also be applied in relation to aspects of Christian practice: this form of worship is the right one because it is the most meaningful to me. The ministry can be conducted along the same line: we ought to follow this or that course of action because it works out best in the actual experience of the individual or Church. Even biblical interpretation can be subjected to the same canon: the right meaning of a verse or passage is that from which I derive doctrinal, devotional, or practical benefit. Fortunately, experience has seldom, if ever, been set up as a final or sole authority, for it obviously gives rise to rampant individualism and anthropocentricity with its assertion that God exercises his authority specifically through me and Scripture is an infallible rule of faith and practice according to my particular interpretation. At the same time, the chaos of conflicting experiences produces an inevitable crisis of authority when God is apparently saying different things to different individuals, and thousands of "popes" are claiming infallible discharge of the teaching office.

Roman Catholicism, under the pressure of its new stress on biblical study, has been forced to do some rethinking on the matter of authority. The interrelation of oral and written tradition has come under new discussion, especially in relation to early patristic thinking. Sharp differences have arisen on the sources of revelation, and the view has even been advanced (e.g., by Hans Küng) that Scripture has always been the primary source according to true Catholic theology. The infallibility of the pope has also been called in question, either in itself, or in its exercise apart from the official participation of other bishops, priests, or even the Church as a whole. If few positive results have thus far been achieved in this process, the rigidity of the Tridentine statement and the Infallibility Definition has been broken and important modifications are by no means out of the question.

Possibly the most constructive of recent dogmatic contributions to the theme of authority is to be found in the section that Karl Barth devotes to it in his *Church Dogmatics, I/2*. This section falls within the chapter on Holy Scripture as the second of the three forms of the Word of God (the Word revealed, written, and preached). Authority is thus considered specifically in relation to the Word—first as the authority *of* the Word and secondly as authority *under* the Word. (The parallel section on the freedom of the Word and freedom under the Word offers some important complementary insights.)

As regards the authority of the Word, Barth first deals with the question whether Scripture can claim precedence of authority simply by virtue of its historical position as the apostolic deposit. He concludes that at best this argument can yield only an indirect, formal, and relative authority, which can make Scripture only the first among equal competitors. Final authority resides with the revelation event itself, the first form of the Word of God. Nevertheless, this revelation stands in a unique relation to the prophets and apostles, and therefore to their writings too, since both the men and their works were raised up by God specifically to be witness to revelation, and hence to be God's written Word. In virtue of this unparalleled relationship between event and witness, Scripture has then a direct, material, and absolute authority that marks it off from all its competitors. Even preaching, as the third form of God's Word, cannot be its rival in this regard, since the preached Word is known only from the written Word. Thus the written Word has a normative function in relation to the preached Word.

As regards authority *under* the Word, Barth's main point is that subsidiary authorities cannot be in competition with the authority of the written Word but are in fact established by it. This applies primarily and prototypically to the Church, which undeniably has authority but which derives this authority wholly from the Word, i.e., by authorization. This authority then comes to focus in the Church's confession, which is not a rival authority, nor a hermeneutical norm, nor indeed a sum of biblical teaching, but the Church's hearing of the Word. Finally, it takes historical form in the canon, in fathers old and new, and in the historical confessions. All these are relative, indirect, and formal authorities. All stand under, and must be tested by, the supreme authority of the Word. All are thus reformable in principle, as the written Word, in virtue of its unique relation to revelation, is not.

4. Civil Authority

Concentration on the problems of ecclesiastical authority should not cause us to overlook the fact that civil authority has also constituted a difficulty throughout Christian history. The New Testament, in Romans 13, gave recognition to the divinely given authority of civil office-bearers. However, it was not long before conflicts arose between the authority of Church and state—especially with the rise of professedly Christian rulers from the time of Constantine, and consequent approximations to the Old Testament model—and a demarcation of authority was demanded.

In the Middle Ages the divine authorization of rulers found expression in the idea of the Holy Roman Empire and in the impressive coronation rituals. At the same time, however, the popes resisted the attempt of temporal rulers to interfere in ecclesiastical matters, since such interferences usually made the Church subservient to political and material interests. This was the reason for the drastic medieval principle of a separation of Church and state, which went to the length of excluding the clergy from secular justice and taxation as well as ensuring that churches and monasteries would not come under military attack. Rulers, of course, opposed this obvious threat to their own supremacy, finding in the pretensions of the clergy an infringement on their rightful temporal and spiritual authority and responsibility; and they constantly played a part in church matters wherever these had obvious civil implications.

The more powerful popes tried to solve the problem by arguing that while the powers are separate, the ecclesiastical power is superior. Gregory VII (1073–1085) was already claiming the right, as the vicar of Christ, to depose or set up rulers. Innocent III (1198–1216), who imposed this right more successfully, compared Church and state to the two lights of Genesis 1, the Church being the greater light, the sun, and the state the lesser light, the moon, which draws its radiance from the sun. Boniface VIII (1294–1303) put the matter even more forcefully in his bull *Unam Sanctam* (1302), when he stated that the two swords—the temporal and the spiritual—are both in the hands of Peter, the one to be used *by* the Church and the other *for* it. He failed dismally, however, in his attempt to bring England and France under this rule.

A sharp reversal of this position came with the Reformation period when the reformers, often finding civil rulers more ready to instigate reforms than the clergy, recalled the godly princes of the Old Testament and saw it as within the authority of Christian magistrates, and indeed as their duty, to take action for the spiritual welfare of their subjects. Thus Luther leaned on the electors of Saxony; Zwingli brought about reformation through the city council of Zurich; and Henry VIII set a pattern in England that led ultimately to the authorization of the prayer book and articles by crown and parliament as well as by convocation.

Nevertheless, the reformers were not unaware of the dangers of this course. Rulers might be ill-disposed to the gospel, or to some aspects of it, as Calvin found in his dealings both with the Geneva councils and with the French crown. They might also use reformation to their own selfish ends, as Cranmer and Ridley learned to their own cost when Northumberland would not permit the proper redeployment of ecclesiastical endowments. Furthermore, even in their exercise of civil authority they might indulge in wicked or despotic actions. An attempt was thus made to set the limits of temporal power by subjecting it plainly to God, from whom it derives, and to the Word of God, which is its norm. Heinrich Bullinger of Zurich states the position forcefully and clearly in *Decades* 2. He argues that distinctions should be made between "the office, which is the good ordination of God, and the evil person."

Tyranny should not be tolerated on the ground that "it is of God." As every magistrate "is ordained of God, and is God's minister, so he must be ruled by God, and be obedient to God's holy word and commandment."

In the last resort this means that an evil power may be resisted or, finally, overthrown, so long as this is done responsibly. Unlike the Lutherans and Anglicans, the Reformed were thus prepared for the extreme action of civil revolt as this found historical expression in the overthrow of Mary Guise in Scotland, the war of independence in Holland, and the unfortunate civil wars in France. It was emphasized, however, that resistance to the powers is justified only when the gospel is threatened or excessive tyranny is enforced. Patient submission to authority, or, at the most, passive resistance in religious matters, was seen to be the biblical rule.

The Reformed understanding, as Bullinger succinctly states it, tries to avoid the clash of ecclesiastical and civil power by relativizing both in the same way. As the Church derives its authority from God, so does the state. Neither has inherent power. Neither, indeed, has power that can ever become independent of the God who gives it. The freedom of God is not restricted by the authorization that he grants. The human institution thus authorized is no autonomous competitor. If it draws its right and power from God, it does so only in subjection to the rule which God still exercises by his Word.

The so-called radical reformers, of course, approached the matter very differently. Certain violent leaders attempted a fusion of religious and civil authority in Münster, the "new Jerusalem," the kingdom of the saints; but when this proved to be illusory, the dominant motif became the strict separation advocated and practiced by the Swiss and South German Anabaptists. On this view the secular authorities are ordained by God, but their function of restraint and force is incompatible with true Christianity. They are to be honored and obeyed in virtue of their divine ordination, but Christians can have no part in their work and must not become entangled in the evils of temporal office. If a conflict arises between civil authority and true Christianity, no resistance is to be offered; but the authority of God must also take precedence, so that patient endurance of persecution is the only legitimate course. In no circumstances are the children of the light to make use of the weapons of the present world, since their victory will come in and through affliction and by the weapons of spiritual warfare. With the emergence of the modern secularist state and pluralist society, the thinking of the radical reformers has taken on new relevance today, although whether or not there should be abstraction from all temporal exercise of power is a question to which very different answers obviously will be given.

5. Conclusion

It might be accepted as a basic principle that God exercises authority through the Word. In the ultimate sense, since Christ is the Word, the Word is God himself. God exercises his own authority. Nevertheless, the Word takes form not only in the Incarnation but also in the words spoken and written by the prophets and apostles, that is, in the Scriptures of the Old Testament and New Testament. These words or Scriptures, having divine authorization, carry the authority of God himself. Similarly, being God's Word, they have the freedom of God, not innately or inherently, but in virtue of their divine authorship or authorization.

God also exercises his authority through the Church and its confessions, rulings, and teachings. Here again one might say that since the Church is Christ's body, Christ himself is the Church. In the Church, therefore, Christ exercises his own authority. At the same time, in terms of its human members and structures, the Church does not have the same immediate authorization as the apostles and prophets. It has indirect authorization by the Word of God that gave it birth and that comes through the prophetic and apostolic words. Hence the freedom it enjoys is, as Barth observes, freedom under the Word, not freedom from or over the Word. The Church achieves its true authority not when it makes a direct claim to declare the voice of God, but when it seeks to speak God's Word in accordance with the Word already spoken and written, so that the authority with which it is invested is authentically that of the Word.

In another sense and sphere, civil authorities are also means by which God exercises his authority. Outside the sphere of revelation, rulers have only an indistinct and perverted apprehension of this truth. They thus tend to think in terms of absolute or inherent power or to confuse divine authorization with a transferred right to do all things at will. This can raise acute problems for the Church and can produce the clash of authority that brings tension, persecution, or compromise. Even where rulers are Christians and know clearly the source of their authority, they may still fail to see that this authority can be properly exercised only according to the Word of God and within the sovereign authority that God always reserves for himself. This is equally true no matter what the human form of authority might be.

God grants authorization, but in so doing he does not reduce or transfer his own divine authority. Neither church nor state, then, has any mandate for tyranny. Neither church nor state can issue any edict it pleases and demand absolute submission on the basis of divine authorization. Indeed, even Holy Scripture, for all the uniqueness of its origin and role, is not to be treated as though it had autonomous authority apart from God himself, who is its ontic, noetic, and dynamic basis. God indeed rules through Scripture. The ultimate stress, however, lies not on Scripture but on the God who rules. "To the only God, our Savior through Jesus Christ our Lord, by glory, majesty, dominion, and authority, before all time and now and for ever. Amen" (Jude 25).

NOTES

1. *Adversus omnes haereses* III.ii.1.
2. *Contra Gentes* 1.
3. *Homiliae in Jeremia* 1.
4. *Moralia* xxvi.1.
5. *Contra Cresconium grammaticum Donatistam* ii.32.
6. *De fide orthodoxa* 1.
7. *De praescriptione haereticorum* 19.
8. *De Spiritu Sancto* 27, 66; cf. Epiphanius, *Adversus lxxx haeresus* Lxi.6.
9. *Commentary on Haggai* 1.
10. *Dialogus contra Luciferianos* 8.
11. *Homily 4 on 2 Thessalonians.*
12. *Church Dogmatics*, I/2, pp. 550f.
13. Toland, *Christianity Not Mysterious* (1696).
14. M. Tindal, *Christianity As Old As the Creation* (1730).

2: On "Q" and the Cross

CHARLES E. CARLSTON

1. A Synoptic Overview

Several years ago I read a story of a student who was suspected of cheating on exams. The evidence became conclusive, it seems, when the student from whom he was apparently copying his answers wrote on a particular question, "I don't know." The hapless copyist wrote, "I don't know, either," and the case was closed.

It is something like this that has led practically all New Testament scholars to recognize that the gospels of Matthew, Mark, and Luke must somehow be related to one another literarily. Though Jesus probably understood Greek, he almost certainly preached in Aramaic; and when Greek translations of his words agree almost verbatim, it is neither wise nor necessary to assume that such translations were all made independently. In other words, if our gospels were all Aramaic documents, we might assume that they agree in wording precisely because the words are simply identical with Jesus' own words, transmitted—under the guidance of the Holy Spirit—unchanged throughout the decades until they were finally written down in our gospels. But since our present gospels are in Greek, this explanation will not do. Most of us have some idea of the meaning of non-English sayings like *sic semper tyrannus* or *honi soit qui mal y pense;* but the likelihood is not great that any three of us would produce nearly identical translations of even these brief phrases, to say nothing of whole paragraphs. What we are dealing with in the gospels is, to return to our story, something like the "I don't know, either" phenomenon.

If this is as evident as it seems to most people to be, it should be fairly easy (at least in theory) to deduce what that necessary literary relationship is. And most, though by no means all, New Testament scholars hold that at least one item in solving the puzzle is fairly clear: Matthew and Luke both read Mark and used Mark's gospel as a major source in constructing their own words. Hence, when either Matthew or Luke or both agree in wording of events with Mark, we may assume that they are following that source in their work.

Yet when one reads the first three gospels side by side it is evident that while most of Mark (statistically, nearly 90% of it) is in either Matthew or Luke or both, there is still a great deal of material in both Matthew and Luke which does not occur in Mark and which therefore can hardly have come from there. How shall we explain that? Obviously, *if* this material, common to Matthew and Luke but not found in Mark, is so nearly identical in the first and third gospels that some literary relationship must be postulated,[1] there are, logically, only three possibilities: (a) Matthew used Luke, (b) Luke used Matthew, or (c) they both used something else. For various technical reasons it does not seem likely that either evangelist used the other, in which case only (c) remains. It is this something else, this second source (besides Mark) of Matthew and Luke, that scholars have dubbed "Q" (from the German word *Quelle,* source).

Q, in other words, is a construct, a source which seems a necessary postulate in explaining why at so many places Matthew and Luke agree in both order and wording in material that they could not have gotten from Mark and apparently did not get from one another. It would be nice, of course, if some itinerant archeologist were to discover a copy of the document; but it seems highly improbable that such a discovery will ever be made. Thus we are restricted in our questioning of this presumed document to logic and careful literary analysis. Obviously, such analysis is not easy, and competent scholars differ on details as the analysis is pursued. Yet it is fair to say that the great majority of New Testament scholars today think that such a document once existed and that much of its content can be approximately reconstructed.

A rough sketch of Q's contents would run something like this:[2] It begins with the warning of John the Baptist (Luke 3:7–9 = Matt 3:7–10) and ends with promises and warnings about the coming of the Son of Man (Luke 17:23–27, 33–37 = Matt 24:26f., 37–39, 40f., 28; 10:39), though conceivably it could have ended with the parable of the Talents (Luke 19:12–26 = Matt 25:14–29) or the short saying about the Twelve Thrones (Luke 22:28–30 = Matt 19:28). (It could also have been very much longer than this and ended with a narrative of the passion, since endings of ancient documents were easily lost and since Matthew and Luke *might* have read the ending of Q and simply preferred some other sources for the conclusion of their gospels. What is important to note, however, is that there is no clear evidence that Q ever had a passion narrative.) Q includes narratives of the Temptation (Luke 4:1–13 = Matt 4:1–11) and of the visit of John's disciples (Luke 7:19–23 = Matt 11:2–6) as well as two healing miracles, the centurion's servant (Luke 7:1–10 = Matt 8:5–10, 13) and the (blind and) dumb demoniac (Luke 11:14–23 = Matt 12: 22–30). All the rest of what we may plausibly postulate as Q, except for a few very short and rather unimportant phrases, is sayings-material, most of it without any historical context or geographical setting.

It is this latter detail that has caused the greatest interest almost since Q's existence was first postulated. We are familiar with four gospels in the New Testament that contain sayings of Jesus; but such sayings are encased in a narrative framework, with occasional notices of time and place and a distinct movement from beginning to end, from Galilee to Jerusalem. In Q such a narrative framework—indeed, most narrative of *any* kind—is missing. What kind of document was Q, then, and what kind of community might have created or used it and for what purpose?

2. The Purpose of Q

To this question, unfortunately, no unanimously acceptable answer has yet been given. Its purpose, for example, has been variously described as providing instruction for preachers or for new converts, "wisdom," ethical instruction, consolation, and much else. Some scholars think of it as coming from a group of Christians who had formerly been Jews; others think the original community behind it was probably made up largely of Gentile Christians; some think it impossible to decide between the two; and some think a sharp distinction between "Jewish-Christian" and "Gentile-Christian" is either misleading or meaningless in any case.[3]

At one significant point, however, something like a consensus seems to be emerging; and this point raises a theological question of some interest. In this emerging consensus[4]—if we may speak somewhat more unambiguously than the data really justify—Q's *theological* purpose may be sketched somewhat as follows: In the early church there were many who collected and used the sayings of Jesus primarily as wisdom-sayings. For such people, the framework within which Jesus was interpreted was the Wisdom-myth, a very widespread view with both Jewish and non-Jewish elements according to which Wisdom came to earth, was rejected by those whom she sought, and returned again to the place from which she had come. The developed form of this myth, it is held, can be seen in Gnosticism, particularly in many of the documents discovered at Nag Hammadi. But fragments of it can be seen in the Old Testament, in post-biblical Jewish literature, and even in the New Testament itself, as well as in some second- and third-century Christian literature. On this view, Jesus is first understood as Wisdom's envoy (Q) and then as identical with Wisdom itself (Matthew).[5] In other words, Q reflects a tendency, known elsewhere in early Christian literature but particularly clear in Gnosticism, to concentrate not on the death of Jesus but on his teaching and to understand the resurrection not as the overcoming of sin and death but as the vindication of God's envoy and the validation of his ministry.

What shall we say to these things? Clearly the interpretation has much to commend it. A substantial amount of material in the first three gospels clearly fits into the category of "wisdom-sayings": "He that hath, to him shall more be given"; "Where the carcass is, there the vultures will gather"; and so on. Naturally, those who saw no special significance in Jesus' ministry put such sayings alongside those proverbs and axioms known in all cultures for setting forth a general ethos if not always a concrete rule of conduct.[6] But those who saw him as God's special messenger could hardly rest content with this; and ready to hand, as an abundance of widely scattered and disparate materials show, was a view that Wisdom can be thought of as a person. Readers of Proverbs had long noticed chapter 8: "Does not Wisdom call? . . . 'To you, O men, I call, and my cry is to the sons of men.' . . . The Lord created me at the beginning of his work, the first of his acts of old" (vv. 1, 4, 22). And scholars have found varied uses of this scheme in practically every kind of ancient thought from which the early Christians might have drawn in working out fitting expressions of their convictions about who Jesus Christ was. When one notes in addition that second- and third-century Christian thought, both "orthodox" and "heretical," did the same thing, one can hardly have any objection to the possibility, even probability, that wisdom-materials of various kinds may have served in the construction of Christian thought in its earliest formative stages.

In addition, this "consensus" enables us to interpret a few very difficult texts that otherwise do not yield easily to careful analysis. Luke 7:35 (= Matt 11:19), for example, "Yet wisdom is justified by her children," is best perceived as seeing both John the Baptist and Jesus, in different ways, as "justifying" not an abstraction but a "person." Not, of course, a human being with a datable past and a concrete present, but a non-historical personified power who is ordinarily rejected by those to whom she comes but "justified" by John and Jesus. A very similar pattern can easily be discerned behind the passage in which the Wisdom of God notes that those whom she has sent have commonly been rejected by God's people (Luke 11:49–51; 13:34 = Matt 23:34–37). And even passages where Wisdom is mentioned only indirectly (Luke 11:31f. = Matt 12:41f.) or not at all (Luke 10:21f. = Matt 11:25–27) make very good sense when one understands a pattern of wisdom-thought behind them. After all, the earliest Christians had to use what conceptual categories were available in expressing their understanding of Christ—no multi-volume systematic theologies were available for the purpose, a fact that does not seem seriously to have incapacitated them!—and just as they wrote Greek instead of English, so also they used ancient rather than twentieth-century materials as building blocks.

Yet two theological problems arise for the Christian who would try to use these particular categories. One is that Wisdom somehow never quite touches ground, never really becomes a part of human history in all its concrete reality. The other is that seeing Christ as Wisdom's envoy leaves open the possibility that he is one among others, perhaps at most *primus inter pares*, not ultimately different from those who have gone before and perhaps not really distinguishable from some who might come after. It is probable that even those who compiled Q were aware of this problem, as we shall see below; but first a closer look at a text might be useful.

The description of Wisdom in *Sirach* 24 is justly famous:

> I came forth from the mouth of the Most High,
>   and covered the earth like a mist.
> I dwelt in high places,
>   and my throne was in a pillar of cloud.
> Alone I have made the circuit of the vault of heaven
>   and have walked in the depths of the abyss. . . .
> Along all these I sought a resting place;
>   I sought in whose territory I might lodge (vv. 3–5, 7, RSV).

This passage, which, as Conzelmann has shown,[7] is surely related somehow to the myth of Isis, portrays Wisdom as acting in both earth and heaven. Most early Christian theology understood Jesus similarly. But the "earth" is not understood in quite the same way, and even those Christians who (like Paul) paid comparatively little attention to the details of Jesus' life in Galilee would have found it difficult to understand Jesus as having shared human experience only in so tangential a fashion as this. Sirach, to be sure, is not a "gospel"; but neither was Q, and it must be asked whether any community collecting sayings about Jesus would have felt free to construct *any* kind of writing which has so completely lost contact with the ordinary world.

There is not much narrative in Q, and even what little there is, is often subordinated to the surrounding sayings or minimized almost to the vanishing point. But it does not quite vanish. And at the end of history Jesus comes as Son of Man to judge "this generation," to separate out those whose "wisdom" is shown in their having watched for his coming. In other words, even if the Son of Man sayings represent a late stage in the tradition behind Q, these sayings reflect already a partial corrective to a totally non-historical understanding of Jesus as well as to any theology that would leave open the possibility of Wisdom's embodiment in some other, later figure. Analysis of other forms of the Wisdom-myth or its antecedents or components[8] would show pretty much the same differences.

3. Conclusion

And thus we return to the theological question. Suppose that what we have sketched here is approximately correct. Then some early Christians selected fragments of wisdom-traditions for expressing their understanding of Jesus' significance, seeing him first as Wisdom's envoy and then as identical with Wisdom itself. Q goes slightly further even than this, adding some stress on Jesus' coming as Son of Man in judgment, associating Jesus in some way with John the Baptist (note the possibility that the *beginning* of Q, as well as its ending, has been partially lost), and a bit of narrative material. Matthew and Luke complete the process, inserting Q into a basically Marcan framework and thus rendering very difficult any more development in a "mythological" direction. Now Jesus is seen primarily within a narrative framework that includes his life and death, the reality of his suffering, and (in baptism, the Eucharist, and preaching) some spelling out of the implications of these events for the life of believers. How are we to decide whether this development was a happy one?

Surely not by historical means. On historical grounds one can say only that one form of the faith rather than another was preserved. And on theological grounds one can concede that Christianity itself has probably always been somewhat broader than any particular theological definition might suggest; this, given the theological climate in some evangelical circles, would probably be salutary for us anyway.

But in the last analysis we would do well to affirm, with Catholic

Christianity, that the Scripture as a whole, not some part of it and certainly not the *sources* of some part of it, provides the "canon" of the faith by which we live. Let us by all means be grateful for this new historical insight into a hitherto unsuspected tendency in primitive Christianity, and let those who would usurp the divine prerogatives judge the community behind Q as fully Christian. But in doing our own theology we should keep in mind that what has commended itself to God's people as their rule of faith and practice is not all early Christian literature or the beliefs of all early identifiable Christian groups or even all good and pious and edifying first-century writings, but a particular collection of writings in which the teaching of Jesus is encased within a fairly concrete history, a history that culminated on a particular cross at a particular moment, and a death that for most Christians in all times and places has been understood as the central event in human history.

NOTES

1. Some scholars believe that the material common to Matthew and Luke came to them as oral tradition or as a mixture of oral and written materials. The statistical evidence that the materials must have been written is given in Charles E. Carlston and Dennis Norlin, "Once More—Statistics and Q," *HTR* 64 (1971), pp. 59–78.
2. A convenient English reconstruction of Q is given in A. M. Hunter, *The Work and Words of Jesus* (1950), pp. 131–146.
3. For bibliography on these and other generalizations about Q, see Ronald D. Worden, "Redaction Criticism of Q: A Survey," *JBL* 94 (1975), pp. 532–546.
4. An excellent sketch of this view may be found in James M. Robinson, "Jesus as *Sophos* and *Sophia*: Wisdom Tradition and the Gospels," in Robert L. Wilken, ed., *Aspects of Wisdom in Judaism and Early Christianity* (1975), pp. 1–16. (Many other essays in this volume are also of value.) A much more technical and detailed discussion will be found in several of the essays in James M. Robinson and Helmut Koester, *Trajectories through Early Christianity* (1971). See also the next note.
5. See particularly M. Jack Suggs, *Wisdom, Christology, and Law in Matthew's Gospel* (1970). Note that Robinson himself sees the identity between Jesus and Wisdom implied already in Q ("Jesus as *Sophos*," pp. 9f.), but in what he considers the latest strata of Q's tradition.
6. Contradictory advice is given in proverbs in all cultures. In English, for example, we have "Look before you leap" but "He who hesitates is lost." Clearly no universal rules are to be expected.
7. Hans Conzelmann, "The Mother of Wisdom," in James M. Robinson, ed., *The Future of Our Religious Past* (1971), pp. 230–243.
8. For an Isis-"aretalogy," see Frederick C. Grant, *Hellenistic Religions* (1953), pp. 131–133. Note that a single discrete "myth" is neither suggested by the "consensus" nor required by the evidence; see Elisabeth Schüssler Fiorenza, "Wisdom Mythology and the Christological Hymns of the New Testament," in Wilken, *Aspects*, pp. 17–41.

3: The Impotence of the Law:
Toward a Fresh Understanding of Romans 7:14-25

RONALD Y. K. FUNG

Rom 7:14–25 has, without exaggeration, been described as "perhaps the most discussed and fought over part" of the epistle.[1] The question at issue here, as also in the immediately preceding section (vv. 7–13),[2] concerns the temporal reference of the passage and the identity of the subject. This essay attempts to make a contribution to the continuing debate by proposing a relatively new interpretation of the passage.

1. The Prevailing View:
The Passage Refers to the Non-Christian

Some have seen in it a description of the pre-conversion experience of the apostle Paul.[3] But this interpretation is contradicted *both* by the explicit testimony of Paul himself (Gal 1:13f.; Phil 3:4–6), which shows that he regarded his own Jewish past as corresponding most exactly to the Pharisaic ideal, *and* by what is known of the attitude of Pharisaism toward the law and fulfilment of its moral demands.[4]

Others, without seeing a biographical reference to Paul, take the "I" generally as a stylistic form representing man under law, sin, and death and described from the standpoint of the Christian,[5] or specifically as referring to the pre-Christian existence of the believer understood from the vantage-point of his new existence in Christ.[6] This "non-Christian" interpretation, however, involves a number of difficulties.

Heavily weighed against it is the strong contrast between the past tenses in verses 7–13 and the present tenses in verses 14–25. This change of tense is explained by exponents of the view in question in terms of a close logical connection between the two sections: the later section merely describes the result of the irrevocable history narrated in the earlier section, but both the history and the result belong to the believer's past.[7] But it has rightly been maintained that "the only natural way for Paul's readers to interpret the present tenses of vss. 14ff. is as having a present reference," since "there is no recognized linguistic idiom which will account for the change of tense."[8]

It has also been objected that the cry of verse 24 would have to be characterized as theatrical, if it did not refer to the present,[9] though the force of this argument will be variously regarded.

A more cogent objection is that the order of the sentences in verses 24f. is an embarrassment to those who view verse 24 as the cry of an unconverted man, and see in verse 25a an indication that the desired deliverance has actually arrived; since, coming after the thanksgiving, verse 25b is then "*prima facie* a *non sequitur*, and a shattering anticlimax into the bargain."[10] The suggestion that verse 25b is to be transposed to an earlier place[11] has no manuscript evidence in its favor; and while the possibility of verse 25a being parenthetical[12] cannot be ruled out, the suggestion involves supposing a drastic change in the subject between verse 24 (non-Christian) and verse 25a (Christian).

The weightiest argument against the "non-Christian" interpretation is that, on this understanding, the text contradicts Paul's view of the natural man elsewhere, since the present passage then speaks of a non-Christian having a natural affinity with the law of God whereas elsewhere (for example, in the immediately succeeding context, Rom 8:5, 7) such affinity is categorically denied. Despite the plausibility of attempts made by W. G. Kümmel and others to get over this difficulty,[13] they do not carry conviction. Thus, it may be questioned whether the *nous* (with the *esō anthrōpos*) is to be understood (as by Kümmel) in purely psychological terms; for it is surely more natural, and more in keeping with Paul's usage elsewhere, to recognize in the "mind" which serves the law of God (vv. 25b, 23) and the "inner man" which delights in God's law (v. 22) the human self which is being renewed by God's Spirit (cf. Rom 12:2; 2 Cor 4:16), not the self of the still unconverted man.[14] And while in Hellenistic tradition *nous* is indeed sometimes equivalent to *pneuma* and represents the highest element of man's spiritual life, and the notion of the *esō anthrōpos* was current in Paul's day,[15] it is likely that Paul has used these expressions not in their current meaning but in his own sense.[16] We must conclude, therefore, that Rom 7:14–25, if understood of the non-Christian, represents not just (in Kümmel's terms) a "formal deviation" or "relative departure" from Paul's view of the natural man as found elsewhere, but a radical difference, a direct contradiction; and that, despite the overwhelming support it currently enjoys, the "non-Christian" interpretation of our passage does not really do justice to the text.

2. The Passage Refers to the Christian

The opposite view, namely, that the passage is to be understood as referring to the Christian, is, among recent interpreters, upheld by, *inter alia*, A. Nygren, C. K. Barrett, J. Murray, F. F. Bruce, and, most recently, C. E. B. Cranfield.[17] The chief considerations urged in its support have already been mentioned in the form of objections to the "non-Christian" interpretation of the passage. In turn, the "Christian" interpretation has met with many objections, and the main ones must now be discussed.

It has been maintained that the "caesura-less continuation" from verse 13 to verse 14 forbids the view that the thought here advances from the state of the non-Christian to that of the Christian.[18] This, however, is surely an overstatement of the case; for, quite apart from the change of tense from verse 14 onwards, there now lies on the surface an inward tension which is absent from verses 7–13. Since this is not satisfactorily explained in terms of a psychological dualism which is present in the natural man, it would seem a reasonable suggestion that what emerges here is the tension in the Christian life which reflects his existing in two aeons simultaneously.[19] In this connection, appeal is sometimes made to Gal 5:17 as supporting a Christian reference in our passage. But it is necessary to examine whether, and if so in what sense, the text does provide this support.

In this text, it is clear that the flesh and the Spirit are diametrically opposed to each other. But what is the meaning of *hina mē ha ean thelēte tauta poiēte*? Taking *hina* in the final sense as indicating the purpose of both the flesh and the Spirit would yield some such meaning as this: "Does the man choose evil, the Spirit opposes him; does he choose good, the flesh hinders him."[20] However, since it is difficult to regard these two opposing principles as the common subject, both together realizing this purpose, or to regard as purpose a state of continuous opposition,[21] the consecutive sense of *hina* may be preferred.[22] The meaning of the clause, though, has still to be determined. The view that the clause has "definite reference to the restraint which the Spirit exercises on the flesh"[23] is in harmony with the explicit promise of verse 16;[24] but it is "logically inconsistent with *tauta gar all[ēlois] antik[eitai]*, which seems rather to point to the *opposition* incurred than the victory gained by the

Spirit";[25] and it does not accord well with the adversative *de* at the beginning of verse 18, which suggests that victory is achieved only when the Christian is actually led by the Spirit. A second interpretation takes *ha ean thelēte* to refer to "the promptings of the conscience" or "the purpose fixed by spiritual impulse, namely, the achievement of love (cf. v. 14f.),"[26] so that the picture is of the believer whose good desires are overcome by the desires of the flesh—a picture, in that case, which irresistibly recalls that of Romans 7 (esp. vv. 15, 19).[27] Taken as a unit, however, Gal 5:16–18 undoubtedly places the emphasis on the positive aspect of victory through obedience to the Spirit. Far from viewing Christians as helpless onlookers in the Spirit-flesh conflict, the passage in reality presupposes their ability to overcome the flesh through the Spirit.[28] A third view refers *thelēte*, not specifically to the carnal will or the moral will, but to "the free-will in its ordinary acceptation";[29] the meaning of Gal 5:17 then is that in the strife between flesh and Spirit neutrality is impossible: one must serve either the flesh or the Spirit.[30]

On either the second or the third view of the text, insofar as it refers to the conflict of the flesh with the Spirit in the Christian, it supports the contention that the Christian lives in two aeons simultaneously, and to that extent provides a point of contact with a "Christian" interpretation of Rom 7:14ff.; but it is difficult to avoid the conclusion that in its context Gal 5:17 refers to a different situation from that envisaged in Rom 7:14ff.[31] Thus, the appeal to Gal 5:17 at best shows that the flesh is something to be reckoned with even in the life of the Christian. At the same time, taken in context it actually raises the question whether the unequal conflict described in Romans 7 can be the normal outcome of the Spirit-flesh conflict in the life of the believer.

An important objection to the "Christian" interpretation of our passage refers to the conspicuous absence of the Holy Spirit therein—in striking contrast to chapter 8, where the Spirit is mentioned over a dozen times in the first seventeen verses. But, as noted above, hints of his presence are not entirely wanting (cf. vv. 22, 23, 25). At the same time, however, comparison with Rom 8:1ff. or with Gal 5:16–18 (as we have seen) would suggest that here the Spirit, even though not absent, is not fully active.

It is considered improbable, even impossible, that a Christian will utter the cry of despair in verse 24, and the interrogative pronoun "who" is taken to show that the man here spoken of does not yet know who can deliver him, but only that he cannot deliver himself.[32] It has been pointed out, however, that *talaipōros* can indicate distress without any implication of hopelessness, and that the use of *tis* does not necessarily imply ignorance of the deliverer, as comparison with Ps 13:7 (LXX) and 52:7 (Ps 14:7; 53:6, MT) will show.[33]

It is also objected that "to take vii. 7–25 of the typical Christian life is to fix upon St. Paul a craven ideal of that life, which he defies in the triumphant cry of victory [of vi. 14]."[34] Again, how could Paul say of the Christian both that he is "sold under sin" (7:14) and that he has been set free from sin and enslaved to God and righteousness (8:2; 6:18, 22)? "That would indeed be a Theology of Yes and No!"[35] The overall contrast of our passage not only with chapter 8 but also with chapter 6, it is claimed, is sufficient to render the "Christian" interpretation of it impossible to maintain.[36] Of all the objections against the view under discussion, this is the strongest: to understand our passage of the Christian entails a picture of the Christian life which in its darkness is incompatible with Paul's description elsewhere of the believer's liberation from sin, just as the weightiest objection against the "non-Christian" interpretation is that it involves a direct contradiction of what Paul elsewhere says about the natural man.

To get over this particular difficulty, it has been suggested, for example, by Cranfield, that the language used of the Christian here is to be interpreted in the light of the fact that

> the farther men advance in the Christian life, and the more mature their discipleship, the clearer becomes their perception of the heights to which God calls them, and the more painfully sharp their consciousness of the distance between what they ought, and want, to be, and what they are.

Paul's language might then be taken to mean that what the Christian actually does never fully corresponds to his will, and that since he still has a fallen nature he remains in a real sense a slave of sin so long as he remains in this present life.[37] Although this interpretation contains an important insight into the nature of the Christian's sanctification (namely, that it is never perfect in this life, on account of indwelling sin), yet it cannot entirely escape the criticism that it "instinctively softens down that which is said by Paul, so as to be able to refer it to the Christian"; that this very attenuation shows that the apostle's words, as they stand, cannot be harmonized with his picture of the Christian given elsewhere; and that to understand Rom 7:14ff. in the way suggested "would be completely isolated and without analogy among all the letters of Paul."[38] One may therefore doubt whether our passage can really be regarded as describing an aspect of the Christian life which is, and as long as the Christian is in the flesh continues to be, a contemporaneous reality with what is described in Rom 8:1ff. or, for that matter, Gal 5:16–18.

3. Other Views

One or two alternative suggestions have sought to do justice to the arguments on both sides by supposing that Paul is here speaking of neither the Christian nor the non-Christian exclusively, or that the experience described here is neither that of the unregenerate nor that of the converted. Thus, to take them in reverse order, D. M. Lloyd-Jones sees in our passage the picture of a man who has been given to see, by the Spirit, the holiness of the law, who feels utterly condemned, but does not know the way of deliverance—a man, in short, who is "not unregenerate," but whose position is only that of "conviction but not conversion."[39] It would seem unlikely, however, that Paul, whose constant practice is to appeal to the consciousness or knowledge of believers in general,[40] is here thinking of some special condition or stage in the conversion experience of Christians (and only of some of them, at that). Moreover, the keynote of the passage seems to be not so much conviction under sin as the conflict between willing and doing and the consciousness of being taken captive by sin. The use of the present tenses throughout the passage, too, remains a difficulty for this view; and so does the order of the sentences in verses 24f., inasmuch as the present view involves a change of speaker between verse 24 (the regenerate but as yet unconverted man) and verse 25a (the Christian).

In view of C. L. Mitton, our passage gives

> a description of the distressing experience of any morally earnest man, whether Christian or not, who attempts to live up to the commands of God "on his own" (*autos egō*), without that constant reliance upon the uninterrupted supply of the resources of God, which is characteristic of the mature Christian. It is especially applicable to a man "under the law", even if he be nominally a Christian. . . . It can also be true of the converted Christian who has slipped back . . . into a legalistic attitude to God and to righteousness.[41]

On such an understanding, "the present tenses describe not merely a past experience but one which is potentially ever present."[42] The fatal objection to this view is that it is exceedingly doubtful whether *autos* can bear such a weight of meaning as is here assigned to it. The rendering of *autos egō* as "I by myself" or the like has rightly been called in question on linguistic grounds. Kümmel points out that while *autos* with the sense of *monos* indeed occurs in profane usage, in the New Testament the word, especially in conjunction with a substantive or personal pronoun, always serves to emphasize the person in question, sometimes in distinction from others; accordingly *autos egō* always means, "I myself, and no one else."[43] And J. B. Lightfoot, though he adopted the rendering "I by myself, etc.," was compelled to admit that "this interpretation is hardly borne out by the usage of *autos egō* in St. Paul."[44] It seems most natural, therefore, to take the words as meaning "I *myself,* and *no other,* i.e. the same *Egō* of which he [Paul] had spoken all along."[45] On this understanding of the phrase, Paul is not talking about both the natural man and the immature Christian, but (as we see it) of the Christian only.

4. A New View of the Passage

As none of the views considered above seems entirely satisfactory, we venture to present our own tentative understanding of the matter. Two points have clearly emerged from our discussion thus far: the description does not fit the natural man; at the same time, in view of Paul's description elsewhere of the Christian and his life as guided and controlled by the Spirit, it is very difficult to regard the picture here as that of the believer in whose life the Spirit is fully at work. While, for the reason stated above, C. L. Mitton's view cannot be accepted just as it stands, we believe that it yet points to the right solution when it is said that the description can be "true of the converted Christian who has slipped back . . . into a legalistic attitude to God and to righteousness."

That Paul is concerned in this passage to illustrate the relation between sin and law is beyond reasonable doubt (cf. the references to the law in vv. 14a, 16b, 22, 25b, and to sin in vv. 14b, 17, 20b, 23, 25b). In particular, it would appear from the context of the chapter that Paul's purpose is to show that the law is powerless to sanctify the Christian. Thus, verses 7–13 have demonstrated the connection of sin and law in the case of the natural man to be as follows: the law in itself is holy, but as an instrument wielded by sin it operates on the natural man to entice him to sin and condemn him to death; verses 14–25 now show that even in the case of the man whose nature has been renewed by the Spirit of God and who is therefore able to acknowledge the goodness of the law, delight in it, and serve it with his mind, the law (spiritual and good as it is) is powerless to deliver him from his bondage to indwelling sin,[46] so long as he is not placing himself under the full control of the Spirit but tries to overcome sin or to live a holy life by endeavoring to observe the law—so long, that is, as he fails to act in accordance with the truth stated in 6:14b, that the Christian is not *hypo nomon* but *hypo charin.*

It has been suggested that Paul's meaning in 6:14 is not that believers have been freed from the authority of the law, but only that they have been freed from its condemnation and curse and also from it as a basis of righteousness.[47] Certainly there are passages in Romans (3:31; 7:12, 14a; 8:4; 13:8–10) which clearly imply that the law retains its validity as a revelation of God's will and to that extent as obligation. Yet the point of the antinomian retort immediately quoted by Paul (Rom 6:15) shows that in the statement of verse 14b he has in view, not simply the initial justification by faith, but the ongoing course of Christian life; so that the implication of his statement seems rather to be that believers are not under law even as a rule of life.[48] The thought of Rom 6:14 is taken up again and made somewhat more specific in 7:6, where believers are said to render their service to God *en kainotēti pneumatos* and not *palaiotēti grammatos*. If *kainotēs* and *palaiotēs* point to the distinction between the new aeon and the old, the distinguishing characteristic of each is designated by, respectively, *pneuma*, a reference to the Holy Spirit,[49] and *gramma*, a reference to the law in its character as that which is merely written and which as such has absolutely no power to bestow new life[50] (cf. 2:29). The advent of the Holy Spirit is the *kainotēs* which gives rise to the *palaiotēs*, and shows that the new covenant prophesied by Jeremiah is realized in the new aeon. Hence, not the written code, but the enabling Spirit, is to be the new regulative principle in the life of the believer.

In Rom 6:14, the Spirit is not mentioned; the contrast there is between *hypo nomon* and *hypo charin*. It is significant, however, that in Gal 5:18, which occurs in a context similarly dealing with the believer's moral life, *hypo nomon* is contrasted with *pneumati agesthai;* and that two verses before *pneumati peripatein* is stated to be the way to avoid *telein epithumian sarkos*. The implication is plainly that the desire of the flesh cannot be overcome by the Christian remaining *hypo nomon,* but only as he walks or is led by the Spirit. It is also significant that Paul's statement seems to be polemically oriented to the Judaizers' claim that the only way to moral victory was to place oneself under the restraint of the law; if the Judaizers uphold the law as the only safeguard against becoming slaves to the flesh, Paul asserts as an adequate safeguard the guidance of the Spirit.[51] The latter, to him, constitutes "a third way of life," a highway distinct from, and above, both legalism and antinomianism.[52] The proposition stated in verse 18 is substantiated by verse 23 where, after listing the works of the flesh (vv. 19–21) and then, in contrast, the harvest of the Spirit (vv. 22f.),[53] it is said of the latter, *kata tōn toioutōn ouk estin nomos*. Burton is probably right in regarding this as "an understatement of the apostle's thought for rhetorical effect": the mild assertion as it stands "has the effect of an emphatic assertion that these things fully meet the requirements of the law (cf. v. 14)."[54] But as "these things" are the fruit of the Spirit, Paul's words really mean that "the law is not against those who walk by the Spirit because in principle they are fulfilling the law."[55]

Thus Paul argues in Gal 5:14ff. for the guidance of the Spirit as a superior alternative to a life of self-indulgence than restraint by law. In the course of his argument it emerges that, on the one hand, to be *hypo nomon* is not only not the way to overcome the desire of the flesh, but leads instead to the works of the flesh, and, on the other hand, *peripatein agesthai pneumati* is the way both to overcome the flesh and to fulfill the law. Now, in view of the close similarity between Romans and Galatians generally,[56] and in particular of the similar orientation toward the law in what Paul says in both Galatians 5 and Romans 7, we submit that Rom 7:14–25 may best be understood in the light of what we have just discovered from Galatians 5, as a theological description,[57] from the standpoint of Christian maturity, of the state of the Christian who lives *hypo nomon,* as an illustration of the truth that the law cannot overcome indwelling sin or give release from its bondage; Rom 8:1ff., on the other hand, describes the state of the Christian who walks *kata pneuma* (v. 4b) and *pneumati agontai* (v. 14a), thereby both prevailing over the flesh (v. 13b) and fulfilling the law (v. 4a). On this understanding, the first person singular would refer to any Christian who does or would live *hypo nomon* instead of walking by the Spirit (such as was probably not unfamiliar to Paul); the present tenses would be in place; the conspicuous absence of the Spirit's activity (as distinct from his presence) would be explained; and the difficulty posed by the description here (if understood as a normal Christian experience) with the picture of the Christian elsewhere would be resolved. If this interpretation is not entirely free from difficulty, we yet venture to believe that it goes a considerable way in doing justice to the text of Paul and to the strongest arguments on either side of the debate as to whether the description is of the natural man or of the Christian. It is from the standpoint of this interpretation that we proceed to study the passage below.

5. Exegesis of the Passage

Paul is here substantiating (*gar*) the thesis of the whole preceding argument (vv. 7–13), summed up in verse 13, namely, that it was sin, not the law, which brought about death for the man under law. The logical connection appears as follows: while the law is holy in itself, it is an instrument of sin and the effect of its operation on the natural man is to entice to sin and condemn to death. That this is the actual effect of law is now further illustrated (*gar*) by the fact that, even in the case of the Christian, the law is powerless to overcome indwelling sin. Over against the law as *pneumatikos,* divine in origin and spiritual in nature, the Christian here is *sarkinos,* which in this instance means "carnal."[58] The use of this word in 1 Cor 3:1, 3 (where also it is opposed to *pneumatikos*) shows that to be *sarkinos* in the sense of *sarkikos* is to be *hōs nēpios en Christō,* to be subject to *zēlos* and *eris* (both of which, though in reverse order, figure in Gal 5:20 among the works of the flesh), to walk *kata anthrōpon* and not (one is irresistibly tempted to add) *kata pneuma.* A Christian who is carnal is, in other words, an immature Christian who does not yet know how to live by the Spirit and (consequently) fails to subdue the flesh. It is of such a one, it seems, that our passage speaks.

Being carnal, he is sold under sin, subject like a bondslave to *hamartia,* which rules over him as an evil power. His bondage is elaborated upon in the rest of the passage (vv. 15–25). Both the general context of the whole chapter and the narrower context (vv. 14a, 16b) combine to indicate that the point at issue in verse 15 is the Christian's performance in relation to the law;[59] his *thelein—* which denotes "definite purpose and readiness to do the divine will"[60] —is, however, irreconcilably opposed by his *poiein.* From this an inference is drawn in favor of the law (v. 16); and it follows from this state of things (*nyni de*) that it is no longer the Christian who performs what he does not want (v. 16a) but sin which dwells within him (v. 17). Paul's intention is not, however, to exonerate him from responsibility for his actions, but rather to show how completely he is under the thraldom of indwelling sin.

Repeating verses 14–17 with certain variations, verses 18–20 further describe the inner conflict which this Christian experiences. In support (*gar*) of the implication of verse 17 that the self is powerless for good, verse 18a gives expression to the Christian's confession that nothing good dwells within him, that is, in his flesh—*sarx* standing for man in his totality apart from the sanctifying influence of the Holy Spirit. *Tout' estin,* which introduces the additional phrase, has been taken as having a merely explanatory force, defining or identifying "me" as "my flesh";[61] but more probably it has a corrective or restrictive sense, qualifying *en emoi.*[62] This qualification implies that the Christian here is aware of his not being entirely *sarx* and may be aware of the presence of the Holy Spirit within him. Still, the fact remains that neither here nor anywhere else in the passage is the Holy Spirit so much as explicitly mentioned, let alone described as working, so there is little evidence that the Christian here is experiencing the help of the Holy Spirit in his predicament. Thus the situation remains as described in verses 18b–19. If in verse 15b the objects of the *thelein* and the *prassein* are not yet named, here they are specified as *to kalon* (v. 18b) = *agathon* (v. 19a) and *kakon* (v. 19b) respectively. Now, as O. Michel remarks, it is natural "to refer the 'good' (*agathon, kalon*) to the fulfilling of God's demand, the 'evil' (*kakon*) to the performance of man which conforms to lust"[63] (cf. v. 16b, where the law is acknowledged as *kalos*); and so the picture here is of the Christian who, despite his will to keep the law and satisfy God's requirements, falls into acts which are contrary to God's will. Verse 20 repeats, in almost identical words, the reasoning already expressed in verses 16a and 17, and thereby emphasizes the controlling power of indwelling sin.

From the foregoing (vv. 14–20) the logical position concerning this Christian is summed up in terms of the principle or rule of verse 21,[64] which is more precisely described in verses 22f. (cf. NEB). The *heteron nomon* which the Christian sees in his bodily members and the law that is in his bodily members are one, and this is the law of sin.[65] Over against this is the law of his mind, the law which his (renewed) mind acknowledges, even the law in which he delights in his inner man (v. 22).

Thus the victory in this unequal conflict clearly belongs to the law of sin; and the Christian here, despite his approval of the law (v. 23), his acknowledgment of its goodness (v. 16b), his delight in it (v. 22), and his will to keep it (vv. 18b, 19, 21), finds himself inextricably in the grip of indwelling sin. He is therefore constrained to utter the cry of distress (v. 24): "Wretched man that I am! Who will deliver me from *tou sōmatos tou thanatou toutou?*" If *toutou* is taken with *sōmatos,* the cry is for deliverance from the condition of life in the body under the occupation of sin, a life which must succumb to death on account of sin.[66] It is more natural, however, to take the words as they stand and connect *toutou* with *thanatou.*[67] The "body of this death" then signifies the body which is dominated by that "death" which has been described in the preceding verses, namely, the condition of bondage to sin. What follows in verse 25a is not a direct, but only an indirect, answer to the question of verse 24b, Christ being regarded as the mediator through whom thanks is given. On the view that the passage is dealing with the "normal" Christian, it is most natural to refer this thanksgiving to God's future deliverance in the resurrection (cf. 8:23; 1 Cor 15:57). It is possible, however, to regard this thanksgiving as a parenthetical ejaculation on the part of Paul, by which he indicates that deliverance for the Christian here described is indeed available—deliverance, that is, not actually from the physical body itself, but from that "death" which so dominates the body of the Christian here that he longs to be delivered from that body itself. Since Paul's object (as we understand it) is to illustrate the impotence of the law in the case of the Christian who is living *hypo nomon*, he does not expatiate on this deliverance which is effected by a different power but returns immediately to summarize that Christian's position, already described in verses 14—24, in the concluding statement of verse 25b.

6. Conclusion

We are aware that the above exegesis involves supposing a change of speaker between verse 24 (the Christian) and verse 25a (the apostle), and that this might fairly be regarded as a difficulty in our interpretation. It may be said, however, (a) that the very abruptness of the exclamation in verse 25a (particularly if the original lacks the *de*[68]) might be an indication of its parenthetical nature, and (b) that the present difficulty appears less serious than some of the difficulties with which the other alternative suggestions are faced.

If the understanding of Rom 7:14—25 proposed here is anywhere near the truth, then we have in this passage Paul's description of a Christian who, instead of living *kata pneuma*, seeks to keep God's law by his own efforts but finds that, for all his delight in it and desire and determination to keep it, he is firmly in the grip of indwelling sin; a Christian, that is, who (in terms of 6:14b), though objectively already *hypo charin*, subjectively still lives *hypo nomon*, and who (in terms of 7:6), though already transferred to the new aeon, serves God (cf. v. 25b, *douleuō*) still in *palaiotēti grammatos* instead of *en kainotēti pneumatos*. Paul thus illustrates his point that the law, in spite of its being spiritual and good (vv. 14, 16), is powerless to restrain or overcome sin—over against the Jewish theory (with which Judaizers may well have agreed) that the law was given both to provide the Jew with the legal basis whereby justification may be achieved and to strengthen him to gain victory in the conflict between the good and evil *yētzer*. In accord with our understanding of Rom 6:14; 7:6; and Gal 5:14ff. in their bearing on the Christian's relation to the law, the implication of the present passage would seem to be that the Christian is not to live *hypo nomon*, submitting to the law of God as a legal code and trying to keep it by his own efforts, for neither these nor God's law can enable him to overcome his indwelling sin; but that rather he is to walk *kata pneuma*, who imparts that power which the law cannot supply, and who alone can break the domination of sin and flesh in the Christian's life and enable him to fulfill the righteous requirement of the law (8:4).[69]

NOTES

1. A. Nygren, *A Commentary on Romans* (1952), p. 284.
2. If one may simply state one's understanding of this similarly controversial passage, Paul is here describing, from the Christian perspective, the believer's pre-Christian existence under sin and law and illustrating it in terms of the experience of Adam. Cf., e.g., K. Kertelge, "Exegetische Überlegungen zum Verständnis der paulinischen Anthropologie nach Römer 7," *ZNTW* 62 (1971), pp. 105–114 (p. 108); G. Bornkamm, *Early Christian Experience* (1969), p. 93; E. Käsemann, *An die Römer* (1974), p. 187.
3. E.g., C. H. Dodd, *The Epistle of Paul to the Romans* (1970), pp. 125, 126.
4. Cf. W. G. Kümmel, *Römer 7 und die Bekehrung des Paulus* (1929), pp. 111–117; C. E. B. Cranfield, *A Critical and Exegetical Commentary on the Epistle to the Romans*, 1 (1975), p. 344.
5. E.g., Kümmel, op. cit., pp. 118ff., 138; *Man in the New Testament* (1963), pp. 49ff.
6. Cf. Kertelge, op. cit., p. 112.
7. Cf. Kümmel, *Römer 7*, p. 126; Kertelge, op. cit., p. 108; Bornkamm, op. cit., p. 95; O. Kuss, *Der Römerbrief* (1963), p. 440.
8. J. I. Packer, "The 'Wretched Man' of Romans 7," *StudEv* 2 (1964), pp. 621–627 (p. 624). "The use of the historic present in the gospels to give vividness to narrative does not provide a parallel, for here the narrative part is in the aorist, and what is in the present is not narrative, but generalised explanatory comment" (ibid.).
9. So, e.g., Nygren, *Romans*, p. 286.
10. Packer, art. cit., p. 625. Cf. Cranfield, *Romans*, 1, p. 345.
11. So, e.g., O. Michel, *Der Brief an die Römer* (1966), p. 179.
12. Cf., e.g., E. Stauffer, *TDNT* 2, p. 359.
13. Cf. Kümmel, *Römer 7*, p. 136ff.; *Man in the New Testament*, pp. 57ff.; Bornkamm, op. cit., pp. 98f.; Kertelge, op. cit., pp. 111ff.; H. Ridderbos, *Paul: An Outline of His Theology* (1975), pp. 126–130.
14. Cf. Cranfield, *Romans*, 1, p. 363 with n. 2, p. 346. Of verse 22, Henry Alford, *The Greek Testament*, revised by E. F. Harrison (1958), 2, p. 383a, remarks: "It is *absolutely necessary* to presuppose the *influence of the Holy Spirit,* and to place the man in *a state of grace before this assertion can be true.*"
15. Cf. J. Behm, *TDNT* 4, pp. 954–958; J. Jeremias, *TDNT* 1, p. 365.
16. So Cranfield, *Romans*, 1, p. 363, n. 2. Cf. C. K. Barrett, *The Second Epistle to the Corinthians* (1973), p. 146, for a similar conclusion. Pace Jeremias, op. cit.; Käsemann, *Römer*, pp. 196, 198.
17. Cf. Nygren, *Romans*, pp. 284–296; C. K. Barrett, *The Epistle to the Romans* (1973), pp. 146ff., esp. pp. 151–153; J. Murray, *The Epistle to the Romans* (1968), 1, pp. 257–259; F. F. Bruce, *The Epistle of Paul to the Romans* (1963), pp. 150–153; "Some Thoughts on Paul and Paulinism," *Vox Ev* 7 (1971), pp. 5–16; Cranfield, *Romans*, 1, pp. 344–347, 356–358. Cf. also Packer (see n. 8 above), and J. D. G. Dunn, "Rom. 7:14–25 in the Theology of Paul," *ThZ* 31 (1975), pp. 257–273.
18. So P. Althaus, "Zur Auslegung von Röm. 7:14ff.," *ThLZ* 77 (1952), pp. 475–480 (p. 477). Cf. C. L. Mitton, "Romans vii Reconsidered," *ExpT* 65 (1953–54), pp. 78–81, 99–103, 132–135 (p. 100a).
19. So, e.g., Nygren, *Romans*, pp. 34, 293; Bruce, *Romans*, pp. 151, 156.
20. E. de W. Burton, *A Critical and Exegetical Commentary on the Epistle to the Galatians* (1968), p. 302. Cf. E. Schweizer, *TDNT* 6, p. 429.
21. So, rightly, H. N. Ridderbos, *The Epistle of Paul to the Churches of Galatia* (1968), p. 203, n. 9; and D. Guthrie, *Galatians* (1969), p. 144, respectively.

22. So, besides Ridderbos and Guthrie, also M. Zerwick, *Biblical Greek* (1963), p. 122.
23. G. S. Duncan, *The Epistle of Paul to the Galatians* (1934), p. 168. Cf. F. Rendall, *EGT* 3, p. 187a; S. J. Mikolaski, *NBCR*, p. 1102b.
24. "*Ou mē telesēte* is equivalent to an emphatic promissory future expressing, not a command, but a strong assurance" (Burton, *Galatians*, p. 299). The RSV is almost alone in taking the clause as an imperative.
25. C. J. Ellicott, *St. Paul's Epistle to the Galatians* (1867), p. 115a.
26. J. B. Lightfoot, *The Epistle of St. Paul to the Galatians* (1962), p. 210a, and G. Schrenk, *TDNT* 3, p. 50, respectively.
27. So, e.g., Ridderbos, *Galatians*, pp. 203f.; I. H. Marshall, "Preparation for exposition: Galatians 5:16–20," *TSF Bulletin* 70 (Autumn 1974), pp. 7–10 (p. 9).
28. Cf. Kümmel, *Römer* 7, p. 106; Althaus, op. cit., p. 478. Cf. also K. Prümm, "Rom 1–11 und 2 Kor 3," *Bibl* 31 (1950), 164–203 (p. 193, n. 3).
29. Ellicott, *Galatians*, p. 115a.
30. Cf. Kümmel, *Römer* 7, p. 106.
31. Cf. Bornkamm, op. cit., pp. 100f.; Ridderbos, op. cit., p. 127.
32. Cf. D. M. Lloyd-Jones, *Romans. An Exposition of Chapters 7.1–8.4* (1973), pp. 223, 255; Kümmel, *Römer* 7, p. 115.
33. Cranfield, *Romans*, 1, p. 366.
34. A. Robertson, "Christian Ethics and the Spirit," *Exp* 5 (1899), p. 349.
35. Althaus, op. cit., p. 479.
36. Cf. Käsemann, *Römer*, p. 190; Kuss, *Der Römerbrief*, p. 483.
37. Cf. Cranfield, *Romans*, 1, pp. 365f. (whence the quotation), 361, 370.
38. Althaus, op. cit., p. 479.
39. Lloyd-Jones, op. cit., pp. 255f. (cf. p. 187), 261f.
40. Cf. *oidamen hoti* (Rom 2:2; 3:19; 7:14; 8:22; 8:28) and *ouk oidate hoti* (6:16).
41. Cf. Mitton, op. cit., pp. 132–135; quotation from p. 133b.
42. A. M. Hunter, *The Epistle to the Romans* (1955), p. 74.
43. Kümmel, *Römer* 7, p. 66.
44. J. B. Lightfoot, *Notes on Epistles of St. Paul* (1895), p. 305.
45. C. Hodge, *A Commentary on Romans* (1972), p. 239.
46. Cf. Althaus, op. cit., p. 477, who rightly sees the train of thought from verses 7–13 to verses 14–25 as advancing "from the law as a medium of sin to the law as powerless in the face of sin."
47. Cf. Cranfield, *Romans*, 1, pp. 319f.; J. Murray, *NBD*, p. 772b; C. F. D. Moule, "Obligation in the Ethic of Paul," in W. R. Farmer, C. F. D. Moule, and R. R. Niebuhr (eds.), *Christian History and Interpretation: Studies presented to John Knox* (1967), pp. 389–406 (p. 397).
48. Cf. F. F. Bruce, "Paul and the Law of Moses," *BJRL* 57 (1974–75), pp. 259–279 (p. 266).
49. 7:6b is an anticipation of 8:1ff., in which *pneuma* clearly refers to the Holy Spirit.
50. So G. Schrenk, *TDNT* 1, p. 766. Cf. Prümm, op. cit., p. 188; E. Käsemann, *Perspectives on Paul* (1971), p. 147; H. Seesemann, *TDNT* 5, p. 720.
51. Duncan, *Galatians*, pp. 168f. Cf. R. P. Martin, *1 Corinthians–Galatians* (1968), p. 122.
52. Burton, *Galatians*, p. 302. Cf. Guthrie, *Galatians*, pp. 144f.
53. This very contrast, in the light of the preceding one in verse 18, implies that the works of the flesh are closely associated with being *hypo nomon*.
54. Burton, *Galatians*, p. 318. Cf. H. Schlier, *TDNT* 2, pp. 501f.
55. Ridderbos, *Galatians*, p. 208. Cf. R. Bultmann, *Theology of the New Testament, 1* (1971), pp. 340f., where *toioutōn* is taken as masculine.
56. On this cf. Lightfoot, *Galatians*, pp. 45–49; Dodd, *Romans*, p. 23; Michel, *Römer, p. 25.
57. By a "theological description" we do not mean that the description does not to any degree correspond to actual experience, but rather that Paul's primary concern is to illustrate the limitation of the law by referring to the case (real or hypothetical) of a Christian who puts himself *hypo nomon*. It is not irrelevant to observe that, while holding to opposite interpretations of our passage in respect of the identity of the speaker (Christian

versus non-Christian), Barrett (*Romans*, p. 152) and F. J. Leenhardt (*The Epistle to the Romans* [1961], p. 198) agree in regarding the description here as basically of a theological nature.

58. That Paul can use the terms *sarkinos* and *sarkikos* interchangeably is suggested by 1 Cor 3:1–4. In the present instance, "*sarkinos* is used in the full Pauline sense" (E. Schweizer, *TDNT* 7, p. 144).

59. Cf. Käsemann, *Römer*, pp. 192f. Cf. n. 63 below.

60. G. Schrenk, *TDNT* 3, p. 50.

61. So Michel, *Römer*, p. 178; Bornkamm, op. cit., p. 95; Kertelge, op. cit., p. 109; Käsemann, *Römer*, p. 195; E. Stauffer, *TDNT* 2, p. 359 with n. 140.

62. So W. Sanday and A. C. Headlam, *A Critical and Exegetical Commentary on the Epistle to the Romans* (1962), p. 182; Kümmel, op. cit., pp. 60f.; A. Schlatter, *Gottes Gerechtigkeit. Ein Kommentar zum Römerbrief* (1965), p. 244.

63. Michel, *Römer*, p. 186. Cf. n. 59 above.

64. The addition of *tou theou* to *ho nomos* in verse 22 shows that here in verse 21 (and also in v. 23) *nomos* is probably not a reference to the Mosaic law, but rather used "in the non-literal, figurative sense" to denote "the coercive law of sin" (Michel, *Römer*, p. 178), which is called a "law" "because there is no evading its validity" (W. Gutbrod, *TDNT* 4, p. 1071).

65. So, e.g., Kümmel, *Römer* 7, p. 63; Kuss, *Der Römerbrief*, p. 457; Cranfield, *Romans*, 1, p. 364 with n. 2. *Pace* H. W. Beyer, *TDNT* 2, p. 703.

66. Cf., e.g., N. Turner, in J. H. Moulton, *A Grammar of New Testament Greek*, 3 (1963), p. 214; Michel, *Römer*, p. 180, n. 3; Cranfield, *Romans*, 1, p. 367.

67. Cf., e.g., Schlatter, op. cit., p. 247; Alford, op. cit., 2, p. 384b; Murray, *Romans*, 1, p. 268.

68. The inclusion of *de* is defended on the grounds that "the absence of *de* . . . seems to represent a natural development in the light of liturgical usage (*de* is present in the same ascription at 6.17; 2 Cor 2.14; 8.16 . . .)" (B. M. Metzger, *A Textual Commentary on the Greek New Testament* [1971], p. 515); on the other hand, the addition of *de* after *charis* gives a less abrupt text, and is explicable as an attempted improvement of *charis tō theō* (so Cranfield, *Romans*, 1, p. 367, n. 1). We prefer the shorter reading, as do also Sanday and Headlam, *Romans*, p. 184; Michel, *Römer*, p. 180, n. 4; and Kuss, *Der Römerbrief*, p. 459.

69. Since completing this essay, I have noticed that according to Ridderbos, op. cit., p. 129, "the opinion has also been defended that Paul here speaks of a kind of transitional period in which the man finds himself who, although already confessing Christ, still struggles to hold fast to the law," though this conception is said to have found very little acceptance. It is interesting to note also that J. C. O'Neill, *Paul's Letter to the Romans* (1975), p. 136, regards Paul's argument in chapter 8 as "the culmination of his plea to the Roman Christians *not to live under the Law*" (our italics).

4: Why Did God Inspire the Bible?

GEORGE ELDON LADD

All scripture is inspired by God and profitable for teaching, for reproof, for correction, and for training in righteousness (2 Tim 3:16).

If one reads the modern literature about the Bible produced by those of us who are heirs of the fundamentalist theology, one would be likely to conclude that the main reason God inspired the Bible was to give modern theologians the opportunity of debating the meaning of inerrancy or infallibility. Many evangelical scholars assume that if God inspired the Bible, it must as a matter of course be perfect and without any errors of any kind. It is not my purpose in this essay to debate this issue. It is rather to point out that, in this clear statement about biblical inspiration, nothing is said about inerrancy or infallibility. On the contrary, the Bible is inspired that it in turn may inspire the reader. It is inspired that it may be *profitable.*

Of course, from Paul's perspective "all scripture" refers to the Old Testament. But if this statement applies to the lesser, it is also to be applied to the greater, the New Testament. Therefore, although it is not within Paul's perspective, we must understand this statement to be descriptive of the entire Bible.

It is not our purpose to discuss at length what inspiration means. The word "inspired" means "God-breathed." It should be noted, however, that it is the Scripture that is inspired, not the prophets. In other words, this verse demands a view of verbal inspiration. God inbreathed not only the writers, he inbreathed what they wrote. He did this that the words of Scripture might be useful—that they might do something.

From one point of view, the Bible is a book of history, and can be studied as such. When the Bible is studied in the university, it is usually studied as the words of men which tell a continuous story. It

49

tells the story of Abraham, the father of Israel, and of his sons and grandsons, the patriarchs. It tells of Israel's journey to Egypt and eventual enslavement there. It tells of Israel's deliverance from Egypt under Moses and the repossession of the land under Joshua. It tells of the time when Israel was ruled by charismatic judges, and then of the establishment of a monarchy under Solomon and David. It tells of the division of the people into two nations—Israel and Judah, and after sketching the history of each, it tells how they were removed from the land and carried into captivity in Assyria and Babylon. It tells of the return of some of the southern tribes from Babylon to repossess the land under Ezra and Nehemiah.

There follows a silent period of several centuries for knowledge of which we are dependent on non-canonical Jewish literature. Then the New Testament tells the story of the appearance of John the Baptist, then of Jesus of Nazareth, including his deeds and teaching. It tells of his crucifixion as one politically dangerous to Rome. It tells of the rise of the resurrection faith and the formation of the Christian Church. It tells of the spread of this Church from Jerusalem to Rome, particularly as it occurred through the ministry of Paul. It contains considerable correspondence between Paul and other Christian leaders and their churches, which must be studied historically. It concludes with a vast imaginative drama, in which the Church is assured that no evil, no persecution, can destroy her.

All this is history. We have no need of inspiration to produce such historical books. The so-called books of the Apocrypha and Pseudepigrapha are also historical books reflecting the historical, social, and religious thought of the intertestamental period. However, the biblical writers were writing more than history. They were reciting *the acts of God in history.* It was *God* who called Abraham. It was *God* who delivered Israel from Egypt. It was *God's* judgment which sent Israel and Judah into captivity. It was *God* who appeared among men in the person of Jesus Christ. It was *God* who raised him from the dead and gave birth to the Christian Church. Therefore the Scripture tells a story that history as such cannot tell. It relates the redemptive acts of God. But more: it relates the redemptive meaning of those acts.

Modern historical criticism has confirmed the basic accuracy of the Bible's historicity. But one thing history cannot do: it cannot say that it was God who was acting in Israel's history. And again: it cannot explain the divine meaning of these historical events. So great a scholar as Rudolf Bultmann has said, "Today we cannot claim to know the end and goal of history. Therefore the question of meaning in history has become meaningless."[1] However, this is not the Bible's view of itself. The Bible is the trustworthy historical record and the normative, authoritative interpretation of what God has done in history. This requires inspiration—the inbreathing of God—that the Scripture may be and do what God intended. Because the Bible is inspired, it is not a book of *mere* history, nor is it merely a record of revelation that occurred in the distant past. The Word is a living Word which continues to reveal God. It is contemporary with every age. I should read the book not only to learn what happened in the past; I should read the book to learn what God wills to happen to me in the present. Therefore, when it is read only as history it is misused. The Bible is inspired that it may be profitable to generation after generation of readers.

1. Scripture for Teaching

Our text says that the Bible is inspired that it may be profitable in four dimensions. The first of these is *teaching.* The Bible is the only source-book in which we find answers to our most profound questions about life. The Bible contains instruction primarily about three themes: God, man, and destiny. "In many and various ways God spoke of old to our fathers by the prophets; but in these last days he has spoken to us by a Son" (Heb 1:1–2). It is of course impossible in a brief essay adequately to summarize what God has said about himself. Suffice it to say that the Bible pictures God not only as creator and sustainer of the universe, but as one who longs for fellowship with his people. Perhaps the most central fact about God in the Bible is that he has continually been creating a people. He called Abraham that he and his descendants might be God's people. He raised up Moses and gave the law that Israel might be God's people. The prophets are full of divine heartbreak that Israel has rejected her role as God's people. "How can I give you up, O Ephraim! How can I hand you over, O Israel!" (Hos 11:8). God finally sent his Son that he might create a new people. "You are a chosen race, a royal priesthood, a holy nation, God's own people" (1 Pet 2:9). God has done everything in his power to persuade men that their most important role in life is to belong to the people of God—to belong to God. One thing he has not done: he does not compel; he does not drive; he does not coerce. He treats us as responsible moral agents. He longs for our love, but it can only be *given;* it cannot be forced. As he was on his way to the cross, Jesus wept over Jerusalem, and in his words we hear the voice of God, "O Jerusalem, Jerusalem, killing the prophets and stoning those who are sent to you! How often would I have gathered your children together

as a hen gathers her brood under her wings, and you would not"
(Matt 23:37).

The second major revelatory theme in the Bible is man. Who is
he? What is his nature? Many modern students of human behavior
see man as little more than an animal. He necessarily and inevitably
reacts to his physical and social environment as animals do. Now it is
true that man is an animal; he is a physical creature, and he can react
to his environment like an animal. But the Bible reveals something
that psychology cannot prove: man is also spirit. "For what person
knows a man's thoughts except the spirit of the man which is in
him?" (1 Cor 2:11). Because I am spirit, I can know my own
thoughts as a mere animal cannot. I can know myself. I can ask
questions about the meaning of myself which no other animal can
do.

Because I am spirit, I can relate to other spirits. Because I and my
friend are spirits, we can enjoy a fellowship—a relationship which
transcends my love for my cat or my dog. And finally, because I am
spirit, and because God is spirit (John 4:24), I can enter into
personal fellowship and relationship with God.

The Bible reveals something else about men which evangelical
Christians have too often neglected. It is that both I myself and every
other man are created in the image of God, and this fact should be
determinative of my relationship to other men, whatever their status
in life. Paul stressed this fact in his sermon at Athens. God

> made from one blood every nation of men to live on all the face of the
> earth. . . . Yet he is not far from each one of us, for in him we live and move
> and have our being; as even some of your poets have said, For we are indeed
> his offspring. Being then God's offspring, we ought not to think that the
> Deity is like gold, or silver, or stone, a representation by the art and
> imagination of man (Acts 17:26–29).

In other words, God is not less than his creatures, and since man is
more than an idol, God is more than an idol. Here is a staggering
thought. There is something divine about all men. And the divine
element consists in the fact that we are God's offspring; we are
created in the image and likeness of God; we are living spirits, as God
is a spirit.

One important fact must be noted lest we be misunderstood.
Paul is talking about man seen as creature, not man seen as redeemed. He is speaking of the order of creation, not redemption. It
remains true that man, although a creature of God, is in rebellion
against his God. However, this passage must not be overlooked.
There *is* a biblical doctrine of the universal fatherhood of God. "For
we are indeed his offspring" (Acts 17:28). God is the father of all

men as their creator; he wills to become their father as their redeemer and savior. If all men are by creation the offspring of God, then it follows that there is a universal brotherhood of man. All men, whatever their race or social status, yes, even whatever their religion, are like us, the offspring of God. It follows, therefore, that I should regard every man and treat him as my brother, whoever he may be. Here is a biblical basis for a social ethic. I must be concerned about the welfare of my fellow man, for he, like myself, is God's offspring.

The third thing the Bible reveals is human destiny. One of the most prevalent themes running throughout the Bible is the Kingdom of God. The prophets continually look forward to a day when God will become the only recognized King among men. This Kingdom involves three things: the conversion of God's people so that they become perfectly obedient to the divine will; the suppression of all who would oppose God's will; and the transformation of the world so that it provides a suitable dwelling place for God's people. This expectation is vividly expressed in Isaiah 11, where the prophet sees a new King arising from the family of David:

> And the Spirit of the Lord shall rest upon him. . . .
> And his delight shall be in the fear of the Lord. . . .
> With righteousness he shall judge the poor,
> and decide with equity for the meek of the earth;
> and he shall smite the earth with the rod of his mouth,
> and with the breath of his lips he shall slay the wicked (Isa 11:2–4).

There follows a description of a redeemed earth:

> The wolf shall dwell with the lamb,
> and the leopard shall lie down with the kid . . .
> and a little child shall lead them. . . .
> They shall not hurt or destroy in all my holy mountain;
> for the earth shall be full of the knowledge of the Lord
> as the waters cover the sea (Isa 11:6–9).

Here in poetic language is described a state of earthly bliss where there shall be no more violence, cruelty, or death, where God will bring salvation to the poor and the weak of the earth, where every hostile force shall be subdued, where God shall be known, loved, and served in all the earth.

The New Testament complements this promise. Throughout the New Testament, the Kingdom of God is seen as the divinely intended goal. This is explicitly stated in Rev 11:15: "The kingdom of the world has become the kingdom of our Lord and his Christ, and he shall reign for ever and ever." It is equally explicit in Paul. "For he [Christ] must reign until he has put all his enemies under his feet" (1 Cor 15:25). Paul is equally explicit about the redemption of creation: "Because the creation itself will be set free from its bondage to decay and obtain the glorious liberty of the children of God" (Rom 8:21).

The New Testament ends with a prophetic vision of a new heaven and a new earth with God's (and man's) enemies abolished. "The last enemy to be destroyed is death" (1 Cor 15:26), with God's people redeemed from all evil, dwelling in perfect fellowship with God. All this is encapsulated in the brief saying, "They shall see his face" (Rev 22:4).

This means that history is going somewhere. It is moving surely toward the Kingdom of God. This is not because of any powers resident in history; it is due solely to God. We have already quoted Bultmann to the effect that we do not know the goal of history and that the search for meaning in history is meaningless. On the contrary, the theme of the goal and meaning of history is one of the central themes of the Bible. However, this meaning does not reside in history as history, but in God who acts in history. Bultmann makes the above comment because he considers himself a modern man who has a "scientific outlook" and cannot envisage such an event as the New Testament describes as the Second Coming of Christ. However, the evangelical Christian is sure that the Kingdom of God will come because in the historical mission of Jesus, the Kingdom of God has already come. Jesus said, "If it is by the Spirit of God that I cast out demons, then the kingdom of God *has come* upon you" (Matt 12:28). We have already tasted the powers of the Age to Come (Heb 6:5). Furthermore, the believer knows that Christ is already enthroned as King even though the human eye may not behold it. "When he had made purification for sins, he sat down at the right hand of the majesty on high" (Heb 1:3). "Sit at my right hand, till I make thy enemies a stool for thy feet" (Heb 1:13). In Jesus' historical mission, God has acted to bring to men in advance the blessings of Christ's reign, and this same Jesus will come again in power and glory as the Davidic King and the heavenly Son of Man to consummate his redemptive reign and to fulfill the biblical hope of the Kingdom of God.

These, then, are the three main themes of the Bible: God, man, and destiny. These constitute the substance of Christian teaching and preaching.

2. Scripture for Reproof

A second reason according to our text that God inspired the Bible is that it may be profitable for *reproof.* We have said that one

of the functions of the Kingdom of God is to subdue God's enemies—to judge wicked men. Something has gone wrong with human
society. We have pointed out that the Bible has a high view of man.
He was created in the image of God, and is a created child of God.
However, this is not the whole story. Men do not act like the
children of God. As we survey the conduct of contemporary man,
one would never guess that he is in the image of God. Indeed, his
conduct reflects evil—oftentimes demonic evil. Men often act as
though they were possessed by evil demonic powers.

Here is a tragic contradiction: men made to be the children of
God but often acting like children of the devil. The answer of the
Bible is clear. Man's evil plight has not come about because he is a
creature, or because as a creature he stands at important points in
solidarity with the animal world. While in his physical and emotional
being he is an animal, he stands apart from the animal world as the
crown and glory of God's creation.

> When I look at the heavens, the work of thy fingers,
> the moon and the stars which thou hast established,
> what is man that thou art mindful of him,
> and the son of man that thou dost care for him? (Ps 8:3—4).

It is true that when man compares himself with the vast powers
evidenced in the physical creation he seems weak and puny. But that
is only half the story.

> Yet thou hast made him a little lower than God,
> and dost crown him with glory and honor.
> Thou hast given him dominion over the work of thy hands;
> thou hast put all things under his feet (Ps 8:5—6).

Man stands both in continuity and discontinuity with the totality of
creation. He has been given superintendence over the works of
creation; that is, he is the lord of creation, overseeing it for God.

Yet something has gone wrong. Oftentimes man acts more like an
animal than a child of God. In our "advanced" scientific world,
numerous bloody wars are taking place. The Los Angeles area
witnesses about four homicides a day, many of them senseless,
irrational killings. The main theme of many of our current motion
pictures is violence for its own sake. This is not because of man's
physical nature or weakness. It is not because he has bodily ap-
petites, like the other animals. Indeed, Paul says, "Whether you eat
or drink, do all to the glory of God" (1 Cor 10:31). Again, speaking
of sexual matters, he exhorts, "Glorify God in your body" (1 Cor
6:20).

The evil which is seen in human conduct has come about because man has rebelled against God. His sin is first of all a sin of the spirit, of the human will. "For the wrath of God is revealed from heaven against all ungodliness and wickedness of man" (Rom 1:18). *Asebeia*—ungodliness, impiety, irreverence—here is the root of sin. All kinds of wickedness follow man's rebellion against God.

This is not something which can be detected by the scientific study of man, nor by psychological analysis. It can be known only by revelation—the revelation given in God's inspired Word. All Scripture is inspired of God and is profitable for *reproof.* To the man who will read the Bible as the Word of God, it will rebuke him for his godlessness. It will disclose to him that his heart, his affections, have turned him away from God—indeed, against God. Here is the fount of all evil—the perverted will of man.

According to the Bible, the root of sin is self-centeredness rather than God-centeredness. It is pride in one's own achievements. It is boasting of one's self instead of starting out where the Bible does— man as a convicted sinner. Left to himself, there is no way out. Left to himself, he can only face the wrath of God.

Here again is freedom. God has placed man in a position of superiority over his entire creation. But when a man exercises this mastery for self-glorification and self-exaltation, instead of as a steward responsible to God, he falls into sin. God has inspired the Bible to make man's fallen and rebellious condition clear.

3. Scripture for Correction

All Scripture is inspired of God and is profitable for *correction.* The good news of the gospel is that God has taken the initiative to do something about man's helpless and hopeless state. He has acted in Jesus Christ to restore man to the position he ought to fill. The Greek word is used only here in the New Testament and means restoration or correction. God is not satisfied to rebuke us for our rebellion; he would restore us to a position of favor.

Here is another truth which can be discovered only by divine revelation: how to find the way that leads to salvation. Paul has just written, "From childhood you have been acquainted with the sacred writings which are able to instruct you for salvation through faith in Christ Jesus" (2 Tim 3:15). Apart from the Word of God, man is lost. He cannot find his way. The Bible is a divinely inspired book whose purpose is to direct lost men in the faith that leads to salvation. Undoubtedly the salvation spoken of here is eschatological. The way to salvation in God's eschatological Kingdom can be found only by divine revelation. Indeed, sometimes it seems as though evil powers are so predominant in human experience that the salvation pictured in the Bible seems almost to be a vain hope, an empty dream. The Bible says that Jesus is even *now* the ascended, enthroned Lord over all. Confession of Jesus as Lord was the most popular primitive Christian profession (Rom 10:9). God has even now seated Jesus at his right hand and bestowed on him the status of Lord. Yet history does not look like it. Even as these words are being written, wars are raging in several quarters of the earth. Where is God's salvation?

The Bible has been inspired to lead us through the confusing experiences of life to God's salvation. We should not be disappointed that we do not *see* it. Now we walk by faith, not by sight (2 Cor 5:7). Even though human experiences and the contemporary events of human history seem to contradict it, the man of faith finds in the inspired Scripture a sure guide to the eschatological salvation.

I am reminded of an experience I had the first time I took a long flight in an airplane. I was flying down the west coast from Portland to Los Angeles late in the afternoon. From a height of 20,000 feet, the sunset was nothing less than spectacular. I watched the lights in the towns below us twinkle on while the sun still rested on the western horizon. As we flew over the San Gabriel mountains and the Hollywood hills, I could see that the entire Los Angeles area was "socked in" with low clouds and fog. It was bright with a luminescence because of the thousands of lights on the ground. At that time I knew nothing about aerial navigation, and I assumed the fog reached to the ground. This was during the time of the famous Berlin airlift, when planes flew in all kinds of weather, even at ground zero, and I remembered seeing on television pictures of planes missing the runways and cracking up. Frankly, I was scared. We descended into the clouds, and I sat glued to the window, straining to see through the clouds. I was literally sweating from fear. It seemed as though we were in the clouds for half an hour. I had never been so frightened in my life. But suddenly we broke out of the clouds and fog, and found ourselves directly over the end of the runway, with just enough clearance for a perfectly safe landing.

I have learned since then that both the pilot in the plane and the people in the control tower have electronic instruments so that the pilot always knows where he is "on the beam." The point is that because of these instruments, both the pilot and the tower knew all the time where we were, in complete safety. But I did not know that. I was lost.

The Word of God is inspired to be such a guide to us, to guide us safely into our salvation. Many times we cannot see or understand why life is like it is. All we can see is clouds and fog. This is true in the world as a whole; it is all too often true in the world of individual experience. He whom we honor in this volume has been through his share of clouds and fog in which it was impossible to see and understand. However, we have the inspired Word of God, which serves as a beam, unseen by the world, which will surely bring us to our divinely intended destination—salvation.

4. Scripture for Training in Righteousness

Finally, the Word is inspired that it might be profitable for *instruction in righteousness.* This is an emphasis much needed in our day of "situational ethics," when even theologians tell us that all conduct is acceptable if it doesn't hurt anyone.

The conclusion cannot be avoided that much of the New Testament is devoted to ethical teaching. Some scholars would separate ethics from theology. Peabody said that Jesus' first demand was not for orthodox instruction or for ecstatic religious experience but for morality.[2] The Jewish scholar Klausner said, "If ever the day should come and this ethical code be stripped of its wrappings of miracles and mysticism, the Book of the Ethics of Jesus will be one of the choicest treasures of the literature of Israel for all time."[3] However, this cannot be done. The ethics of Jesus cannot be divorced from his person and preaching about the Kingdom of God. But not only the teachings of Jesus but the whole Bible is the inspired Word of God. In Evangelical theology, all ethics is theologically grounded. Right is right because God has spoken; wrong is wrong because God has said, "Thou shalt not."

This does not mean a literalistic, wooden, proof-text approach. We must recognize progressive revelation, that the New Covenant reinterprets the Old Covenant. Furthermore, it is clear that even in the New Testament, much ethical teaching is culturally conditioned. The problem of meats offered to idols is as such no problem to the modern North American or European Christian as it was in Corinth. Even so, Paul's instruction about meats offered to idols contains principles which transcend their cultural situations and have a modern application. Peter's injunction to women, "Let not yours be the outward adorning of hair, decoration of gold, and wearing of robes" (1 Pet 3:3), has nothing to do with the question of women going to beauty parlors. Furthermore, some ethical questions are not explicitly discussed even in the New Testament. The letter to Philemon appears to sanction slavery as an institution even though it insists upon a new relationship within the institution. A biblical basis for our ethic of liberation cannot be found in the letter of Scripture. When such questions have been recognized, it remains true that the Word of God contains an ethic which is the will of God for Christian conduct. Ultimately right is right because God is God.

God has inspired the Bible that it may *become the Word of God to me.* Let the reader not misunderstand this statement. The Bible *is* the Word of God whether anyone recognizes it or not. But because the Bible *is* the Word of God, it must *become* the Word of God to me, who lives in an entirely different age and culture.

God desires that "the man of God may be complete, equipped for every good work" (2 Tim 3:17). This is the book we preach and teach. This is the book by which he whom we are honoring has conformed his life. He is a man of God, thoroughly equipped for every good work.

NOTES

1. R. Bultmann, *History and Eschatology* (1957), p. 120.
2. F. G. Peabody, *Jesus Christ and Christian Character* (1905), p. 103.
3. J. Klausner, *Jesus of Nazareth* (1925), p. 414.

5: Worthy Is the Lamb

ROBERT H. MOUNCE

Dr. Harrison once remarked in class that while some scholars study the text of Scripture, others study one another. This was in no way intended to deny the importance of familiarity with the secondary literature. It was, however, a clear challenge to keep it just that—secondary literature. The article which follows is an attempt to write freely about chapter 5 of Revelation. Commentaries and journals have been read in general preparation, but then they were laid aside. The author alone is responsible for what happens in this highly individualistic experiment.

1. Grammatical Observations

I have always felt that syntax has been slighted in exegesis. Words have received the tender care of philologists until they have been worn smooth by constant handling. How many times, for instance, have we been reminded that *kairos* means "a decisive moment," while *chronos* denotes time in a "general sense." And so it does. But *kairos* may be used in the sense of "from time to time" (John 5:4) or "about that time" (Matt 11:25). Undue attention to individual words tends to obscure the fact that a word means only what it means in a specific context. In English, the word "fast" is essentially meaningless until you place it in a sentence. A sprinter runs "fast"; color that doesn't fade in the washing machine is "fast"; a person bound hand and foot is tied "fast"; the dieter who goes without food is said to "fast." What does "fast" mean? Put it in a sentence and I will tell you!

Arranging words to convey an idea is what intelligent speech is all about. Without syntax our literary efforts would be at best a series of unconnected one word grunts. It is words in concert with one another that give meaning to the whole. And the whole—that is, the sentence or the paragraph—determines the meaning of each word *in that setting,* and that setting alone. Obviously, words do not have opposite meanings in different contexts, but the variation in meaning is sufficiently significant that while appreciating the help of the dictionary, we must insist that its broad categories are much too clumsy to do justice to the text of Scripture.

One of the better ways to become aware of the syntactical idiosyncrasies of an author is to diagram his sentences. This I did with Revelation 5. The first thing I noticed is that every verse in the chapter (except v. 12, which carries on the sentence begun in the previous verse) begins with *kai.* While this may not be very important, it does tell us something about the style of the author. It suggests a Semitic influence in which clauses tend to follow one another without being dependent or subordinate. Thus it is no surprise to learn that the chapter contains only two *hoti* clauses: John weeps *because* no one is found worthy to open the book (v. 4) and the four living creatures and elders declare the Lamb to be worthy *because* he was slain, purchased men, and made them kings and priests (v. 9). Apart from these two occurrences there are no subordinate clauses in the chapter (I take infinitives as extensions of the verbal idea). Only one appositional phrase is to be found: the Lion who conquered is at the same time the Root of David. Two relative clauses are used: the seven eyes of the Lamb are further identified as the seven spirits of God (v. 6) and the incense which fills the golden bowls of the heavenly attendants is the prayers of the saints (v. 8). The question that could arise is, How, with such a simple syntax, can the Seer do justice to the majesty and wonder of a heavenly throne-room experience? Since chapter 5 is widely accepted as a magnificent example of rhetorical skill, the answer must be that complicated sentence structure and syntactical subtleties are unnecessary for stylistic achievement. As in so many other areas, artistic achievement lies along the line of utter simplicity.

Since John is often accused of writing barbaric Greek, we need to look at his two "grammatical errors" in chapter 5. The first is in verse 12. The antecedent of *legontes* apparently is *angelōn pollōn* (of v. 11) or perhaps *phōnēn.* Why did John use a nominative masculine plural? The obvious answer is that the more distance one places between a participle and its antecedent the weaker the tie becomes. Here, nineteen words separate *legontes* and *angelōn pollōn.* The parenthetical remark about the number of angels (11b) serves to separate even further. So when John begins verse 12 he moves naturally to a nominative plural and assumes his readers will subconsciously adjust. Only a pedant would insist that this constitutes a grammatical error. The other example is in verse 13 where John writes *pan ktisma . . . legontas.* How does he get from the neuter singular to the masculine plural? In this case twenty-two words separate participle and antecedent. In between we learn that included in "every creature" are those in heaven, on earth, under the earth, and upon the sea (and all that is in them). Since this great multitude gives praise, honor, glory, and power to God and the Lamb, they must be intelligent beings, or at least personified as such. Is there any question, then, why the masculine plural *legontas* is used?

Several of the variants are interesting in that they reveal how scribes reacted to or tried to rearrange in a more satisfactory manner the text as it stands.

In the first verse of the chapter we learn of a seven-sealed book which was written "within and on the back" (A 1), or "before and behind" (ℵ), or "within and without and in front and on the back" (2073; no chances taken here!). One manuscript of Andrew of Caesarea has "written on the inside and the outside: and on the back sealed with seven seals." Apparently the word *opisthen* bothered the later copyist. Terminology appropriate for a scroll appeared strange when applied to a codex. Perhaps "completely covered with writing" would be the nearest contemporary equivalent.

In verse 4 *ego* is added before *eklaion* to show that it was John, not those implied in the previous verse as unable to open the book, who broke out weeping (taking the verb as an inceptive imperfect). The KJV addition "to open *and to read* the book" follows inferior manuscript evidence. The problem in verse 6 is whether the seven eyes of the Lamb (A) or the seven spirits of God (ℵ) have been sent out into all the earth. The Byzantine text reads the present participle (*apostallomena*) rather than the perfect, suggesting that the activity is continuing in the present time. The perfect passive nominative plural *apestalmenoi* has as its antecedent *ophthalmous*, while the neuter *apestalmena* takes *pneumati. Ophthalmous* is the first and more basic term from a syntactical point of view (it completes the *echōn*, which in turn modifies the direct object *arnion,* of the main clause) and hence determines the case of *apestalmenoi.* It is difficult, however, to think of "eyes" being sent out into the earth, so the variant *apestalmena* assigns the activity to the "seven spirits."

The various ways that *hēmas* is added after *ēgorasas* in verse 9 show the scribes' uneasiness about leaving the verb without a specific direct object. When omitted (as it is **A** and the Ethiopic) there is no direct indication of who is purchased.

Verse 10 has two important variants. The Textus Receptus reads *hēmas* rather than *autous* and *basileusomen* rather than *basileusousin* (or *basileuousin*) which places the twenty-four elders among the redeemed. (It also includes the four living creatures among the redeemed—they are coordinate with the twenty-four elders and fall before the Lamb in worship [v. 8] and sing a new song [v. 9]—but no one seems to be troubled by this unusual circumstance!) Textual evidence strongly favors the readings which distinguish the elders from those who are the redeemed. The King James, following the Byzantine text, has led many interpreters astray in their attempt to identify the twenty-four elders.

The most interesting observation coming from a survey of John's vocabulary in the book of Revelation is his use of *arnion*. It occurs twenty-nine times in Revelation and only once elsewhere in the New Testament (John 21:15). The glorified Christ in Revelation is not the *amnos tou theou*—the Lamb of God who dies innocently and representatively—but the *arnion tou theou*—the messianic leader who has conquered by the power of selfless love and leads his followers in triumph over the powers of evil. While the figure is taken from the vocabulary of Jewish apocalyptic, its specific meaning in Revelation is determined by the way it is employed by John in its many contexts.

2. Rhetorical Observations

Rhetoric is usually defined as the art or science of using words effectively. Rhetorical skill is not simply vocabulary or a grandiose style but the effective use of words. Words may be said to be used effectively when they accomplish the aim or goal of the speaker or writer. I consider the opening sentence of a well-known book ("My name is Asher Lev") to be an eloquent example of rhetorical skill. It is powerful in its simplicity and utterly clear. It anticipates in a poignant way the intensely personal drama to follow. Is the Seer of Revelation rhetorically sophisticated or do the words from his pen lack the power to captivate and move? We will examine several characteristics of his style, and you be the judge.

The first thing I notice is his habit of joining words or phrases in couplets, threes, fours, and sevens. The parallel words and phrases may be emphasized by the following format:

The scroll is written
   within and
   on the back (v. 1).

John saw the book
   written
   sealed (v. 1).

The strong angel asked who was worthy to
    open the book and
    loose its seals (v. 2; cf. v. 9).

No one was able to
    open the book or
    look into it (v. 3; also v. 4).

But the Lion has conquered to open
    the book and
    its seven seals (v. 5).

John saw a Lamb
    in the midst of
        the throne and
        the four living creatures, and
    in the midst of the elders (v. 6; the parallel use of *en mesō* is
        obscured by the RSV's change from "between" to
        "among").

The Lamb
    went and
           the scroll (v. 7).
    took

The four living creatures and ⎫
The twenty-four elders   ⎬ fell before the Lamb (v. 8).

They had
    harps and
    golden bowls (v. 8).

They sang a new song to the Lamb because
    he was slain and
    did ransom men (v. 9).

He made them
    a kingdom and
    priests (v. 10).

The number of worshipers was
    myriads of myriads and
    thousands of thousands (v. 11).

All creation honors
    the One sitting upon the throne and
    the Lamb (v. 13).

The elders
    fell down and
    worshiped (v. 14).

I count seventeen couplets in thirteen of the fourteen verses in the chapter. Only verse 12 has no parallel passage, and that is certainly because it is taken up with a climactic sevenfold ascription of praise to the Lamb. This constant use of parallel words and phrases is a major distinguishing characteristic of the writer's rhetorical method.

There are within the chapter three incidents of a threefold grouping:

No one
> in heaven or
> on earth or
> under the earth
>> was able to open the book (v. 3).

John heard the voice of many angels around
> the throne and
> the living creatures and
> the elders (v. 11).

It is also possible to see a three-part expression in verse 7 where the Lamb takes (the scroll)

> *ek tēs dexias*
> *tou kathēmenou*
> *epi tou thronou*

and in verse 9 and 10 where the Lamb

> *esphagēs*
> *ēgorasas*
> *epoiēsas*

Verses 9 and 13 provide three good examples of groupings of four elements:

The Lamb ransomed men from every
> tribe and
> tongue and
> people and
> nation (v. 9).

John hears every creature
> in heaven and
> on earth and
> under the earth and in the sea (v. 13; note that the first three elements parallel v. 3).

Three creatures ascribe to God and the Lamb
> blessing

honor
glory
might (v. 13; all but *kratos* are included in the sevenfold list
   of v. 12).

Finally, in verse 12 we learn that the Lamb is worthy to receive

power and
wealth and
wisdom and
might and
honor and
glory and
blessing.

What does this all mean? While the couplets are equally dis-
tributed throughout the chapter, the other combinations are
clustered toward the latter part of the chapter. Seen graphically, they
are as follows:

```
1  2  3  4  5  6  7  8  9  10  11  12  13  14
   III                       III
                        IV             IV
                            VII
```

Whether consciously or intuitively, the chapter builds in rhetorical
intensity to a climax in verse 12 with the sevenfold ascription of
worth to the Lamb. When the chapter is read aloud with this in
mind, there can be no doubt where the high point of the chapter lies
and how skillfully the author leads his readers to grasp the central
significance of verse 12.

Perhaps the most obvious rhetorical device in the chapter is the
use of direct quotations. Three of the six quotations are connected
with the Lamb as worthy to open the scroll. In verse 2 the strong
angel asks, "Who is worthy to open the scroll and break its seals?" In
verse 9 the heavenly worshipers say to the Lamb, "Thou art worthy
to take the scroll and open its seals." In verse 12 the angelic hosts
proclaim with a loud voice, "The Lamb who was slain is worthy to
receive power and wealth and wisdom and might and honor and
glory and blessing!" These direct quotations add vividness to the
heavenly throne-room scene. The other three examples are found in
verse 5 where one of the elders instructs John not to cry, verse 13
where all creation praises God and the Lamb, and verse 14 where the
four living creatures (almost in the fatigue of exaltation as it were)
bring the scene to a close with a simple "Amen."

Other rhetorical devices employed by the Seer include repetition (cf. "open and break/look into" in vv. 2, 3, 4, 5, 9 [reversed]), assonance (*myriades myriadōn kai chiliades chiliadōn*), dramatic contrast ("Lo, the *Lion* of the tribe of Judah" and "I saw a *Lamb* standing," vv. 5–6), and doxologies (vv. 12–13). In view of the rhetorical skill which lies behind the dramatic power of chapter 5 it is hard to agree with those who insist that the Greek of Revelation is barbaric and ungrammatical. That it doesn't pay unwarranted respect to rules laid down by grammarians is quite obvious, but the reason for this lies more in the exalted state of the writer than in any lack of ability to compose acceptable Greek prose. "Rules" are broken both by those who don't know them and by those whose message causes them to transcend normal patterns. John fits the latter category!

3. Theological Observations

The theology of chapter 5 is primarily a Christology. In the previous chapter the adoration of heaven is directed toward the indescribable One seated on the heavenly throne. The four living creatures give him glory and honor (4:8–9), and the twenty-four elders fall down before him to sing his praises as Creator (4:10–11). In chapter 5 the focus moves to the Lamb as Redeemer.

First the problem is set forth: no one in heaven, on earth, or under the earth is able to open the scroll or look into it. No one is able because no one has conquered (v. 5). Knowledge of the outcome of human history and the privilege of setting into motion the events that lead irreversibly toward the consummation are privileges reserved for the One who entered into history and conquered it by his death (v. 9). The uniqueness of this great redemptive act is underscored by the fact that *no one* in heaven or on earth (or under the earth for that matter) was worthy to perform the one crucial act necessary to bring history to its appointed goal. No wonder John wept much!

The Gordian knot is cut by One who bears three titles in Revelation 5. He is the Lion of the tribe of Judah. Gen 49:3–27 predicts what is to happen to each of the tribes of Israel in the days that would follow. Jacob refers to Judah as "a lion's whelp" (v. 9) and declares that "the scepter shall not depart from Judah, nor the ruler's staff from between his feet, until he comes to whom it belongs (or "until Shiloh come" [ASV])." The authority to rule is to remain as the prerogative of the tribe of Judah until the One comes to whom all sovereignty is given. He is the Lion of the tribe of Judah, a title taken from the common stock of Jewish messianism and applied appropriately to Jesus the Christ.

The Lion of Judah is also the Root of David. This second title is an allusion to Isa 11:1 ("There shall come forth a shoot from the stump of Jesse, and a branch shall grow out of his roots") which looks forward to an ideal king of the line of David who will judge with righteousness and usher in an era of peace. These two titles unite the Christ of the New Testament with the messianic expectations of the Old. He becomes the theological link which makes the Christian faith the authentic fulfillment of all that God promised to his ancient people of Israel.

The Lion and the Root are also the Lamb. Most commentators consider this a dramatic contrast. The Lion is pictured as a mighty beast symbolizing power and dominance while the Lamb is set forth as meek and unassuming. Verse 6 says that John sees a Lamb "standing, as though it had been slain." This apparently strengthens the picture of a sacrificial lamb. But slain lambs do not stand! The comma which translators quite regularly place after "standing" recognizes that the larger phrase contains two separate ideas. The Lamb that John sees is standing. He also bears the marks of having been offered in sacrifice. That he stands indicates his victory over sin and death by virtue of his resurrection from the dead. The Lamb in Revelation should not be thought of as innocent victim but as conquering leader. Earlier it was mentioned that *arnion* is regularly used to designate a messianic leader. The *arnion* of Revelation is not a dramatic contrast to the figure of the Lion but an extension of the same powerful figure. The Lamb is pictured as having seven horns (perfect or complete power) and seven eyes (absolutely nothing escapes his observation). The seven eyes are then designated as the seven spirits of God sent out into all the earth. The Lamb knows all because he sees all. He sees all because the seven spirits of God go out into all the earth. The seven horns and seven eyes are symbols of perfect power and knowledge.

Verse 5 tells us *why* the Lamb is worthy and what follows as a result. He is worthy because he has conquered. "Has conquered *what?*" can be asked. The answer is given in verse 9, "Worthy art thou—for thou wast slain and by thy blood didst ransom men for God." The Warrior-Messiah has already fought and won the decisive battle. By the sacrifice of his life he defeated sin and Satan. He accepted their ultimate stroke and rose victorious. He gathered into himself the full fury of evil and crushed it by the sacrifice of his life. When he rose victorious over the grave, there remained nothing in the arsenal of Satan which could in the least way touch him. He conquered, and is therefore worthy to set into motion the final sequence of events leading to the ultimate destruction of the forces of evil and the eternal vindication of those who follow in his train. His great redemptive act brought to God men from every tribe, tongue, people, and nation. This great universal multitude has been made by his ransom a kingdom and priests to God. As a kingdom they constitute a community under the sovereign reign and rule of God. As priests they enjoy immediate access to God and the privilege of bringing others into his presence. And they shall reign on earth! Not only do they reign now in a spiritual sense, but in the consummation they shall be declared victorious and share in the universal acclamation to the Lamb and his followers. Little wonder that all the hosts of heaven declare, "Worthy is the Lamb who was slain, to receive power and wealth and wisdom and might and honor and glory and blessing!" (v. 12). A sevenfold ascription is appropriate for the perfection of the Lamb in his role as Redeemer.

When the Lamb takes the scroll from the right hand of him who is seated on the heavenly throne, the four living creatures and the twenty-four elders fall before him in adoration. The golden bowls they carry are full of incense which represents the prayers of the saints. Thus even those who as yet belong to this life join in the activity of heaven. The Lamb is worthy of all praise. His exaltation in the book of Revelation is best revealed by the fact that the final doxology of the chapter is directed to "him who sits upon the throne *and to the Lamb* (v. 13). The Redeemer Lamb and the Creator God share equally in the praise given by the adoring universe. No Christology could possibly go beyond this.

6: A Third Alternative: Scripture, Tradition, and Interpretation in the Theology of G.C. Berkouwer

JACK ROGERS

In the late nineteenth and early twentieth centuries two move-ments had a decisive effect on American evangelical theology, espe-cially in its Reformed expression. One of these movements was liberalism, which denied central doctrinal affirmations of orthodoxy, discounted supernaturalism, and introduced new scholarly methods of biblical criticism.[1] The second movement was Reformed scholasti-cism, particularly as presented by the old Princeton theology of Archibald Alexander, Charles Hodge, and B. B. Warfield. Following the Scottish Realist philosophy of Thomas Reid and the post-Refor-mation scholastic theology of Francis Turretin, they dug in to oppose all the tendencies of liberalism. They repeated doctrinal forms rigidly. Wary of every human element in Scripture, they exalted the whole of Scripture as divine. They opposed the use of biblical criticism and minimized attention to the historical and cul-tural context in the interpretation of biblical materials.[2] For many Reformed evangelicals that turn-of-the-century dichotomy still pre-vails. The assumption is that if we wish to avoid the debilitating effects of a liberal subjectivism, we must adopt the scholastic ration-alism of the Hodge/Warfield doctrine of Scripture. These are not, however, the only alternatives.

Many, indeed most, evangelical scholars have long been aware of data in and about Scripture which do not fit the older Hodge/War-field model of the doctrine of Scripture. But without a new paradigm into which to fit their facts they have been reluctant to pursue their findings, or to publish them. It has been demonstrated that in any field of scholarly study, new facts are not enough to cause people to abandon old theories.[3] A new theory must be advanced which takes account of all the available data and makes better sense of them than the outmoded model.

This article intends to suggest that our own American history has left us with a distorted picture of our theological options. The liberal-scholastic dichotomy forced to prominence by the Fundamentalist-Modernist controversy in the early part of this century was not and is not the only option for Reformed evangelicals.[4] There is a third alternative, a different doctrine of Scripture, a more adequate model of what the Bible is and how it works. It is not a new alternative, but an old one—as old as Augustine and Calvin. This model focuses not on the nature, but on the function of Scripture. But because of the peculiarities of our own American evangelical history, it has been overlooked. That was not the case outside this country.

In Europe, in addition to those who in the nineteenth century tried to hold on to a scholastic orthodoxy and those who reacted against it and became liberals, there were others who never became involved in that unfruitful dichotomy. In England there were highly respected evangelicals such as James Orr who rejected the Hodge/Warfield theory about Scripture as unnecessary and unhelpful in dealing with the biblical data.[5] As one result there is a healthy tradition of evangelical biblical scholarship in England which is not preoccupied with formalistic questions. Evangelical scholars such as F. F. Bruce hold to the full authority of Scripture *and* to the necessity of using biblical criticism in interpreting the Bible.

Another illustration, which I would like to develop more fully, comes from the Dutch Reformed tradition in the Netherlands. During the height of nineteenth-century liberalism in the Netherlands there were two splits from the national Reformed Church, each endeavoring to recover Calvinistic orthodoxy. One was a spontaneous pietistic movement, whose greatest theologian was Herman Bavinck (1854–1921). Bavinck took his doctorate at Leiden under Scholten, the father of Dutch theological liberalism. Bavinck studied the Reformers, however, and wrote his dissertation on *The Ethics of Ulrich Zwingli.* He later taught at a small theological seminary of his denomination and produced a four-volume systematic theology, *Gereformeerde Dogmatiek,* between 1895 and 1901. Only a part of volume two was published in English under the title *The Doctrine of God.*[6] His doctrine of Scripture in volume one has never been available to American readers.

The other split from the state church was deliberate and well organized. Its leader, politically and theologically, was Abraham Kuyper (1837–1920). Kuyper also studied at Leiden under liberal teachers and also researched the reformers. He wrote his doctoral dissertation on the idea of the Church in John Calvin and Johannes à

Lasco. Kuyper was brought back to an orthodox Augustinian-Calvinist orientation both through his studies and the piety of the common people in his first pastoral charge. Kuyper wrote voluminously, but few of his writings have been translated into English. Kuyper's organizing genius was expressed in creating institutions based on Christian principles. He founded the Free University of Amsterdam, edited a daily newspaper, led a political party, and eventually became the prime minister of the Netherlands. Later, these two splinter denominations merged, in 1892, to form the *Gereformeerde Kerken* (the Reformed Churches).

When Kuyper left for government leadership in 1902, Bavinck succeeded him as Professor of Dogmatics at the Free University. Both Kuyper and Bavinck were respected in America as evangelicals and Calvinists. Each gave the celebrated Stone Lectures at Princeton, Kuyper in 1898 on *Calvinism,* and Bavinck in 1908 on *The Philosophy of Revelation.* Warfield contributed enthusiastic introductions to the English translations of a part of Kuyper's *Principles of Sacred Theology* in 1898, and to Kuyper's *The Work of the Holy Spirit* in 1900. Later, in 1903, Warfield expressed concern about Kuyper's view of apologetics.[7] Together, Kuyper and Bavinck perpetuated a theological method which, particularly with regard to Scripture, followed in the line of Augustine and the Reformers rather than adopting the post-Reformation scholasticism preferred by the Princeton theology. The Dutch Reformed tradition held to the Augustinian method that faith leads to understanding rather than the medieval scholastic view that reasons were necessary prior to faith. Thus, the primary issue for the Dutch Reformed tradition was the functional one of how God relates to us rather than the philosophical issue of whether God's existence can be proved. In relation to the Bible that meant the Holy Spirit moved us to accept Scripture as authoritative because of the saving message it expressed rather than that our reason compelled us to believe the Bible because of evidential or logical proofs of its divine character.

A brief detour from the Reformation stance at the Free University occurred when Bavinck was succeeded in the Chair of Dogmatics by Valentine Hepp in 1922. Hepp shifted the emphasis to apologetics and adopted the Princeton model for doing theology. For Kuyper, apologetics was the last theological discipline. For Warfield, it was the first.[8] Hepp agreed with Warfield and attempted to develop a distinctively Reformed apologetics. In his Stone Lectures at Princeton, *Calvinism and the Philosophy of Nature,* Hepp expressed an affinity with the theology of the First Vatican Council (1870), that

God could be known from the world of created reality through the natural light of reason.[9]

One of Hepp's doctoral students was Gerrit Cornelis Berkouwer (1903–). Berkouwer grew up in a devoutly Reformed home and a Reformed community committed to subjecting all of life and culture to the authority of the Bible.[10] He went to the university intending to study mathematics, but the preachers in his home church had so captivated his interest that he switched his course of study to theology—an unusual and difficult decision in the Dutch educational system.[11] During his years of study, his denomination, the *Gereformeerde Kerken*, was rent with strife over the doctrine of Scripture. In 1926, a prominent minister was ejected for denying that the serpent had literally spoken to Eve in the garden. Berkouwer and his fellow students were deeply involved in discussion of these matters.

Hepp wanted Berkouwer to write his dissertation on Karl Heim, a German theologian who had devoted himself to the apologetic confrontation between faith and modern science and philosophy. Berkouwer corresponded with Heim, but became convinced that theological attention in Germany was shifting to dialectical theology.[12] He received his doctorate in 1932, shortly after beginning his second pastorate. His subject was *Faith and Revelation in the Newer German Theology.* He treated the views of Ritschl, Herrmann, Wobbermin, Troeltsch, Rudolf Otto, Barth, and Brunner.[13] In 1938, after an early book on Karl Barth, Berkouwer wrote a work in defense of the divinity of Scripture, *The Problem of Biblical Criticism.*[14] It expressed in part the apologetic concerns of Hepp. In a speech which Berkouwer gave to a ministers' conference at this time he stressed the radical commitment of the Reformed view of Scripture to "It Stands Written." One preacher remarked to him that another dimension should be added to this theme, namely, the work of the Holy Spirit in connection with scriptural authority and biblical faith. Berkouwer later commented: "The minister's remark had more to it than I realized when I first heard it, though I certainly was ready then to admit its truth."[15] A deepening awareness that, for the Reformers, the Holy Spirit convinces us of the authority of Scripture was part of Berkouwer's finding his way back to his own tradition.

In 1941 Berkouwer began lecturing in modern theology at the Free University, interacting especially with the developing theology of Barth and the "Crisis Theologians," and Roman Catholicism. When Berkouwer succeeded Hepp as Professor of Dogmatics after the war years, he reaffirmed the theological tradition of Kuyper and Bavinck and began writing a series of monographs designed to bring that tradition into relationship with ongoing discussions in contemporary theology. Beginning with *Faith and Justification* in 1949, his series of Studies in Dogmatics extended to fourteen volumes, the last four of which were published in Dutch as two-volume works.[16] Berkouwer's work *Heilige Schrift* was published in two volumes in 1966 and 1967, with the edited English translation appearing as *Holy Scripture* in 1975.[17] This work received criticism from some evangelicals who had previously lauded Berkouwer's theology. The question arose: Had Berkouwer changed? Or was the problem that the approach to Scripture which had enriched his volumes on other doctrines simply was not in accord with the more scholastic theory bequeathed to American evangelicals from the Hodge/Warfield school? My hope is that an examination of the doctrine of Scripture of Kuyper, Bavinck, and Berkouwer will give us perspective on these questions.

1. The Authority of Scripture in Kuyper, Bavinck, and Berkouwer

Berkouwer's theological method roots in the Augustinian tradition which accepts Scripture in faith and then seeks further understanding of the Bible through a regenerated reason. He is convinced that the purpose or function of Scripture is to bring us to salvation in Christ. Scripture was not given to satisfy our curiosity about philosophical questions. Therefore, Berkouwer, with Calvin, is concerned with Scripture in a functional, not a philosophical, way. The primary issue is, Are we rightly related to the Christ of Scripture?

Berkouwer declares that it is not theologically appropriate "to discuss Scripture apart from a personal relationship of belief in it."[18] He then expands this view, saying:

> Faith is not and cannot be based on a theoretical reflection on what, according to our insight, must be the nature of the divine revelation and on which ways and forms it must have come to us in order to be a guarantee of certainty. The way of Christian faith is . . . a subjection to the gospel, to the Christ of the Scriptures; and from this alone can a reflection on Holy Scripture proceed.[19]

Berkouwer thus reflects Bavinck's attitude that no formal theological method guarantees faith in Scripture. Bavinck wrote: "In the period of dead orthodoxy unbelief in Scripture was in principle just as powerful as in our historico-critical age."[20]

The authority of Scripture, in Berkouwer's tradition, is affirmed to us by the internal testimony of the Holy Spirit. Kuyper said: "The

Reformers wisely appealed on principle to the 'witness of the Holy Spirit.' By this they understood a testimony that went out directly from the Holy Spirit, as author of the Scripture, to our personal *ego*."[21] Kuyper specifically positions himself with the Reformers in denying the efficacy of external evidences to prove the authority of Scripture:

> In this connection the so-called *internal* proof for the Divine character of the Holy Scripture must be understood. In a later period it has been made to appear that "the heavenly majesty of the doctrines, the marvellous completeness of the prophecies, the wonderful miracles, the consent of all its parts, the divineness of the discourse," and so much more formed a system of outward proofs able to convince the reason without enlightenment; but our first theologians at least, did not attach such meaning to them.[22]

Bavinck spoke to the same subject succinctly: "Scripture is the word of God because the Holy Spirit witnesses of Christ in it, because it has the incarnate Word as its subject matter and content."[23]

> The real object to which the Holy Spirit gives witness in the hearts of the believers is no other than the *divinitas* of the truth, poured out on us in Christ. Historical, chronological and geographical data are never, in themselves, the object of the witness of the Holy Spirit.[24]

For Bavinck, the witness of the Spirit to the authority of Scripture was inseparably related to rebirth and conversion. He said: "The *testimonium Spiritus Sancti* is first an assurance that we are children of God."[25] Berkouwer notes with approval that for Bavinck, "our faith in Scripture increases and decreases according to our trust in Christ."[26] Berkouwer in turn positions himself with Calvin and the Reformed confessions, saying that according to them, "faith in Scripture is possible and real only in connection with the witness of the Spirit to Christ and his salvation."[27]

Throughout all of this it can be seen that the purpose or function of Scripture is a central concern for Berkouwer. He cites Bavinck's point that biblical criticism became a problem when the critics lost sight of the purpose of Scripture.[28] Bavinck was unequivocal that the purpose, goal, or "destination" of Scripture "is none other than that it should make us wise to salvation."[29] He declared: "Scripture is the book for Christian religion and Christian theology. For that end it is given. For that end it is suited. And therefore is it the word of God, poured out upon us through the Holy Ghost."[30] Scripture is, therefore, not meant to give us technically correct scientific information:

The writers of Holy Scripture probably knew no more than their contemporaries in all these sciences, geology, zoology, physiology, medicine, etc. And
it was not necessary either. For Holy Scripture uses the language of daily
experience which is always true and remains so. If the Scripture had in place
of it used the language of the school and had spoken with scientific
exactness, it would have stood in the way of its own authority.[31]

Berkouwer comments: "Scripture itself in a very explicit way speaks
about its intention and directedness." That goal, he notes, is salvation (John 20:31), which yields hope (Rom 15:4) and equipment for
every good work (2 Tim 3:16).[32]

Because of their clear understanding that the purpose of Scripture was to bring us to salvation in Christ, the Dutch Reformed
tradition responded very differently to science than did the Princeton theology. In the nineteenth century while Hodge and Warfield
were rejecting biblical criticism, Kuyper and Bavinck were meeting
the issue openly and constructively. Kuyper wrote:

If in the four Gospels, words are put in the mouth of Jesus on the same
occasion which are dissimilar in form of expression, Jesus naturally cannot
have used four forms at the same time, but the Holy Spirit only intended to
create an impression for the church which perfectly answers to what went
out from Jesus.[33]

Bavinck could accept textual problems without feeling shaken in
faith:

The reports concerning the most important events, for example, the time of
Jesus' birth, the duration of his public activity, the words which he spoke at
the institution of the Lord's Supper, his resurrection, etc. are far from exact
copies and allow room for various conceptions.[34]

None of the problems with the form of Scripture changes the fact
that it communicates God's saving content to us. Berkouwer rejects
"an artificial view of revelation" which forgets "that Scripture is
written in human words and consequently offers men legitimate
freedom to examine these words and try to understand them."[35] We
must not dictate God's methods to him by declaring that Scripture
had to come in what seems to us a perfect form. Such a demand on
our part is impious according to Berkouwer. He says: "We may not
risk tarnishing the mystery of Scripture by disqualifying the God-
ordained way in which it came to us."[36] A fundamentalism which
denies the human form of Scripture as prophetic-apostolic testimony
and wants to substitute a divine form may be good-intentioned, but
presents serious problems, "for it is God's way with and in Scripture
that is at stake."[37] Just as serious is Bultmann's view, for example,

which also focuses on the form of Scripture although in a different way than fundamentalism. Bultmann believes that an ancient world view is presupposed into the very heart of the gospel. Thus when Bultmann demythologizes, the "content of the *kerygma* is continually at stake."[38]

For Berkouwer our central concern must be hearing and obeying the divine message of salvation, rather than in deifying or demythologizing the human milieu in which that message came. The New Testament writers had this focus of Scripture's saving purpose as they dealt with the Old Testament. Berkouwer comments: "We find a unique kind of Scripture proof in the New Testament, alien to our standards of exactness."[39]   That should be instructive for us in our use of Scripture because "the background of this large freedom is an unprecedented concentration on the matter, the *content* of the gospel."[40]   Berkouwer finds this same ability to distinguish between the human form and the divine content in Calvin. The Reformer

> evidently did not worry very much about the different methods of quotation in the New Testament, and he underlined the freedom which the apostles displayed in their quotations. He merely wished to stress that the "main point" was decisive for them.[41]

Bavinck, like Calvin, recognized that God had accommodated himself to our human forms of thought and speech in communicating his divine message. Bavinck noted: "Even in historical reports, there is sometimes distinction between the fact that has taken place and the form in which it is set forth."[42]   This does not deflect from the truth of Scripture for Bavinck. He said: "Then finally it appears that Scripture is certainly true in everything, but this truth is absolutely not of the same nature in all its component parts."[43]   Standing in this tradition, the findings of science pose no threat to Berkouwer. He comments that "certain results of science, be it natural science or historical research, can provide the 'occasion' for understanding various aspects of Scripture in a different way than before."[44] Science is not an authority superior to Scripture, but an "occasion" to suggest the real questions we should be asking of Scripture. It also may be the "occasion" for questioning the validity of some of our traditional exegesis. The Word of God remains authoritative with science properly used as an aid in enabling us to approach Scripture with a new openness to what God is saying in it.[45]

For the Reformed tradition which Berkouwer continues, the Bible is a functional, not a philosophical, book. Its function is to present Christ as our Savior. Our conversion to Christ and our commitment to Scripture are caused, not by our reason, but by the

Holy Spirit. Not our rational grasp of evidences, but our response to God in Christ moves us to accept Scripture as authoritative. Our focus as Christians and as theologians should remain on the divine content of Scripture, not on its human form. The Bible's function is to give us encouragement in salvation, not information about science. Therefore, the human forms in which Scripture's message comes can be examined by scholarship. Scientific findings are not an obstruction to faith, but an occasion to understand more fully the ways in which God has revealed himself through human means.

2. The Interpretation of Scripture
in Kuyper, Bavinck, and Berkouwer

A functional view of Scripture's divine message gives freedom for scholarly investigation of Scripture's human form. Scripture is allowed to be its own interpreter rather than being subject to philosophical a prioris of what it can and cannot contain. The relativities of human culture are no hindrance to our coming into a relationship to God in Christ. Thus we are responsible to study the weak human words and deeds through which God's wonderful revelation came. God accommodated himself to our human forms of communication. We are called faithfully to interpret the means of God's communication in order fully to understand the message of God's salvation.

Berkouwer sees his hermeneutics, or principles of biblical interpretation, as clearly in harmony with the Reformers'. He rejects allegorical exegesis and adheres to the grammatical-historical interpretation of the text. According to Berkouwer, the problem with allegory was that it lost the "sense" of Scripture in a multiplicity of meanings.[46] At the same time, appeal to a single sense of Scripture "is not a level literalism devoid of all reliefs, designed to rob Scripture of its depth and riches."[47]

The basic interpretative principle of the Reformation has been stated in several ways: the analogy of faith, or Scripture is its own interpreter. The meaning of these phrases is that each part of the Bible is to be understood in relationship to the overall saving message of Scripture. Bavinck attempted to express this relationship of the parts to the whole through the image of the human body. Berkouwer assumes the validity of Bavinck's concept of "organic inspiration," which draws attention to the fact that there is a center and a periphery to Scripture. Bavinck said:

> In the human organism nothing is accidental, neither the length, nor the breadth, nor the color, nor the hue; but all does not therefore stand in the same close connection with the life center. Head and heart have a much

more important place in the body than hand and foot, and these again stand in worth above nails and hair.[48]

This does not imply differences or grades of inspiration for Bavinck, but just that each part has its own function and some are more centrally important than others:

> The hair of the head participates in the same life as heart and hand. . . . It is one Spirit, out of whom the whole of Scripture has come forth through the consciousness of the writers. But there is a difference in the way in which the same life is immanent and active in the various parts of the body. There are varieties of gifts, also in Scripture, but it is the same Spirit.[49]

Informed by this perspective, Bavinck denied the post-Reformation emphasis on each word and letter of Scripture:

> In the thoughts are included the words, and in the words, the vowels. But from this it does not follow that the vowel points in our Hebrew manuscripts are from the writers themselves. And it does not follow that all is full of divine wisdom, that each jot and tittle has an infinite content. All has its meaning and significance very certainly, but there in the place and in the context in which it comes forth.[50]

When each word and letter is viewed as having its own divine content, according to Bavinck, that "leads to the false hermeneutical rules of the Jewish Scribes, and does not honor, but dishonor Scripture."[51]

For Berkouwer and his tradition from Kuyper and Bavinck, the Reformation concept that Scripture is its own interpreter does not take away the need for interpretation, but focuses on the way in which interpretation must be done. The Reformation rule "is its own interpreter," according to Berkouwer, "is mostly seen as concerning the intention of the author whom one seeks to know in every text."[52] Historical criticism is, at its best, a protest "against every form of Scripture exposition which went to work with *a priori* and external standards. It wanted to proceed from the Scripture as it actually existed."[53] For Bavinck, every kind of scholarly study of Scripture is necessary because the Word of God, Scripture, like the incarnate Christ, has "gone into the creaturely . . . into humanity, weak and despised and ignoble; the word became writing, and has, as writing, subjected itself to the fate of all writing."[54] This circumstance led Kuyper to call for "freedom of exegesis." This is necessary "if theology is to discharge her duty to the confessional life of the Church."[55] Kuyper set forth the reason in simple imagery:

> For this provides the constant stimulus to turn back from the confession to the Word of God, and so prevents the Church from living on the water in

the pitcher, and allowing itself to be cut off from the Fountain whence the water was drawn.[56]

These Reformed theologians do not fear scholarly investigation but consider it an essential aspect of a responsible faith. Berkouwer says sharply: "One can indeed say that those who, because of hesitancy and wariness, abandon new hermeneutical questions contribute to the relativizing of scriptural authority."[57] At the same time, Berkouwer states firmly:

> The discussion about Scripture, its God-breathed character and authority, cannot take place via a coerced concession to a new hermeneutical method and the "occasion" of science. It can only take place in the perspective of that trustworthiness of Scripture which enables us to abandon ourselves in complete trust to its authority and to preach its message.[58]

Berkouwer, therefore, agrees with Kuyper that hermeneutics is a "mixed science." On the one hand, it must deal with the Bible by the same rules of interpretation used with any other book. On the other hand, we are listening for what God has to say to us and therefore interpretation cannot be separated from faith in Scripture.[59]

The clarity of Scripture is therefore continually related to its central saving message, not to the particular words and sentences. Berkouwer notes that for the Reformers the doctrine of perspicuity "did not aim at the clarity of the words as such, but at the message, the content of Scripture."[60] The problem comes in a later twist in history. Berkouwer comments:

> It is not until the post-Reformation theology that a shift occurred: for the idea of perspicuity is then applied to the *words* of Scripture. . . . In this manner Scripture is isolated from its context of salvation.[61]

According to Bavinck, the central truth of salvation is set forth in a form so simple and intelligible "that someone in search of salvation will come to know the truth."[62] For the Reformers, says Berkouwer, "behind this connection of message and words is the power of the Spirit." He concludes:

> For that reason the confession of perspicuity is not a statement in general concerning the human language of Scripture, but a confession concerning the perspicuity of the gospel *in* Scripture.[63]

In this context, then, Berkouwer confronts the question of error in Scripture. He first defines "error" in a biblical manner. When error in the sense of incorrectness is used on the same level as error in the biblical sense of sin and deception:

Thus we are quite far removed from the serious manner in which error is dealt with in Scripture. For there what is meant is not the result of a limited degree of knowledge, but it is a swerving from the truth and upsetting the faith (II Timothy 2:18).[64]

Berkouwer continues:

The supposition that limited human knowledge and time-boundness of any kind would cause someone to err and that Holy Scripture would no longer be the lamp for our feet unless every time-bound conception could be corrected is a denial of the significance of historical development and of searching out as the "unhappy business that God has given to the sons of men to be busy with" (Ecclesiastes 1:13).[65]

Berkouwer acknowledges the "serious motivation" of advocates of scientific and historical inerrancy, but goes on: "In the end it will damage reverence for Scripture more than it will further it."[66] He concludes: "It is not that Scripture offers us no information but that the nature of this information is unique. It is governed by the *purpose* of God's revelation."[67]

Berkouwer emphasizes that Chrysostom and Calvin adhered to the concept that God accommodated himself to our human forms of thought and speech.[68] He notes a similar acknowledgment "in Scripture itself, such as the wording of John 16:12: 'I have yet many things to say to you, but you cannot bear them now.'"[69] For Berkouwer, the essential fact to remember is this:

For the purpose of the God-breathed Scripture is not at all to provide a scientific *gnosis* in order to convey and increase human knowledge and wisdom, but to witness of the salvation of God unto faith.[70]

In the context of Scripture's saving purpose, Berkouwer finds interpretative principles which allow him to take seriously the cultural context into which the Word comes. It is the saving message of Christ which is normative, not the cultural milieu. Bavinck had affirmed "that certainly not everything recorded in Scripture should be of normative authority for our faith and life."[71] Berkouwer, for example, deals in this way with the issue of Paul's statements regarding women. He says:

Paul . . . did not in the least render timeless propositions concerning womanhood. Rather, he wrote various testimonies and prescriptions applicable to particular—and to a certain degree transparent—situations against a background of specific morals and customs of that period.[72]

Berkouwer is intent on finding the *meaning* of biblical statements. He comments: "One must . . . take note of the cultural context and

intent of the words within that period precisely *in order* to hear the
Word of God."[73] He says, "Obedience to the Word of God is
impossible, even an illusion, if it is not a listening discovery of the
meaning of the words, of their essential goal."[74] He concludes that
one must "walk the road of biblical research in the way of the
Spirit," the way of continued association with Scripture—"Scripture
that is *time-related* and has *universal* authority."[75] He can thus
freely acknowledge that Paul uses arguments drawn from his culture.[76] Sometimes Paul interprets the Old Testament by constructing a midrash like that used in the synagogue. But Berkouwer's
conclusion is significant:

> The schism between church and synagogue is not found in the technique or
> the methods of scriptural usage in itself, but in the total and central
> understanding of the Old Testament as witness to the promise of Israel's
> God and in the reality of Jesus as Messiah.[77]

Berkouwer reminds us by the example of the Pharisees that one can
know the words of Scripture and claim to believe all of them and still
miss their saving purpose.

> When Christ accuses the Pharisees of not knowing Scripture (Matthew
> 22:29), he is not saying that they are strangers to it. For he asks, "Have you
> not read?" (Matthew 22:31), and they in turn appeal to Moses. But they do
> not know or understand Scripture and do not discern its deep intent. They
> err (Matthew 22:29) and miss the message of Scripture.[78]

Berkouwer's Reformed tradition freely acknowledges that Scripture comes to us in the form of a servant "as a human phenomenon
of language."[79] He affirms that not only Scripture but preaching is
the Word of God, as stated in the Second Helvetic Confession.[80] He
notes that Paul does not make the preaching of the Word a problem,
"yet he does not forget the nature of this weak medium, the
weakness of man."[81] Human words may be imperfect, but the divine
message is communicated when the preacher submits to the apostolic
norm of the gospel. Similarly, translation of Scripture from one
language to another involves interpretation. Translation is not a
simple matter of matching the word in one language with its exact
equivalent in another.[82] The translator must be willing to change the
form of words and expressions precisely in order that the message of
the gospel may be communicated. According to Berkouwer, "One
may exhaust every aspect of Scripture study in the expectation that
limited and inadequate words will not undermine the secret of
Scripture."[83]

Berkouwer's view is a comfort and encouragement to scholars.
Further, he provides all persons an incentive to take study seriously

because, he contends, it is "for a good reason" that "God's Word was given to us in a form that called for research."[84] The necessity of scholarship for a full understanding of God's Word is coupled with the priority of faith in understanding its central message. Berkouwer thus exemplifies the Reformed tradition which can be traced back through Bavinck and Kuyper to Calvin and Augustine. That tradition accepts the saving message of Scripture in faith and then proceeds to a scholarly understanding of the details. He notes that "Christians throughout the centuries acknowledged Scripture to be God's Word, and thus one does not need to wait until all questions are answered and all difficulties solved."[85]

By distinguishing between the center and the periphery in Scripture, Berkouwer's tradition frees us *from* scholarship and *for* scholarship. The central saving message of Scripture can be received in faith without waiting for scholarly reasons. The supporting material of Scripture, the human forms of culture and language, are open to scholarly investigation. A scholarly interpretation of the human forms of Scripture can yield dividends of deepened faith. Scripture fulfills God's intention to reveal saving truth. No human mistakes could frustrate that divine motivation. It is not meaningful, therefore, to equate human inaccuracy with error in the biblical sense of intent to deceive. Human scholarship can deal with the methods by which God accommodated his message of salvation to our means of understanding.

3. Conclusion

What may we learn for contemporary theological method from this study of the Reformed tradition on Scripture from Augustine and Calvin through Kuyper, Bavinck, and Berkouwer? The basic premise of this tradition is that Scripture is accepted in faith as authoritative because Scripture is the vehicle for bringing us to salvation in Christ. The saving *function* of Scripture is in focus. Then we are free and obligated to use critical scholarship to understand the human *forms* through which God has spoken. These premises provide a contemporary meaning of the Augustinian maxim: Faith leads to understanding.

In the Reformed branch of American evangelical theology we are in need of a new theory, model, or paradigm by which to understand Scripture. Our best biblical scholars often are reluctant to publish all of their conclusions, not because they do not accord with Scripture, but because they do not accord with the older Hodge/Warfield theory about Scripture. We are now beginning to realize how severely limited that theory is because it was formed in a polemic against biblical criticism, in an uncritical dependence on Scottish Realist philosophy and in a slavish adherence to the post-Reformation scholastic theology of Francis Turretin.

We must take care that in rejecting one philosophical system and theological method we do not come into the thrall of another—as has often happened in the history of theology. Berkouwer's tradition has taken precisely that care and therefore has much to teach us. We may use whatever are the language and thought forms of our time and culture in order to communicate the gospel in them. But we should not be fundamentally committed to or dependent on any particular philosophical system as necessary to the gospel. This distinction is evident in Berkouwer's Reformed tradition. Scripture is not a book designed to answer our philosophical questions. The Bible is a book which answers our basic need for salvation. That is its purpose, or function. Berkouwer says emphatically: "It is possible to live with Scripture only when the message of Scripture is understood and is not considered 'a metaphysical document,' but a living instrument serving God for the proclamation of the message of salvation." [86] Scripture's function is not to give technical philosophical information to solve our epistemological problems. Rather, it provides a message of salvation in Christ to meet our deepest human need—the need to be rightly related to God.

The model by which we understand Scripture should be a functional, not a philosophical one. The Bible is not meant simply to communicate objective information about God's essence, but to tell us how God is related to us. Berkouwer is quite clear about the functional character of Scripture. While speaking of the central text usually used to develop a doctrine of Scripture, 2 Tim 3:16, 17, Berkouwer points to Paul's accent on the "usefulness" of Scripture: "One may well speak of the 'functional character' of the God-breathed writing in both translations of Paul's words." He continues: "The scriptures of the Old Testament which Paul had in mind are holy and thus 'functional' and of utmost importance."[87] Berkouwer notes that "It is good to remember the unconcerned way in which the New Testament writers speak of the Scripture as 'profitable' without anxiety about pragmatism and functionalism." He points as well to the Heidelberg Catechism, Questions 49 and 59, for the same emphasis.[88]

In his recent reflections on theology in the last fifty years, Berkouwer comments on our growing awareness of the functional character of Scripture. He says:

The gospels, it was discerned, were not cool reports of facts, but reports in which the purpose of writing played and sounded through the story in all sorts of ways. Thus we could speak of a "religious pragmatic," an expression that has been used in reference to the way the historical accounts of the Old Testament were influenced by the purpose for which they were written.[89]

Berkouwer is confident that the Reformers had a "functional" view of Scripture. In discussing Calvin's view of faith, he declares:

Faith, for Calvin, was not a leap in the dark; it was a form of knowledge, the knowledge of God's benevolence toward us. It was not an assent to something pressed on us, nor a mere believing *that* something is true; it was a personal trust that negates blind obedience (cf. *Institutes*, III.ii.1, 2).[90]

For Berkouwer, as for Calvin, faith involves knowledge. The crucial issue is: what kind of knowledge? Religious knowledge is personal, relational knowledge, or it is not worthy of the name knowledge. Berkouwer again cites Calvin:

Calvin used the word *cognitio*, but did not reduce faith to intellectual knowledge with it because he insisted that this *cognitio* was directed to "the benevolence of God toward us" and was more an affair of the heart than the head.[91]

If a functional view of Scripture can be found in the New Testament and was held by the Reformers, why have evangelicals been so committed to a philosophical view of Scripture? Berkouwer points to an historical cause:

In our time, the central point at issue has again become the post-Reformation theology in connection with the emerging Aristotelianism in theology, which has also begun to influence the doctrine of Scripture. This faulty view has occurred as theologians, in immediate relation to affirmation and certainty, began to interpret the word *est* in the expression *Sacra Scriptura est Verbum Dei* in such a manner that Scripture's divinity was thought to be found in its inner substantial form and had become an essential predicate of Holy Scripture as an inspired book that was elevated to the level of a source of supernatural truths.[92]

Unfortunately the desire of Christians often has been to find religious certainty prior to and apart from the message of Scripture. The post-Reformation theology provided a system of so-called proofs which promised such certainty. Berkouwer notes:

They saw this whole system of philosophical concepts and theoretical objectification as the result of an establishing of a basis of certainty whereby the inspiration already guaranteed certainty quite apart from the witness—the message—of Scripture, whose certainty could rest only on a preceding certainty regarding the source of this witness—Holy Scripture.[93]

Berkouwer rejects this search for a priori certainty as unbiblical and false to the Reformation tradition regarding Scripture. He stands with Kuyper in saying that "Experiencing the *divinitas* of Scripture takes place through experiencing God's *benevolentia.*"[94] Berkouwer emphasizes that in the Reformed tradition neither reasons nor the witness of the Holy Spirit authenticate Scripture *prior* to our encountering the message of Scripture. He states:

> It is important that both Bavinck and Kuyper reject the idea that Scripture is the object of the *testimonium* apart from its message, for as Kuyper points out, such a view is contrary to the way in which faith works, which excludes such a formalization. . . . To formalize Holy Scripture in this way is as nonsensical as to praise a book without reading it; to do so violates the word-character of Holy Scripture.[95]

It is also possible to change the function, the meaning, the message of the gospel. That change is wrong. Berkouwer declares:

> There is another kind of preaching in which the gospel itself is at stake and whereby a different gospel comes forward as a threat to salvation and the way of Christ (Phil. 3:2f.). This preaching is judged according to its content, for it blurs the gospel message and can no longer be approached in terms of motivation alone.[96]

A true doctrine of Scripture must be developed in our interaction with the saving message of Christ in Scripture, not with some other theme or function supposedly found in Scripture, nor with some external proofs for Scripture derived from philosophical arguments about its form.

This means that we cannot construct a philosophical theory about what Scripture ought to be and then expect Christian experience to conform itself to this abstract model. A true doctrine of Scripture cannot be built in the abstract, using "logical inference" from a few verses. Our Christian interaction with the Word of God in faith must precede and shape our theory about Scripture. This is completely appropriate according to Berkouwer since it takes into account the nature of Scripture. Scripture has a practical, not a theoretical, purpose. "Scripture has not been given to the church primarily as a study book for 'theology' as such."[97] Indeed, according to Berkouwer:

> Faith is not and cannot be based on a theoretical reflection on what, according to our insight, must be the nature of the divine revelation and on which ways and forms it must have come to us in order to be the guarantee of certainty. The way of Christian faith is not one of a possibility becoming more clear on its way to the reality of certainty, but a subjection to the

gospel, to the Christ of the Scriptures; and from this alone can a reflection on Holy Scripture proceed.[98]

Not a priori proofs, but Christian faith should be the foundation of our doctrine of Scripture. One of Berkouwer's favorite biblical passages is the incident in John when Philip witnesses to his brother Nathanael concerning his newly discovered Messiah. In response to Nathanael's objection, "Can anything good come out of Nazareth?" (John 1:46), Philip simply replies with the urgent call to "Come and see." Berkouwer comments on the passage:

> Here we are not dealing with a subjectification of authority, which might only become reality through acknowledgment. But we are referred to the fact that the unique authority can only be acknowledged and experienced on the way; it is not acknowledged on the ground of a preceding consideration, and the way then followed as a conclusion.[99]

Berkouwer is also impressed with the fact that Satan quoted Scripture to Christ in the temptation. What was the difference between Christ's appeal and interpretation and that of his adversary?

> The fact that Satan himself cited Psalm 91 in his temptations shows how close the connection is between the appeal to the written word and the right understanding of it. The words themselves, as isolated and unrelated things, can be used as pawns in a game of interpretations. Christ's appeal has the background of his own relationship with the Father, his ministry in the business of his Father; it has nothing to do with a formal declaration of authority or with a blind faith.[100]

For Berkouwer, therefore, our experience of God's authority in our lives mediated through Scripture precedes and should shape any theory about Scripture which we develop. He comments, on the last page of his book, *Holy Scripture:*

> It may seem like a roundabout way to go from the message of Scripture to its unique authority. In reality, it is the true and only way to obedience.[101]

We must not fear that we will fall into subjectivism if we move away from the model of Scripture created by scholastic rationalism. That fear has always been the defensive fortress of the rationalists. Berkouwer demonstrates that there is a third alternative between rationalism and subjectivism. It is the way of Augustine, Calvin, and Luther. It is the way of beginning in faith, but proceeding with a regenerate mind, through scholarly study to understanding. It is a way which distinguishes between the central saving message of Scripture and all of the difficult surrounding material which supports that message. It is a way which holds in balance the objective and the subjective, the Word and the hearing of the Word. The union is a personal one. We know God in his Word in a relationship which he initiates. This is not some kind of "Barthianism." Berkouwer specifically rejects any notion that "Scripture *becomes* God's Word 'through its use.' "[102]   He knows that Scripture "does not and cannot derive its authority from the fact that *we* use it, not even when we use Scripture in faith."[103]   The Augustinian stance of faith seeking understanding is neither spiritualism, subjectivism, blind submission, nor a sacrifice of the intellect.[104]   Thus Berkouwer plainly declares: "Faith in terms of a sacrifice of the intellect is a perversion of Christian faith and obedience."[105]   A sacrifice of the intellect is a bowing before external authority. Christian faith in Scripture is rather "an inner conviction regarding the object and content of the faith to which man is called."[106]   The object is Jesus Christ as Savior. The conviction is wrought by the Spirit as one encounters Christ in the Word. As Berkouwer says, "In this way the Spirit conquers the dangers of an objectivism that misunderstands the Spirit and of a subjectivism that loses perspective on the reality of Christ."[107]   For him, "These dangers are overcome in the relationship between the heart and Scripture."[108]   He concludes *Holy Scripture* by citing another of his favorite biblical texts:

> In spite of all differences, this road for the church is the same as that of the walkers to Emmaus. After they had recognized the stranger and encountered the living Lord just prior to the dispensation of the Spirit, they came to themselves and said to each other: "Did not our hearts burn within us while he talked to us on the road, while he opened to us the Scriptures?" (Luke 24:32).[109]

Berkouwer offers us a third alternative. His Reformed doctrine of Scripture is neither rationalistic nor subjectivistic. It is a view which correlates the saving message of Scripture and our faith in it. We are not being offered a philosophical fideism. We are being urged to acknowledge the Bible's saving function.[110]   Evangelicals need a doctrine of Scripture which accords with the purpose of Scripture— "that you may believe that Jesus is the Christ, the Son of God, and that believing you may have life in his name" (John 20:31).

NOTES

1. See William E. Hordern, *A Layman's Guide to Protestant Theology,* chapter 2, "The Threat to Orthodoxy," and chapter 4, "Liberalism: The Remaking of Orthodoxy" (rev. ed., 1968).
2. For documentation of these background influences on the Princeton Theology see my

chapter, "The Church Doctrine of Biblical Authority," in *Biblical Authority*, Jack Rogers, ed. (1977).
3. See Thomas Kuhn, *The Structure of Scientific Revolutions*, 2nd ed., International Encyclopedia of Unified Science, Vol. 2, No. 2 (1970). Ian Barbour, *Myths, Models and Paradigms* (1974), makes creative application of Kuhn's work to the field of theology.
4. For a detailed discussion of the controversy over the Bible, particularly in the United Presbyterian Church, U.S.A., see my *Scripture in the Westminster Confession* (rev. ed., 1977). I have recorded my own earlier commitment to the Hodge/Warfield theory and my surprise in discovering its divergence from the Reformation tradition on Scripture in *Confessions of a Conservative Evangelical* (1974), chapter 8.
5. See James Orr, *Revelation and Inspiration* (1910), pp. 199, 209–217.
6. Translated by William Hendriksen (1951).
7. John H. Gerstner, "Warfield's Case for Biblical Inerrancy," in *God's Inerrant Word* (1974), pp. 121–122.
8. Gerstner, p. 122.
9. G. C. Berkouwer, *Een Halve Eeuw Theologie: Motieven en Stomingen van 1920 tot heden* (1974), p. 31; E.T. pp. 26–27. A translation has been prepared by Lewis B. Smedes under the title, *A Half Century of Theology: Movements and Motives* (Eerdmans, 1977).
10. The only introduction to Berkouwer's life and thought available in English is Lewis B. Smedes' article, "G. C. Berkouwer," in *Creative Minds in Contemporary Theology*, Phil E. Hughes, ed. (1966), pp. 63–97.
11. An excellent interview with Berkouwer is found in the volume *Gesprekken Over Rome-Reformatie*, G. Puchinger, ed. (1965), pp. 299–319.
12. Berkouwer, *A Half Century*, pp. 32ff.
13. Puchinger, p. 303.
14. *Het Probleem der Schriftcritiek* (1938).
15. Berkouwer, *A Half Century*, p. 138.
16. All of them have been published in English by Eerdmans as one-volume works, with some of the more recent larger works being abridged.
17. Translated by Jack Rogers (1975).
18. *Holy Scripture*, p. 9; hereafter cited as *HS*.
19. *HS*, p. 33.
20. Bavinck, *Gereformeerde Dogmatiek*, 1, p. 411; hereafter cited as *GD*. All translations are my own from the fourth Dutch edition (1928).
21. *Principles of Sacred Theology*, trans. J. Hendrik De Vries (reprint, 1968), pp. 556–557; hereafter cited as *PST*.
22. *PST*, p. 558.
23. *GD*, p. 414.
24. *GD*, pp. 564–565.
25. *GD*, p. 564.
26. *HS*, p. 241; citing *GD*, p. 569.
27. *HS*, pp. 54–55 and 46.
28. *HS*, p. 26; citing *GD*, p. 415.
29. *GD*, p. 416.
30. *GD*, p. 416.
31. *GD*, p. 417.
32. *HS*, p. 125.
33. *Encyclopaedie der Heilige Godgeleerdheid*, 2 (1894), p. 499. Interestingly, this is the only statement of Kuyper's which Bavinck quotes in *GD*. See p. 415.
34. *GD*, p. 419.
35. *HS*, pp. 19–20.
36. *HS*, p. 19.
37. *HS*, p. 22.
38. *HS*, p. 258.
39. *HS*, p. 228.
40. *HS*, p. 228.

41. *HS*, p. 227.
42. *GD*, p. 420.
43. *GD*, p. 419.
44. *HS*, p. 133.
45. *HS*, pp. 294–295.
46. *HS*, p. 129.
47. *HS*, p. 129.
48. *GD*, pp. 409–410.
49. *GD*, p. 410.
50. *GD*, p. 409.
51. *GD*, p. 409.
52. *HS*, p. 128.
53. *HS*, p. 130.
54. *GD*, p. 405.
55. *PST*, p. 596.
56. *PST*, p. 597.
57. *HS*, p. 137.
58. *HS*, p. 138.
59. *HS*, pp. 112–113.
60. *HS*, p. 274.
61. *HS*, p. 275.
62. *GD*, p. 447, cited in *HS*, p. 274.
63. *HS*, p. 275.
64. *HS*, p. 181.
65. *HS*, p. 182.
66. *HS*, p. 183.
67. *HS*, p. 183.
68. *HS*, pp. 175–176.
69. *HS*, p. 176.
70. *HS*, p. 180.
71. *GD*, p. 428, cited in *HS*, p. 191.
72. *HS*, p. 187.
73. *HS*, p. 187.
74. *HS*, p. 188.
75. *HS*, p. 194.
76. *HS*, pp. 187–188.
77. *HS*, p. 234.
78. *HS*, p. 109.
79. *HS*, p. 205.
80. *HS*, pp. 335–336.
81. *HS*, p. 207.
82. *HS*, p. 216.
83. *HS*, p. 237.
84. *HS*, p. 238.
85. *HS*, p. 347.
86. *HS*, p. 333.
87. *HS*, p. 142.
88. *HS*, p. 142, note 9.
89. *A Half Century*, pp. 120–121.
90. *A Half Century*, p. 157.
91. *A Half Century*, p. 175.
92. *HS*, p. 32.
93. *HS*, p. 32.
94. *HS*, p. 45.
95. *HS*, p. 45.
96. *HS*, p. 339.
97. *HS*, p. 11.

98. *HS*, p. 33.
99. *HS*, p. 348.
100. *A Half Century*, p. 139.
101. *HS*, p. 366.
102. *HS*, p. 317.
103. *HS*, pp. 317–318.
104. *HS*, pp. 349–351.
105. *HS*, p. 351.
106. *HS*, p. 352.
107. *HS*, p. 366.
108. *HS*, p. 366.
109. *HS*, p. 366.
110. I am not the first to describe Berkouwer's view with the term "functional." Even before the publication of Berkouwer's *Holy Scripture*, John Timmer, a Christian Reformed pastor, had noted the transition from ontological to functional thinking in Berkouwer's theology. "Berkouwer's theology, in other words, is functional; it is relational. It is this that makes Berkouwer an influential theologian." See John Timmer, "G. C. Berkouwer: Theologian of Confrontation and Co-Relation," *RefJ* (December, 1969), p. 19.

7: The "Analogy of Faith" and the Intent of Hebrews

CALVIN R. SCHOONHOVEN

1. Introduction

One of the striking structural patterns in The Epistle to the Hebrews is the alternation between doctrinal and hortatory sections.[1] The doctrinal segments lay the foundation for and give rise to the sections of exhortation. This is not dissimilar to the other epistolary literature of the New Testament and especially the Pauline letters wherein quite inevitably the statement of doctrine is followed by the ethic of command.[2] The notable difference in Hebrews is that the alternation is sustained for a longer time and each section of doctrine and exhortation becomes fuller as it subtly interlaces concepts only briefly introduced in the earlier sections. The writer is not haphazard in his literary effort, but very methodical and deliberate. Indeed, though at the first reading it may seem awesomely difficult to capture the intent of the writing, this difficulty can be lessened considerably by recognizing the above-noted sections and attempting the application of proper hermeneutical principles.

The hortatory segments are among the most dramatic and direct in the New Testament. It is not that the things said are unique or in conflict with the rest of the literature, but only that some segments are cast in language conspicuously construed to frighten and warn the reader. Luther so felt the sting of these sections that he disavowed the book. Not only the dramatic pointedness bothered him, but more so what was actually said. Subsequent commentators have struggled rather much to ease the violent impact of this material.[3] Thus it is that Luther and other commentators follow the "analogy-of-faith" hermeneutical principle, which we are convinced obstructs precise exegesis by demanding that all the biblical literature be read in the light of so-called ruling concepts derived from supposed clear statements of other Scripture. By so doing they have done great disservice to the text. Luther understood well what the text said, but he felt that he could not relate this harmoniously to the rest of the Bible. This surely indicates that something extraordinary is articulated by this writer. It also suggests that there is a profound deficiency in Luther's hermeneutical procedure and theological understanding. What is it in this material that so disturbs Luther and other commentators?

Hint of the answer is given in the very first hortatory section (2:1–4). "Therefore we must pay the closer attention to what we have heard, lest we drift away from it" (2:1). Here the possibility of drifting away is suggested. In the next parenetic section (3:1–4:16) the idea is intensified. "And we are his house if we hold fast our confidence and pride in our hope" (3:6). In 3:14 it is restated as "For we share in Christ, if only we hold our first confidence firm to the end." Care must be taken not to be "hardened by the deceitfulness of sin" (3:13) as were the Israelites who were disobedient (3:15–4:16).

These warnings to Christians are again soberly and very dramatically articulated in the third hortatory section (5:11–6:20). Here language of an effusive but clear sort is employed to stress the terrible danger of spiritual ruin. It is quite clear that there is no repentance for the Christian if after being enlightened he then commits apostasy. In such an instance he crucifies the Son of God and holds him up to contempt (6:4–6). To be this way is the exact opposite of Abraham, who, "having patiently endured, obtained the promise" (6:15).

In the fourth and last section (10:19–13:17) the emphasis is similar. If the Christian commits deliberate sin, he will know the fury of God that will consume him. There is no escape (10:26–31). Consequently, there is need for endurance so that the Christian may do the will of God and receive what is promised (10:36). If one does not persevere, then his lot will be like Esau, who after he sold his birthright found no chance to repent, though he sought it with tears (12:16, 17).

2. The Problem

It becomes evident now as to why these passages caused consternation among the Reformation theologians and later exegetes. There are two reasons. The first is that of a sustained emphasis in all this material upon the unbreakable connection between faith and obedience. Apparently in the mind of this writer the glorious inheritance is secured only if one perseveringly obeys. Thus, in these hortatory sections there is a consistent stress on the necessity of having confidence, of enduring, obeying, persevering, and standing firm. If one does this, if one holds fast his confidence, then, and only then, will there be a sharing in Christ. So then, contrary to some Reformation thinking, grace or the blessing of God seems to be conditioned on obedience. And here is the nub of the problem. The Reformation and later theologians were so intent on obliterating the "works" idea of the Roman Church that they read the texts in such a way as to conform to what they falsely regarded as a radical grace theology, a grace with no conditions attached whatever. This is a patent application of the "analogy-of-faith" principle.

Secondly, this material is a problem because it stipulates that lack of obedience can become so pervasive that the professing but disobedient Christian can actually fall away so as no longer to inherit the blessing. And it is even taught that there is a sin so severe that repentance is impossible. Here the exhortation to obedience is intensified. It is difficult, and some would maintain impossible, to fit this in with the soaring concepts of grace given in the other New Testament literature.

3. The Primary Command—Assurance

Above we have noted that the exhortation of these sections has to do with obedience. This idea of obedience is important to the writer. But this is not the lone command and not even the primary command. If it were the single command with no contextual modification, it would be a "works" teaching or theology.[4] If this were so, we should acknowledge this and admit that in the canon are contradictory statements about God's redemptive dealings with men. This would mean the end of a viable Christian position and, to be sure, the end of Christianity. For such a dichotomy of grace/works could not be construed as a minor flaw or friction in the primitive revealed truth, but rather should have to be regarded as a crucial contradiction at the very heart of Christian proclamation. This would be unacceptable.

But the stress is of another sort. The overriding concern of this author is to bring about assurance or confidence in the lives of his readers. This is the first and foremost exhortation. For "if we hold our first *confidence* firm to the end" (3:14), we share in Christ. He further affirms, "And we desire each one of you to show the same earnestness in realizing the *full assurance* of hope until the end, so that you may not be sluggish, but imitators of those who through faith and patience inherit the promises" (6:11, 12). Another similar command is in the tenth chapter. "Therefore do not throw away your *confidence,* which has a great reward. For you have need of endurance, so that you may do the will of God and receive what is promised" (10:35, 36).

If invoking confidence or assurance is of concern to the writer, we must know what he really means by this term and idea. Light is cast on this when we note that the doctrinal sections have as their one purpose to establish the credibility and greatness of Christ (1:1–14; 2:5–18; 5:1–10; 7:1–10:18). This has long been recognized. These sections are composed of statements that point up the marvels of our great salvation in Christ. Christ died that we might be redeemed from sin. He is the mediator of a new covenant. He makes promise of an eternal inheritance. In sum, God has provided a redemption in Christ that is final and complete. Now, because of this, we are exhorted to have assurance.

But what really is the anatomy of this assurance? Surely it centrally contains the idea of reliance or dependence upon Christ. It is finding God so trustworthy that we are free from anxiety and elated with happiness. It is having our hearts happy and resting in God. It is finally the exercise of faith that gives confidence of unseen things. But one cannot have the subjective experience of "full confidence" or assurance unless he has the unassailable conviction that the object of his confidence is all that it purports to be. When the text affirms that "faith is the assurance of things hoped for . . ." (Heb 11:1), it surely connotes the idea that faith rests in the assurance that the things hoped for are real. If we are convinced that God is trustworthy, that the promises of God in Christ are real, then we experience "full assurance." This is an existential involvement that inevitably results in joy.[5] This is not a leap of faith, but an involvement predicated upon a reasoned conviction that God is all that he is purported to be.

4. Endurance

This full assurance is so much stressed because it is axiomatic with this writer that the only way to endure or persevere is to have precisely this assurance. The exhortation is: "realize the full assurance of hope until the end, so that you . . . through faith and patience inherit the promises" (6:11, 12). Here and in other places (10:35, 36) assurance is depicted as the *sine qua non* for the strong, enduring life of faith and obedience. This must be the kind of assurance that enabled Noah to build an ark on the desert (11:7), that impelled

Abraham to leave the land of his kindred and to offer up his only son (11:8, 17). It is this full assurance that caused others to undergo torture, death, and deprivation and be like Moses, who steadfastly endured (11:27, 32–37). It is finally that quality that enabled the recipients themselves to endure a great conflict of suffering (10:32–33). And why all this? Because they were assured of a better possession and an abiding one. Such assurance leads to endurance that inevitably leads to doing the will of God.

So a condition for belonging to Christ is that one endure to the end. Now all of us undergo suffering. And there are various kinds of suffering. Great mental anguish, the suffering of purposelessness, realization of a futile life, remorse, regret, and, to be sure, physical suffering that finally ends in death. Boredom alone is enough to utterly debilitate one. Life continues, but there is despondency and despair because the end of it all is so pathetic. If there is any joy, it is only momentary and quite immediately suffocated by an awesome realization that the pendulum of time is swinging and will finally cripple the most intense of our hearty pleasures.

But in this context and in this tract the writer is not concerned with a generalized kind of suffering; he is not first of all concerned with the overall and pervasive suffering of the world. He writes to a community of believers who have made a commitment to Christ. They have been challenged in this commitment; it seems as though in this context they are struggling and are having a rather bad time of it. They are on the brink of a terrible tragedy. They need help. Constantly, therefore, the writer stresses that they should endure. They must endure temptation (2:18; 4:15). This should not be construed as temptation to a particular sin, but rather as temptation to place confidence and trust in something other than Christ. Insofar as specific sins are indicative of man's seeking for happiness and joy elsewhere than in the provision of God, they are here included. But the primary idea is that men should never succumb to the temptation to seek joy in the things that he can do or the things he can obtain. This is unbelief. And this was the problem of the Israelites in the wilderness. They looked elsewhere for the contentment of life. They wanted the joy that possession of land could provide and the security that constant access to food could insure (3:7–14).[6] God was provoked with that generation (3:10) because they no longer relied on him, no longer cast all their cares upon him. Indeed, they did not endure. In a word, they were not trusting Jehovah God. This is why the recipients of the letter are to take care lest there be in any of them an evil, unbelieving heart, leading them to fall away from the living God (3:12).

In order for this emphasis not to become a meaningless mockery, we must know that the writer is speaking of the ultimate of issues. It is not some reward that may be lost, rather it is one's very soul. John Calvin spoke of the perseverance of the saints, and it is precisely of this that the writer of this treatise speaks. Whether the word be perseverance or endurance,[7] it is one's eternal destiny that is here involved. We must not here apply some external theological concept to this writer's formulations. Whether other biblical writers are teaching what this writer teaches or not, we should never utilize the "analogy-of-faith" principle to make him say something other than that which he really intends to say and thereby force conformity to what we think he should say. This is precisely where hermeneutics and the application of certain false principles forthrightly frustrate thinking an author's thoughts after him.

5. The Threats

Why do the recipients need to be threatened into carrying out the purposes of God? There they were carrying on in the daily responsibilities of life as best they could. No awesomely great sin had yet decimated their ranks and Christian commitment. Indeed, they were continuing in brotherly love (13:1); they were those who were of such nature that the writer says "we feel sure of better things that belong to salvation" (6:9). He could even say that "God is not so unjust as to overlook your work and the love which you showed for his sake in serving the saints, *as you still do*" (6:10). Yet, terrible and exacting threats are leveled against them of such a kind as to cause awe in the most stalwart of believers and to impress upon all the reality of God's wrath. They exist in danger of experiencing the full fury of the wrath of God. And why is this? Because their lives are being eroded by the enticements of an easy life wherein the latent anxiety of the spirit is seeking its resolution in the immanent and tangible realities that are all about. The recipients of this letter had to be threatened because in this way, and only in this way, would they be enabled to swerve from a potentially destructive course. Apparently, there is nothing more deadly to meaningful human experience than the peculiar lethargy that enshrouds one when the *status quo* is so much appreciated that there is no awareness as to the consequence of a given deed in terms of one's future experience and destiny. Hence, they were "dull of hearing" (5:11). They were so dull of hearing and so elementary in Christian teaching and experience that they had difficulty distinguishing "good from evil" (5:14). It is needful that they "go on to maturity" (6:1). Now, all of this means that they were not yet beyond the boundary of hope. The threatenings and warnings are indicative of hope. They yet can hear and respond. But the threats must be heeded, there must be response; there must be reconciliation to the fact that a collision course is being held and destruction is imminent.

It is quite clear, then, that in the view of this writer the anger of God that results in threats made upon man is an indispensable link in the justification-sanctification sequence. And however much we may think this to be contrary to our customary theology, to the other books of the New Testament, or to proper Rogerian psychology or counseling, the fact is that this is what is plainly taught here. However much man may seek to avoid the reality and, indeed, the need for these threats, they are nonetheless a real and indispensable aspect of the salvation process. This is only tantamount to saying that sin is real and that the consequences of sin are very real. The recipients are warned not to sin because when they do sin, they at that very moment and in that very act are violating the holiness of God and living in discord with the reality of the grace into which they have entered. The threats are so grave because the act of sin is so serious. It partakes of a realm that is wholly contrary to God; it is in another sphere of existence, the demonic sphere. And to the extent that it is participated in, even though it be slight, it is an offense to the holiness of God. Therefore, the threats are in every section of exhortation in the book. They are summed up in words of sober renunciation, "They shall never enter my rest" (3:11), and given intense expression when it is catalogued that there is a "fearful prospect of judgment, and a fury of fire which will consume the adversaries" (10:27).

6. The Condition

For the experience of salvation the condition, then, must be met. What is this condition? How really does one obtain salvation and avoid the threats described above? Various terminology is employed to clarify the condition for acceptance, but it is perhaps best summed up in the statement ". . . we share in Christ, *if* only we hold our first confidence firm to the end . . ." (3:14). Now this seems clear enough and sufficiently to the point so that we should not be immensely perplexed as to what is intended, especially when this is coupled with other similar statements that give equally clear indication of meaning.[8] Quite clearly and much to the point the author utilizes strong imagery and language to assert that there will be a functionalizing of that experience by full confidence in (6:11; 10:22) or reliance upon God. This is to say that such a one will have faith, will believe and thereby be saved. But the author cannot continuously use just the word faith to describe those who will be participants in the rest of God. When he stipulates the condition for belonging to Christ, it all hinges upon the thought of holding our first confidence firm to the end. And by so doing we are made to know not that an academic affirmation of belief in God is important, but that a functional expression of the "God reality" is the *sine qua non* for participation in the "church of the first born." To put it another way, faith always functionalizes itself existentially by confidence in God, which is reliance upon him and his promises. And this is what Heb 11:1 affirms: "Now *faith* is the *assurance* of things hoped for, the *conviction* of things not seen."

It is because of this assurance or confidence which is a functional expression of faith that the recipients "endured a hard struggle with sufferings, sometimes being publicly exposed to abuse and affliction" (10:33), and why they joyfully accepted the plundering of their property (10:34). Speaking in the second person he says, "you knew that you had a better possession and an abiding one" (10:34). And as we have already discussed, this is what confidence really is, knowing that we have something that we can and must finally rely upon. All other supports of comfort, good health, freedom, possession of property cannot hold up the enormous weight of human need. This can alone be adequately supported by the resources of God. And if we possess this full confidence in God and his resources, then, and only then, will we share in Christ.

There is no way that this emphasis on a necessary condition can be diminished. Though not absent from the other New Testament writings,[9] it is represented so forthrightly and dramatically here that it forces a careful reevaluation of all traditional theological categories. Indeed, salvation is by faith alone; but the very faith that saves is only such if it is or includes the obedience of faith. There is simply no way that the "analogy-of-faith" principle can modify or eradicate the conditional nature of salvation.

7. The Joyous Life

But this should not be taken to infer that the life of the Christian wayfarer is gloomy and sad. This would be totally to misconstrue the intent of Hebrews. We here have every indication that the life of the one who belongs to Christ is a profoundly happy and joyous life. This surfaces in a peculiar way in this book. By means of an odd juxtaposition of seemingly conflicting and paradoxical concepts the author suggests that which should be abundantly clear to all who perceptively read these words. The idea is capsuled when he says, "For you had compassion on the prisoners, and you *joyfully* accepted the plundering of your property, since you knew that you yourselves had a better possession and an abiding one" (10:34). This should not be interpreted to mean that there was delight in the plundering itself as though in some strange and morbid fashion those so ill-treated felt better because of this negative event than if it had not happened. Rather, as the context suggests, their joy and reliance was upon realities that transcended the immediacies of this life and world. Here in another world was their support and in this they rejoiced even though publicly exposed to abuse and affliction. Here there is no polarizing of joy and suffering. They are so brought together that joy is experienced not despite the suffering, but precisely in the context of suffering and deprivation. The obvious temporality of all possessions is underscored by the "plundering of their property" with a consequent greater reliance on the promise of God. It is then that their joy is made more effusive through the loss of the realities that could preempt their dependence upon God. This kind of happening causes them to acknowledge that they are "strangers and exiles on the earth," and that they are "seeking a homeland" (11:13, 14).

8. Motivation One—The Reward

These people are not commended to follow Christ with the expectation that their lives will then be spiritless, sad, and lacking in dynamic participation in the life of this world. Rather, because of sure and certain promises of a transcendent but wholly satisfying sort, they are exhorted to pay "closer attention" to what they have heard (2:1). Indeed, it is the prospect of reward that plays such a large part in the attempt of this author to stabilize and recall this community to whom he so ardently writes. There is a reward to be had, there is a promise to be received; it is the eschatological hope, "For yet a little while, and the coming one shall come and shall not tarry . . ." (10:37).

It is because of this reward, this hope, this "rest" (11:6, 10, 26), that the Old Testament personages are represented as having steadfastly proceeded along the pilgrimage of life in continuity of faith in the victorious eleventh chapter. By such lives of sacrifice they were gaining the greatest good for themselves both now and in that future day. In this sense, then, they were not heroes, but simply seeking out good for themselves. They had come to that fortuitous and most profound conception that joy is accessible only in dependence upon the living God. And though very many terrible things happened to them in this stance of dependence, they relied upon the promises of God and thus endured. They were tortured, mocked, scourged, put in chains, imprisoned, stoned, sawn in two, killed with the sword, afflicted, ill-treated. But they endured. Why? The reason is given clear and forthright expression when the text speaks of Moses and in so doing sums up the attitude of all these incredible people. "He considered abuse suffered for the Christ greater wealth than the treasures of Egypt, *for he looked to the reward*" (11:26). That this is not an isolated strand in the presentation of the writer is clear when he says even of Christ, "who *for the joy that was set before him* endured the cross . . ." (12:2). That this has direct applicability to the original readers and to all Christians is established by the words "let us go forth to him outside the camp, bearing abuse for him. For here we have no lasting city, *but we seek the city which is to come*" (13:13, 14).

Put simply, endurance in the contest of life is only possible if one has the certain expectation of receiving a "reward," a good that makes all the suffering dim or become worthwhile in the attainment of that final ecstasy. The readers are exhorted to patience and steadfastness not because this is the noble or essentially right thing to do in a moral universe; they are told to be this way not because there will be a natural increment of good for themselves and their posterity; surely they are not to think that they will gain a trouble-free life, have success, gain the respect and recognition of others, or have good health.[10] Rather, because they will receive a marvelous promise that gives to them joy even in the midst of suffering, they are to manifest the virtues of love, patience, ethical propriety, and peace. In this kind of distraught world there is nothing else that is big enough in motivational capabilities to do the job of lifting drooping hands and strengthening weak knees (12:12).

But what precisely is the nature of this "reward" that should so renovate one's life as to enable one to endure, be steadfast, and do God's will? No mean or petty thing is spoken of here. It partakes of grandeur and glory, it relates the recipient to the past grand manifestations of God in history and to the further exhibition of God's purpose and power. The writer's concept of reward is not an isolated, narrow, provincial, nationalistic one that would stifle and restrict the entire human enterprise. Rather, in all the significant arenas of human involvement this concept stimulates.

The reward stimulates and is to be sought because it is locked in with and quite inseparable from familiar human history. In no other book of the New Testament is history so important as in the book of Hebrews. Indeed, it is a holy history, but this in no way places restricting perimeters about the concept. It soars freely and breaks out beyond any nationalism that may be inferred from the many references to a particular people in a particular time and at a particular place; i.e., the Hebrew people. Not an ideal people, but a people mixed; both evil and good make up the matrix out of which a new humanity emerges. This history of the Hebrew people is not arbitrary, but it is a chosen history and a limited history. It is chosen and limited because in this, and only in this, can its familiarity and universal applicability be possible. Through the concretions of the real life of a particular people is it possible for the universality of God's purpose and plan for all peoples to be realized, actualized, and consummated. This truth and realization made up an important ingredient of the "reward" theology of Hebrews. The sojourner on earth who endures and does the will of God has happy company. He is not alone, isolated, a meaningless fragment that is finally to be absorbed through a terminal dissolution of all personality into a beingless state of oneness. This holds no attraction for the human spirit. Since it holds no attraction, neither does it have character-forming power. The writer knows, because it is true, that only a representation of a final good that possesses familiarity, personality, and solidarity can possibly be sufficiently attractive to induce any man to lay aside every weight and sin which clings so closely (12:1). To speak in this way is to speak in the way of substantial history, substantial history that is limited and fragmented but that has universal signification. It is not enough to be an individual, solitary participant in the working and reward of God. This is meager. To be part of a movement, of a history, of a destiny that finally will include nations, and men, and power and glory, this is the only anticipation worth talking about according to this writer. Man as man can only be satisfied when everything is put in subjection to him (2:8). This means that the finitude of life must be overcome, and this is alone possible in company with Jesus. And this Jesus is concerned "with the descendants of Abraham" (2:16). A direct spiritual, corporate entity is envisioned here. Constantly these connections are established. And they are not established just randomly, but quite purposefully. This is so because it is of fundamental importance to this literature that redeemed man will experience that redemption not in isolation but in continuity and company with a host of others. This is at the same time reward and great motivation.

9. Motivation Two—Judgment

The threat of God's wrath must be an inducement to faith and faithfulness. It must be this because, unless it were so, the many references to the uncompromising wrath of God would not play such a prominent part in this writing. Indeed, "we know him who said, 'Vengeance is mine, I will repay.' And again, 'The Lord will judge his people.' It is a fearful thing to fall into the hand of the living God" (10:30, 31). This is stressed to an extreme degree when the text reads, "Let us offer to God acceptable worship, with reverence and awe; for our God is a consuming fire" (12:28b, 29). There is "a fearful prospect of judgment, and a fury of fire which will consume the adversaries" (10:27). The nature of the human order is such that punishment plays an indispensable part in its order and continuity; likewise, the divine order is such that punishment is the indispensable reality without which the divine order would be less than divine. Axiomatic it is that when one disobeys, punishment invariably follows. Therefore, one should not disobey. This is the simple but very direct reasoning of the writer. Any additional finesse and subtlety of reasoning alludes him. This is quite true even for the Christian; "God disciplines us for our good, that we may share his holiness" (12:10).

The sobriety of this whole matter is brought to the fore in the very first hortatory section (2:1–4). "For if the message declared by angels was valid and every transgression or disobedience received a just retribution, how shall we escape if we neglect such a great salvation?" (2:2, 3a). In the second section of command the escalation of disobedience reaches an ultimate level when a nation is excluded from a pursued destiny. It is said of disobedient Israel, "They always go astray in their hearts; they have not known my ways. As I swore in my wrath, they shall never enter my rest" (3:10, 11). Finally, the application of this to those who belong to Christ is such that a radical affirmation of the disobedient one's total personal exclusion from God results then in complete ruin and catastrophe.

10. Irremediable Judgment

The threat of judgment upon such as commit apostasy is not only severe, but can be for the Christian absolutely irremediable. It is impossible to restore this kind of person again to repentance (6:4–6). In the final hortatory section this idea is again repeated with equal vigor. It is simply stated, "For if we sin deliberately after receiving the knowledge of truth, there no longer remains a sacrifice for sins, but a fearful prospect of judgment, and a fury of fire which will consume the adversaries" (10:26, 27). This is "deserved by the man who has spurned the Son of God, and profaned the blood of the covenant by which he was sanctified, and outraged the Spirit of grace" (10:29). These verses teach that no man is exempt from the judgment of God. Men and nations have a destiny, but this destiny is achieved only within the context of and proper regard for the God of love *and* wrath. It is through judgment that God effects his purpose. This has ever been so. The history even of the chosen people, that special strand of human struggle, both heroic and deplorable, is a history of judgment. God interposes himself constantly in drastic and formidable fashion to bestir a people to holiness and godliness. Whole nations as well as individuals are chastised, brought to their knees by the heavy hand of God.

However much out of keeping with contemporary trends this may be, we at least must acknowledge that this writer speaks from a tradition and standpoint that in no way minimizes the terrible anger of God. Indeed, in this very context he directly states, "A man who has violated the law of Moses dies without mercy at the testimony of two or three witnesses" (10:28). And it is because God has been this kind of God and continues to be this kind of God that the recipients are in terrible danger when they "sin deliberately" (10:26). It is indisputable that the Christian recipients of this severe warning are in such a spiritual condition that the threat has direct applicability to them. The writer does not waste words; he is not erecting a hypothetical specter just to frighten them; nor is he unaware of the tragic implication of his statements. It is an ultimate and irrevocable exclusion from the rest of God that makes up the critical point of his alarm. This is terrifying. Every Christian should know that the path to open "falling away" or forthright apostasy is wide, comfortable to traverse, and easy of access. The beginning is disobedience. This disobedience easily becomes a fashion of life which then is tantamount to practical apostasy. In the majority of life's decisions and acts such a one is not so much guided by reliance upon God, but rather upon the support immediate gratification can provide. This is deadly and, if nurtured, irreclaimably destructive. It is also subtle. To say, as Calvin did, that to make this applicable one must in blunt manner deny Christ, is wrong.[11] The language of these verses (10:26–39) can be construed to convey the idea of an abrupt, verbal, attitudinal denunciation of Christ. But it need not be. Actually, the context prohibits this as the sole category of person who is irredeemable. The material here encompasses the idea of need for obedience in the hard struggle of life. It has to do with endurance. It has to do particularly with a continuing reliance upon God and his provision. It has to do with doing the will of God, because this is the way to receive the promise. The rather forthright teaching here is that although one may make claim to faith and affirm his participation in the community of faith, he may yet consistently and continuously be "dull of hearing" (5:11), and may irretrievably "drift away." Extended disobedience, which is the functional equivalent of "shrinking back" (10:38), brings one into irremediable jeopardy of soul. God says, "My soul has no pleasure in him" (10:38).

Although the "analogy-of-faith" devotee may assert that whatever these texts say they cannot teach that a "saved" person could be forever lost so as never again to be able to experience repentance, this is precisely what is taught here. These statements must not be interpreted in the context of other teachings; they must be interpreted in the context of Hebrews and from the perspective of this writer. Such strong words should not be distorted by some sort of "illumination" from other passages. They must stand as they are, and in so standing give more profound understanding of an emphasis to the enormous evil of relying on anything other than God. By doing this one forthrightly tells God that neither he nor his sacrifice in Christ can be trusted. One who does this calls God a liar. There is no greater sin. And if persisted in, this brings one into such spiritual ruin that there can be no repentance (6:4–6).

11. The Dual Motivation

Now it becomes quite evident that the two motivations mentioned above are really quite inseparable. They are two sides of the same coin. We should not think that the writer is using only negative reinforcement when he warns of the wrath of God, when he speaks of the terrifying consequence if one does not obey. It is finally and most clearly maintained that the traversing pilgrim will be made happy when he seeks the way of God. Seek after happiness, avoid suffering and pain. This is the dual motivation that coalesces into one. Great joy will be had only through reliance upon the steadfastness and high-priestly ministry of Christ. Misery will attend the way of rebellion and disobedience. So see that which will make you happy. "Whoever would draw near to God must believe that he exists and that he rewards those who seek him" (11:6). The writer is so solicitous for the good and ultimate joy of the reader that he wishes at much cost to motivate to godliness.

The situation is similar to that of an earthly father with his children. "For the moment all discipline seems painful rather than pleasant; later it yields the peaceful fruit of righteousness to those who have been trained by it" (12:11). The child learns from threats, warnings, and discipline the proper conduct in life; he learns conduct that will serve him in good stead in the future. He will learn the way of life that issues in joy and peace. So it is that at the very time that he is being denied, scolded, warned, and chided, he is simultaneously being prepared for a life of steadfast joy. The implication here is that if a father really loves a son, he will discipline him. It is out of love, and because of love, that the father exerts a heavy hand.[12] This is made abundantly clear in the context of our epistle. The soaring concepts of the high-priestly ministry of Christ, the sacrifice of his person, the forgiveness of sins through his blood, all conspire together to underscore the fact of God's love. It is the most positive reinforcement imaginable when the author indicates his strong conviction that through all the varying circumstances of the sojourn, the rest will be obtained. Indeed, even though they are "dull," his confidence is strong, for he affirms "we feel sure of better things that belong to salvation" (6:9) and that the recipients are "not of those who shrink back and are destroyed but of those who have faith and keep their souls" (10:39).

How could one avoid being raised to an ecstatic level of positive appreciation of the reality of God and salvation after reading the initial confident victorious statements of the opening verses of the last great hortatory section (10:19–13:17)? "Therefore, brethren, since we have confidence to enter the sanctuary by the blood of Jesus, by the new and living way which he opened for us through the curtain, that is, through his flesh, and since we have a great priest over the house of God, let us draw near with a true heart in full assurance of faith, with our hearts sprinkled clean from an evil conscience and our bodies washed with pure water" (10:19–22). Finally, the only motivation is to find happiness. This means that the writer is simply telling the reader how distress and anguish of soul may be avoided and how ultimate joy may be achieved. And he is furthermore concerned in the teaching sections (1:1–14; 2:5–18; 5:1–10; 7:1–10:18) to show that it is in Christ that joy and spontaneity of life is captured.

12. Faith—Obedience

If we were to inquire of this literature as to how one really obtains rest, the answer would be given in simple monosyllabic syntax: by faith in Christ. This is quite to the point and, we think, glorious in simplicity. The message given to the house of Israel did not benefit them "because it did not meet with *faith* in the hearers" (4:2). But those "who have *believed* enter that rest" (4:3). Simple belief ensures the rest. This assured rest is the same as becoming a recipient of the inheritance. So the exhortation is, do "not be sluggish, but imitators of those who through *faith* and patience inherit the promises" (6:12). Since Christ has made such marvelous provision for us, "let us draw near with true heart in full assurance of *faith* . . ." (10:22). That this priestly Jesus is concerned with our faith is clear, for he is the "perfecter of our *faith*" (12:2). Finally, the eleventh chapter is obviously centrally concerned with the power of life and dedication of men of old—patriarchs, prophets, and just regular, everyday, trusting people. And how were they regarded by God? They were pleasing to God. They received divine approval. How? By faith: "Without *faith* it is impossible to please him" (11:6). By *faith* "the man of old received divine approval" (11:2).

But what is the nature of this faith? It is most interesting that in the chapter most devoted to faith, the answer is inevitably of a functional kind. Faith is depicted not so much in the theoretical sphere, as in the practical sphere. It is not so much an abstract belief of the heart as enduring a hard struggle and suffering abuse and affliction. Here moves to the fore a pragmatic understanding of faith. It is more doing than being, or better, it is a being that issues quite surely in doing. Faith is that internal reality that enables works of righteousness to be accomplished. "*By faith* Abraham obeyed when he was called to go out . . ." (11:8). The consistent pattern here is that of a direct and unbreakable correlation between the man of faith and the man of obedience. The obedience is possible because the faith is real. So, for this writer, faith is the principal term utilized to describe the experiences of reliance upon God that enables and, indeed, demands obedience. This is why any rupture in the obedience segment of the man of faith is looked upon with such horror and described in such ultimately serious terms.[13] Faith, then, is not a term that can be divorced from the concreteness of life. Faith cannot be separated from obedience. Obedience is included in and a part of the faith experience. Thus when the author says faith, he at the same time says obedience, for the terms are interchangeable.

Indeed, even the two terms utilized to describe those who will not enter the rest are coextensive and mutually precise and unqualified. They are grammatical variations of the infinitives "to disobey" and "to disbelieve." It is extraordinary but nonetheless true that these two ideas and consequent conceptualizations are also used interchangeably.[14] In the context of this writer's thought there is an interlocking and indisputable connection of an equative kind between disobedience and unbelief. If he were asked why the Israelites of old did not enter the rest of Canaan and, more contemporaneously, why the recipients of the letter might not enter the rest of salvation, the answer is, because they did not or will not *obey*, because they did not or will not *believe*. This is clearly highlighted when he says, "And to whom did he swear that they should never enter his rest, but to those who were *disobedient?* So we see that they were unable to enter because of *unbelief*" (3:18, 19). This alternation and equivalence between disbelief and disobedience is carefully sustained throughout the entirety of the epistle. Those who are to enter the rest are the ones who believe and obey.

The writer never even conceives of an obedience apart from faith. All of the obedience of which he knows anything, and which is worth emulating, is a God-connected obedience or a faith-obedience. Once he has established the axiomatic truth that "without faith it is impossible to please him [God] " (11:6), it is only a logical step to conclude that if the "men of old" pleased God by such noble, obedient lives, they did so by faith. The absolute essential for participation in the promise is that God be pleased. Here again is established a definitive division between obedience and legalism or works. Abraham and the other worthies did not obtain the favor of God by doing certain things, but rather by being a certain way. The certain way in which they were in being (a faith way) quite simply and quite inevitably resulted in a "doing way," or in obedience. This is why it is repeatedly said, "*By faith* Abel offered . . ." (11:4), "*By faith* Noah . . . constructed an ark" (11:7). "*By faith* Abraham obeyed when he was called to go out . . ." (11:8). They found God to be trustworthy. And this is all they needed for this life and the next.

It is exactly in regard to this discussion of faith and obedience that the problem of an "analogy-of-faith" hermeneutic is most acute. Though Paul and the other New Testament writers in a different and less dramatic way say the same as the writer of Hebrews,[15] yet somehow in many theological circles a wrong radical of revelation has achieved normative status; namely, that man is saved by faith alone and that this faith does not *necessarily* include "obedience." This simply cannot be squared with the book of Hebrews, nor for that matter with the other New Testament writings. There is nothing more dangerous to accurate and truly biblical interpretation than the imposition of external categories on a specific or individual writing. Each writing must be construed in its own terms and not in the light of some other radical of revelation supposedly derived from some other book that makes up the corpus of divine and authoritative revelation.

The writer of this book, then, gives us authoritative ideas, most of which cause "fear," jar and disturb us, but all of which are utterly essential in the experience of faith and practice as the traversing pilgrim achieves joy now and that ultimate "rest" of the celestial city.[16]

NOTES

1. The doctrinal sections are 1:1–14; 2:5–18; 5:1–10 and 7:1–10:18. The hortatory sections are 2:1–4; 3:1–4:16; 5:11–6:20 and 10:19–13:17.
2. For example, see Eph 1:3–3:21 (doctrinal), 4:1–3 (ethical), 4:4–21 (doctrinal), 4:22–6:20 (ethical) and Col 1:5–2:5; 2:9–15 (doctrinal) and 3:2–4:6 (ethical).
3. See H. A. Ironside, *Studies in Hebrews and Titus* (1932), pp. 79–82; L. S. Chafer, *Systematic Theology*, (1948), pp. 296, 302; E. C. Wickham, *Hebrews* (1910), p. 42; Thomas Hewitt, *Hebrews* (1960), pp. 106–111; C. I. Scofield, *Reference Bible* (1917), p. 1295.
4. "Works" as a negative and useless quality is always defined in the Scripture as that righteous activity of man done to secure favor and acceptance with God. The obedience of faith is radically different, for it connotes the fact that trust always issues in obedience, though obedience is never engaged in to obtain favor with God. It is impossible to earn God's favor (Deut 10:17).
5. Our writer uses two different words for "assurance." *Plērophorian* (Heb 6:11; 10:22) has the sense of "full assurance" or "certainty" which is attained by appropriating salvation through Christ. Cf. G. Delling, *TDNT* 6, p. 311. This salvation results in a subjective experience of assurance. On the other hand, *hypostasis* (Heb 1:3; 3:14; 11:1; reality, assurance) is not describing the subjective experience of faith, but rather *defines* "the character of the transcendent future things . . ." (H. Köster, *TDNT* 8, p. 587). Thus, faith rests in the assurance that the things hoped for are real. These two terms come together in the experience of the believer. When one sees that the future and transcendent things that are hoped for are indeed real (11:1; 1:3; 3:14), this knowledge then produces full assurance (10:22; 6:11). The author tells us that this assurance comes from considering the person and ministry of Christ (12:2, 3; 3:1), in whom the reality of the things hoped for rests.
6. Israel looked for contentment of life in things rather than in God. For example, when they were being pursued by the Egyptians, they stated that they would rather serve the Egyptians in slavery than face the possibility of death in the wilderness (Exod 14:10–12). The security of the status quo also played a part in their refusal to enter the promised land (Deut 1:26–28). They also sought contentment in food (Exod 16:2–3), water (Exod 15:23–24; 17:2–3), and other gods (Exod 32:1–6).
7. The ideas of "endurance" and "perseverance" are contained in the same Greek word. *hypomenō*. Cf. 10:32, 36; 12:1, 2, 3, 7. Other Greek words are employed which convey this same meaning. See *makrothumeō* (6:12, 15); also *katechō* (3:6, 14; 10:23). According to this, one could as well speak of the "endurance of the saints."
8. Cf. Heb 3:6; 6:4–6; 10:26–27.
9. Cf. Matt 13:1–8; 18:35; 24:13; John 8:31; Rom 11:21; 1 Cor 15:1–2; Col 1:23; Gal 5:4.
10. Nothing like religious science, so called.
11. Calvin says, "Those who sin, mentioned by the apostle, are not such as offend in any way, but such as forsake the Church, and wholly alienate themselves from Christ. For he speaks not here of this or of that sin, but he condemns by name those who wilfully renounced fellowship with the Church. But there is a vast difference between particular failings and a complete defection of this kind, by which we entirely fall away from the grace of Christ. . . . The apostle then refers to those alone who wickedly forsake Christ, and thus deprive themselves of the benefit of his death." *Loc. cit.*
12. This "heavy hand" must be applied only in the context of radical love, otherwise the filial relationship becomes grotesque.

13. As discussed above.
14. The following illustration can perhaps help us understand the relationship between "disbelief" and "disobedience." A certain tight rope walker publicized that he was going to walk across Niagara Falls. A large crowd gathered. He dusted his hands and feet with powdered chalk, grasped with both hands the pole he used for balance, and proceeded confidently across the rope. He not only went across but also made a return trip. The crowd stood amazed and responded with cheers. The man proclaimed he would do it again, this time without his pole. Again he successfully went over and back. As he stepped off the rope, he turned to the crowd and asked how many thought he could make a third trip, this time with a wheelbarrow. Some responded with confidence while others with skepticism. He set off on his task and completed it with the greatest of ease. He then inquired of the crowd as to whether they believed he could do the same thing with the wheelbarrow full of cement. This time the crowd responded with great confidence. Again, he performed this feat with unbelievable ease. Having completed these four trips successfully, he asked the spectators if they believed he could wheel a human being across the dangerous expanse. The response was unanimous. He could do it. Upon their reply he turned to a gentleman and said, "All right, my friend, let's go." In this illustration it is clear that if the man appointed to ride in the wheelbarrow refused, his refusal would constitute a lack of trust in the tight rope walker. So it is with us in our relationship with God. If we disobey him, we really don't trust him. It is in this sense that distrust and disobedience are terms capable of being used interchangeably. Other New Testament literature reflects this same use. Cf. John 3:36; Acts 14:2; 19:9; Rom 15:31; 2:8; 1 Pet 2:8; 3:1.
15. Cf. the references given in note 8 above.
16. That joy and a proper "fear" of God are not just permissible but necessary correlates can perhaps be illustrated in the following manner. When one drives along a narrow two-lane highway, there is always a certain sense of fear because of what might happen if the vehicle should veer into the lane of oncoming traffic. This is a very real fear and causes the driver to be alert. But it is not antithetical to joy, happiness, peace, and assurance. In part, it is necessary to these experiences. The fear of the possibility of veering into oncoming traffic is a means to the end of diligence in driving, of "making one's calling and election" sure as a safe driver. Now, if the car should, through lack of "fear and trembling," through lack of alertness, swerve into the other lane, then adrenalin-inspired horror grips the entire person; real consternation and profound fear and terror develop. This is a disquieting state. Now there is no peace. There is only turbulence, uncertainty, and frustration. If the driver continues in this way, sooner or later, no one can tell when, disaster will be experienced. But if he heeds the warnings, recognizes the error of his way, and gets back into his own lane, he will be saved and will, as he exercises caution and has appropriate fear, know once again quietness of soul and peace of mind. So is it with the Christian. As he obeys God and trusts him, as he fears unbelief above all things else, and trembles at the prospect of disobedience which is unbelief and deliberate sin, then he is joyful and happy, at rest in the Lord. But when he disobeys God, which means a faltering of trust, then life begins to be disjointed. Now it is at this point that the true church reminds him of the promises of God and of the wrath of God. A disobedient, "wrong side of the highway" Christian must be told that his way is the way of destruction, that he has veered off into the other lane, and that unless he heeds the warnings there will be final, even irrevocable, disaster (Heb 6:4). And indeed, the true Christian, the elect, will heed the warnings of God's wrath. Such a one will be divinely enabled to hear and heed the words of promise and the words of wrath, and he will turn from his wicked way and live.

II. Tradition

8: Tradition and Citation in the Epistle of James

PETER H. DAVIDS

New Testament scholarship knows well that the New Testament does not necessarily follow the rules of grammatical-historical exegesis in its use of the Old Testament material. We are well aware that Hebrews often uses a typological exegesis, Paul can allegorize, and Acts can use *pesher* exegesis.[1] When we turn to the Epistle of James, then, we are curious to discover what we will find, for James is doubly significant for this issue: (1) in five short chapters James cites no less than four Old Testament narratives, those of Abraham, Rahab, Job, and Elijah; and (2) the Abraham narrative is used in a way significantly different from the way Paul applies it. We wish to analyze these citations to demonstrate that our author, although he neither allegorizes nor uses typology, cites not only the biblical narrative, but also the wider collection of traditional embellishments and theological reflection, which he assumes his reader knows. James, perhaps more than any other author in the New Testament, shows the awareness he and his church had of the Jewish haggadic tradition.

1. Abraham

The citation of Abraham in James 2 is one of the best-known features of the epistle, for it has formed the center of the Paul-James controversy over the relationship of faith and works.[2] The issues which concern us form the background to this theological discussion, for they concern the relationship between the citation and its context which gives the clue to James' method.

Jas 2:14–17 sets the stage for a discussion of faith and works by citing the all-too-realistic case of a poor Christian coming to a richer one, sharing his need, and being turned away with a prayer. James obviously desires a response of sharing (charity). This passage forms

113

part of a major theme in the epistle, the relationship of the rich and poor;[3] it also introduces the Abraham citation. But how does this citation fit with the cited example? The works called for in 2:14–17 are charity, but in the citation one finds Abraham offering his son, a work of a different type indeed, which Christians are not expected to emulate.

The solution to this apparent *non sequitur* lies in the context of the binding of Isaac in Jewish tradition, for this work of Abraham is not the only work with which this tradition credits him. For example, in the *Testament of Abraham* we read,

> Abraham lived the span of his life, nine hundred and ninety-five years, and having lived all the years of his life in quietness, gentleness, and righteousness, the righteous man was extremely hospitable. For having pitched his tent at the crossroads of the oak of Mamre, he welcomed all, rich and poor, kings and rulers, cripples and helpless, friends and strangers, neighbors and travelers—all alike did the devout, all-holy, righteous, hospitable Abraham welcome.[4]

This tradition that Abraham was meritorious for his charitable deeds is not limited to the one pseudepigraphon, for it is repeated in a variety of Jewish sources. In Tg. Ps.-J. Gen 21:33 we read,

> *And he planted* an oasis at the Well of the Seven Lambs, and he prepared in it food and drink for those who passed by and returned, and he used to declare to them there, "Acknowledge and believe in the name of the word of *the Lord, the Everlasting God.*"

Again, a similar tradition appears in *Aboth de Rabbi Nathan* 7:

> [discussing "And let the poor be members of your household" in answer to Job in Job 21:16–20] But the Holy One, blessed be he, said to Job: "Job, you have not achieved a half of Abraham's achievement. You sit and wait in your house until travellers come to you. To a man used to eating good bread you give good bread. To a man used to eating meat you give meat. To a man used to drinking wine you give wine. But Abraham was not like that, because he went out looking all around, and when he found any travellers he brought them to his house. To a man not used to eating good bread he gave good bread. To a man not used to eating meat he gave meat. To a man not used to drinking wine he gave wine. In addition he set himself to building great houses by the way, leaving in them food and drink so that travellers could eat and drink and give thanks to heaven. . . . And whatever a man asked for was found in Abraham's house, as it is written, *And Abraham planted a tamarisk tree in Beer-sheba.*"[5]

This tradition naturally spread beyond rabbinic circles,[6] and there is no reason to doubt that our author knew of it.

But how does the charity of Abraham relate to the passage in

James? Does our author not refer to the binding of Isaac? That is in fact the case; but for Jewish tradition the *'Aqedah* (binding of Isaac) is the culmination of the testing of Abraham. It is the capstone of ten tests and thus must be seen in the context of the others.[7]

The text in Jas 2:21 states (in the form of a question with implied agreement) that Abraham *ex ergōn edikaiōthē anenenkas Isaak ton huion autou epi to thysiastērion.* It is clear in the text that the point at which Abraham was declared righteous, the point at which the legal pronouncement was made, was the time of the "sacrifice" (taking *anenenkas* as a temporal participle). Our author is probably referring to the statement made in Gen 22:12, "For now I know that you fear God, seeing you have not withheld your son, your only son from me." This "for now I know" formula is the normal formula pronounced over those passing the test of faith. The test is ended, and Abraham is declared righteous at its end.[8]

In Genesis this test may stand alone,[9] but in Jewish thought this final declaration does not stand without the context of the previous life. A typical rabbinic view appears in the following expansion of the text:

> The angels broke into loud weeping, and they exclaimed: "The highways lie waste, the wayfaring man ceaseth, he hath broken the covenant. Where is the reward of Abraham, he who took the wayfarers into his house, gave them food and drink, and went with them to bring them on the way? The covenant is broken, whereof Thou didst speak to him . . . , for the slaughtering knife is set upon his throat."[10]

In other words, the *'Aqedah* was the end test of a righteous life. The life of Isaac was spared and Abraham was declared righteous because this act was consistent with the previous righteous life of Abraham.

James indicates in three ways that he, too, is thinking of the total situation of the life of Abraham. First, he uses the plural *ex ergōn*— not a single great work but the works of Abraham in general are in view. Second, he cites Gen 15:6 ("And he believed the Lord; and he reckoned it to him as righteousness") in verse 23. This sentence was spoken during another of the tests of Abraham, and our author now sees it "fulfilled" in the result of the *'Aqedah.*[11] Third, our author sets this citation of Abraham into a context stressing charity or hospitality, which would call to mind for a Jewish reader the total context of the works of Abraham. Thus we conclude that James sees this one test as indicative of the whole; the pronouncement in the end is not the pronouncement on a single act alone, but on that act as the culmination of a series of works stemming from faith.[12]

What, then, may we say about the use of the Abraham tradition in James? Our author indeed cites the biblical details as part of his argument, but at the same time he intends that the reader will see the connection between Abraham and charity. The reader must supply this connection from his own acquaintance with the multitude of tradition surrounding the life of Abraham. James expects that the reader shares his extrabiblical thought-world and will thus make the proper connections.

2. Rahab

Immediately after his citation of Abraham, our author mentions the example of Rahab. Again the Old Testament contains the details he mentions, but there is more to the citation than what appears on the surface. First, James may well see a parallel between Rahab and the Christians to whom he writes in that the works of both are the fruit of repentance. Rahab repeatedly appears in Jewish tradition as the archetypical proselyte, as one who was "brought near."[13] Thus, as in the case of Abraham (who was also considered a convert from idolatry), works of righteousness flow naturally from repentance: they are the evidence of the repentant heart. This concept fits James' main point that the one who truly repents will demonstrate the fact through charity.

Second, Rahab's deed, which is the focal point of our author's interest, explicitly points the reader to the epistle's theme of charity (in the form of hospitality);[14] for in her personal concern for the spies Rahab does "deeds of lovingkindness" (gemîlût hasadîm), which were the highest form of charity known to the rabbis: "Almsgiving and deeds of lovingkindness are equal to all the commandments of the Law."[15] The value of this deed of Rahab is enshrined in later Jewish tradition as part of Israel's treasury of merit.[16]

Third, the close connection of Abraham and Rahab is of more than passing significance, for the same connection is found in 1 Clement 10–12. Clement first calls Abraham "the Friend" (ho philos as in Jas 2:23), stating: "Because of his faith and hospitality a son was given to him in his old age, and in his obedience he offered him as a sacrifice to God on the mountain which he showed him."[17] In the next chapter Lot appears as an example of "hospitality and piety."[18] The following section turns to Rahab: "For her faith and hospitality Rahab the harlot was saved."[19] This teaching in turn becomes the basis for ethical exhortation. We observe, then, the following facts in this citation: (1) Abraham and Rahab appear together as examples in a second work of early Christian literature, a work which is probably independent of James, (2) the same deeds of both characters are recalled, and (3) the virtue of hospitality is specifically named as the reason for the citation. Thus we agree with H. Chadwick when he argues that this points to a traditional use of Abraham and Rahab as examples of hospitality (or charity) in Christian (and in all likelihood Jewish) circles.[20]

We may draw several conclusions from this Rahab citation. First, here again—although not so emphatically as in the previous case— traditional material helps to establish the relevance of the citation and may be assumed to have been a part of the author's and readers' common culture. Second, this citation, coming as it does *after* the example of Abraham, reinforces our impression that hospitality is the subject of both citations. This reinforcement strengthens our argument in the previous section. Third, it is probably precisely the element of hospitality which linked the two names together in the Christian parenetic tradition. This traditional association in turn determined the use of the two together here. Our epistle draws upon an earlier tradition of ethical exhortation, possibly a pre-Christian one.[21]

3. Job

James cites the example of Job in a rather difficult context as part of his conclusion (chap. 5):

> As an example of suffering and patience, brethren, take the prophets who spoke in the name of the Lord. Behold, we call those happy who were steadfast. You have heard of the steadfastness of Job, and you have seen the purpose of the Lord, how the Lord is compassionate and merciful.[22]

The first part of James' dual example is clear enough. The prophets certainly do serve as examples of endurance during persecution (which the context in Jas 5:1–6 suggests to be the situation of the Christian community), whether one cites the canonical accounts of Micaiah, Jeremiah, or Daniel or whether one includes such extra-canonical examples of suffering as the martyrdom of Isaiah. The reference to the prophets may have in turn suggested the example of Job, for Jewish tradition considers him one of the seven Gentile prophets. But the reference to Job is surprising in this context, nevertheless, for he is cited as an example of patient endurance, *hypomonē*. In the canonical book of Job this virtue is only evident if one stops reading at chapter 2, and even there the stress is on uprightness rather than patient endurance. Did James mechanically include Job as a prophetic example without considering his merits vis-à-vis his theme, or has he more than the book of Job in mind? The latter appears to be the case.

The theme of patient endurance is not lacking in Jewish traditions about Job, especially those coalescing in the *Testament of Job*. Indeed, this pseudepigraphal work is hardly begun when the author boasts, "I am your father Job, who exhibits complete endurance" (*ho en pasē hypomonē genomenos*).[23] The author then presents the suffering as a contest with Satan, a battle in which Satan will have the upper hand (having been angered by Job's destruction of an idol). "But [says God] if you endure (*hypomeinēs*), I shall make your name renowned in all earthly generations until the consummation of the age."[24]   After the contest is joined and Satan has done his worst for some seventeen years, he is forced in the end to admit in tears that Job has conquered him, leading Job to comment, "Now then, my children, you must also be patient in everything that happens to you, for patience is superior to everything."[25]   In the following discussion with his comforters (who arrive three years after the defeat of Satan) Job demonstrates a perfect trust in God to the point of refusing all medical help.[26]   Such is the patience of Job. James certainly had plenty of precedence in this tradition for citing Job as an example of patient endurance.

But it would be superficial to end our discussion about the contact between James and the *Testament of Job* at this point, for there are other areas of contact as well. For instance, if James wishes to incite Christians to share their goods, the Job of the *Testament* is also an example of a great giver, a model of charity to shame all others. Job recites his various charitable acts to his children on page after page. Every conceivable need of every class of poor was cared for in a magnificent manner. Indeed, his charities were virtually industries in themselves. His servants, he claims, were worn out from serving the poor, so Job had to refresh them in turn. Naturally, this is a side of the tradition virtually absent from the biblical account, only occurring as scattered examples during Job's defense of himself (which passages may well be the roots of these legends),[27] but it is a side which is not unimportant to James. The epistle has two themes which interact at this point: (1) the call to charity and (2) the call to endurance. James never suggests that the Christians are suffering because of lack of charity. Rather, he seems to be calling loosely attached community members, particularly those with some wealth, to the deeper commitment of sharing we may assume the majority of the community already practiced. Thus righteousness has not preserved the Church from suffering, for suffering appears to come irrespective of just deserts. The same theme occurs in the *Testament of Job*, for despite his magnanimous charity Job suffers. The fact that he suffers in a contest with Satan is probably also meaningful to James. Now there is reason to believe that Jas 5:7–20 is a recapitulation of the major themes of the work, drawing the loose ends back together. If this is indeed the case, James' reason for citing Job becomes clear: Job combines in his person the two major themes of charity and patience in undeserved suffering.[28]

We do not wish to imply that our author knew and used a Greek form of the present *Testament of Job.*[29] Although several scholars accept the not-unlikely hypothesis that this form of the legends originated among the Therapeuts in Egypt, one doubts that the Greek version was current in Palestine when James wrote—if indeed it even existed then. Yet there is a large amount of agreement among scholars that a Semitic tradition lies behind the Greek document. Most estimate that this originated around the first century B.C. (Naturally this date depends upon how late the canonical book is dated.) Thus our author may have known a *Vorlage* for the *Testament of Job.* Even if this were not the case, similar legends about Job or hints that such legends were current have been preserved in both the Dead Sea Scrolls and the rabbinic literature. The legends are in fact so widespread in Jewish literature that it would be surprising if James were ignorant of them. We conclude, then, that James had adequate opportunity to know the tradition later embodied in the *Testament of Job,* either as an oral tradition or possibly as an Aramaic document, and that he certainly draws upon this tradition in his epistle.[30]

In his citation of Job as well as those of Abraham and Rahab our author calls upon Jewish haggadic tradition to complete the example he cites from the Old Testament. In the case of Job, both he and the prophets occur in the Old Testament narrative, but the author expects the reader to supply a wealth of detail to the illustration from the stories he has heard since a child. While in chapter 2 the contextual flow of the passage would be interrupted by the citation of Abraham if one did not know the tradition, here in chapter 5 the citation without those stories is strained and artificial (leading to the atomized approach many exegetes take toward James); with its traditional accompaniment the reason for the citation becomes crystal clear.

4. Elijah

When James turns to Elijah as an example, he writes,

The prayer of a righteous man has great power in its effects. Elijah was a man of like nature with ourselves and he prayed fervently that it might not rain, and for three years and six months it did not rain on the earth. Then he prayed again and the heaven gave rain, and the earth brought forth its fruit.[31]

Now this statement is interesting in itself when compared with the Old Testament account. It is true that the ascension of Elijah into heaven in 2 Kings 2 and his expected return in Mal 4:5, 6 might explain the emphasis on Elijah's being "a man like us," but in the Elijah cycle in 1 Kings 17–18 we do not find prayer playing the part specified in James. Elijah prays for a boy's life to return and for fire to descend upon his altar (although one gains the impression that the author believes the prayer is more for dramatic effect than the real cause of the wonder), but he never prays for rain. He simply appears and announces the judgment of God at the beginning of the narrative and later turns from slaughtering the prophets and priests of Baal to announce that the judgment is over. From where does James obtain his idea about the rôle of prayer?[32]

Again we find help in Jewish tradition, for Elijah plays a large rôle in the traditions of late Judaism. Our interest, however, is not in his activity as the predecessor of the Messiah nor in his eschatological action as judge and as the bringer of the resurrection, but in his work as a man of prayer.[33] Significantly in the Mishnah (*Ta'an.* 2:4) when Elijah is cited after the fourth additional benediction, God is blessed for answering prayer. The rabbis may have been thinking more about the fire on Mt. Carmel than the rain which cooled its smouldering ashes, but the identification of Elijah with prayer is indicative, for in the Jewish tradition prayer plays a large rôle in Elijah's activities. In the expansion of 1 Kings 17–18, for instance, Elijah is said to be reacting to the wickedness of the people (especially the rebuilding of Jericho described in 1 Kgs 16:34). He prays for the keys to rain, and God gives them to him (not without reservations). True to his severe nature, Elijah gets angry and causes a drought. In fact, in some versions of the tale God cannot persuade Elijah to release the rain again and the incident of the widow's son becomes God's trick by which he can bargain with Elijah to release the rain in exchange for the boy's life.[34]

Quite probably this highly developed tradition arose long after the book of James, but one does not need to posit such a developed tradition to recognize that many forms of Jewish teaching connect the name of Elijah with prayer. He is, for instance, called the intercessor for Israel.[35] And his prayer is specifically connected with the drought in 4 Ezra 7:109 ("and Elijah [prayed] for those who received the rain"). So James is claiming no more than contemporary Jewish works were claiming.

Two other aspects of the Elijah traditions were probably in the mind of the author of our epistle beyond the reference to prayer. First, James describes Elijah as a normal human being, "a man of like nature with ourselves." This qualification means that James is probably defending his argument from the way many of the traditions behind the rabbinic literature present Elijah (often identified with Phinehas, Aaron's son) as a semi-divine intermediary between God and men, working in heaven as well as on earth, appearing as a somewhat-human Holy Spirit (although rather irascible and severe as well).[36] A caution to "bring him back to earth" fits well in such a context and would be necessary if his example as a man of prayer were to be at all meaningful to ordinary mortal Christians.

Second, James could hardly have been ignorant of the fact that according to the Jewish tradition (and one may be assured that this tradition was very popular) one of Elijah's chief activities on earth is assisting the poor or defending the oppressed. Sometimes this means helping a poor scholar out of his poverty; sometimes this means helping someone to bear his poverty. But Elijah is often pictured as the helper of the helpless, the one who delivers and the one who judges.[37] Now in the immediate context of James the help required by the neighbor is intercession rather than material goods, but in the wider context of the epistle one cannot help but think that the fact that Elijah often acted to "fulfill his own prayers" was a welcome feature of the narrative which James would wish his readers to recall and follow.

The Elijah citation, then, as well as the other citations in James, combines both canonical and extra-canonical tradition. The Old Testament provides the character and the framework of the narrative, but certainly the stress on prayer and perhaps also an allusion to helping others came from the oral tradition the author had received and which had already predisposed the readers to understand his point.[38] On the other hand, our author handles the material critically enough that he can insert a corrective at a point where he feels the tradition might weaken instead of strengthen his argument. Yet without the traditional knowledge it would be difficult for the reader to pick up the full force of the citation.

5. Conclusion

We can now draw some conclusions about James' method in citing Old Testament characters and events. In each of the references to a biblical character which we have examined, the author of James needs the reader to supply the traditional embellishments of the biblical account to fully understand the passage. How else would one know, for instance, that Abraham, Job, and Elijah were all helpers of the poor? And where else would the reader discover that Elijah was a man of prayer, even an intercessor? The freedom with which James combines the canonical with the extra-canonical means that he apparently had no firm boundary in his mind between the two. The amount of his reliance on the oral tradition varies: in the case of Job it is probable that the extra-canonical materials are the primary reference our author has in mind, but in the case of Rahab his dependence on them may be minimal. So for James the apocryphal and canonical are not sharply divided, and his apparent biblical references are not so entirely biblical at all.[39]

This fact enables us to place these stories within their wider exegetical context both within the epistle and within the whole New Testament. Every one of these accounts concerns a character known for his charity. This unanimous feature is suggestive, since solidarity with the poor is a major theme in James. Consciously or unconsciously James returns to his theme in every example, even when it is admittedly not the primary reason for the citation. Widening our scope, we see that James' method is not entirely different from that of other New Testament writers, such as Jude in Jude 9 and 14–15: they feel almost as free to take examples from non-canonical as from canonical tradition, and they mix the two. The evidence from James, then, must be included when one discusses canon-formation or canon-consciousness.[40] Moreover, since the author must have known and expected his readers to know the traditional material upon which he draws, these citations either form supporting evidence or else disprove any theory about the authorship and intended readership of this epistle. Finally, these citations remind us again of the necessity of placing the New Testament in its context before interpreting it: the authors were not writing to twentieth-century Westerners, but to first-century Near Easterners with a wealth of tradition stored in their minds. Well known though this may be, we need to constantly remind ourselves, pricking the balloon of Western scholarly interpretive arrogance, that rude peasants of 1900 years ago had interpretive tools in their store of legend and tradition which we can only recover in part by years of painful work and study.

NOTES

1. Perhaps the most complete recent treatment of this subject is Richard Longenecker's *Biblical Exegesis in the Apostolic Period* (1975).
2. Few if any scholars at present believe that James is directly attacking Paul. The only really live issue over the relationship between Jas 2:14–26, Galatians 3, and Romans 4 is

whether a later, misunderstood Paulinism is the object of attack (implying a later date for James and probably a non-Palestinian provenance) or an early Jewish-Christian "dead orthodoxy" (implying a date before the Pauline terminology became known, probably before A.D. 50). J. H. Ropes, *A Critical and Exegetical Commentary on the Epistle of St. James* (1916), p. 35, represents a classical statement of the former position (which the majority of scholars hold today); and G. Kittel, "Der geschichtliche Ort des Jakobus-briefes," *ZNTW* 41 (1942), pp. 71–105, and "Der Jakobusbrief und die apostolischen Väter," *ZNTW* 43 (1950–51), pp. 54–112, represents a scholarly defense of the latter.
3. At a minimum the following passages discuss this theme: 1:9–11; 1:27; 2:1–26; and 4:13–5:5.
4. M. E. Stone, trans., *The Testament of Abraham in Texts and Translations* (1972), recension A, chapter 1; see also chapter 17.
5. J. Bowker, *The Targums and Rabbinic Literature* (1969), pp. 222 and 223. The tradition of Abraham's hospitality to strangers also appears in the *Fragmentary Targum* and *B. Soṭah* 10a–b. In Midr. Teh. Ps 37:1 we read:

> If Abraham had not sought to rival God he would not have become the possessor of heaven and earth. When did Abraham seek to rival God? When he said to Melchizedek, "Because of what righteous deed did you come out of the ark alive?" He said, "Because of the alms which we gave in the ark." Abraham said, "How could you do so if there were no people there? If no one except Noah and his sons was there to whom did you give alms?" Melchizedek said: "We gave alms to the cattle, wild animals and birds. We had no sleep because we were setting food before them one after another." Abraham at once thought, "If they had failed to give alms to the cattle, wild animals, and birds, they would not have come out of the ark alive. The deed will be even greater if I give alms to the children of men." Thereupon Abraham established an inn at Beer-sheba, that is to say, he gave food, drink and lodging to all the children of men.

It should be noted that several of the interpretations of Abraham's activity in Beersheba are based upon a play on the word *'eshel*, "tamarisk tree."
6. Josephus, for instance, refers to the tradition obliquely in *Antiquities* i.200.
7. This tradition is born out in *Pirke de Rabbi Eliezer* 26–31; *Aboth de Rabbi Nathan* 32; *Midr. Teh.* Ps 18:31; *Jub* 17:17; and *Jub* 19:8.
8. On the formula "now I know" see B. Gerhardsson, *The Testing of God's Son* (1966), p. 27. On the fact that *dikaioō* indicates a final judgment in a court "declared on the basis of the proven character of the defendant " see S. S. C. Marshall, *The Character, Setting, and Purpose of the Epistle of James* (unpublished B.Litt. thesis, Oxford University, 1968), p. 148.
9. This is not the place for a redaction-critical study of Genesis, but it is not our immediate impression that the author in Genesis views the test as one of a series.
10. L. Ginzberg, *The Legends of the Jews*, 1 (1913), p. 281. This work has a large collection of material pertinent to our theme on pp. 221–281.
11. It is possible that the connection is even deeper than this. Although James cites the LXX and not a targum, it could well be that he knew Aramaic traditions. In this tradition righteousness was often considered a merit (this interpretive twist was made possible through translation from Hebrew to Aramaic and through shifts in the meaning of the key Aramaic terms under the influence of the developing tradition). So *Tg. Ps.-J.* Gen 15:6 reads: "And he had faith in the word of the Lord, and it was reckoned to him for merit because he did not argue before him with words." Thus James may be citing a connection between faith and meritorious deeds, the former producing the latter. The dating of both the developing doctrine of merit and the Epistle of James must be more settled, however, before such a line of thought can be anything more than tentative.
    Related to this question is the citation of Abraham as the friend of God (Jas 2:23). While the title is found in Isa 41:8 and 2 Chron 20:7, it (and the related "beloved of God") is also widely found in Judaism. It may have been the formula used when the Jews called upon God to have mercy upon them for Abraham's sake (i.e., because of his merit), as, for example, in Dan 3:35 (LXX). If this is the case, one could argue that James calls his readers to recognize that they appeal to the fact of Abraham's faith's producing meritorious works

in this phrase. For the references for both these lines of argument see Bowker, *Targums,* pp. 201–202 and 212 respectively.

12. Much of this discussion of Abraham was first suggested by R. B. Ward, "Works of Abraham: James 2:14–26," *HTR* 61 (1968), pp. 283–290 (which is an excerpt from his 1966 Th.D. Dissertation at Harvard). We differ from his conclusions principally in believing that the *'Aqedah* is also considered by James to be a work, not just evidence of the other works (the time at which he was rewarded for them). Otherwise his argument expands upon what we have presented and the reader is referred to it for further details.

13. E.g., *Numbers R. Bemidbar* III 2; cf. *Midr. Ruth* 2 (126a).

14. Hospitality in Israel was a form of charity, charity toward the foreigner (who together with the Levite, widow, and orphan was a central recipient of charity) or others without a home. For further discussion see H. Bolkestein, *Wohltätigkeit und Armenpflege im Vorchristlichen Altertum* (1967), pp. 38ff. and 402ff.

15. Cited from *J. Peah* 15b–c. See also *B. Sukkah* 49b and G. F. Moore, *Judaism* (1927), 2, p. 171.

16. See further A. Marmorstein, *The Doctrine of Merit in Old Rabbinical Literature* (1920), p. 86. We are not entirely convinced that the value of Rahab's merits for future generations was taught as early as the Epistle of James. If the tradition preserved in *Mekilta Vayehi* 4 is accurate, the doctrine of Abraham's merits may have existed before Christ (the passage in question presents a discussion between Shemaiah and Abtalion, who flourished before and at the beginning of the reign of Herod the Great, over the question of whether Abraham's merits or some other cause procured the deliverance from the Red Sea); but in that case it was a disputed doctrine. Certainly the destruction of the temple gave the doctrine a new importance and place in Jewish doctrine. It is possible that Rahab's value developed at this later time from her close association with Abraham. James, we should note, appears to interact only with the value of the deeds in question for the individual, not for later generations.

17. *1 Clement* 10:7.

18. It is worth noting in this connection that Jewish traditions concerning Lot and Sodom do not pick up so much on the sexual evils of the city as on the statement in Ezek 16:49: "Behold, this was the guilt of your sister Sodom: she and her daughters had pride, surfeit of food, and prosperous ease, but did not aid the poor and needy." Lot's act of hospitality to the angels, then, was an act of lovingkindness worthy of salvation. Jewish amplification of this tradition may be found in Bowker, *Targums,* pp. 212–213, and in Ginzberg, *Legends.*

19. *1 Clement* 12:1.

20. H. Chadwick, "Justification by Faith and Hospitality," *StudPat* 4, pt. 2, in *Texte und Untersuchungen* 79 (1961), p. 281. Naturally we would have to modify our conclusions if it were likely that Clement knew and used James. The fact that he cites Lot between Abraham and Rahab makes a dependence upon James unlikely, even if one would agree with Bo Reicke, *The Epistles of James, Peter, and Jude* (1964), and S. S. Marshall, *Character, Setting, and Purpose,* that James came from Rome. Yet should one assume the dependence of Clement upon James, then one would have an example of a reader of James who did understand the reference to Abraham in its wider context in Jewish tradition and was able to cite it in its fuller form and rightly apply it to hospitality.

21. This is not the only place where James probably draws upon pre-existing material. For a convenient, if too atomistic, analysis of many further examples see M. Dibelius, *James* (1975). One example which may indicate pre-Christian origins for the parenetic material in James is Jas 3:17ff., which has closer affinities with the virtue-list in 1QS 4 than with any Christian virtue-list (e.g., Galatians 5).

22. Jas 5:10–11, RSV. The RSV is translating *hypomonē* by "steadfastness" and *telos* by "purpose." (A better translation for this latter word would have been, "the outcome which the Lord brought about," as Arndt, p. 819, renders the phrase.) By using these two Greek terms the author of James portrays a miniature eschatological situation with a tribulation leading to a consummation, for both terms are most widely used in Christian literature to refer to Christian tribulation and its final, eschatological conclusion.

23. *Test. Job* 1.2a. We cite Robert A. Kraft, ed., *The Testament of Job* (1974), and we are using his notation, for this is the most easily available form of the *Testament* today. It

agrees with the earlier edition of K. Kohler in G. A. Kohut, ed., *Semitic Studies in Memory of Rev. Dr. Alexander Kohut* (1897), pp. 264–338, which uses a chapter-verse style of division.

24. *Test. Job* 4.5–4.6.

25. *Test. Job* 27.3a–27.10.

26. *Test. Job* 39.11–39.13b. This refusal, of course, is quite natural in the mouth of one who earlier so accepted his state that he could report, "There were many worms in (my body) and if a worm fell off, I would pick it up and return it to the same place saying: Stay in the same place in which you were put until you receive instructions from the one (i.e., God) who commanded you" (*Test. Job* 20.10a–b).

27. Job 29:12–17; 31:16–23. A negative example in the form of an accusation is in Job 22:1–11.

28. Unfortunately we do not have room in this essay to discuss the structure of the Epistle of James and prove our assertion, but one of the best presentations of the evidence for the structure we have assumed here appears in F. O. Francis, "The Form and Function of the Opening and Closing Paragraphs of James and I John," *ZNTW* 61 (1970), pp. 110–126.

29. F. Spitta, "Das Testaments Hiobs und das Neue Testament," in *Zur Geschichte und Literatur des Urchristentums* (1907), 3/2, pp. 139–206 (pp. 170–177 concern James), corrects his omission of a mention of the *Testament of Job* in his commentary of eleven years earlier and makes just such a claim of literary dependence. Most scholars are not so confident as he about dating the *Testament* so early, made doubly early in his case because he believes James to be pre-Christian.

30. Among others who argue that the *Testament of Job* (in its final form) originated among the Therapeuts are the following: R. H. Pfeiffer, *A History of New Testament Times* (1949), p. 71; K. Kohler, "The Testament of Job," pp. 265–281; and M. Philonenko, "Le Testament de Job et les Thérapeuts," *Sem* 8 (1958), p. 42. A minority, led by M. R. James, *Apocrypha Anecdota* in *Texts and Studies,* 5, ed. J. A. Robinson (1897), pp. xciii–xciv, see Christian editing in the Greek form of the text, which would mean that it comes from a Christian, not a Jewish, community. But only a very few scholars (e.g., F. Spitta) believe Jas 5:11 is an allusion to the Greek work itself. James just does not make enough use of such a powerful tradition to warrant claiming more than a passing allusion to a well-known group of legends. Those interested in the rabbinic and Qumranic references to the legends should consult Kohler and Philonenko respectively. See also Marmorstein, *Doctrine of Merits,* p. 183. A complete bibliography on the issue of provenance appears in R. A. Kraft, *Testament of Job,* pp. 17–20.

31. Jas 5:16b–18, RSV.

32. This silence in the Old Testament includes the Apocrypha, for Sirach 48:1–11 never refers to Elijah as praying, but rather as speaking a powerful word from God. Of course, the bowed posture of Elijah in 1 Kgs 18:42 could indicate prayer, yet its causal relationship to the rain is not stressed at all, for the promise of rain had already been given in 18:41.

33. The Elijah traditions are so common in rabbinic literature that one entire book, *Tanna debe Eliyyahu* (or *Seder Eliyyahu Rabba*), is given over to a collection of some of them. This work, formerly considered only a witness to later traditions, is now considered to contain early traditions, according to J. Bowker, *Targums,* p. 90. See also the long Elijah bibliography in J. Jeremias, *"Ēl(e)ias,"* in *TDNT* 1, pp. 929–930.

34. B. Sanhedrin 113a; J. Sanhedrin 10, 28b. On God's tricking Elijah see J. Berakoth 5, 9b (= 5:1) and J. Ta'anith 1, 63d (cf. B. Berakoth 113a). A running collection of these legends as well as others may be found in Vol. 4 of L. Ginzberg, *Legends of the Jews,* pp. 195–235.

35. J. Jeremias, *"Ēl(e)ias,"* p. 931.

36. See, for example, *B. Baba Bathra* 121b and *Aboth de Rabbi Nathan* 38 and 103 (pp. 17 and 139 respectively in Goldin's translation). This all fits the rabbinic assessment of his character cited in S. Schechter, *Some Aspects of Rabbinic Theology* (1909), pp. 52–53 and 204–205.

37. See *B. Kiddushin* 40a, *B. Nedarim* 50a, and *B. Sanhedrin* 109a. This tradition is reflected in the New Testament in Mark 15:34–36 and parallels. For further examples and literature see J. Jeremias, *"Ēl(e)ias,"* p. 930 and H. L. Strack and P. Billerbeck, *Kommentar zum Neuen Testament* (1956), 4, p. 769.

38. Other marks of dependence upon the oral tradition include the length of the drought. See F. Mussner, *Der Jakobusbrief* (1967, ed. 2), p. 229. There is also a tradition which cites Elijah as the one who overcame the evil *yētzer* (see S. Schechter, *Some Aspects*, p. 271) which, if it existed in our author's time, would be another possible point of contact between James and the Elijah traditions.

39. There is a quite natural reverse parallel to this phenomenon: how many preachers stop to discover if an idea about an Old Testament narrative really occurs there or if it actually comes from James (or another New Testament book)? The illustrations one cites may in fact combine quite a large range of biblical and traditional (including exegetical traditions) quite unbeknown to the preacher.

40. The virtually unanswerable psychological question is the following: Did the author accept or expect his readers to accept these legends on a par with the Old Testament? Or did he and other authors cite Old Testament characters and legends simply because they illustrate a point they want to make, not because they accept them as true or particularly historical? Pre-scientific cultures often prove to be more discerning and skeptical in their use of even their own legends than the modern layman credits them for being. The study of what legends meant to their users is an expanding field in anthropological study, and these insights need to be applied to our study of biblical authors and their citations.

9: John and the Synoptic Tradition

HAROLD E. FAGAL

It has long been recognized that differences exist between the accounts of the life of Jesus presented in the Synoptic Gospels and that found in the Gospel of John. Eusebius reports that Clement of Alexandria in the second century said: "Last of all, aware that the physical facts had been recorded in the gospels, encouraged by his pupils and irresistibly moved by the Spirit, John wrote a spiritual gospel."[1] This has often been taken to mean that the synoptists wrote an account of the external factors in the life of Jesus, while John wrote that which was in the realm of spiritual interpretation. It should be noted that to an Alexandrian such as Clement, who was steeped in the allegorical method of biblical interpretation, the Fourth Gospel with its "spiritual" approach would come closer to being considered a real history of Jesus than would the more "historical" Synoptics. However, today it is impossible to know exactly what Clement meant by his use of the term "spiritual." The word conveys to us an idea of detachment or remoteness from that which can be said to be "historical" in a factual sense of the word, and as such it creates an unfortunate impression of the Fourth Gospel.

In the literature of this century, the distinctiveness of the Gospel of John has been described in various ways. William Manson (1923) said:

> In passing from the Synoptic Gospels to the later work which bears the name of John, the reader is conscious of entering into a new atmosphere. It is as if he had turned from some busy street of the world's life and entered the quiet spaces of some cathedral close.[2]

W. F. Howard (1931) said that the element of interpretation in John is universally recognized, but that this can be explained by comparing the work of a portrait painter with that of a photographer. The

127

former is no less true to the subject than the latter, and he may, in fact, come nearer to the truth.

The debate on the question of history and interpretation in the Fourth Gospel can be traced back to the Tübingen scholars F. C. Baur and D. F. Strauss, who abandoned the traditional views concerning John's Gospel for dogmatic reasons. Baur rejected the apostolic authorship of John and saw its theology in a different light when he applied the Hegelian dialectic to the history and literature of the early Church. If the Johannine theology contains dogma purveyed as history which became the mediating synthesis between the faith of the Jerusalem Church (thesis) and Paulinism (antithesis), then the date for the writing of the Fourth Gospel whould have to be somewhere in the middle of the second century, far beyond the lifetime of the apostle John. It could no longer be considered an apostolic work of one who was an eyewitness of the events he reported.

1. The Relationship of John and the Synoptic Gospels

In 1938, P. Gardner-Smith published a small volume which he entitled *St. John and the Synoptic Gospels* and which has exerted an influence far greater than its modest size would suggest. In it the author sought to reopen the question of the relationship between the Fourth Gospel and the Synoptic Gospels, a question that was thought to have been settled long before. Since the time of Clement of Alexandria the almost unanimous opinion was that the author of John was acquainted with, and to some extent dependent on, one or more of the Synoptic Gospels. Detailed studies by men such as V. H. Stanton and B. H. Streeter resulted in the belief that John knew the Gospel of Mark fairly well but that he did not know Matthew or Luke.[3] Gardner-Smith was not convinced on this point, and after conducting his own investigation he was led to conclude that those who saw literary dependence in John on any other Gospel were victims of a wrong method that put too much concentration on the points of agreement, and not enough on the many more points of disagreement between John and Mark. He concluded that the similarities in John with the general scheme of Mark were not the result of literary borrowing but resulted from the arrangement of the early Christian tradition into some kind of order to meet the needs and conventions of the apostolic preaching, and that this Christian tradition was first presented orally in accordance with a definite plan. In addition to this oral tradition, there may also have been certain works, now lost, such as Luke mentions in his prologue, that were an influence toward a uniform tradition. This uniform tradition accounts for the few instances in which the Gospel of John is similar to that of Mark.

Gardner-Smith's study of the dissimilarities between John and the Synoptics led him to this conclusion:

> The present author finds it inconceivable that St. John was content wantonly to contradict the testimony of "standard works" in matters dogmatically indifferent. Sometimes he may have known himself to have been better informed than other teachers, sometimes he may have rejected a tradition because he did not like it, just as Matthew and Luke did, but there are many passages in which he differs from the Synoptics for no apparent reason, and of them the easiest explanation is certainly ignorance.[4]

Furthermore, he believed that since John's Gospel contains the beliefs and traditions of a source independent of the other gospels, it should be regarded as a work in its own right and its historical value judged on its own merit and not in comparison with any other work. There is every reason to believe that in some cases, where John differs from the Synoptic Gospels, it may be right.

The low view that many scholars of the time took of the value and historicity of John may be illustrated by what C. H. Dodd wrote in 1928:

> We may now say with confidence that for strictly historical material, with the minimum of subjective interpretation, we must not go to the Fourth Gospel. . . . But it is to the Synoptic Gospels that we must go, if we wish to recover the oldest and purest tradition of the facts.[5]

However, some years after Gardner-Smith's work was published, Dodd began to change his mind; and in 1953 he wrote:

> Definite evidence pointing to documentary relations between John and the Synoptics is seen to be singularly sparse, when once the presumption in favor of such relations is abandoned. The *prima facie* impression is that John is, in large measure at any rate, working independently of other written gospels.[6]

Ten years later, in his study *Historical Tradition in the Fourth Gospel* (1963), Dodd's thesis was that "behind the Fourth Gospel lies an ancient tradition independent of the other gospels, and meriting serious considerations as a contribution to our knowledge of the historical facts concerning Jesus Christ." Other scholars who reexamined their positions and changed their minds, as Dodd did, would include scholars of such different views as W. F. Howard (1943),[7] Rudolf Bultmann (1955),[8] and T. W. Manson (1956). Here is Manson's statement:

Forty years ago it was possible to write off John as having been discredited once and for all by Strauss. . . . Today we are not so sure. There is a growing body of evidence that the Fourth Gospel enshrines a tradition of the Ministry which is independent of the Synoptic accounts, bears distinct marks of its Palestinian origin, and is on some points quite possibly superior to the Synoptic record. The question of the historical value of the Fourth Gospel is wide open again.[9]

Not all scholars by any means have accepted the conclusions regarding John first suggested by Gardner-Smith. C. K. Barrett in his 1955 commentary on John said:

It may be laid down at once that John did not use any of the synoptic gospels as, for example, Matthew used Mark. The most that may be claimed (and will be claimed in the present discussion) is that John had read Mark, and was influenced both positively and negatively by its contents—that is, that he reproduced in his own way some Marcan substance and language, and also emended some of the Marcan material—and that a few of John's statements may be most satisfactorily explained if he was familiar with matter peculiar to Luke.[10]

E. K. Lee (1957)[11] argues for John's dependence on Mark, and J. A. Bailey (1963)[12] believes that John knew Luke's Gospel.

In an attempt to break out of the impasse that existed, Raymond Brown in 1966 made this suggestion in his Anchor Bible Commentary on John:

To decide the question [of the relationship between John and the Synoptics] one must study each of the scenes and sayings shared by the two traditions to see wherein John and the Synoptics are the same and wherein they differ. One must also observe whether John consistently agrees with any *one* of the Synoptic Gospels in material peculiar to that Gospel, or with any significant combination of the Synoptic Gospels, for example, with the material proper to Matthew and Luke. In such a study the differences are even more significant than the similarities; for if one posits Johannine dependency, one should be able to explain every difference in John as the result of a deliberate change of Synoptic material or of a misunderstanding of that material.[13]

This paper attempts to follow Brown's suggestion by studying the relationship that exists between the Fourth Gospel and the Synoptics, using the material concerning John the Baptist as a test case. Our aim is to study comparatively the Johannine and Synoptic accounts to see if, at this one point at least, John is sharing material previously used by the Synoptists, whether he is deliberately changing it or has misunderstood that material, or whether he is using a differing strand of the Christian tradition from that which was used by the Synoptists. It should be emphasized that this is only a test case involving a limited amount of gospel material and that any conclusions drawn from it are only valid with regard to this portion of the tradition alone. It is hoped, however, that this study may help in clarifying the relationship that does exist between the Synoptic Gospels and the Fourth Gospel and may even shed some light on the historical value of the Johannine material vis-à-vis the Synoptic material.

2. A Test Case: John the Baptist
in the Johannine and Synoptic Traditions

a. The Prose Portions of the Prologue (John 1:6–8, 15)

The Prologue to the Fourth Gospel is unlike the beginning of any other Gospel; it is even different in form and content from the rest of the Gospel of John as well. Since it bears striking resemblances to the kind of Semitic poetry found in the Old Testament and, more specifically, to certain early Christian hymns,[14] it has been suggested that John used a hymn which he himself had written (either for the occasion or previously); or it is possible that he used a hymn that was written by someone else and that he found it useful for his present purpose. The important consideration, however, has to do with the fact that there is some non-hymnic prose material that is interjected into the poem that disrupts both the thought and style of the Prologue. At a minimum this would include verses 6–8 and 15, all verses that have to do with John the Baptist. It is possible to account for this prose material in an otherwise poetic passage by saying that the author originally began his work with a prose introduction concerning John the Baptist, and that before his work was finished he revised it to include this hymn that traces the activity of Jesus to his pre-existence with the Father before the world was created.

The Gospel of Mark begins with a reference to John the Baptist that includes the *testimonium* from Mal 3:1 and Isa 40:3 concerning the messenger who would come as a voice crying in the wilderness in order to prepare the way of the Lord. If the Fourth Gospel originally began with verses 6–8 and 15 of chapter 1, then it, too, would begin with the witness of John the Baptist to Jesus. However, as it now stands the Gospel of John begins in a strikingly different manner from the Gospel of Mark. It is possible that Mark was writing to those who had some preparation for the subject about which he was writing, and therefore he does not need to explain to them who Jesus was. The author of the Fourth Gospel, on the other hand, was writing for a non-Christian audience, and he begins with a Prologue in which the idea of the eternal Logos and the testimony of John, a man sent from God, to the Logos are introduced. John was not the Logos, but he did come to bear witness to the Logos and to identify the One who was the Logos.

John makes three points in his Prologue concerning the Baptist. (1) He is a man and not a divine being in any sense (1:6–8). Although he was "sent from God," indicating that he had a divine commission, his human personality is emphasized. (2) The one great purpose of his mission was to bear witness to the One who would come after him. He is not mentioned as a baptizer, or as a preacher of righteousness; his one great act was to present the Logos to men and to prepare them to accept him (1:7). (3) His role was subordinate to that of the Logos. "He was not the light, but came to bear witness to the light" (1:8). John showed that he recognized his subordinate role when he said, "This was he of whom I said, 'He who comes after me ranks before me, for he was before me' " (v. 15). The emphasis in the Fourth Gospel is quite different from that which we find in the Synoptic Gospels, where John appears as a preacher of repentance in the tradition of the prophets of old. In Mark, John is introduced immediately as a divinely appointed herald whose function is to announce the coming of the Messiah. In the Fourth Gospel the emphasis is on John as a witness to Christ.

Barrett accounts for the differences between the opening of the Fourth Gospel and that of Mark as "John's rewriting of the synoptic material" which "may have been due in part to a desire to counteract an excessive veneration of the Baptist."[15] He follows here the position first suggested in 1898 by Baldensperger that the references to John the Baptist in the Prologue were first and foremost a polemic against those who were exalting John the Baptist at the expense of Jesus. However, this position has not been sustained by any real evidence that a sect of John the Baptist's followers existed late in the first century. Barrett refers to the twelve disciples Paul met in Ephesus who knew only the baptism of John (Acts 19), and says that it is possible that from this and similar groups exaggerated claims were made concerning the Baptist. Strachan, who reasons along similar lines, suggests that an apparent canonization of John in the church at Ephesus led to the rise of an influential party that regarded him as a more noteworthy person than Jesus himself. He supports his view by citing Acts 19 and other sources outside the New Testament, such as the *Clementine Recognitions*,[16] in which he finds evidence of a Baptist party with which there was active controversy in the Church.[17] But his argument is weakened by the fact that the

Clementine Recognitions come from the third century, although it is possible that they were drawn from second century sources.

Even if this much is conceded, that the negations about John the Baptist in the Fourth Gospel may reflect exaggerated claims made about him by certain of his followers who attributed to him a more exalted position than to Jesus, it is hard to agree with Barrett that this represents "John's rewriting of the synoptic material" which may have been due in part to a desire to counteract an excessive veneration of the Baptist." There is no indication that the author of the Fourth Gospel, in his references to John the Baptist, is rewriting Synoptic material at this point. John refers to the Baptist as a witness to Christ. He does not record the actual baptism of Jesus as the Synoptists do, nor do they record the statement of his that the Baptist referred to Jesus twice as "the Lamb of God" (John 1:29, 36). It is John, and not the Synoptists, who tells us that the Baptist encouraged some of his disciples to follow Jesus, and it is he who alone records a ministry of Jesus in Judea before the Baptist was imprisoned by Herod. The Synoptists place emphasis on the apocalyptic nature of the Baptist's preaching in which he summoned the Jews to repentance in view of the coming crisis, while John emphasizes the subordinate role of the Baptist to Jesus. This does not appear to be a rewriting of the Synoptic material as far as John is concerned.

While there are differences in the two accounts, there are also underlying points of harmony that must not be overlooked. The emphatic negative, "He was not the light" (John 1:8), and the statement, "This was he of whom I said, 'He who comes after me ranks before me, for he was before me' " (John 1:15), harmonize with the words of the Baptist that Mark records: "After me comes he who is mightier than I, the thongs of whose sandals I am not worthy to stoop down and untie" (Mark 1:7). The words are not the same, but there is a basic unity of thought present in both statements. It is true that the Fourth Gospel does not contain the saying of Jesus found in Matt 11:11: "Truly, I say to you, among those born of women there has risen no one greater than John the Baptist; yet he who is least in the kingdom of heaven is greater than he." However, this does not contradict in any way what John says about the importance of John the Baptist, who was "a man sent from God. . . to bear witness to the light" (John 1:6, 7). Rather than seeing John as having rewritten Synoptic material, one should see John as preserving a different tradition concerning the Baptist, a tradition that is not contradictory in any way with the Synoptic tradition but which has as much claim to being authentic in its own right as does the other. The underlying harmony leads one to see these traditions as complementary rather than contradictory.

b. *The Testimony of John (John 1:19–34)*

All four gospels record an account of John the Baptist whose work was an introduction to the ministry of Jesus. However, in John 1:19–34, which contains John's witness to himself (vv. 19–28) and his witness to Jesus (vv. 29–34), there is a different emphasis, almost a different picture, from that found in the Synoptic Gospels. First, let us look at the points of similarity.

(1) All four writers introduce the *testimonium* of Isa 40:3 into their account of the mission of the Baptist.[18] The significant difference is that where the Synoptists have the *testimonium* as a part of their own comment about the Baptist, John has it on the lips of the Baptist himself, who makes the application of the verse in Isaiah to his own ministry. At this point John is not dependent upon the Synoptics for the form in which he passes on this tradition. It is entirely possible that the Baptist did use this verse with reference to his own ministry, for we now know that the Qumran community used it to explain why they had withdrawn from the Jerusalem priesthood and temple and established themselves in the desert.[19] It is all the more probable that John spoke these words if some sort of contact is postulated between John the Baptist and the Qumran community prior to the start of his ministry.[20]

(2) Common to all four gospels is the prediction of One who would come after John the Baptist and who would be much greater than he, so much so that John would not be worthy to untie his sandals.[21] But when the four accounts are compared, there are differences in all of them. John is distinctive in his use of *axios* where the other three have *hikanos*, his use of the singular *hypodēmatos* where they have the plural, his use of a *hina* clause where they have the infinitive, and the entire section *mesos hymōn stēkei hon hymeis ouk oidate* which they do not have. In addition, he uses the emphatic *egō* in connection with *eimi* and places the *autou* differently. All three Synoptists refer to Christ as *ischyroteros mou*, but John does not have this. Surely there is no evidence that John is dependent on any one of the Synoptics for this saying.

(3) The Fourth Gospel records a conversation between John the Baptist and certain priests and Levites who were sent by the Pharisees to inquire of him his identity and his right to baptize. To these men John emphatically denies that he is the Messiah ("I am not the Christ," v. 20) or any other messianic figure such as Elijah or the Prophet. This disclaimer, although not found in Matthew or Mark, is

found in the second volume of Luke-Acts (Acts 13:24–25) in the version of the apostolic *kerygma* that is attributed to Paul: "Before his coming John had preached a baptism of repentance to all the people of Israel. And as John was finishing his course, he said, 'What do you suppose that I am? I am not he. No, but after me one is coming, the sandals of whose feet I am not worthy to untie.' " The setting of this passage is in a historical resumé that is cast in a different form from that of the Synoptic tradition.

(4) The reference to the Holy Spirit descending on Jesus like a dove is common to all four gospels, but the verbal agreements between them are not very close. In referring to "the Spirit" without the modifier "holy," John is closest to Mark, and in the manner in which he describes the descent he is closest to Matthew. However, he differs from all three Synoptics in not describing the baptism itself, which is such a central feature of their account. John also has the Baptist witness the descent of the Holy Spirit on Jesus; whereas Mark and Matthew seem to limit this to Jesus alone, and Luke treats it as an objective occurrence "in bodily form." The Synoptics all mention the voice from heaven that proclaims Jesus as God's "beloved Son"; but in John it is the Baptist who bears witness that Jesus is "the Son of God" (1:34). Although John does not refer to the voice from heaven, he does use the same words Luke uses in connection with the voice (*ex ouranou*) but with regard to the descent of the dove-like Spirit "from heaven."

In addition to these points with which there are some similarities with the Synoptic accounts, there are sections in John that are peculiar to this Gospel alone.

(1) It is clear that the author of the Fourth Gospel makes it most emphatic that the Baptist is not to be equated with Elijah whose return was foretold in Mal 3:1; 4:5, 6. It is equally clear that in the Synoptic accounts Jesus equates John the Baptist with Elijah (Matt 11:14, "and if you are willing to accept it, he is Elijah who is to come"; Matt 17:12, "I tell you that Elijah has already come, and they did not know him, but did to him whatever they pleased"). Mark 1:6 and Matt 3:4 represent John as dressing in a similar manner to Elijah (cf. 2 Kgs 1:8), and Luke in his account of the birth of John records that the angel said to his father concerning his son that "he will go before him in the spirit and power of Elijah, to turn the hearts of the fathers to the children . . ." (Luke 1:17).

In order to understand what is meant by the Baptist's disclaimer to being Elijah, it must be remembered that the Jews were expecting the return of Elijah "before the great and terrible day of the Lord comes" (Mal 4:5). This expectation, based on Malachi's prophecy, was repeated in certain Jewish literature of the second century B.C. and later.[22] This expectation was also prevalent in Palestine in the first century A.D., as Mark 8:28 and 9:11 indicate. John's denial that he was Elijah is exactly the response we would expect from one who knew what the Jews were expecting and wished to make it absolutely clear that he was not Elijah *redivivus*. In that sense the statement attributed to the Baptist in the Fourth Gospel was correct—John was not Elijah in the sense in which the Jews looked for him. But in another sense, he was Elijah as foretold by Malachi, for he fulfilled the prophecy of Mal 3:1: "Behold, I send my messenger to prepare the way before me, and the Lord whom you seek will suddenly come to his temple. . . ." It is in this sense that the saying of Jesus recorded by the Synoptics, "Elijah has come, and they did to him whatever they pleased . . ." (Mark 9:13), is true. John the Baptist did not come as Elijah *redivivus*, as the Jews expected, but he came "in the spirit and power of Elijah, to turn the hearts of the fathers to the children, and the disobedient to the wisdom of the just, to make ready for the Lord a people prepared" (Luke 1:17). John the Baptist was Elijah, but not in the sense in which the Jews were looking for him.[23]

(2) Another point of difference in John from the Synoptics is the reference to the unrecognized Messiah. In place of the Synoptic phrase, "one who is mightier than I" (Mark 1:7; Matt 3:11; Luke 3:16), John has the words of the Baptist, ". . . among you stands one whom you do not know" (John 1:26). Rather than being a rebuke for the lack of perception on the part of the people, this may be a reference to one of the messianic beliefs of the time. There was a generally accepted belief that the Messiah would be born in Bethlehem and be a descendant of David (John 7:42; Matt 2:4). But there was also an apocalyptic strain of messianism in which the claim was made that the Messiah would be unknown until such time as he would be shown suddenly to his people. This doctrine is very clear in Justin Martyr's *Dialogue with Trypho* (c. A.D. 150), where Trypho, the representative of Judaism, says: "Even if the Messiah should have been born and be living somewhere, yet he is unknown; indeed, he does not even know himself; nor has he any power, until Elijah comes, anoints him and reveals him to all."[24] That such an expectation was known also in the first century is indicated in John 7:27: "Yet we know where this man comes from; and when the Christ appears, no one will know where he comes from." The Synoptics make no reference to this apocalyptic strain of messianism that the Fourth Gospel apparently refers to, which may be another indication that John was following an independent tradition concerning the

Baptist in which it was remembered that he was acquainted with the apocalyptic expectations of a hidden messiah and the coming of Elijah.

(3) In John 1:29 a title for Jesus is introduced for which there is no parallel in the Synoptics: "Behold, the Lamb of God, who takes away the sin of the world." The meaning of the term "lamb" (*amnos*) used here is uncertain. It may be a reference to the Passover lamb, or the lamb of the sin offering, or the lamb to which the Suffering Servant is compared in Isa 53:7, or the horned lamb of both Jewish and Christian apocalypses that is a symbol of the messianic leader of God's people, or it may even be a mistranslation of an Aramaic original *talya'* that means either "lamb" or "boy, servant."[25] It is not within the purpose of this article to come to a conclusion regarding the meaning of this title. It is possible to say, however, that its use by John the Baptist as recorded in the Fourth Gospel does not need to be attributed to the Evangelist's theology put on the lips of the Baptist, as some have insisted. It is possible to see in the title the apocalyptic point of view that was prevalent at the time in which the Baptist lived, as well as a reflection of his Old Testament eschatological outlook. The testimonies to Christ in John 1:29–34 are taken from traditional material about the Baptist that the Fourth Evangelist has made the vehicle of a deeper Christian insight into the person and work of Christ.

c. The Call of the Disciples (John 1:35–51)

Another point of difference between John and the Synoptic Gospels has to do with the accounts of the calling of the first disciples. According to the Gospel of John, the Baptist was in the company of two of his disciples when Jesus walked by. He repeated his witness to Jesus as the "Lamb of God," with the result that the two disciples began to follow Jesus. In answer to their question, "Rabbi, where are you staying?", Jesus said, "Come and see." It was then about the tenth hour, and they spent the remainder of the day with him. Only the name of Andrew is given, and he is referred to as "Simon Peter's brother" (1:40). There follows the account of Andrew bringing his brother to Jesus and saying to him, "We have found the Messiah," and when he came Jesus changed his name from Simon to Cephas (1:35–42).

The first mention of disciples following Jesus in the Synoptic Gospels is found in a completely different setting. Mark says that the time was "after John was arrested" (Mark 1:14) and that it took place "along by the Sea of Galilee" (v. 16). Simon and Andrew were invited to follow Jesus and to become fishers of men, "and immediately they left their nets and followed him" (v. 18). Similarly, and at the same time, James and John, sons of Zebedee, were called and followed him (Mark 1:14–20).

There are similarities in the two accounts. Both attribute disciples to Jesus; and the same names—Andrew and Simon—appear, although in different order and under different circumstances. But there are also noticeable differences. (1) The locale for the Johannine account is the Jordan valley, and for the Synoptic account it is the shore of the Sea of Galilee. (2) Only John makes any reference to the Baptist's witness to Jesus as the "Lamb of God" as providing the stimulus for the action that followed on the part of his two disciples. (3) The implication in John is that the time is a day or two after the imprisonment of John the Baptist by Herod Antipas, while in the Synoptists the temporal reference is given as "after John was arrested" (Mark 1:14). (4) In John the initiative is on the part of the disciples who attach themselves to Jesus, while in the other Gospels Jesus distinctly calls the men to follow him. (5) John mentions five who became disciples—Andrew and his unnamed companion, Simon, Philip, and Nathanael (the locale for the call of the last two changes from Judea to Galilee), while the Synoptists mention two pairs of brothers—Peter and Andrew, James and John.

It is possible to harmonize these two accounts and to claim historical accuracy for both by explaining that they happened at different times. First, Jesus called five men to be his disciples, as recorded in the Johannine account; but these men soon returned to their former life in Galilee until such time as Jesus recalled them to full-time service, as the Synoptists record. However, there is no verification of this in the gospels themselves. The Fourth Gospel never intimates that these five disciples returned to Galilee without Jesus, nor does the Synoptic account intimate that the disciples who were called by the Sea of Galilee had had any previous contact with Jesus in the region of the Jordan.

Disagreeing with this harmonization are two recent commentators who state that there is no possibility of harmonizing the two accounts as they now stand. C. K. Barrett says: "It is impossible to harmonize the Johannine and synoptic narratives. . . . That John knew the Marcan story is probable in view of his other contacts with the second gospel, but his own is quite different."[26] Alan Richardson (1959) says: "There is no possibility of harmonizing St. John's account with those of the Synoptists."[27] He bases this in part on the fact that in the Johannine account the titles "Son of God," "Lamb of God," "the Messiah," "the King of Israel," and "the Son of Man" are all used in referring to Jesus in the first chapter; but in Mark a considerable amount of time elapses before the disciples acknowledge Jesus as the Messiah, and even then Jesus "charged them to tell no one about him" (Mark 8:30). In the Gospel of John, the Baptist is the recipient of a revelation from God that reveals to him the mystery of the person of Jesus (1:33), but in the Synoptics John sends some of his disciples while he is in prison to inquire of Jesus whether he was the One who should come or whether they should look for another. He believes that the Johannine and Synoptic accounts cannot be harmonized because John "is concerned not to tell the historical story" but rather "to bring out the truth of history. . . ." However, he fails to tell us how it is possible for something to be unhistorical and yet to bring out the truth of history.[28]

The modern study of the gospels has brought out the fact that interpretation is found in all four gospels and not only in the Gospel of John. All four Evangelists were more than historians—they were primarily theologians who were interested in the *kerygma*.[29] Leon Morris says that "there is no history without interpretation,"[30] and to support his view he quotes Alan Richardson, who said in another place: "The facts of history cannot be disentangled from the principles of interpretation by which alone they can be presented to us *as history*, that is, as a coherent and connected series or order of events."[31] Dodd, too, has said that there are some events "which can take their true place in an historical record only as they are interpreted."[32] Interpretation of itself does not rule out historicity, for there are times when, by the nature of the event being described, there must be interpretation in order for the event to be understood historically.

Morris comments that "there is not the slightest doubt but that the Baptist is depicted in a certain way in order to attain a theological end. This is conceded by all and is plainly stated by the Evangelist. But it now appears that when he wrote about the Baptist John is accurate."[33] If Morris is as correct as I believe him to be, then the dichotomy Richardson makes between the Synoptics that "tell the historical story" and John whose "aim is to bring out the truth of history" is not substantiated. We cannot assume that John is less historical than the Synoptics simply because his purpose in writing is to lead his readers to believe in Jesus as the Savior of the world and by believing find life in his name (20:30, 31).

Neither does a comparison between John and the Synoptics regarding the call of the first disciples need to lead us to conclude, as Barrett would have us do, that John is rewriting Synoptic material while at the same time misunderstanding it. The evidence points rather in the direction of two separate accounts, each independent of the other, but each deserving of consideration when the historical facts concerning the life of Jesus are sought. They are interlocking traditions that connect with each other at certain points. Morris says this regarding the two traditions of the call of the first disciples: "The events of Matthew 4 are more intelligible if they follow after those of John 1 than if they represent the first contact that the men there spoken of had had with Jesus. Once more John helps us to understand a Synoptic narrative."[34] If that is the case, then these two incidents, coming as they do from two separate and independent traditions represented by John and the Synoptics, in this case complement each other and together present a more complete picture of what actually happened than either one does separately.

d. John's Last Testimony to Christ (John 3:22–36)

The testimony that John the Baptist bore concerning Jesus in John 1:29–34 is resumed again in chapter 3:22–36. The theme of John 3 is Christian baptism, and some thoughts about the mission of John the Baptist are added to the reference to the necessity of being born "of water and the Spirit" as a prerequisite to entering the Kingdom of God (v. 5). One of the problems posed by this passage is that of its chronology. The narrative has as its setting the "land of Judea" (v. 22), where Jesus and his disciples were baptizing (although in 4:2 the point is made that "Jesus himself did not baptize, but only his disciples"). John the Baptist was also baptizing in the same general region at a place called "Aenon near Salim, because there was much water there" (v. 23). The Fourth Gospel speaks of the ministries of Jesus and John as concurrent at this time, but the Synoptics record that it was only "after John was arrested" that "Jesus came into Galilee, preaching the gospel of God" (Mark 1:14, 15).

When B. F. Westcott wrote his commentary on John (1881), he said, "At this point then the work of Christ and of his forerunner met."[35] Hoskyn also saw in this, evidence of a concurrent ministry of John and Jesus that is "reminiscent of a time (overlooked or at least not recorded by the earlier evangelists) when Jesus, at the beginning of His ministry, associated Himself with John's call to repentance, and baptized as he did."[36]

Barrett, however, takes a different view, as does Richardson. Barrett writes:

> This may be a correct representation, but it is not necessary to suppose that it was given because John possessed a historical tradition divergent from

that of Mark; it was rather his intention to bring out the truth expressed in 3:30 ["He must increase, but I must decrease"], possibly with some polemical intention against the adherents of the Baptist.[37]

Richardson finds the idea presented in John that the ministries of the Baptist and Jesus were going on at the same time impossible to reconcile with the material in the other gospels. The confusion, he says, is compounded by two things: the correcting statement in John 4:1, 2, which attempts to clear up any misunderstanding about Jesus himself actually baptizing, and the improbability that there was any such baptism by the disciples of Jesus before the ascension, since John 1:33 says that Jesus was to baptize with the Holy Spirit and John 7:39 says that "the Spirit was not yet given, because Jesus was not yet glorified."

> How then can we explain these difficulties? They can be explained only by recognizing the true character of St. John's Gospel: it does not purport to give a rival history and chronology to those of the Synoptists: it frankly reads the historical issues of St. John's own times back into the story of Jesus and his ministry. The historical situation at the end of the first century was that in various parts of the world, including Ephesus (Acts 19:1–7), the disciples of John the Baptist were administering a rival baptism to that of Christ. The testimony of the Baptist that he is not the Messiah but only the one sent before him (v. 28) is repeated from 1. 20–23, and the Baptist is made to declare that his followers must decrease while those of Christ increase (v. 30).[38]

Such skepticism regarding the historicity of the Gospel of John does not seem to be required as long as another reasonable explanation can be offered on this point. Such an alternative has been suggested by Vincent Taylor, who sees the possibility that between Mark 1:13 and 14 there is room for the special tradition on which the Fourth Evangelist drew.[39] Accordingly, if the Fourth Gospel records a Judean ministry preceding the Galilean ministry covered in the Synoptic accounts, it is possible that this chronological reference is to events that took place before John had been imprisoned and during this Judean ministry that only the Fourth Gospel records. This would mean that we have here another instance in which the Fourth Gospel supplements rather than corrects the Synoptic account. This would mean that at this point the two traditions become interlocking. John seems to be working with a tradition separate from the Synoptic tradition, but it is not inferior to it nor any the less "historical."

Dodd's analysis of the passage under discussion leads him to conclude that 3:22–36 is an explanatory appendix to the dialogue with Nicodemus and the discourse that grows out of it, the whole of ch. iii being concerned with the idea of initiation into eternal life (or rebirth), in conjunction with a rich complex of ideas which are required for its proper understanding.[40]

This explanation, linking the passage with the dialogue with Nicodemus that precedes it and the discourse that grows out of it, offers in my opinion the best understanding of the text in its present form. His conclusion that "it is highly probable that we are here in touch with pre-canonical tradition"[41] indicates again that John was in possession of a Gospel tradition that, in spite of its differences from that followed by the Synoptists, is in no way inferior to it. In some respects his tradition is fuller than theirs at the points at which they come together, but it is not contradictory to it. The two traditions supplement each other, and for a more complete understanding we need them both.

3. Conclusion

The material presented in this essay has been an attempt to analyze the relationship that exists between the Fourth Gospel and the Synoptics by using the account of John the Baptist as a test case. It has sought to test the thesis put forth first by Gardner-Smith, and followed by Howard, Bultmann, Manson, and Dodd, *inter alia,* that the Fourth Evangelist did not follow the same Gospel traditions that were known to the Synoptists but followed a tradition that was separate but deserving of equal consideration in deciding matters of history. Holding an opposite view are such scholars as Barrett, Richardson, R. H. Lightfoot, and others, who believe that John was acquainted with Mark (and possibly Luke) and that he rewrote the Marcan material in certain places and at times even misunderstood it.

The evidence studied, limited to the traditions concerning John the Baptist in the Fourth Gospel as compared with those in the Synoptics, leads to the conclusion that the thesis first proposed by Gardner-Smith and later expanded and refined by Dodd and others is essentially correct at this point. There is no evidence that requires us to conclude that John set out to correct Mark, nor did he reproduce in his own way Marcan substance and language even to the point of misunderstanding it. The Gospel of John was written by one whose purpose was to present a work based on faith in order to produce faith in his readers, but his theological motif did not in any way affect the trustworthiness of that which he wrote. The Fourth Gospel is a theological work, and as such it is concerned with the meaning of the events it records from the life of our Lord. It does not purport to give a clear chronology of events from Jesus' birth to his ascension, but neither is the author careless in the way he handles the tradition. He did not aim to present history for history's sake, but history for the sake of establishing faith on the part of his readers in the world's Redeemer. His account of John the Baptist depicts him as a witness to Christ. Nothing is allowed to distract the reader from seeing the Baptist in this role. There is a theological motive behind this portrayal, but the author is not any less historical because of it. The life of John the Baptist is an event in history that can only be rightly understood as it is interpreted, and the Fourth Evangelist has supplied that interpretation.

NOTES

1. Eusebius, *Historia Ecclesiastica* VI.xiv.7 (trans. G. A. Williamson) (Penguin Classic), pp. 254–255.
2. William Manson, *The Incarnate Glory* (1923), p. 13.
3. V. H. Stanton, *The Gospels as Historical Documents*, 3 (1920), p. 220: "The parallels with St. Mark certainly seem to afford evidence of an amount and kind sufficient to prove that the fourth evangelist knew that Gospel fairly well. That he knew either of the others seems more than doubtful. . . ." B. H. Streeter, *The Four Gospels: A Study of Origins* (1924), p. 400: "Clearly the facts so far stated amount to little short of a demonstration that John knew the Gospel of Mark, and knew it well. But they suggest doubts as to his acquaintance with the other two Synoptics."
4. P. Gardner-Smith, *St. John and the Synoptic Gospels* (1938), p. 92.
5. C. H. Dodd, *The Authority of the Bible* (1928), p. 215.
6. C. H. Dodd, *The Interpretation of the Fourth Gospel* (1953), p. 449.
7. W. F. Howard, *Christianity According to St. John* (1943), p. 17, n. 2. The one reservation he expressed is "that before the Gospel was published there was some verbal assimilation to a few of the Marcan and Lucan narratives (such as the Anointing, and the Feeding of the Multitude) by the hand of the Editor."
8. R. Bultmann, *Theology of the New Testament*, 2 (1955), p. 3.
9. T. W. Manson in *The Background of the New Testament and Its Eschatology*, D. Daube and W. D. Davies, eds. (1956), p. 219, n. 2.
10. C. K. Barrett, *The Gospel According to St. John* (1955), p. 34. Barrett refers to the evidence set forth by Creed, *The Gospel According to St. Luke* (1930), pp. 318–321, on the matter of the use of Luke by John. Creed says: "It appears, however, to be almost certain that John knew and used Luke. . . ."
11. E. K. Lee, "St. Mark and the Fourth Gospel," *NTS* 3 (1956–57), pp. 50–58.
12. J. A. Bailey, *The Traditions Common to the Gospels of Luke and John* (1963).
13. Raymond E. Brown, *The Gospel According to John, I–XII* (1966), p. XLV.
14. Eph 5:19 and Col 3:16 mention "hymns to Christ," and the following passages are thought possibly to be early Christian hymns or hymnic fragments: Phil 2:6–11; Col 1:15–20; 1 Tim 3:16.
15. Barrett, op. cit., p. 142.
16. Recognitions 1, 54, and 60 have to do with John the Baptist.
17. "If such a party was active in Ephesus, we can understand why this Evangelist emphatically points out that the Baptist directed his followers away from himself to Jesus (i.26, 29); why he nowhere calls John, 'the Baptist'; why he relates that John is said to be only a 'lamp', burning and shining indeed, but 'for a season'. . . ." R. H. Strachan, *The Fourth Gospel* (1951), pp. 111–112.

18. Matt 3:3; Mark 1:3, 4; Luke 3:4–6; John 1:23.

19. The passage pertaining to this is found in the *Manual of Discipline:* "When these things come to pass for the community in Israel, by these regulations they shall be separated from the midst of the session of the men of error to go to the wilderness to prepare there the way of the LORD; as it is written, 'In the wilderness prepare the way of the LORD; make straight in the desert a highway for our God.' This is the study of the law, as he commanded through Moses, to do according to all that has been revealed from time to time, and as the prophets revealed by his Holy Spirit" (1QS 8:13–16, translation by Burrows).

20. Brown, op. cit., p. 50.

21. Matt 1:1; Mark 1:7; Luke 3:16; John 1:27.

22. E.g., Ecclesiasticus 48:10: "It is written that you are to come at the appointed time with warnings, to allay the divine wrath before its final fury, to reconcile father and son, and to restore the tribes of Jacob" (NEB). Justin Martyr's *Dialogue with Trypho,* chapter 8, refers to the Jewish doctrine of the anointing of the Messiah by Elijah. See also J. Klausner, *The Messianic Idea in Israel* (1956), pp. 451–457, for evidence that this doctrine continued into the second century A.D.

23. J. A. T. Robinson has suggested a different answer from the one suggested here. He says that John the Baptist never gave any indication that he thought of himself as Elijah; rather, he thought of the one coming after him as the fulfillment of the Elijah prophecy. It was Jesus who made the identification of John the Baptist as Elijah (Matt 11:3–14), an identification that became traditional in the Church; but there is no reason to believe that John himself was even aware of it. Robinson says: "If John saw anyone as Elijah, it was *not* himself but the one coming *after* him. To be sure, this figure remains anonymous, though it is just possible that there may be an allusion to his identity in the fourth Gospel, which preserves, I am persuaded, in the Baptist material some very good independent tradition." In a footnote at this point, Robinson gives his opinion that "whatever the circumstances and the environment in which this Gospel was eventually put out, there is little doubt in my mind that it rests upon oral tradition with a southern Palestinian milieu prior to A.D. 70, parallel to, and independent of, the Synoptic tradition." "Elijah, John and Jesus: an Essay in Detection," *NTS* 4 (1957–58), p. 264. Reprinted in *Twelve New Testament Studies* (1962), pp. 28–52.

24. Justin Martyr, *Dialogue with Trypho,* chapter 4. This same idea appears in *2 Esdras* 13 (late 1st century A.D.) where the messianic figure is called the Son of Man who comes up from the heart of the sea (v. 25). This is interpreted to mean: "Just as no one can explore or know what is in the depths of the sea, so no one on earth can see my Son or those who are with him, except in the time of his day" (v. 52). See also S. Mowinckel, *He That Cometh* (1951), pp. 304–308; E. Stauffer, "Agnostos Christos," in *The Background of the New Testament and Its Eschatology* (Davies and Daube, eds.), pp. 287–291.

25. W. Zimmerli and J. Jeremias, *The Servant of God* (rev. 1965), pp. 83–84. Raymond E. Brown discusses the context of the final judgment in Jewish apocalyptic writings in which a conquering lamb destroys evil in the world (e.g., *The Testament of Joseph* 19:8 and *Enoch* 90:38) and says: "We suggest that when JBap called the one to come after him 'the lamb of God who takes away the world's sin,' he was speaking in the framework of this Jewish apocalyptic expectation: the lamb to be raised up by God to destroy evil in the world" (*New Testament Essays* [1968], p. 180). However, he does not rule out the possibility that the reference could also be to the lamb in Isa 53:7, since the Baptist surely knew Isaiah.

26. Barrett, op. cit., p. 149.

27. Alan Richardson, *The Gospel According to Saint John* (1959), p. 45.

28. Ibid., p. 46. Cf. A. Richardson, *History, Sacred and Profane* (1964), for a fuller discussion of this point by the author.

29. B. Gerhardsson speaks of the "extremely tenaciously-held misapprehension among exegetes that an early Christian author must *either* be a purposeful theologian and writer *or* a fairly reliable historian." *Memory and Manuscript* (1961), p. 209.

30. Leon Morris, *Studies in the Fourth Gospel* (1969), p. 72.

31. Alan Richardson, *Christian Apologetics* (1963), p. 150.

32. C. H. Dodd, *History and the Gospel* (1938), p. 104.

33. Morris, op. cit., p. 112.

34. Ibid., p. 53.
35. B. F. Westcott, *The Gospel According to St. John* (1881), p. 58.
36. Edwyn C. Hoskyns, *The Fourth Gospel* (1943), pp. 225–226.
37. Barrett, op. cit., p. 182.
38. A. Richardson, *The Gospel According to Saint John,* pp. 70, 71.
39. V. Taylor, *The Gospel According to St. Mark* (1952), p. 165. Cranfield has a similar comment: "While according to Jn the ministries of John and Jesus overlapped, the Synoptic Gospels date the beginning of Jesus' Galilean ministry after John's imprisonment. Mark's statement, however, does not altogether rule out the possibility of an earlier activity of Jesus alongside that of John, room for which could be found between i.13 and i.14." *The Gospel According to Saint Mark* (1959), p. 61.
40. Dodd, *Interpretation,* p. 311.
41. Ibid., p. 287.

10: Nineteenth-Century Roots of Contemporary New Testament Criticism

W. WARD GASQUE

1. The Problem

One does not have to read very far in contemporary New Testament studies before being confronted with a very startling fact: there is a great diversity of opinion among scholars concerning nearly every detail of New Testament criticism and interpretation. The layman who turns to this study of academic theology thinks that he will have all his questions answered; he thinks that he will now be in a position to decide between varying interpretations which he has heard put forward in church concerning various biblical texts and problems. But, alas, he soon learns that there is no more agreement among scholars than there is among pastors and ordinary lay Christians concerning even the most basic matters. Not only does he not have *all* his questions answered, but he also discovers many *new* questions!

The problem is confronted when one turns to the standard New Testament introductions, for example, Kümmel[1] and Guthrie.[2] Each author has his own point of view and gives you his own conclusions, but along the way he refers to a bewildering variety of opinion offered by hundreds of other scholars; and on many issues the two compendiums themselves disagree. The problem is even more complex when one refers to the briefer and more popular introductions which do not have space to list all the alternative views and often give the uninformed reader the impression that they are listing "the assured results of criticism," when, in fact, they are simply giving their own opinions on the various issues—opinions which are often hotly debated by other scholars.

Now, there are understandable reasons for the differences of opinion among New Testament scholars. For a start, there is the uncertainty caused by the distance which lies between us and the New Testament documents, a small body of Greek literature written some nineteen centuries ago. So much of what scholars would like to know—and sometimes think they have discovered!—simply cannot be known. As the distinguished English literary critic, C. S. Lewis, once quipped, the reason why the so-called "assured results of criticism" are so assured is that all the people who really knew the facts are dead! Then, there are the differences in philosophical presuppositions among the critics. While one should never dismiss the views of a scholar simply because one discerns in his writing a certain bias which one finds personally uncongenial, it is extremely naive to think that such biases are unimportant. Finally, there are differences in critical methodology: different scholars represent different traditions of criticism. And these different critical approaches sometimes lead to radically differing conclusions.

The problem becomes obvious when one turns to the study of the Acts of the Apostles, the New Testament book upon which I have focused the bulk of my research. When, for example, one compares the two major commentaries on The Acts in recent years— by F. F. Bruce[3] and E. Haenchen[4]—one finds radically differing conclusions on many issues, particularly on the matter of the historical value of Acts.

According to Haenchen, Acts is primarily a theological composition rather than a historical work. The author, who belongs to a generation far removed from that of the earliest apostles, is concerned to give us a portrait of early Christianity as he thought it should be, rather than as it actually was. He is concerned to preach the gospel in his own day rather than to tell how the apostles preached it in their day. And in so telling the story of early Christianity as he wishes to understand it, he both twists the historical facts which he knows and invents materials which did not exist but which suit his own special purposes. Thus very little of what is included in his work gives us a historically reliable picture of early Christianity.[5]

According to Bruce, the Book of Acts, though certainly theological, gives us a first-rate historical account of the first three decades of the Church's existence. Although it does not tell us everything—it focuses primarily on the earliest days in Jerusalem and then on the missionary activities of Paul—what it does tell us is reliable. In fact, when Acts is tested by the ordinary canons of historical research, the result is positive: it is vindicated on every point which can be tested. Bruce goes on to argue not only for the traditional authorship by "Luke the beloved physician" and sometime travelling companion of Paul but also for the plausibility of an early date of origin (c. A.D. 62), though neither point is necessarily fundamental to the book's essential historical reliability.[6]

How can two internationally esteemed scholars reach such radically different conclusions on this basic issue? How do we explain their differences? The answer is, briefly, that they represent two almost totally different scholarly traditions of the study of the Acts of the Apostles. Building on different foundations, they thus erect different superstructures.

2. Sixteenth-, Seventeenth- and Eighteenth-Century Roots

The roots of modern criticism, of course, go very deep—at least as far back as the Renaissance. I would suggest three basic steps in the development of the biblical criticism up to the period with which we are concerned, namely, the nineteenth century. First, there was the rediscovery of the ancient world by the scholars of the renaissance. The study of the Greek language and literature was revived, and with this came the recognition that one could not be satisfied to read the New Testament in its traditional Latin form. Then came the recovery of the knowledge of Hebrew by Christian scholars, a language which had been lost by the early fathers (except for Jerome) but kept alive by Rabbis. At the same time doubts began to be raised concerning legends, traditions, and pseudonymous ecclesiastical writings by the new historical consciousness which was developing.

Second came the Protestant Reformation and the call to return to the Bible as the primary document of the Church's theology (*sola scriptura*). The supremacy of Scripture over tradition was asserted (not that tradition was unimportant), and traditions which had replaced biblical truth came to be increasingly rejected. Then, there was the reformers' rejection of the allegorical method of biblical interpretation with its three- or fourfold meaning in favor of the historical-grammatical method of exegesis. There was also the rejection of the Apocrypha as being on the same level as the books of the Hebrew Bible, as well as the challenge of traditional views concerning some canonical books (e.g., Hebrews not by Paul; Song of Solomon not by Solomon). Luther went beyond any of the other reformers with his idea of a "canon within the canon" and rejection of some New Testament books (e.g., James, Jude, Hebrews, Revelation), suggestions which were rejected by other leaders of the Reformation but which have reappeared as influential in our day.

Third, came the Enlightenment with its rejection of the historic Christian faith. Man became the measure of all things and the sufficiency of human reason was thought to be self-evident; therefore, there was no longer any need for revelation, for a Word from God. With this came the enthronement of deism in the place of theism, i.e., the rejection of God in the historic Christian sense. A concomitant of this is, of course, anti-supernaturalism (no miracles, thus no incarnation or resurrection). In this way historic Christian orthodoxy was rejected.

At first, the assumptions of the Enlightenment were rejected by all theologians. They were seen to be obviously anti-Christian and quite incompatible with the Christian faith. But gradually toward the end of the eighteenth century one or two theologians began to move toward these assumptions and seek to reinterpret Christianity in terms of the *Zeitgeist*. However, it is only in the nineteenth century that this compromise with the views of the Enlightenment becomes very influential. Thus the nineteenth century becomes a watershed in the history of biblical criticism. From about the middle of the nineteenth century onward two parallel streams of criticism begin to emerge, one of them from within Christian orthodoxy and the other in conscious reaction to it.

3. F. C. Baur and the Tübingen School

To return to our original starting point, the commentary by Professor Ernst Haenchen of Münster represents the critical tradition which has its roots in the work of Ferdinand Christian Baur (1792–1860) and the so-called younger Tübingen School. Baur, whose ghost still exerts an eerie influence over contemporary German scholarship, was certainly one of the most influential figures in nineteenth-century German theology. Insofar as the history of New Testament criticism is concerned, he is *the* single most important individual. He has been called "the father of historical criticism," though a case could be made for the honor going to one or two other German scholars (unless one takes a very narrow definition of the subject). Baur was not primarily an exegete or a New Testament critic, but rather a theologian, specifically a historian of dogma. Yet he published five books[7] and a similar number of significant essays[8] in the area of New Testament research. His basic thesis concerning the nature of early Christianity, which forms the environment of the writings of the New Testament and other non-canonical books, was first put forward in 1831 in an essay devoted to the problem of the "Christ party" of Paul's correspondence.[9]

His thesis is basically this: In spite of the impression which one gains from a superficial reading of the New Testament documents, namely, that the early Church was essentially uniform in its doctrine and practice, a closer examination of the literature demonstrates that this was not the real situation. Rather than being united in its confession of faith, early Christianity was marked by a severe conflict between two groups representing two very different conceptions of Christianity: a Jewish (Petrine) Christian party and a Gentile (Pauline) Christian party. A large part of the early Christian documents can be understood in the light of this basic division of thought and action.

In his essay Baur used the method which later came to be known as *Tendenzkritik*—"tendency criticism" is the usual translation—the study of a New Testament writing in terms of its special theological point of view in the context of the history of primitive Christianity. His point of departure is 1 Cor 1:12, which mentions four factions in the Corinthian church, identifying them respectively with Paul, Apollos, Cephas (Peter), and Christ. These four represent actually only two parties: the basically Gentile part of the Church (represented by Paul and Apollos) and the Jewish Christians who remained faithful to Judaism and the law (represented by Peter and James). Concerning the Jewish-Christian party, Baur comments:

> It called itself *tous Kēpha* because Peter had the primacy among the Jewish apostles; *tous Christou*, because it made direct connection with Christ the chief mark of genuine apostolic authority and, therefore, would not recognize Paul as a true apostle of equal rank with the others, since he made his debut as an apostle later and in an entirely different manner from the others; it believed that it was necessary to consider him far inferior to the least of the other apostles.[10]

These Jewish Christians, the Cephas-party, are the opponents of Paul in Corinth, before whom he defends himself, especially in 1 Corinthians. The same group is to be identified with his opponents referred to in Galatians.

In addition to the New Testament data which Baur adduces in support of his theory, he finds evidence for this basic division of thought in the primitive Church in an Ebionite tradition concerning Paul and in the so-called *Clementine Homilies*.[11] In the former tradition Paul is said to have been a Gentile who became a proselyte because he wanted to marry the daughter of the Jewish high priest; this being refused, he left Jerusalem in anger and began preaching against the Sabbath, circumcision, and the law. In the *Clementine Homilies* he found evidence for a polemic against Paul, veiled as an imaginary debate between Peter and Simon Magus. Baur argues that both these imaginary and tendentious stories provide evidence for his view that a strong and significant part of the early Church, a Petrine party, rejected the work and the teaching of the apostle Paul.

Baur does not discuss the book of Acts in this early essay, but his formulation of the nature of early Christianity is of supreme importance for an understanding of the Tübingen criticism of the book. It is important to recognize the fact that when Baur and his disciples turn to the study of Acts it is the book of Acts in the light of Baur's theory of the nature of primitive Christianity that they study, not the text of Acts in its own terms. In this way this basic dichotomy between Petrine and Pauline Christianity, between Jewish and Gentile Christians, between the original apostles and Paul, becomes the basic presupposition of the Tübingen conception of Acts, as indeed for the whole of their consideration of the early Christian writings.

Five years later in an article in which he applied the method of *Tendenzkritik* to the Epistle to the Romans,[12] Baur brought forward the hypothesis that Acts was written by a "Paulinist" in order to defend the mission of Paul to the Gentiles against the criticisms of the Jewish Christian party. The author of Acts argues his point by portraying Paul as everywhere preaching to Jews and only turning to the Gentiles when the Jews had rejected his message. The idea is only mentioned in passing and is not developed. Two years later he developed the idea slightly in a few brief comments in an essay on the origin of the episcopacy.[13]

> Whatever one may think of its historical trustworthiness, the Book of Acts, according to its basic conception and inmost character, is the apologetic attempt of a Paulinist to initiate and bring about the rapprochement and union of the two opposing parties. Thus Paul is made to appear as Petrine as possible, and Peter, as Pauline as possible, thereby throwing a veil of reconciliation over the differences which we know, according to the clear statement of the Apostle Paul in the Epistle to the Galatians, without any doubt really existed between the two apostles, and causing both parties to forget their mutual hostilities in their common enmity toward the unbelieving Jews, who had made the Apostle Paul the constant object of their transigent hatred.[14]

An understanding of this important parallelism between Peter and Paul, insists Baur, is fundamental to any attempt to solve the other historical and critical problems related to the book of Acts.

4. The Legacy of Baur and His School

The influence of Baur, which extended far beyond the walls of the lecture rooms of the at-that-time rather insignificant university on the Neckar, was due to the development of a small band of fervently loyal disciples around him.[15] Of primary importance was his son-in-law, Eduard Zeller, who was to leave the sanctuary of theology for philosophy and make significant contributions to both subjects. Then there was Albert Schwegler, the melancholic

Schwabian who expanded the seminal ideas of his master into a brilliantly conceived and written *History of the Post-apostolic Age* (1846), thus offering the world the only comprehensive account of Baur's all-encompassing re-interpretation of the history of the early days of the Church. Then there were lesser known disciples such as Karl Christian Planck, uncle of Max, who is said to have been "best known for his extremely complex philosophical system which no one but he himself was ever able to understand."[16] And though they later parted company with him, the men who really put Baur and his School on the academic map were his most famous disciples: David Friedrich Strauss, Albrecht Ritschl, and Adolf Hilgenfeld.

In the area of New Testament criticism, the legacy of Baur and his School is at least sixfold: (1) the conception of biblical criticism as an attempt to formulate a comprehensive total-view which seeks to explain *all* the available data; (2) the principle of a purely historical (i.e., non-supernatural) interpretation of the origins of Christianity; (3) the assumption of a radical dichotomy in the early Church between Paul and the primitive apostles, as well as between Gentile and Jewish Christianity; (4) a negative judgment concerning the value of the Acts of the Apostles as a source for the history of the Church during the first three decades of its existence; (5) an antipathy for the theological emphases of the Lucan writings; and (6) the tendency for German biblical scholarship to divide up into various schools (e.g., the Bultmann School of the recent period). All of these assumptions and tendencies can be observed to have an abiding influence in contemporary New Testament scholarship.

5. J. B. Lightfoot and Nineteenth-Century British Scholarship

F. F. Bruce, in contrast to Haenchen, represents the British tradition of New Testament scholarship which has its roots in the work of J. B. Lightfoot (1818–1889) and his colleagues, B. F. Westcott (1825–1901) and F. J. A. Hort (1828–1892), and, from a later period, Sir William M. Ramsay (1851–1939). Two major differences between the German and British tradition are worthy of note: (1) British criticism has rarely been anti-orthodox in its theological orientation (*contra* the Tübingen School, and the contemporary Bultmannian School); and (2) early British criticism was firmly rooted in historical (rather than theological) research.[17] In contrast to Baur and his disciples in Germany, Lightfoot and the early British critics were trained in classical philology and history rather than speculative philosophy and theology. A little later, the man who almost single-handedly founded the academic discipline of classical archaeology in Great Britain, Sir William Mitchell Ramsay,[18] applied his great expertise to the study of Acts, with the result that he became a champion of "Luke the *historian.*" It is interesting to note in passing that Bruce began his career as a classicist, being educated first at the University of Aberdeen, where Ramsay was professor for many years, under Alexander Souter, who was a student of Ramsay.[19]

Space will not allow a detailed exposition of the work of Lightfoot,[20] but it may be useful to include a brief outline of his contribution to the study of Acts as an illustration of his critical method. Lightfoot's first work related to Acts was written as a criticism of a book entitled *Supernatural Religion: An Inquiry into the Reality of Divine Revelation,* published anonymously in 1874 (the author was W. R. Cassels) and which attempted, *inter alia,* to impugn the historical trustworthiness of the Acts of the Apostles on the grounds which had been suggested by the Tübingen critics. Lightfoot's careful and dispassionate rebuttal of Cassels' book [21] prevented the approach to Acts put forward by Baur and his disciples from ever being established in British scholarship. But it was not simply his lengthy criticism of this otherwise rather unimportant book which carried the day but rather his nonpolemical works, his great commentaries on the Pauline epistles[22] and the Apostolic Fathers,[23] which demonstrated so clearly that the Tübingen reconstruction of early Christianity was simply a castle built in the sky without any real foundation in historical research.

Lightfoot had planned to write a full-scale commentary on Acts, but this was never completed. He did, however, publish two important essays on the subject,[24] in which he pointed out (1) how difficult it was for an ancient writer to be accurate in matters of historical detail and (2) how carefully accurate the author of Acts shows himself to be. Take, for example, the details of Roman government in the first two centuries. From the time of Augustus' reorganization of the Empire, there were two types of provincial governors: provinces administered by the Senate were ruled by a proconsul (*anthypatos*), and provinces under the direct responsibility of the Emperor as the head of the army were ruled by a propraetor (*antistratēgos*) or legate (*presbytēs*). This terminology was quite different from earlier republican times, and the original subdivision of the provinces between the Emperor and the Senate underwent constant revisions. Thus at any given time it would be impossible to say without either personal, or at least very exact historical, knowledge whether a particular province was governed by a proconsul or propraetor. The province of Achaia is a case in point. A few years before Paul's visit to Corinth, and some years thereafter, it was ruled by a propraetor. At the time of Paul's visit, however, it was ruled by a proconsul on behalf of the Senate, precisely as represented by Acts. Again, Cyprus was also under the rule of a proconsul during the time of Paul's visit, even though at a later date the situation was different; and this is precisely what Acts indicates (13:17).

Lightfoot was writing at a time when the important archaeological researches which would throw important light on the New Testament were just being made, and he is the first New Testament scholar of note to see the importance of these. Discoveries at Ephesus, for example, had indicated the dominance of the city of Ephesus by the cult of Artemis exactly as presented in Acts. In fact, many of the newly discovered inscriptions, Lightfoot suggests, form almost a running commentary on the narrative of Acts 19. And the same proves true for what was being discovered concerning the other cities of Asia Minor and Greece which were visited by Paul, down to the smallest item of historical and geographical detail. When compared with other ancient historical works, it is unlikely that any other offers so many tests of historical accuracy or contains so many points of contact with contemporary history, politics, and geography. What Lightfoot suggested and gave incidental illustration of was to be demonstrated in detail by Ramsay and others.[25]

6. The Legacy of Lightfoot

The legacy of Lightfoot has been equally important as Baur's for modern New Testament scholarship. A. C. Headlam once observed that Lightfoot had accomplished exactly what he had set out to do: bring the study of Christian antiquity back from the realm of speculation and fantasy to the sober realities of genuinely critical investigation. Insofar as British scholarship is concerned, Stephen Neill points out that Lightfoot had, in a sense, done his work too well:

> Every elementary text-book of church history today takes for granted the authenticity of the letter of Clement and the seven letters of Ignatius, and uses them as primary source material for the history of the sub-apostolic age. As a result the majority of theological students do not even know that their authenticity was ever seriously questioned, and that one of the greatest critical battles of the century was fought about them.[26]

For British scholarship, at least, Lightfoot assured a New Testament criticism which (1) weds literary criticism with authentically historical research (i.e., study of the classics, archaeology, etc.); (2)

emphasizes exegesis and the writing of detailed commentaries rather than speculative reconstructions of alleged historical backgrounds; (3) is cautious in its rejection of traditional views and in the acceptance of new hypotheses; (4) does not assume that criticism and faith are necessarily mutually exclusive; (5) recognizes an essential unity of conviction in the apostolic Church; and (6) accepts the basic historicity of the Acts of the Apostles as a source for the earliest developments within the Christian Church.

7. Conclusion

Thus I have briefly traced the historical development of two differing traditions of New Testament criticism.[27] I should conclude by pointing out that these traditions are not necessarily entirely exclusive. That is to say, scholars like Haenchen and Bruce who follow more or less in the two different traditions I have outlined do not always disagree regarding either method or conclusions. There is a great common ground existing among scholars of all traditions and viewpoints, and this often leads to a very fruitful interchange of ideas and real progress in biblical interpretation. Furthermore, there are many scholars who cannot be neatly classified as representing either the "Tübingen" or "Cambridge" traditions: they represent a bit of both, mixed together like oil and water. So it will not do simply to label scholars as belonging to *this* school or to *that* school as though that should determine whether they should be taken seriously or not. We must beware of the danger of our labels becoming libels. However, I do think that the isolation of these two traditions of criticism helps one to understand the reasons lying behind at least some of the radically different approaches and conclusions one finds in modern New Testament scholarship. A close look at the nineteenth-century roots of New Testament criticism does not explain everything. But it does explain *some* things. Or so I believe.

NOTES

1. W. G. Kümmel, *Introduction to the New Testament* (ET, rev. ed. 1975).
2. D. Guthrie, *New Testament Introduction* (rev. ed. 1970).
3. F. F. Bruce, *The Acts of the Apostles* (1951; rev. ed. 1952); and *Commentary on the Book of Acts* (NICNT) (1954). Note that these volumes supplement one another. The first is on the Greek text and focuses on historical, grammatical, and critical details; the second uses the ASV as a starting point and has an orientation more toward theology.
4. E. Haenchen, *The Acts of the Apostles* (ET, 1971).
5. On Haenchen's treatment of Acts, see W. W. Gasque, *A History of the Criticism of the Acts of the Apostles* (1975), pp. 235–247.

6. For more on Bruce's views regarding Acts, see Gasque, *History*, pp. 257–264.

7. On the Pastoral Epistles (1835), Paul (1845), the four Gospels (1847), the Gospel of Mark (1851), and the theology of the New Testament (posthumous, 1864).

8. Notably, on the Christ party in the Corinthian church (1831), Apollonius of Tyana and Christ (1832), the purpose and occasion of the Epistle to the Romans (1836), the origin of the episcopacy (1838), and the composition and character of the Gospel of John (1844).

9. "Die Christuspartei in der korinthischen Gemeinde, der Gegensatz des petrinischen und paulinischen Christenthums in der ältesten Kirche, der Apostel Petrus in Rom," *Tübinger Zeitschrift für Theologie* 5 (1831), 4. Heft, 61–206.

10. Ibid., p. 84.

11. "Die Christuspartei," pp. 115, 116ff.

12. "Über Zweck und Veranlassung des Römerbriefs und die damit zusammenhängenden Verhältnisse der römischen Gemeinde," *Tübinger Zeitschrift für Theologie* 9 (1836), 3. Heft, pp. 59–178.

13. "Über den Ursprung des Episcopats in der christlichen Kirche," *Tübinger Zeitschrift für Theologie* 11 (1838), 3. Heft, pp. 1–185.

14. Ibid., p. 142.

15. See the brilliant recent study by Horton Harris, *The Tübingen School* (1975).

16. Harris, op. cit., p. 89.

17. Compare, for example, the parallel histories of modern New Testament criticism by S. Neill, *The Interpretation of the New Testament, 1861–1961* (1964), and W. G. Kümmel, *The New Testament: A History of the Investigation of Its Problems* (ET, 1973).

18. See the present author's *Sir William M. Ramsay: Archaeologist and New Testament Scholar* (1966).

19. Cf. F. F. Bruce, "The New Testament and Classical Scholarship," *NTS* 22 (1976), pp. 229–242.

20. Since I have dealt with Ramsay elsewhere and since I am concerned primarily with nineteenth-century roots, I have omitted him from the present discussion.

21. *Essays on the Work Entitled "Supernatural Religion"* (1889), first published in series of articles in *The Contemporary Review* (1874–1877).

22. *Galatians* (1865); *Philippians* (1868); *Colossians and Philemon* (1875). Each of these is, I believe, still in print today.

23. *The Apostolic Fathers*, 5 vols. (1885–1890); includes Clement of Rome, Ignatius, and Polycarp. An earlier edition of Clement was published in 1869 and 1877, but this was revised in 1890.

24. "Discoveries Illustrating the Acts of the Apostles," first published in *The Contemporary Review* (1878) and then as an appendix to his *Essays on . . . "Supernatural Religion,"* pp. 191–302; and "Acts of the Apostles," *Dictionary of the Bible*, W. Smith, ed. (1893), 1, pp. 25–43.

25. Cf. Gasque, *History*, pp. 136–163.

26. *Interpretation*, p. 57.

27. For further detail, see my *History of the Criticism of the Acts of the Apostles*.

11: The Composition of the Fourth Gospel

LEON MORRIS

The Johannine literature continues to fascinate students of the New Testament, and there seems no end to the spate of books or articles on one or another of these writings. One of the topics which arouses interest is the milieu in which the Fourth Gospel was written and the way in which it was composed. It is to this that I wish to address myself.

1. Gnosticism

First, let us notice the view that we must look to some gnostic milieu for the origin of this writing. Probably no one has done more to make this point in recent years than Rudolf Bultmann. This great scholar sees John as giving expression to what Lindars calls "a Christianized form of Gnosticism";[1] he has taken a gnostic source and applied what it says to Jesus. Bultmann attaches special importance to Mandaism. The Mandaeans survive as a non-Christian, gnostic sect, and Bultmann finds in them the same kind of thinking as that which he discerns in the "revelation" source he postulates for John. Others do not accept Bultmann's full position but go along with the view that the book cannot be understood apart from some form of Gnosticism. Thus Ernst Käsemann sees John as putting forward what he calls a "naive docetism" in his portrait of Jesus.[2]

Whether Gnosticism is thought of as in the sources or in the mind of the evangelist, there are not inconsiderable objections. First, no one has yet shown conclusively that Gnosticism antedates Christianity; and there are still good reasons for holding that it should be understood as a Christian heresy. Johannes Munck thinks that if we retain the word "Gnosticism" to denote "the heretical movements that arose in the second century . . . we shall reach a clarity that will be to the benefit of scholarship."[3] His point is that far too many apply the word "Gnosticism" to anything with any of the elements that in due time went to make up Gnosticism, but that the term would be better confined to the systems that eventually emerged and not to any of the foreshadowings. It is, of course, true that some of the ideas put out by developed Gnosticism are to be found also in pre-Christian writings. But this does not make those writings gnostic. Gnosticism did not appear all at once with a monopoly on all the ideas in its various systems. It was a syncretistic movement, gathering in from a variety of sources, some earlier than others. Raymond E. Brown points out that "when Gnosticism appears in the 2nd century A.D., it is an amalgamation of different strains of thought, and certain of these strains are truly ancient." Then he asks an important question, "But were they really *joined* in the pre-Christian era? For it was the joining of the strains that produced Gnosticism."[4]

Central to the various forms of Gnosticism that we know is the idea that there is a high, good God who could not possibly have contact with anything so evil as matter. Gnosticism postulates a series of intermediate beings to bridge the gap and eventually in the series comes to the *demiourgos,* a being powerful enough to create and stupid enough to be able to see that creation is evil. There is often the figure of a Revealer or Redeemer who teaches men the way whereby they may be delivered from the evils of matter and of ignorance. There is no trace of the *demiourgos* in John. And despite the confident assertions of some, there is no real evidence that John based his portrait of Jesus on some gnostic Revealer. None of the gnostic systems we know is early enough for us to say that John drew his portrait of Christ from it, but the opposite is possible in every case. It seems to have been part of the genius of Gnosticism to take some of the features of the Christian portrait of Jesus and combine them with ideas taken from elsewhere. The fact that these ideas are sometimes pre-Christian does not give a reason for holding that the whole system is pre-Christian. And when we cannot find in any pre-Christian source a picture anything like that of the Jesus of the gospels, including the Fourth Gospel,[5] we must beg to be excused from holding that John's essential picture is derived from anything gnostic.

Let us give attention to two specific areas, the gnostic Redeemer myth and the Mandaeans. As to the first, Charles H. Talbert has recently pointed out[6] that there are serious problems in the way of the popular view that the Christian idea of Jesus "as a descending-ascending saviour figure" derives from gnostic sources. He sees three which are widely noted: our sources for the gnostic myth are late;

the Redeemer myth is not essential to Gnosticism (so that even if a pre-Christian Gnosticism could be demonstrated, that would not be enough; it would still be necessary to show that there was a Redeemer myth in it); and "in the Christian sources where the gnostic myth has been assumed to be influential (e.g., the Fourth Gospel), there is no ontological identity between Christ and the believers as in gnosticism."[7] He adds a fourth, "myths of descending-ascending redeemers are found elsewhere in the Mediterranean world prior to and parallel with the origins of Christianity."[8] He cites examples of this from Greco-Roman mythology before proceeding to argue that a similar pattern is to be found in pre-Christian Judaism and that this is probably the source of the Christian idea. This is a weighty article and its argument must be considered carefully.

Schnackenburg has an excursus in which he notes the work of C. Colpe on this subject. Colpe discerns three types of gnostic doctrine: one which sees need only of knowledge and which a prophet might proclaim, a second which refers to the descent of a Redeemer but only to a lower heaven, and a third which has the Redeemer on earth, but a Redeemer of a docetic type. Often there is no Redeemer. In view of this kind of research, Schnackenburg is not prepared to affirm that Gnosticism was moved to evolve the concept of a Redeemer only when confronted by Christianity (though Christianity gave impetus to this kind of thinking and supplied it with some ideas).

> But it is equally difficult to maintain that Gnosis presented Christianity with a ready-made and consistent myth of a redeemer. It would certainly be premature to ask when and how the Gnostic redeemer-myth or the various forms of it arose. Our effort here was merely to show how difficult it is to speak of a "Gnostic Redeemer Myth" prior to Christianity in a clear and definite form.[9]

It cannot be said that the view that John was indebted to Gnosticism for his idea of the Redeemer rests on any solid foundation.

When he compares the gnostic myth, as far as it is known, with what John says, Schnackenburg finds a number of essential features lacking. In the Fourth Gospel

> Christ is not the prototype of man in need of redemption; he is not a "Primordial Man", neither *salvator salvatus* nor *salvandus*. He has no typical significance as "man". . . . There is no trace of the "Paradisaical Man" in John and the protological role of Christ is not reflected in it. His activity as mediator of creation, which appears only in the Logos hymn (1:3,10b), is anything but a cosmogony intended to explain the nature of man . . . there is no speculation on the essential kernel of man's "self."[10]

This combination of a lack of anything early enough to serve as a model for John with a portrait in John which lacks a not inconsiderable number of traits characteristic of the gnostic Redeemer when he eventually does appear, surely forms a demonstration that this is not a helpful area in which to search for clues to John's method and meaning. John's Christ and the gnostic Redeemer belong to different worlds.

The Mandaeans are, as already noted, surviving non-Christian Gnostics. They have sacred scriptures, notably a book called the Ginza and another, the Book of John. But C. H. Dodd points out that there is no manuscript of either that goes back beyond the sixteenth century. The originals would, of course, have been much older; but there is no reason for seeing them as older than the early Islamic period. Dodd doubts whether the compilation of the Mandaean canon can be dated "much, if at all, before A.D. 700."[11] It is precarious to reason back from a hypothetical A.D. 700 to a time early enough to be influential on Christian writings. Many scholars see the dependence as the other way and think that Christian writings have influenced the Mandaeans. They may or may not be right, but clearly we have a long way to go before Mandaism can be proved to be part of John's background.

Indeed, it is not even certain that Gnosticism is original to Mandaism. Lindars objects in these terms: "Though there is some evidence for Baptist groups in Syria at this time, from which Mandaism is derived, it is virtually certain that the Gnostic elements are due to later syncretism."[12] I am not clear as to what makes Lindars "virtually certain" about this (though he cites the work of Colpe) and would not wish to be so definite myself. But the fact that the claim can be made is important. The lateness of all our Mandaean sources presents us with more than one problem. It is not easy to be sure that there is anything in Mandaean contacts with Christian teaching that is early enough to have influenced the New Testament, nor can we be sure that Mandaean Gnosticism was early enough for those who emphasize the importance of a gnostic background. We are moving in a highly speculative area in which it is hazardous to draw firm conclusions.

Sometimes the *Odes of Solomon* are adduced as helping Mandaism by showing that there was early Gnosticism in this general area. But recent study of these documents has weakened the basis for the theory. For example, R. H. Charlesworth has argued that the *Odes* should not be understood as gnostic but rather as another specimen of Jewish mystical apocalyptic.[13] In any case he thinks that their evidence has not been used satisfactorily. In an article written in conjunction with R. H. Culpepper he rejects the views that the *Odes* depend on John or John on the *Odes* in favor of the view that John and the *Odes* come from the same religious environment.[14] Plainly the *Odes* come a long way short of showing that Gnosticism of a Mandaean type is in John's background.

It is true that there is much in the Fourth Gospel that commended itself to the Gnostics[15] and that this Gospel was highly valued among them. The first commentary on John was written by the Gnostic Heracleon, and the discoveries at Chenoboskion show conclusively that this Gospel was widely used by the Gnostics.[16] But the evidence before us is that John was a source for the Gnostics rather than vice versa.

And we must always bear in mind the great differences between John and Gnosticism. There are terminological resemblances, but the basic ideas are quite different.[17] The Gnostics are interested in a kind of religious philosophy with mythological elements. John is concerned with salvation, with God's great act in Christ to deliver men from sin and bring them to himself. The Gnostics are interested in knowledge, John in redemption. Where the Gnostics have a Redeemer, he is one who brings men knowledge; in John the Redeemer lays down his life for his sheep. These are two different worlds. It is not easy to see how anyone could start with the Gnostics and finish with John.

2. The Author a Jew?

For reasons such as these most agree that we should not look to Gnosticism for the origin of this Gospel. These days there is considerable agreement that we should seek the author in a Jewish environment. This has not always been held. In the period up to World War II there was a good deal of emphasis on the Hellenistic features which many discerned in this writing, and it could be viewed as "the Gospel of the Hellenists." Since that war the emphasis has been different, though Bultmann and others have discerned Greek influence in the Gnosticism of which we have been thinking. C. H. Dodd drew attention to the significance of what he called "the higher religion of Hellenism," the Hermetic literature. This is a series of writings in the name of Hermes Trismegistus, who "was represented as a sage of ancient Egypt, deified after his death as the Egyptian Hermes, that is, the god Thoth."[18] Dodd also gave attention to Hellenistic Judaism of the type we see in Philo, to Rabbinic Judaism, to Gnosticism, and to Mandaism. But he worked from the presupposition that the Gospel should be seen as a work "addressed to a wide public consisting primarily of devout and thoughtful persons . . . in the varied and cosmopolitan society of a great Hellenistic city such as Ephesus under the Roman Empire."[19] In view of his openness to the idea that Greek thought is behind this writing, it is significant that Dodd could yet say, "The evidence for an underlying Semitic idiom is irresistible."[20] But he saw the Greek as more significant.

These days not many scholars are ready to put such emphasis on the Greek thinking that earlier scholars discerned in this writing. But perhaps the reaction has gone a little too far. A writing in the Greek language, probably published in a center of Greek culture, cannot but have been interpreted along the lines of Greek thought.[21] A writer sending forth his brain-child in such surroundings must have been mindful of the associations his particular form of expression would arouse. We should accordingly not overlook the Greek element. To take but one example, our author uses the term *Logos* in his opening line. It is true that a case can be made out for seeing this as essentially Semitic;[22] but in the end we are bound to bear in mind that the *Logos* was a concept in use among the Greeks, so that native Greek speakers who first read the book would already have in mind a definite meaning for the term. I find it difficult to think that the author was oblivious of this. It seems much more likely that he used the term as one which could be meaningful to Greeks as well as to Jews.[23] We must bear in mind that there was a considerable penetration of Palestine by Hellenism so that some Greek elements might be expected even in a purely Palestinian production.

But when full allowance has been made for all this, the trend among recent scholars has been to emphasize that the Fourth Gospel is a Semitic writing. Some have held that it was written in Aramaic and that what we have is a translation of the original. This was argued forcefully by C. F. Burney,[24] and espoused also by C. C. Torrey.[25] The whole thesis was subjected to careful scrutiny by Matthew Black,[26] who reached the more cautious conclusion that the Gospel was written in Greek but that there is Aramaic thinking behind it, particularly in the sayings attributed to Jesus. It can scarcely be said that the theory of an Aramaic original has been taken up enthusiastically by Johannine scholars, but there is increasing recognition of the fact that basically this is a Semitic document, and something like Black's position is widely accepted. [27] The author was Jewish. He knew the Jewish scene and thought in Jewish categories.

But in the first century there was Judaism *and* Judaism. C. K. Barrett puts emphasis on Hellenistic Judaism, though warning us that

"Judaism" is a term with many meanings and one which we must use with care.[28] He also draws attention to the importance of apocalyptic and of the rabbinic literature. There was much variety in Judaism, and in particular we must not differentiate it too sharply from Hellenism. There was undoubtedly a good deal of Greek influence in Palestine itself, though we must not hold this in such a form that we blur the line between the two. Granted that there was much Hellenism in Palestine, that does not make Judaism and Hellenism the same thing.

The essentially Jewish character of the Fourth Gospel was given emphasis by many who studied closely the discoveries from Qumrân when in the 1950's and 1960's these discoveries received a good deal of attention. One of the unexpected results of this study was the discovery that the scrolls have more links with the Fourth Gospel than with any other writing in the New Testament. There are many coincidences of language, though, interestingly, similar language is often used to give expression to very dissimilar thoughts. For example, both use the unusual expression, "the Spirit of truth"; but, whereas in the Fourth Gospel this means a divine Person, in the scrolls it is one of two spirits, the spirit of truth and the spirit of error, who strive within men. Sometimes the scrolls indicate a knowledge of the scene in ways we would not have anticipated. For example, almost everything John tells us about John the Baptist can be paralleled somewhere in the Qumrân writings, a fact which has led a number of scholars to alter their estimate of the reliability of John's picture of the Baptist.[29] Such accurate knowledge underlines the Jewishness of this Gospel.

Several scholars point to the accurate knowledge of Palestinian topography shown by the writer, notably W. F. Albright[30] and R. D. Potter.[31] Objection is sometimes made, as by C. K. Barrett,[32] who argues that John shows no great knowledge of the land and who also makes a good deal of the different identifications of some places made by Potter and Albright.[33] But not many have been persuaded by such arguments. It is generally accepted that the topography of Palestine presupposed by this Gospel is reliable. This forms a further indication of the essential Jewishness of its background.

We should not overlook the kind of controversy of which John writes. He tells of discussions about the right use of the sabbath, about true and false Judaism, about the Messiah and his work (Where would he come from? Would he rescue the Jews from the Romans?). We do not find discussions of the problems that preoccupied the second-century Church in its Gentile environment, problems of episcopacy, the date of Easter, gnostic speculations about aeons, and the like. And while there is certainly polemic against the Jews, it is not the kind of polemic we know from the second century. There is an authentic ring about it. This is supported by some detailed studies on particular points. Thus P. Borgen has shown that the sixth chapter is genuinely Palestinian in both subject matter and method,[34] and Severino Pancaro argues that John's use of the category of law is thoroughly Jewish.[35]

C. H. Dodd puts the point well. He notes such things as the reference to the Jewish practice of circumcision on the sabbath so that the law of Moses be not broken (John 7:23), which points to an accurate knowledge of Judaism. He reasons,

> The *Sitz im Leben* of such a tradition must have been within a Jewish environment such as that of the primitive Church, and in all probability it belongs to an early period. Once the Church, by that time mainly Gentile, had ceased to have relations with the synagogue, such discussions would no longer be kept alive, and only isolated traces of them remain, embedded in the gospels.[36]

One such reference might not mean much, but John has a number. Together they convince many that there is good knowledge of Judaism behind this Gospel.

This point is made also by J. L. Martyn. He selects six affirmations about Moses made in this Gospel by the Jews. He finds every one of them attested by "Jewish texts which put us in touch with the first century." He further points out that "these six points are not merely historically reliable. They are also representative of the very life nerve of Judaism, and they are stated in John's Gospel with great precision."[37] A little later he says that these six points "stand proudly among the most accurate statements about Jewish thought in the whole of the New Testament."[38] Such statements should leave us in no doubt but that there is good and accurate knowledge of Judaism behind this Gospel, and knowledge that would scarcely be available to a late, Gentile writer. The writer knows Judaism and is appreciative of many things about it, though of course he emphasizes the way "the Jews" of Jesus' day reacted against his Lord. He does not approve of everything in Judaism, but he is familiar with the Jewish scene.[39]

It is a curious fact that in this Gospel there are no references to "the Gentiles" (*ta ethnē*). When John uses *ethnos* he means the Jewish nation. This does not mean that he had no knowledge of the Gentiles or of the considerable Gentile section of the Church at the time he wrote. But it does mean that when he looked back at the life of Jesus it was Judaism that he saw clearly. J. A. T. Robinson contrasts his attitude with "the assumption reflected throughout the synoptists, Acts and Paul that the rejection of the Jews is to be followed by the in-coming of the Gentiles." This does not mean that there was no mission to the Gentiles at the time John wrote, "but it certainly presupposes a milieu where concentration on the presentation of Jesus as the truth and fullness of Israel was the all-absorbing task of Christian apologetic."[40]

It is noteworthy that scholars who see Judaism behind this Gospel do not represent any one school of thought or outlook. They are very diverse, and their consensus on this point is all the more impressive. For most scholars, it is plain that this Gospel must be seen as essentially a Jewish product, whatever other strains there may have been in the thinking of its author. He must have been a Jew, a Jew who knew Palestine, but who also knew something of the Greek world.

3. Sources

This leads to the important question of how this Jewish author went to work. Here a good deal of attention is given to John's *aporiai* ("perplexities"). These are such things as the reference to Jesus' "second sign" (John 4:54) after we have been told that he did "signs" in Jerusalem (2:23). In the first part of John 3, Jesus appears to be in Judea as he talks to Nicodemus (cf. 2:23); but in 3:22 he came into Judea. In John 14:31, Jesus says, "Rise, let us depart"; but it is another three chapters before the little band leaves the upper room. The Gospel appears to end at 20:31, but another chapter follows. There are other difficulties of this kind which convince most students that the writing has a complex history. A number of solutions have been proposed.

Some have seen the answer in accidental displacement of sections of the completed writing, but such views are not widely accepted. It is more common to find the view that the evangelist made use of a number of sources. R. Bultmann gave such ideas a stimulus with his theory that John had three main sources: a signs source, a discourse source (deriving from non-Christian Gnosticism), and a passion narrative. In addition, there were some smaller units, such as the story of the cleansing of the temple. Bultmann sees the evangelist as combining these three, together with important contributions of his own. Somehow the manuscript got into disorder (Bultmann does not say how this came about), and a final redactor gave it its present shape, making some contributions of his own in the process.[41]

Raymond E. Brown makes four major criticisms of all such

views.[42] (1) The signs and the discourses are "closely woven together."[43] For example, the discourse on the bread of life is an interpretation of the multiplication of the loaves. (2) Sayings of Jesus, which comparison with the Synoptics indicates are genuine, are embedded in the discourses, so that a pre-Christian discourse seems improbable. (3) The work of E. Schweizer, J. Jeremias, P. H. Menoud, and E. Ruckstuhl has shown that there are no differences in style between the postulated sources. (4) There are no parallels to the kind of source that Bultmann postulates.

These and other criticisms have convinced many, though not all. J. Becker, for example, has worked with a sources hypothesis,[44] as have R. T. Fortna[45] and more recently H. M. Teeple.[46] Fortna, as the name of his book implies, sees evidence that there was a source which listed the "signs" of Jesus, to which he thinks a passion narrative was added. Some have felt that the idea that the passion narrative formed one source with the signs narrative takes away from the credibility of the theory. They point out that a major reason for postulating a signs source is the reference to signs in John 20:31, which is felt to follow oddly on the passion. But if the passion was in the source, this argument is taken away. If the words could follow the passion in the source, there is no problem about them in the Gospel.

Others, however, are impressed with Fortna's work. Thus D. M. Smith has written approvingly of it and indicates that he sees a growing acceptance of the theory that there was a signs source.[47] R. Kysar shares this view, as the title of his article, "The Source Analysis of the Fourth Gospel, A Growing Consensus?" suggests.[48] He argues on the basis of a study of John 6 that there is evidence of a general agreement among nine theories which he examines, though he agrees that the whole idea is rejected by scholars of the caliber of E. Schweizer, F. Williams, C. K. Barrett, and E. Ruckstuhl.

But criticisms persist. O. Cullmann, for example, is impressed by "the unity of style, language and purpose" which he finds throughout this Gospel. He is not opposed to the idea that John may have used sources, but this unity makes "problematical all attempts to *identify* their extent, despite Fortna's efforts in methodology and his attempts to contrast his statistics with those of Ruckstuhl." [49] Barnabas Lindars makes a number of points. He draws attention to some assumptions underlying Fortna's work: that a complete Gospel could have existed containing no direct teaching of Jesus (apart from conversation in narrative), and that a creative writer like John would nevertheless have incorporated almost the entire source so that a removal of the non-Johannine elements reveals it. He regards both as false and sees the *coup de grâce* in Fortna's inclusion in the source of the miraculous catch of fish in chapter 21, which Lindars sees as certainly an isolated piece added to the Gospel after the evangelist's death.[50] He finds it difficult to think that much that is common to all Christian literature (predictions of the passion, eschatology, apocalyptic language) should be absent from this source.[51] Lindars also objects to Becker's somewhat similar view of a source depicting Jesus as a *theios anēr*, a wonder-worker of a docetic type, which John took over to express a non-docetic point of view. He argues that this is inherently improbable and that "the reconstruction of the Signs Source has not recovered an authentic independent document, but it is really a filter whereby the Gospel of many colours has all the colours cut out except one."[52] J. A. T. Robinson is another who finds the sources hypothesis difficult: "The unity of style has rendered unconvincing all attempts to analyse out written sources."[53]

We should also mention Teeple's position. He argues for

> four main writers . . . the authors of two written sources, the editor who used portions of the sources in his composition, and the redactor. In addition, the editor and redactor used a few brief written sources, and a later copyist inserted a few glosses.[54]

Most of the criticisms of Fortna's work apply equally to Teeple's. The latter's method inspires no great confidence, and he does not seem to have made real advance. The case for sources is still that of Fortna.

The great difficulty in the way of all hypotheses of sources is the uniformity of style throughout the Gospel. Attempts to minimize this do not seem to have been successful. Allied to this is the point that to most students of this Gospel the discourses bear the unmistakable stamp of the evangelist. It is not easy to think that anyone who could write like this would simply add the discourses to some pre-existing source. The difficulty is compounded by the fact that the signs sections in any case have many of the same characteristics. While recognizing the force of the arguments put forward by those who see sources, most students of this Gospel find the difficulties so great that they cannot accept the hypothesis with any enthusiasm. The evangelist may have incorporated earlier material into his book, but the general feeling appears to be that he is himself responsible for the bulk of his Gospel. There is considerable agreement with Pierson Parker's well-known dictum, "It looks as though, if the author of the Fourth Gospel used documentary sources, he wrote them all himself."[55]

So instead of sources there is agreement among many that it is more likely that the *aporiai* are to be explained by a series of editions or stages dominated, if not written, by the evangelist himself. Thus Parker thought of two editions, first a Judean edition and later a second edition amplified with Galilean material.[56] Others see the evangelist as starting with a collection of signs and adding discourses and a passion narrative (the affinity with the sources hypothesis is obvious; the difference is that here there is no thought of a unified source, but simply of information coming to the evangelist from a number of directions which we cannot identify). But probably more are willing to find a solution along some such lines as those suggested by Raymond E. Brown.[57] He thinks of five stages. First, there was a body of traditional material similar to but independent of the Synoptic tradition. Secondly, there was the preaching of the evangelist[58] and others during which some of the stories "were developed into superb dramas, for example, ch. ix."[59] Thirdly, the evangelist organized some of the material into a Gospel. Fourthly, he re-edited it. He may have done this a number of times, but Brown thinks most of the features can be accounted for by one re-editing. Finally, after the death of the evangelist a redactor put the Gospel into the shape in which we now have it.[60]

Lindars has a somewhat similar view. He sees John as working on traditional material which may have been oral or written or both. This has often been worked up into homilies and is now incorporated into his book. The sermons would have been worked over; and Lindars finds devices like dialogue, putting words into the mouth of Jesus, and so forth.[61] He agrees with the view that John made use of earlier sources, though he finds himself unable to go along with R. T. Fortna's views, concerning which he levels some strong criticisms.

4. Preaching

It will have been noticed that a number of those who advocate sources or editions make some mention of preaching. It is clear that to many this Gospel says "Sermons." Perhaps this could be looked at again. And here let me quote some words of the distinguished scholar in whose honor these essays are written. Everett F. Harrison speaks of a gospel as "a writing deliberately intended to set forth the saving message of the Christian faith as it centers in the historic figure of Jesus of Nazareth."[62] The gospels are not histories. They are accounts of "the saving message."[63]

There must have been many accounts of parts at any rate of the saving message. I am not sure that we have ever taken seriously enough Luke's statement that "many" before him had undertaken to write accounts of the things that had been fulfilled among the Christians (Luke 1:1). We usually agree that Mark was already written but hold that Matthew and John came later. We discern perhaps a Q source and, if we are generous, M and L. But what else is there? It is not easy to see why these four should be described as "many." There must have been much early literature that has perished.

We have, of course, no way of knowing for certain what that was. But we have a few clues. One is in the titles of our Gospels, even though the full titles are apparently late. They are not "Matthew's Gospel," "Mark's Gospel" and so on, but "*The* Gospel," to which we add, "according to ——." This way of speaking is found also in the *Didache,* which speaks of such and such things as found "in his (i.e., Christ's) gospel" or "in the gospel."[64] There seems not much room for doubt that the early Church knew but one gospel (cf. Gal 1:6f.), the gospel which according to Matthew may be put this way, according to Mark that way, and so on.

There is no reason for holding that this "gospel" was an unknown quantity until Mark's book appeared (or whichever was the first to be published). Nor ought we to assume that up till that time the gospel was purely oral. I have no doubt that much was carried in oral tradition, and as an aside I wonder whether we have paid sufficient attention to the work of B. Gerhardsson and H. Riesenfeld on the role of memory in such a society as the early Church. People who are used to relying on their memories habitually commit much more to memory than do we who rely so much on our written memoranda.

But when full allowance has been made for memory and oral tradition, it seems in the highest degree unlikely that people in the early Church waited for thirty or forty years after the death of Jesus before committing anything of the saving events to writing. It is no answer to say that the early Christians formed an eschatological community living in the constant expectation of the imminent return of the Lord which accordingly saw no reason for writing anything. In the first place, it is not as certain as is often assumed that the whole Church expected Jesus to return so soon that writing was a profitless exercise. And in the second, we have the example of the men of Qumrân, men from roughly the same place and time. They certainly had vivid eschatological expectations, but that did not stop them from producing an extensive literature.

In my opinion there is everything to be said for what Luke has put so clearly—many people did write in the early Church, and they wrote "the gospel."

This does not mean that they wrote gospels like our canonical four. The canonical gospels form a remarkable genre, one for which there is no real parallel. We should not expect that all over the early Church people just naturally sat down and wrote comparable documents. We must leave room for the considerable achievement of our canonical evangelists.

But why should not the literary members of the early Church have tried their hands at something on a more modest scale? Students of Mark often say that behind that Gospel they discern a number of *pericopae* which have been strung together. Were these *pericopae* all oral? Is it not possible that some at least were written? And that they were written to set forth the gospel? If *pericopae* might be written, might not also longer sections? As nothing of this survives we have no way of putting limits to the possibilities (and no brake on our imagination!). But it seems reasonable to think that when men preached the gospel in the early Church they sometimes had sermon notes, and that when they had sermon notes they sometimes made them available to others. There seems no reason why aspects of "the gospel" should not in this way have been made available to church members, and I do not see it as recklessly imaginative to postulate some such process behind John as well as the Synoptists.[65]

It has been usual to date John late in the first century or early in the second. As long as everyone agreed that the Gospel dates from some such time it could be argued that it was unlikely that the apostle John survived so long and emphasis could be put on the evidence that the material in the Gospel had been worked over many times, this being regarded as evidence that several hands had taken part in the composition of the work. But if John is early, this must be looked at in another light; and many recent writers are of the opinion that John is early. The evidence is well stated in the article by F. Lamar Cribbs, "A Reassessment of the Date of Origin and the Destination of the Gospel of John."[66] Cribbs has drawn attention to a variety of considerations which lead him to think of a date in the late 50's or early 60's. To this should now be added the discussion by J. A. T. Robinson, who argues that on the basis of the evidence available to us we should see this book as completed by 65+.[67] Robinson discerns a trend which he describes in this way: "There would appear indeed to be a new convergence on a pre-70 dating between those who have given most study to the Jewish background of the gospel and the newer conservative evangelicals. It will be interesting to see if and when others join them."[68]

If we accept such a date for this Gospel (as I certainly do), then the *aporiae* which have worried so many scholars may appear in a different light. They may be evidence not for the work of several hands but for the evangelist's use of records of his preaching. Christian preaching started on the day of Pentecost, and all our evidence is that it was a very common phenomenon thereafter. If we date the Fourth Gospel in the 60's, there would have been thirty years of preaching behind it; and that seems time enough to account for the phenomena. Many sermons can be preached in thirty years, and it is not easy to see what is gained by postulating another generation of preaching.

I am envisaging the evangelist as a preacher who wrote down some of the things he said in his sermons. These sermons may have included stories of things Jesus did or accounts of things Jesus said either in private conversations or in public discourses. These writings may have been made available to others in the early Church, and possibly a similar process lies behind the other Gospels. If so, these early accounts of "the gospel" may have been compared with one another. This would help to account for some puzzling features of our gospels, such as the relation between Luke and John and the fact that sometimes one of our Synoptists seems to have the earliest form of the tradition, sometimes another. Eventually the evangelist decided to write a fuller account of "the gospel" than his sermon notes. He may have done this in stages, producing a preliminary form of his Gospel as well as a final stage (as some scholars hold). In view of our ignorance of the circumstances of the early Church and specifically of the way the first Christians went about their writing projects, I do not see how we can be dogmatic. But a number of stages appears unnecessary. After all, this Gospel is not an extraordinarily long writing and could have been produced with one working over of the material in the evangelist's possession. Be that as it may, the evidence we have that preaching lies behind the composition of this Gospel can be accounted for if we think of the evangelist himself as the preacher.[69] I see no reason for postulating other preachers, though I immediately add that I see no reason for excluding them either. If he came across a good sermon of someone else, there seems no reason why he should not have made use of it; though if he did, the language indicates that he first made it his own and expressed it in his own way.

In his final composition the evangelist would have included some material which he had often preached and other material which he had used more sparingly (most preachers use some sermons more than others). He put it together in his own way with a definite purpose: that readers might come to believe that Jesus is the Christ, the Son of God, and so enter life (John 20:31). We must see this as the avowed purpose of the writing, not the production of a smooth, neatly turned book that conforms to modern canons of consistency. What seems to us like dislocations and the like may be nothing more than the places where matter from different sermons came together.

This is not unlike the position taken up by J. A. T. Robinson in his recent book *Redating the New Testament,* to which I have already referred. Robinson sees the formation of the Johannine tradition in the period A.D. 30–50, with a first edition of the Gospel in 50–55. He sees the Johannine Epistles as coming from the period 60–65 and the final form of the Gospel from 65+. Such a scheme seems to account for the data at least as well as any other hypothesis at present in the field.

One thing this view does is to eliminate the redactor. It has always seemed curious to me that Johannine scholars clung so firmly to this shadowy figure. A redactor is supposed to iron out the unevennesses in a narrative, even if he does it without sufficiently covering his tracks (which, of course, enables scholars to detect him). But a Johannine redactor has performed in a surprisingly slipshod manner, for he has left all the *aporiai* which attract scholarly interest.[70] To put the same point in another way, if it was possible for a redactor to leave the Gospel in this form, it was equally possible for the evangelist to do so. We have no need to postulate a redactor.

Another thing this view does is to call into question the need for seeing a variety of contributors to this writing. Robinson sees "no changes of style and substance which are not better put down to the development of one large mind than to a disciple or disciples slavishly imitating the voice of their master."[71] As I have said, I see no objection in principle to the author's having made use of material originally composed by others. But if so, this is surely small in amount, and the writer first made it his own. The impression left by the Fourth Gospel is that it is the product of "one large mind" rather than the composition of a committee.

And that is where I want to leave it. A book like this Gospel was never produced in the hotch-potch manner some critics postulate. There is "one large mind" behind it. And, granted that the apostle John was a preacher and that this Gospel was written by the 60's, I see no valid reason for denying that John's was the large mind in question.[72]

NOTES

1. *Behind the Fourth Gospel* (1971), p. 20.
2. *The Testament of Jesus* (1968), pp. 26, 45, 70.
3. W. Klassen and G. F. Snyder, eds., *Current Issues in New Testament Interpretation*

(1962), p. 234. He also points out that "the presence in earlier sources of details which are also to be found in later Gnosticism need not lead to the assumption that later Gnosticism in its entirety has therefore been proved to have existed at an earlier date" (ibid., p. 235).

4. *The Gospel according to John*, 1 (1966), p. LV.

5. Referring specifically to the Mandaeans, Schnackenburg speaks of "The confusing relays of mythological figures which merge into each other in Mandaean literature" (*The Gospel according to St. John*, 1 (1968), p. 142). It is not from such material that John derived his portrait of Jesus.

6. "The Myth of a Descending-Ascending Redeemer in Mediterranean Antiquity," *NTS* 22 (1975–76), pp. 418–440.

7. Ibid., p. 419.

8. Ibid.

9. Op. cit., p. 548.

10. Ibid.

11. *The Interpretation of the Fourth Gospel* (1953), p. 115. Cf. W. Nicol, "Bultmann's strong emphasis on the Mandeans has in the last decades, however, more and more been regarded as one-sided. It is very hypothetical to conclude about the first century from books from the seventh century" (*Neot* 6 [1972], p. 13).

12. *The Gospel of John* (1972), p. 41. Cf. Raymond E. Brown, "Literary criticism points to the Gnostic layers of Mandean thought and writing as being relatively late" (op. cit., p. LV).

13. "The Odes of Solomon—Not Gnostic," *CBQ* 31 (1969), pp. 357–369. He thinks that the *Odes* should be classed with "Jewish apocalyptical mysticism (viz., IV Ezra, the Ethiopic Book of Enoch, the Megillat hahodayot (1 QH), the Book of Mysteries (1 QH 27)" rather than with gnostic writings (op. cit., p. 369).

14. *CBQ* 35 (1973), pp. 298–322.

15. Cf. D. M. Smith, "The present form of the Gospel of John may represent neither anti-Gnosticism (Bultmann) nor pro-Gnosticism (Käsemann, Schottroff), but an early stage in the emergence of motifs that had a later flowering in Gnosticism" (*NTS* 21 [1974–75], p. 240).

16. They also show that John was not a Gnostic. Cf. C. van der Waal, "The discoveries at Nag Hamadi have given further proof that the gnostic ideas were as far from the Fourth Gospel as the West is from the East" (*Neot* 6 [1972], p. 28).

17. Cf. G. E. Ladd, "While some of the Johannine idiom does indeed occur in gnostic thought, and while it is probably true that John deliberately used this terminology to interpret the gospel to people with gnostic leanings, we no longer need to feel that the Johannine idiom is derived from gnostic thought" (*A Theology of the New Testament* [1974], p. 229).

18. Op. cit., p. 11.

19. Ibid., p. 9.

20. Ibid., p. 75.

21. The place of publication is, of course, not known; and some hold that it was in Palestine, or at least that a first draft was written in that land. But many still see good reason for favoring Ephesus, the traditional site; and the most widely held alternative is somewhere in the vicinity of Antioch. If both prove to be erroneous, it still seems clear that we must look for the point of origin in some place where the Greek language was the one in use and where Greek culture and thought were dominant or at least deeply appreciated.

22. See, for example, Raymond E. Brown, op. cit., pp. 519–524.

23. Barnabas Lindars emphasizes the Jewish element, but sees the Greek background of the Gospel as important, too: "It is clear that the author derives his thought from the Jewish and Christian tradition; but it is altogether probable that he writes for Greeks, and duly takes their way of thinking into account" (*The Gospel of John*, p. 35).

24. *The Aramaic Origin of the Fourth Gospel* (1922).

25. *Our Translated Gospels* (London, n.d.). Torrey excepts chapter 21, which he thinks was not in the original, but was written in Greek by the translator.

26. *An Aramaic Approach to the Gospels and Acts* (1946).

27. See the useful discussion by Schuyler Brown, "From Burney to Black: The Fourth Gospel and the Aramaic Question," *CBQ* 26 (1964), pp. 323–339.

28. See his *The Gospel of John and Judaism* (1975).

29. See, for example, J. H. Brownlee in K. Stendahl, ed., *The Scrolls and the New Testament* (1958), p. 52; J. A. T. Robinson in K. Aland *et al.*, eds., *Studia Evangelica* (1959), p. 345; A. Wikgren, ibid., p. 124.
30. *The Archaeology of Palestine* (1949), pp. 244–248; see also W. D. Davies and D. Daube, eds., *The Background of the New Testament and its Eschatology* (1956), pp. 158–160.
31. K. Aland *et al.*, eds., *Studia Evangelica*, (1959), pp. 329–337.
32. *The Gospel according to St. John*, p. 102.
33. *The Gospel of John and Judaism*, pp. 36ff.
34. *Bread from Heaven* (1965).
35. *The Law in the Fourth Gospel* (1975). He says of his book, "It is hoped that the present monograph not only casts new light on the role of the Law in Jn, but succeeds in establishing its Jewish character more convincingly than the attempts made to date" (op. cit., p. 3). In his article, "The Relationship of the Church to Israel in the Gospel of St John," *NTS* 21 (1974–75), pp. 396–405, the same author argues that John sees the Church as the new Israel and that "John is not at all concerned with the Gentiles or the manner in which they may be said to have replaced the Jews in God's salvific plan" (op. cit., p. 405). The standpoint is early and Jewish.
36. *Historical Tradition in the Fourth Gospel* (1963), p. 333.
37. *History and Theology in the Fourth Gospel* (1968), p. 92.
38. Ibid., p. 93. Martyn also argues that John has a two-level approach, putting into the time of Jesus problems that arose from contact with a local synagogue in his own day. There is much that is speculative here, and I doubt whether Martyn has made out his case.
39. R. Schnackenburg points out that recent study of the Gospel has led many French-speaking Roman Catholic scholars to see the importance for John of the "great traditions of Israel" (op. cit., p. 121).
40. *Redating the New Testament* (1976), pp. 274, 275.
41. For a good account of Bultmann's views and methods, see D. M. Smith, *The Composition and Order of the Fourth Gospel* (1965), chapter 1.
42. Op. cit., pp. XXVI–XXXII.
43. Ibid., p. XXXI.
44. "Wunder und Christologie" in *NTS* 16 (1969–70), pp. 130–148.
45. *The Gospel of Signs* (1970).
46. *The Literary Origin of the Gospel of John* (1974).
47. "The Setting and Shape of a Johannine Narrative Source," *JBL* 95 (1976), pp. 231–241.
48. *NovTest* 15 (1973), pp. 134–152. We should also mention some considerable and thoughtful reviews of Fortna's book, as by James M. Robinson, entitled "The Miracles Source of John," *JAAR* 39 (1971), pp. 339–348. Robinson sees Fortna's work as "something of a turning point in Johannine studies" (ibid., p. 339), even though modification in detail is inevitable. Fortna is basically accepted also by Ben Johnson, "Another Primitive Literary Source?" (*Ectr* 33 [1972], pp. 393–399), and by E. D. Freed and R. B. Hunt, "Fortna's Signs-Source in John" (*JBL* 94 [1975], pp. 563–579). I have made no attempt to track down the reviews of Fortna's work, but these are sufficient to show that his view has won wide acceptance.
49. *The Johannine Circle* (1976), pp. 6f.
50. *Behind the Fourth Gospel*, pp. 31–35.
51. Ibid., pp. 35f.
52. Ibid., p. 38.
53. Op. cit., p. 297. He also says, "The damaging criticisms of this [i.e., Fortna's *The Gospel of Signs*] in Lindars, *Behind the Fourth Gospel* (1971), ch. 2, would seem to me to apply to any theory, including his own, that presupposes that the evangelist used external sources" (ibid., p. 297, n. 182).
54. Op. cit., p. 249. Teeple's treatment is not helped by his dogmatism nor by his habit of attributing to bias opinions with which he disagrees. For example, he says that C. H. Dodd reaches certain conclusions because he "is determined to show that somewhere in John is authentic tradition of the life of Jesus" (ibid., p. 68). Dodd was far too great and open-minded a scholar to be categorized in this way, however much one may disagree with

what he has to say. Teeple would have done better to have reckoned seriously with Dodd's arguments, and similarly with others whom he finds biased.

55. *JBL* 75 (1956), p. 304.

56. "Two Editions of John," *JBL* 75 (1956), pp. 303–314.

57. Op. cit., pp. XXXIV–XXXIX.

58. Cf. C. K. Barrett, "The hypothesis that they [i.e., the discourses in John] were in the first place sermons delivered by the evangelist and subsequently (perhaps even after his death) arranged in the gospel has much to commend it" (*The Gospel according to St John*, p. 17).

59. Op. cit., p. XXXV.

60. Some think this too complicated, as O. Cullmann who holds that Brown goes "too far in assuming five stages of literary development" (op. cit., p. 9). A. Marcus Ward is also critical of the theory and finds that it "compromises the very historical value on which Brown sets such store" (*ExpT* 81 [1969–70], p. 70).

61. *The Gospel of John*, pp. 51ff., and more fully in *Behind the Fourth Gospel*.

62. *John: The Gospel of Faith* (1962), p. 9.

63. Franz Mussner seems to miss this point when he keeps calling John's Gospel a "life of Christ." In a very narrow compass he refers to it as "the fourth Life of Jesus Christ," "a fourth life of Christ," "a new *Vita Jesu*," " a new sketch of the life of Jesus," and "a new legitimate and orthodox exposition of the history of Jesus" (*The Historical Jesus in the Gospel of St John* [1967], pp. 28f.).

64. *Didache* 8:2; 15:3.

65. Cf. A. M. Hunter, "It is not unjustified to speak of some sort of Johannine 'Q.' " in *According to John* (1968), p. 22.

66. *JBL* 89 (1970), pp. 38–55. In another article, "St. Luke and the Johannine Tradition" (*JBL* 90 [1971], pp. 422–450), he argues that "the Lukan agreements with John against both Matthew and Mark may have been due to Luke's familiarity with some form of the developing Johannine tradition or even to his acquaintance with an early draft of the original Gospel of John" (ibid., pp. 426f.).

67. Op. cit., chapter IX. He has a long list of scholars who have dated this Gospel early (ibid., pp. 307f., n. 218).

68. Ibid., p. 308.

69. D. M. Smith, in an article entitled, "The Sources of the Gospel of John: An Assessment of the Present State of the Problem," published in *NTS* 10 (1963–64), pp. 336–351, concluded, "So it is now possible to speak of a loose, but real, consensus regarding a Johannine tradition relatively independent of the synoptics, a typically Johannine preaching (found especially in the discourses of the gospel and in the First Epistle), and the fundamentally Semitic and even Jewish character and background of this traditional preaching" (op. cit., p. 351). Smith is not arguing for a position anything like mine, but I find his stress on preaching (and the Jewishness of this Gospel) noteworthy.

70. Cf. Robinson, "In fact ironically it is the *lack* of final redaction to which the evidence most powerfully points. The faulty connections and self-corrections do not of themselves argue a multiplicity of hands. They merely show that what was first written, perhaps very early, as homiletic and apologetic material for various occasions has still not at the end been knit into a seamless robe" (op. cit., p. 310).

71. Op. cit., pp. 308f. Robinson also finds in the work of scholars "self-created *aporiai*, or perplexities, in Johannine studies which seem to me so much more baffling than the breaks and discontinuities at which the critics balk." He points out that Brown sees the beloved disciple as the apostle John but not as the author of this Gospel, while Cullmann sees him as the evangelist but not as the son of Zebedee. He goes on, "I believe that both men are right in what they assert and wrong in what they deny" (ibid., p. 310). By contrast with Robinson, D. M. Smith thinks that "efforts to show the traditional character of substantial portions of the Johannine discourses, or of their form, have made it increasingly difficult to think of explaining them as though they were the creations of the mind of a single theological genius" (*NTS* 21 [1974–75], p. 231). With all respect to a distinguished scholar, he does seem to be limiting what a large mind can produce.

72. For reasons for thinking of John as the author may I refer to my *The Gospel according to John* (1971), pp. 8–30, and *Studies in the Fourth Gospel* (1969), chapter 4.

12: The Centripetal Philosophy of Mission

DAVID W. WEAD

The rise and growth of the early Church has always presented some sort of puzzle to scholars and the average reader of the Book of Acts. All sources point to the fact that the early Church would take the message of the Messiah to the world. Jesus had commanded it. We have the record of his Great Commission no less than four times if we count the questionable passage at the ending of Mark. While the details of the commission differ, they agree that the message of the new salvation was to be carried to the entire world.[1] Yet the church seemed to have remained in the city of Jerusalem.

The problem develops because the Church did not enter into the full-scale Gentile mission for many years. The picture we are normally given from Acts is not only that the Church remained centered in Jerusalem but that its leadership was indeed suspicious of any successful evangelism outside of that city (e.g., the deputation sent to Samaria in Acts 8).

Many scholars believe the first great impetus for the Church to spread beyond the borders of Judea was the persecution surrounding Stephen and that this impetus came only to the Hellenistic factions within the Church.[2] This persecution caused the spread of the gospel to areas around Damascus and then beyond to Antioch. Often we are led to picture this persecution as a divine intervention by God to force the Church out of its center into the world.[3] The persecution comes very near to being divine punishment upon the Church for its failure to fulfill the divine commission to bear the message of Christianity to the world. This persecution caused the Church to begin to understand the mission that God would have for it within the world. Thus as a result of the persecution of Stephen and the consequent relocation of Christians, the Church began its divinely intended program of outreach.

In many ways this view is unfair to the early Church. It is unfair

176

because it overlooks the fact that there were two philosophies of world mission within the early Church. There is the "centrifugal" system which most have come to emphasize. This system pictures the message as being forced out from the center in the same manner as spinning the centrifuge forces all away from its center. Indeed, some believe this is the only philosophy of world evangelism. In fact, it is the later-developing of the two and was almost non-existent in the earliest period of the Church. In this system the message is borne by "missionaries" who were sent out from Jerusalem first and then from other important mission centers with the express purpose of bearing the message of Christ to a heathen world. They radiated from a mission center. The missionary journeys of Paul (especially the second and third) are examples of this approach, though we can be sure that Peter and others were also involved in this sort of missionary endeavor and perhaps before Paul began his labors.[4] This method is still alive within the Church in the second century as recorded in *Didache* 11:3–6.

The second philosophy, the centripetal, represented by the forces of gravity, represents men as being drawn to the center of the Church in Jerusalem and then in turn being sent back to their own people to bear the message of Christ so that their own people might be converted. In magnetic terms it is related to attraction, although the concept includes the return of those taught to bear the message to their own. While this method is not as spectacular as the centrifugal system, we would submit that it is the probable source of most of the important and lasting missionary endeavor within the earliest Church. Paul indicates that the Roman church was probably founded in this way.[5] We have no record of a single missionary being sent from Jerusalem leading in the establishment of such Christian centers as Antioch or Alexandria. Moreover, when missionaries did come to a new city, they often found other Christians with whom they might work and with whom they might live and who had been actively evangelizing their community.[6]

In this essay we wish to explore the causes of this centripetal philosophy of mission within the early Church and the effects that it had upon the accounts that we find within the first half of the Book of Acts. While the second half of Acts might emphasize the centrifugal method, it is evident from this study that the centripetal philosophy is most evident within the first chapters of the book.

1. The Prophetic Ideal of Missions

The leadership of the earliest Church saw the Church as the fulfillment of the prophecies of the Old Testament.[7] The Book of

Acts leaves little question of this. Luke pictures the disciples asking about the restoration of the Kingdom (Acts 1:6), showing a consciousness that the crucial time for the fulfillment of the messianic prophecies were present. Peter's action to replace the deceased Judas also comes from a conscious need to fulfill the prophetic character of the Old Testament (Acts 1:15–20). The Pentecost experience of the Church is explained in terms of the Joel prophecy (Acts 2:16) in the same way that Peter refers to David's prophecy of Jesus' death and resurrection (Acts 2:25–28).

In several places within the Old Testament we read the expectation that the light of Judaism will be borne to the Gentiles. The *locus classicus* of this concept is undoubtedly the famous passage from Isaiah 2, which is used almost verbatim in Micah 4:

> In days to come
> the mountain of the Lord's house
> shall be set over all other mountains,
> lifted high above the hills.
> All nations shall come streaming to it,
> and many peoples shall come and say,
> "Come, let us climb up on to the mountain of the Lord,
> to the house of the God of Jacob,
> that he may teach us his ways
> and we may walk in his paths."
> For instruction issues from Zion,
> and out of Jerusalem comes the word of the Lord;
> he will be judge between nations,
> arbiter among many peoples (Isa 2:2–4a; Mic 4:1–3a, NEB).

The prophets clearly state that the nations from afar shall be drawn to the Holy City, where they will be instructed in the Word of God which shall flow from Jerusalem.

The servant songs of Isaiah which were so important to the early Church in their understanding of the prophetic role of the Christ are also a vital factor in this theology. Isa 42:4 says that "the islands wait for his teaching." The second song is addressed to "peoples from afar" and concludes with the words "therefore I make you a light to the nations that my salvation may reach to the ends of the earth" (Isa 49:6). Likewise the fourth song opens with an indication that the message of the servant shall be carried unto the nations (Isa 52:15).

These prophecies seem to reach a climax in Isaiah 60, with its description of the coming of the light of Yahweh's salvation to Israel. Verses 4–7 and 8–9 give us two descriptions of the nations from afar coming to Israel or Zion. The salvation of the Lord draws them so that they might be enlightened. They in turn enrich Israel. The passage following (Isa 60:10–22) tells of the effects of the new state of salvation upon the nation, Israel.[8]

Another key passage is found near the end of the prophecy of Isaiah. Chapter 66:18–19 reads:

> For I know their works and their thoughts, and I am coming to gather all nations and tongues; and they shall come and shall see my glory, and I will set a sign among them. And from them I will send survivors to the nations, to Tarshish, Put, and Lud, who draw the bow, to Tubal and Javan, to the coastlands afar off, that have not heard my fame or seen my glory; and they shall declare my glory among the nations (RSV).

The projection is clear as to how the message of the Lord will be carried to all nations. The influx of foreigners to the city of Jerusalem is the key. They shall see the glory of the Lord and then be sent back to their native lands that they might teach their own nation what they have seen and heard. The key word of the passage is *peléytim*, variously translated as "survivors" or "fugitives." The root underlying the term refers to those who have been delivered or those who have escaped. The LXX translation is significant here. In place of saying, "I will send those who have survived," it says, "I will send those who have been saved (*sesōsmenous*) unto the nations." This version which became so important for the early Church clearly says that the bearers of the message to the world will be those who have come to Jerusalem and have become a part of the salvation of God.

In commenting on this passage the German theologian Claus Westermann notes:

> This is the first sure and certain mention of mission as we today employ the term—the sending of individuals to distant people in order to proclaim God's glory among them. This completely corresponds to the mission of the apostles when the church first began. One is amazed at it: here, just as the Old Testament is coming to its end, God's way is already seen as leading from the narrow confines of the chosen people out into the wide, whole world. The annihilation of all the other nations in a great world-judgment— no, this is not the final word. But equally, it is not that they all journey to Zion and are absorbed into the community there. The final thing is the way taken by the word, borne by the messengers of his glory, to the peoples who are not Israel, all the nations of the world. This not only agrees with what Deutero-Isaiah said in 45:20–25. It also agrees with the places in the servant songs where the Servant is appointed, to be a light to the Gentiles, and is destined to bring God's justice to them. There can be no doubt about it: the people who tell the tidings of God's glory are also characterized as witnesses. As those saved from a castastrophe (the "survivors") and, as saved, having experienced that Yahweh is God, they go to those who have not seen or heard. As his witnesses they can be made into people who proclaim his glory among the nations.[9]

The completed picture shows Diaspora Jews and Gentiles being drawn to Jerusalem, being converted, and then returning to their own people with the message they have received. While we do not find indication from the passages that the converts must return to their own countries, we do find this in each of the examples that we will explore in the early chapters of Acts.

This picture of the centripetal philosophy of missions is much different from that which scholars normally conceive. For instance, Michael Green pictures the prophecies as merely drawing the Gentiles to Jerusalem. Because he does not come to the full conception of their return to their own people, it is easy for him to be convinced that this first philosophy was virtually ineffective. Thus he says:

> In all the passages of the Old Testament without exception in which reference is made to the eschatological pilgrimage of the Gentiles, the goal of the pilgrimage is the scene of God's revelation of himself, Zion, the holy mountain of God. From this it is to be inferred that the movement is always thought of as "centripetal". The Gentiles will not be evangelized where they dwell but will be summoned to the holy mount by the divine epiphany.[10]

Thus Green overlooks the Isaiah 66 passage and does not consider the Gentile mission of the Church as developing out of the process by which the Gentiles are drawn to Jerusalem. When one does not look at the full prophetic picture, it is easy to miss the point of the strategy of the Church. Thus Green can conclude: "The Jewish Christians were mistaken in their hope that Israel would turn to Christ en masse, that the Gentiles would be attracted to Zion and that God's kingdom would be established in that way."[11] Only as one sees the twofold expectation of the centripetal approach does one see the actions of the Church in the Book of Acts clearly.

Equally important is the way the Pentecost passage of Acts 2 recalls the prophecy of Isa 66:18–19. In Acts 2:8–11 we have the curious listing of the nations who are gathered in Jerusalem, showing that they had come from every nation under heaven:

> How is it then that we hear them, each of us in his own native language? Parthians, Medes, Elamites; inhabitants of Mesopotamia, of Judaea and Cappadocia, of Pontus and Asia, of Phrygia and Pamphylia, of Egypt and the districts of Libya around Cyrene; visitors from Rome, both Jews and proselytes, Cretans and Arabs, we hear them telling in our own tongues the great things God has done.

This passage is strikingly parallel to that list of nations which we find in Isa 66:18–19. The close parallel seems to show that to the early Christians the miracle of Pentecost was not only that each man heard in his own language but that this event was also understood as the beginning of the Gentile mission as it appeared in the prophecy of the Old Testament.

This gives us insight into the Church's understanding of God's means of fulfilling the Great Commission. Pentecost was not only intended to be the time when myriads of believing Jews should receive baptism and the Holy Spirit; it was also the impetus for the beginning of the world mission of the Church. At this time those present from many nations of the world would see "signs." From those who had been saved, men would come who would return to their own people with the message of Christ's salvation. A good share of the Church's reticence to move into the world in a "missionary" manner came from their desire to live within the prophetic ideal of God. They believed that it was God's will that his message should be spread to the lands of the world by natives from those lands who came to Jerusalem, were taught, and then returned. Thus the leaders of the Church were in a sense forced to remain within the city so that they might be there to instruct those who came to the city and there received the word.

This goes a long way toward an explanation as to why the apostles felt the need to leave their homeland, Galilee, to make the center of their activity Jerusalem when Jesus had spent so little time in that city. They chose Jerusalem because the prophecies of the Old Testament directed them to that city. The nations of the world would come there for instruction. It also shows why the Scripture should note that they remained there even in time of persecution (Acts 8:3). For the centripetal philosophy of mission, Jerusalem was the key. This also explains to a certain extent why churches established later looked to Jerusalem as their mother church and gave her reverence as the source of their instruction and turned to her in time of trouble.[12]

2. The Development of the Centripetal Mission Philosophy

Within the life of the early Jewish Church there developed two classes of people: Hebrews and Hellenists. These distinctions originally referred to the native languages of the people, though the differences soon became much deeper. The Hebrew-speaking Jews were largely native to Palestine. Galileans were included within this group. The apostolate and the main leadership of the earliest Church were Hebrew-speaking Jewish Christians. To the non-Christian Jew they seemed much more compatible with Judaism than the Hellenists and thus were less violently persecuted.

The Hellenistic Jewish Christian was most noteworthy because he

claimed Greek as his native language. Like Paul, he had probably
been born in an environment outside Palestine but of parents who
were strongly Jewish. Large numbers of these Diaspora Jews lived in
Palestine for one reason or another. Even greater numbers apparently
made regular trips to the Holy City and the temple. Large numbers of
them also became Christians. They developed some theological dis-
tinctives. The major thrust of their theological divergences came in
relation to their depreciation of the worth of the temple.[13] This one
item made them chief subjects of the first major persecution that
arose within the Church (Acts 7 and 8) and caused their scattering.

They fit the prophetic type of Isaiah 66 admirably. Usually they
were born outside of Jerusalem. They had been drawn to the city for
some reason, perhaps education or worship. When they were converted, they often returned to their own people to make the message
of Christ known to their own.

F. F. Bruce is undoubtedly right in calling the Hellenists the
missionaries of the early Church.[14] The passage that describes the
persecution surrounding Stephen (Acts 8:1–3) declares that all except the disciples were scattered abroad. We then move on to examine the evangelistic work of Philip, another Hellenist. His work in
Samaria and with the Ethiopian Eunuch become the thrust of the
eighth chapter of Acts. When one considers that Paul and Barnabas
were also Hellenists, we can understand how nearly all of the Book
of Acts from this point deals with the work of the Hellenists.

Much of the effectiveness of the Hellenists seems to have come
from their ability to return to their homelands to evangelize there.
While the prophecy is not explicit in sending those saved back to
their own people, it is evident that this became the understanding of
the Church. We do not know Philip's homeland, but we do know
that he was living in the same area with his four virgin daughters
twenty years later (Acts 21:8–10). After Paul's conversion and his
study in Arabia, he came to Jerusalem. Very soon it became necessary for him to leave town because of the pressures upon his life. He
went back to his home country of Cilicia and Tarsus. We receive
indication that he preached the gospel there to his own people (Acts
9:30) until called by Barnabas to work in Antioch (Acts 11:25).

Even when the Spirit of God called Paul and Barnabas to a
special mission work, they did not violate the principles of returning
to their own homeland. The first missionary team sailed from
Seleucia to Cyprus, the homeland of their head man, Barnabas. The
major part of their work was done in that island nation. It was not
until they determined to leave Cyprus for the mainland of Asia

Minor that we seem to move beyond the principle of centripetal mission.

At that point John Mark leaves the group. Perhaps there is more than the usual speculations of homesickness involved in this departure.[15] Perhaps the departure reveals a philosophical difference among the missionary party. It is quite possible that John Mark withdrew because he felt that he was overstepping the biblical bounds of his personal mission by leaving the native land of Barnabas. This possibility is magnified when we see that Paul and Barnabas have such a serious dispute following the Jerusalem Council that they go separate ways. The dispute centered around John Mark, who had left them when they left Barnabas' native Cyprus (Acts 15:36–39). Now Barnabas not only desires to take him once more, but when Paul will not consent we find that Barnabas and Mark leave for Barnabas' native Cyprus to do their evangelistic work. Paul also leaves for his native land, Cilicia, at this point (Acts 15:40–41), though he was also bearing the decrees of the Jerusalem Council to those churches. He remained there only briefly, but we cannot overlook that his confirmation of the churches also meant that he was returning to the areas of his labor in his homeland.

The account of the conversion of the Ethiopian Eunuch found in Acts 8:26ff. must be considered an example or a paradigm showing how the early Church expected the gospel to be carried to the world. A pious man, probably not a proselyte because of his status as a eunuch, has journeyed to Jerusalem to worship God.[16] On his return the Spirit of God leads Philip to him. He is converted when Philip shows him that the prophecy of Isaiah points to Jesus Christ. Luke undoubtedly included the story to show that the man then went on his way rejoicing to tell the message he had taken to his heart within his home country. He is one of many who returned to their home countries and there began the proclamation in a very unspectacular way. In this way the message went to the world and Christianity spread.

The Hellenists provided the first major step in this program because there were numbers of them in Palestine with close contacts to their native countries. There were no obstacles of culture and language in their presentations. Most often they needed no financial support to carry out their missions as they did it in conjunction with their regular livelihoods. They continued what they were doing and preached Christ in connection with it. They were able to move back into their own societies and had immediate contacts through their families, friends, and business associates.

Those who were converted could do nothing but establish an indigenous church. When a man returned to his own country with the new message, he soon made converts among his own people. These converts usually had little training and no official standing. They became local congregations with very little outside connection. There were usually no foreigners involved. Even in cases later in Paul's missionary journeys where he had a supervisory relationship, we see the remarkable speed with which Paul moved to set up local governing organization within the congregation (Acts 14:21–23). In times of dispute as within the Corinthian church, Paul would rather have the local governing body make the decision than for them to rely upon his apostolic authority. In areas where there was no apostle (e.g., the early Roman church and, we may presume, Ethiopia), the Christians must have proceeded to establish their own independent local organizations and leadership, probably relying heavily upon the person who originally brought the message into their area.[17]

This goes a long way toward explaining the role of the house church in the developing Church.[18] When a new Christian returned to his homeland, he would most naturally invite those who were converted or were inquirers to his home for worship. As the group of Christians grew, larger homes would be used as centers for worship. Growth would also mean that other homes would become centers for Christian activity as the need arose.

3. Conclusion

We might ask ourselves why this philosophy of world mission seemed to fade from the scene. First and most important, centripetal mission in its purest prophetic sense flourished in direct relation to the importance of the church in the city of Jerusalem. The prophetic base necessitated this. When the church in the city of Jerusalem was strong, the philosophy was viable. When it began to lose its importance because of the political situation within Palestine and because of the rise of other strong centers of Christianity, then the practicality of this approach to world mission decreased. When the Church finally had to flee the city of Jerusalem, the possibility of this approach in its strictest sense ceased to be a possibility.

In addition, with the growth of other centers of Christianity and the spread of its leadership, it ceased to be necessary to send people all the way back to Jerusalem for a proper understanding. With the apostolic leadership removed, an appeal to their authority would come through appeals to their present residence. Neither did many of those converted to the message of Christ find the center of their conversion the city of the mother church but other commercial and educational centers of the world. These people would not see the necessity of returning to the Holy City for their inquiries or the settlement of their problems. The growth of the Church as well as the demise of the Jerusalem church would require that the Church move to other approaches to their task of worldwide mission.

However, our study leads us to make some observations on the Great Commission in light of the centripetal understanding of world mission. Matthew's record of this command is: "Go forth therefore and make all nations my disciples; baptize men everywhere in the name of the Father and the Son and the Holy Spirit and teach them to observe all that I have commanded you" (Matt 28:19–20a, NEB). In the passage there are four verb forms: three participles, *poreuthentes, baptizontes,* and *didaskontes;* and one finite verb, *mathēteusate.* The grammar of the sentence demands that the finite verb (*mathēteusate*) carry the major thrust of the sentence, while the participles must be seen in relation to it. Especially the first of these participles (*poreuthentes,* for "go") is normally translated as an imperative. While such a translation is legitimate under certain circumstances,[19] any exegesis of the passage cannot lose sight of the fact that Jesus' basic command was not to "go" but to "make disciples." All other functions in the commission are subordinate to it.

The centripetal philosophy of mission places the emphasis here. It is evident that the compulsion was on making disciples. The "going" was incidental to it. This earliest missions philosophy of the Church correctly placed the emphasis upon discipleship rather than on being thrust into a new environment for the purpose of evangelism.

NOTES

1. G. B. Caird, *The Apostolic Age* (1966), pp. 50–51, 108–109.
2. D. M. Stanley, "Kingdom to Church, The Structural Development of Apostolic Christianity in the New Testament," *Th Stud* 16 (1955), p. 16.
3. Caird, *Apostolic Age,* p. 90.
4. L. Goppelt, *Apostolic and Post Apostolic Times* (1970), p. 35.
5. Rom 1:11; 15:20.
6. Note the way that Paul found Priscilla and Aquila in Corinth and proceeded to live with them and work with them (Acts 18:1–3).
7. C. H. Dodd, *The Apostolic Preaching and Its Development* (1936), p. 47.
8. C. Westermann, *Isaiah 40–66* (1969), p. 356.
9. Ibid., p. 425.
10. M. Green, *Evangelism in the Early Church* (1970), p. 271.
11. Ibid., p. 425.

12. On the relationship of earliest Christianity to the Jerusalem church see Goppelt, *Apostolic Times*, pp. 68–70. It seems significant that the early Christians would feel such an allegiance to their mother church that they would return to it for a definitive answer (Acts 15) rather than just going their own way. This problem of the relation of the Church to its origins is considered in a significant manner in H. von Campenhausen, *Tradition and Life in the Church* (1968), pp. 13–15.

13. Goppelt, *Apostolic Times*, pp. 52–54, 61–68; F. F. Bruce, *New Testament History* (1969), pp. 217–225.

14. Bruce, *New Testament History*, p. 227.

15. R. Allen, *Missionary Methods: St. Paul's or Ours?* (1962), pp. 10–11.

16. F. F. Bruce, *Commentary on The Book of Acts* (1968), p. 187.

17. H. Turlington, "Paul's Missionary Practice," *Rev Ex* 51 (1954), p. 169.

18. F. V. Filson, "The Significance of the Early House Churches," *JBL* 58 (1939), pp. 105–112.

19. C. F. D. Moule, *An Idiom Book of New Testament Greek* (1968), pp. 179–180.

III. Interpretation

13: The Holy Spirit's Role in Biblical Interpretation

DANIEL P. FULLER

There have been some in the history of the Church who have insisted that the proper understanding of a passage in the Bible is gained only by those who go beyond the wording of the text and seek the illumination that the Holy Spirit provides. For example, Origen (185–254 A.D.), in his *De Principiis*, part iv, argued for this by affirming that the biblical spokesmen wrote under the inspiration of the Holy Spirit. Therefore, the interpreter will miss the meaning of a scripture text unless he, like its human writer, is taught by the Holy Spirit. He will surely miss the text's meaning if he construes it merely from the way the writer used words. So Origen urged people to go beyond a text's historical-grammatical data: "Let us do our utmost endeavor, by abandoning the language of the elements of Christ, which are but the first beginnings of wisdom, to go on to perfection, in order that the wisdom which is given to the perfect may be given to us also" (iv.7). According to Origen, this involved seeking the "spiritual" rather than the literal meaning of a biblical passage: "Now the reason for the erroneous apprehension of all these points . . . is no other than this, that the Holy Scripture is not understood according to its spiritual but according to its literal meaning" (iv.9).

It is well known how Origen, despite his firm belief in the inspiration of the Bible, greatly distorted its intended meaning through his hermeneutical conviction that the proper understanding of Scripture could be gained only through a direct illumination of the Holy Spirit. It was this conviction which led him to allegorize the Bible. For Luther, the rejection of Origen's allegorization was essential for bringing the Church back under the authority of the Bible.

St. Jerome and St. Origen, God forgive them, were the cause that allegories were held in such esteem. But Origen altogether is not worth one word of

189

Christ. Now I have shaken off all these follies, and my best art is to deliver the Scripture in the simple sense. . . .[1]

C. H. Mackintosh, a Plymouth Brethren writer of the last century, provides a more recent example of one who sought the meaning of a Bible passage through the illumination of the Holy Spirit. Regarding the typological interpretation of the details of the tabernacle as outlined in the latter part of Exodus, Mackintosh said,

> Nature can do nothing here. Reason is blind. . . . The most gigantic intellect, instead of being able to interpret the sacred symbols, appears like a bat in the sunshine, blindly dashing itself against the objects which it is utterly unable to discern. We must compel reason and imagination to stand without. . . . God the Holy Spirit is the One Who can . . . expound to our souls the true meaning of all that meets our view. . . . The One who furnished the beauteous symbols [of the tabernacle] can alone interpret them.[2]

The problem with this understanding of the role of the Holy Spirit in biblical interpretation is that the words of the text can play no essential role in conveying its intended meaning, even though it is these very words which the writers were inspired to use in transmitting God's message to men. According to 1 Cor 2:13, biblical spokesmen uttered the divine message "not in words taught by human wisdom, but in words taught by the Holy Spirit."

In the next verse, however, Paul adds, "The natural man receives not the things of the spirit of God, for they are foolishness to him: neither can he know them, because they are spiritually discerned" (1 Cor 2:14). In other words, the message which Paul and others were inspired to transmit can be "received" and "known" only by those who are indwelt by the Holy Spirit. Obviously, then, the Holy Spirit does play an indispensable role in enabling the interpreter to gain the proper meaning of a biblical text. But what is his role? And how does this role urge the exegete always to acknowledge his complete dependence on the Holy Spirit, and at the same time urge him to develop his skill in using valid exegetical means to determine the meanings that were intended by the words which the Holy Spirit inspired the biblical writer to use? We commence our answer to this question by examining 1 Cor 2:14 more closely.

1. Interpreting 1 Cor 2:14

We note that *dechomai* rather than *lambanō* is the Greek word for "receive" in the statement, "The natural man receives not the things of the spirit of God." Whereas *lambanō* means "simply to receive something," *dechomai* means to "accept some requested offering willingly and with pleasure, either because one accepts it with gratefulness and eagerness for himself, or for the purpose of helping and supporting someone else."[3] So in the statement, "The natural man does not receive [*dechomai*] the things of the spirit of God," the meaning is that apart from the Holy Spirit, a person does not accept what the Bible teaches with pleasure, willingness, and eagerness. In other words, the natural man does not *welcome* the things of the Spirit of God.

This refusal to welcome the teachings of the Bible hardly excludes, however, the natural man's having a *cognition* of what he repudiates. To the contrary, the fact that he experiences a revulsion against a biblical teaching presupposes a prior cognition of that teaching, for how can a man hate something without having some knowledge of it?

Likewise, in affirming that "spiritual things are foolishness to the natural man," the meaning is not that biblical teachings are unintelligible, as things spoken in some unknown language would be. Foolishness applies more appropriately to what is understood and yet regarded as false. So when Festus, after hearing Paul's defense in Acts 26:4–23, replies in verse 24, "Paul, you are mad," it is more appropriate to understand this as a response to what Festus understood than to something that was unintelligible. Ernst Haenchen, in commenting on Acts 26:24, says, "Festus must surely have had a surprisingly good understanding of what Paul had been saying, in order to have been able thus to deny the teaching of the resurrection."[4]

First Corinthians 2:14 continues, "Neither can the natural man *know* the things of the spirit of God, because they are spiritually discerned." If this "know" meant "have cognition," then this verse would mean that until regeneration, biblical teachings remain unintelligible. The word for "know" here is *ginōskō,* and it can be used in the sense of *oida,* which in the present tense can represent the idea of mere perception or cognition.[5] But in general, *ginōskō* means not merely perceiving, but "embracing things as they really are."[6] If *ginōskō* is used in this sense, the second half of 1 Cor 2:14 would mean, "The natural man does not embrace the realities represented by the Bible's teachings," and this would be a close parallel to the earlier statement that "the natural man does not *welcome* spiritual things."

At the end of the verse Paul gives the reason that the natural man does not "know" spiritual things: "because they are spiritually discerned." The Greek word for "discerned" is *anakinō,* and it represents an investigative action carried on for the purpose of rendering an appraisal or evaluation. Not being indwelt by the Holy Spirit, the natural man has no ability to see the worth, or value, of biblical teachings; and this is why he does not "know" them. One's inability to welcome spiritual things is supported more aptly by affirming that he cannot evaluate them than by affirming that he cannot even have cognition of them. Therefore, we conclude that the words "cannot know" in 1 Cor 2:14 mean "cannot have an experiential knowledge and appreciation" of the biblical message.

Consequently, the Holy Spirit's role in biblical interpretation does not consist in giving the interpreter cognition of what the Bible is saying, which would involve dispensing additional information, beyond the historical-grammatical data that are already there for everyone to work with. Rather, the Holy Spirit's role is to change the heart of the interpreter, so that he loves the message that is conveyed by nothing more than the historical-grammatical data.

Accordingly, the biblical interpreter does not look to the Holy Spirit to give him the meaning of a biblical text. Instead, he must expend just as much time and energy developing his exegetical skills and applying them to the hard work of understanding a text as others do who seek to determine the intended meanings of some group of ancient texts.

But because the Bible's view of reality clashes with the way people, apart from the work of the Holy Spirit, want to see things, its message will therefore be regarded as foolishness. Naturally, the conclusion that the Bible is foolishness will not affect the accuracy of the exegetical results of those whose only concern is the academic task of describing what the biblical writers intended to teach. An agnostic or an atheist, whose concern is simply to set forth, say, a description of Pauline thought, can make a lasting contribution to this subject, if he has achieved a high degree of exegetical skill. Krister Stendahl argues that

> once we confine ourselves to the task of descriptive biblical theology as a field in its own right, the material itself gives us means to check whether our interpretation is correct or not. . . . Our only concern is to find out what these words meant when uttered or written by the prophet, the priest, the evangelist, or the apostle—and regardless of their meaning in later stages of religious history, our own included.

Therefore, Stendahl continues,

> Both [agnostics and believers] can work side by side, since no other tools are called for than those of description in the terms indicated by the texts themselves. The meaning for the present—in which the two interpreters are different—is not involved, and part of their mutual criticism is to watch

whether concern for meaning or distaste for meaning colors the descriptions where it should not.[7]

But the situation changes radically when one carries on the task of descriptive biblical theology not as an end in itself, but because one is convinced that the biblical message has value for his and others' lives. Since the meaning uttered by the prophet, priest, evangelist, or apostle will be regarded by all who are unregenerated as foolishness, those who nevertheless regard the Bible as having potential for great value will proceed to modify its meanings so they become palatable. Such hermeneutical gambits as demythologizing, or interpreting a passage of the Bible from some religious a priori, or interpreting one biblical passage in the terms of another—these are some of the ways people commonly justify modifying the meaning of a text that would stand simply by letting its pertinent historical-grammatical data speak for themselves. We need now to consider why the unmodified meanings of the biblical spokesmen are foolishness to the unregenerate person.

2. The Offense of the Biblical Message

One way the biblical message may be understood as foolishness is to say that it is absurd from the standpoint of every mode of thinking that is possible to the human mind. As Søren Kierkegaard, the most radical spokesman for this alternative, put it, "The absurd is—that the eternal truth has come into being in time, that God has come into being, has been born, has grown up, and so forth precisely like any other individual human being. . . ."[8] No attempt must be made, Kierkegaard argued, to reduce the absurdity of the Christian message, for then the message would become what someone could *know.* But to the extent that something becomes intelligible and therefore capable of being known, "it is impossible to *believe.* For the absurd is the object of faith, and the only object that can be believed."[9]

Although Karl Barth, after the 1920s, ceased to use Kierkegaard's categories, he has emphasized that the message of the gospel is based "only on the power of God with its self-justifying wisdom," and that the wise "are simply those who accept the Word of the Cross by faith" (*Church Dogmatics,* II/1, p. 437). This understanding of the nature of the biblical message disconnects it from any categories—such as inner coherence, and common ground bases for argument—in which human thinking could detect evidence for regarding it as true. In support of this view, Barth points to Paul's statements in 1 Cor 2:1, 4 that he did not employ "excellency of speech or of wisdom" or "persuasive words of man's wisdom" (II/1, p. 436). Consequently, Paul "must be content with . . . the self-justification of divine wisdom in the face of all the folly of men . . ." (II/1, p. 438).

But there is evidence that "persuasive words of man's wisdom" was a phrase used to denote the distinctive rhetorical style of Greek orators.[10] So in using this phrase, Paul wanted to deny that his purpose in preaching at Corinth was to acquire a following of those admiring his rhetorical prowess. As Leon Morris puts it, "Paul insists that preaching with *wisdom of words* was no part of his commission. . . . A reliance on rhetoric would cause men to trust in men, the very antithesis of what the preaching of the cross is meant to effect."[11] Paul's aim in preaching was to persuade his hearers to worship God and stop glorying in men, and so he avoided an oratorical style which would have implied that he was seeking men's praise.

But if we understand "not with excellency of speech or wisdom" and "not with persuasive words of man's wisdom" (1 Cor 2:1, 4) in this way, then Paul's description in these verses of how he preached at Corinth does not clash with Luke's description of it in Acts 18:4. There Luke says that Paul "argued [*dialogizomai*] in the synagogues every sabbath, and persuaded [*peithō*] Jews and Greeks." And in Luke's understanding, the use of coherency and the appeal to common ground, which is implied in the verbs for "argued" and "persuaded," characterized Paul's preaching both before he came to Corinth (Acts 9:22; 13:16–41, esp. vv. 23, 27, where the argument from fulfilled prophecy is used for a Jewish audience; 17:2–3; and at Mars Hill in Athens, 17:22–31, esp. v. 31), and after he left (Acts 19:8–9; 24:24–25; and 26:26 with its obvious appeal to common ground). All these affirmations that Paul, in his preaching, reasoned with men and based arguments on ground shared in common with his hearers bodes ill for the supposition that the gospel is foolishness in that its message involves categories from which the human mind can make no sense.

But if Paul's preaching did appeal to reason (coherence, and an appeal to common ground) without conforming to a style of oratory used for gaining the praise of men, then another way of understanding his message as foolishness presents itself. Precisely because its message is so comprehensible and yet collides head-on with people's deep-seated desire to exult in themselves, men reject it and seek to justify this by regarding it as foolishness.

There is considerable evidence in the first four chapters of 1

Corinthians to support this way of understanding the gospel as foolishness. Surely Paul emphasizes that the Christian message allows no room for boasting in one's own person or accomplishments. "No flesh should boast before the Lord"; but rather, "He who boasts, let him boast in the Lord" (1:29, 31). The same point is brought out in 3:18–21, where the shift from the wisdom of men to the foolishness of God, or (from another viewpoint) from the folly of men to the wisdom of God, is equated with ceasing to glory in men. It is quite understandable how those who would not relinquish the pleasure of exulting in themselves would find it most convenient to justify their rejection of the Christian message by denouncing it as foolishness.

There is also evidence from Paul's own words in these early chapters of 1 Corinthians that, as Luke indicated in Acts 18:4, Paul's preaching at Corinth was designed to persuade men by an appeal to reason. For one thing, that Paul termed his message as *wisdom* (1:24, 30; 2:6) indicates that he regarded it as possessing those qualities that affirmations must have in order to be termed "wisdom" without transgressing language conventions. Paul's train of thought in 1 Cor 4:6f. reveals a concern for coherence and for argumentation based on common ground—matters that properly belong to what "wisdom" should represent. In verse 6 Paul enjoins the Corinthians "not to be puffed up one against the other." Then in verse 7 he provides an argument for why one is well advised to obey this enjoinder. He calls attention to the fact that anyone's possession, ability, or accomplishment is his only as a gift. "What have you," Paul queries, "which you did not receive as a gift?" The obvious answer is "Nothing," and it is significant that Paul expects his hearers to agree with this, not because he, as an apostle, is a purveyor of special revelation which men ought to believe just because God said it. To the contrary, people should agree with it because its truth is evident to anyone who will reflect on the way things are.

Some might object, however, that they now deserve to enjoy their "good life" because they have not been slothful like so many others, but have worked hard to achieve the standard of living they now enjoy. But as Deut 8:18 says, "You shall remember that it is the Lord your God who gave you the power to get wealth." To be sure, energy, ambition, and intelligence are essential for getting into high-paying vocations. But where do these components for the power to get wealth come from? Obviously, no one has these because he willed them. In the last analysis, they are given and not chosen. So even the power to get wealth belongs to people only as a gift for which they can take no credit.

The knowledge of this fact is available to anyone who will face up to reality. In that it has a claim to universality, it constitutes ground shared in common with all people who are willing to be reasonable. Consequently, the conclusion which Paul draws from this fact, set forth in the last rhetorical question of 1 Cor 4:7, is inescapable. It is that to boast about anything one is or has is nonsensical.

But this highly reasonable conclusion collides head-on with our deep-seated desire to glory in ourselves. If this desire is not replaced with a desire to exult in God, we will reject this reasoning as foolishness, and justify our rejection of it by adhering to some delusion. And what we do with the argument of 1 Cor 4:6f., we will do to other parts of the Bible.

Everywhere one turns in Scripture he encounters the assertion that he ought not to glory in himself but in God, the giver of every good gift. "The haughtiness of man shall be humbled, and the pride of men shall be brought low, and the Lord alone shall be exalted in that day" (Isa 2:17). Jesus pointed to the ego as the crux of whether or not people would glorify God by trusting him. "How can you believe, who receive glory from one another and do not seek the glory that comes from the only true God?" (John 5:44).

Apart from regeneration, however, men do not welcome the reasonableness of the teaching that fulfillment for their deepest yearnings comes from delighting in God's goodness by trusting his promises and thereby rendering him honor. People prefer instead to accomplish things that supposedly provide reasons for delighting in how much they can trust themselves.

In answering the question, "What is happiness?" Spinoza declared, "Joy consists in this, that one's power is increased"; and Nietzsche replied that it is "the feeling that power increases, that resistance is overcome."[12] Heinrich Harrer, a member of the first team to climb the beetle-browed north face of the Eiger in the Swiss Alps, confessed that his reason for undertaking such a risk was to overcome a sense of insecurity.

> Self-confidence is the most valuable gift a man can possess. . . . But to possess this true confidence it is necessary to have learned to know oneself at moments when one was standing at the very frontier of things. . . . On the "Spider" in the Eiger's north face, I experienced such borderline situations, while the avalanches were roaring down over us, endlessly.[13]

As long as one is obsessed with overcoming his finitude so he can delight in trusting in himself, he will find a way to denounce as foolishness the Bible's teaching that man's chief end is to glorify God and enjoy him forever (cf. Mark 12:29). This preference to delight in ourselves rather than in God is the root cause for our antipathy to such biblical doctrines as the substitutionary atonement of Christ, and faith alone as the way to receive God's forgiveness and make progress in living the Christian life. The doctrine of substitutionary atonement hurts the ego by declaring that men's rebellion against God is so serious that nothing less than the Son of God's shedding his blood in an execution like that of a common criminal establishes a sufficient basis for God to forgive men. For the same reason people chafe at the biblical doctrine that only through faith in what God has promised do men receive the forgiveness of sins and the impulse to behave in a way that pleases God. When one's behavior is shaped by a confidence that the Jesus who loved him enough to die for his sins will surely keep his promises to guide him and supply his needs (cf. Gal 2:20), then Christ receives the credit for that life-style, and all boasting is excluded.

Of course these doctrines will present no problem to those whose only concern in biblical interpretation is to give an accurate description of biblical theology. Their desire to gain ego-satisfaction leads them to regard the biblical teachings as foolishness. But since they are concerned only to describe biblical theology and not also to say that the biblical message is true and beneficial, their exposition of the Bible does not clash with their desire for ego-satisfaction. So they have no need to modify the teachings determined by the pertinent historical-grammatical data of the Bible, and to the extent that they are skilled in exegesis, their exposition of what the biblical writers intended to say will be accurate.

But those who expound the teachings of the Bible as true will refrain from modifying the intended meanings of the biblical writers only as their desire for ego-satisfaction is replaced by a delight in God's faithfulness to keep his promises.[14] Otherwise they will take such doctrines as the substitutionary atonement and *sole fide* and modify them in some seemingly justifiable way so that they cease to offend the ego. Only God, working through the Holy Spirit, has the power to replace one's foolish desire for ego-fulfillment with the reasonable, well-advised desire to find peace and joy in depending on God to stand by his promises.

3. Our Utter Dependence on the Holy Spirit

Therefore, those who engage in the task of interpreting the Bible because of a conviction that it sets forth teachings that are true and beneficial must surely spare no effort to perfect their skills of exegesis. But they must also look to God to enable them to have and maintain that humble and contrite spirit (Isa 57:15) that will welcome what the Bible teaches. Otherwise the deceitfulness of sin will cause even the most skilled exegete, by some legerdemain, to modify the meanings yielded up by the historical-grammatical data so they will not offend the ego. Even though the teachings of the Bible are manifestly reasonable, our reasoning powers are not sufficient to suppress the awesome power of sin which predisposes us to glory in ourselves. Only God, through the Holy Spirit, overcomes this power of sin, so that we are willing to love from the heart what our minds can tell us is reasonable.

We can understand, then, why A. H. Francke (1663–1727), one of the founders of the Pietistic revival in Germany, laid down as one of his hermeneutical principles that "to the extent that you are crucified to the world, you will be able to grasp what the holy scriptures are saying."[15] Paul said, "God forbid that I should glory, save in the cross of our Lord Jesus Christ, by whom the world is crucified unto me, and I unto the world" (Gal. 6:14). Since such a resolve leaves no room for ego-satisfaction, we will welcome this teaching, which is so fundamental to biblical theology only as the Holy Spirit maintains within us the reasonable desire to love God rather than the foolish desire to love ourselves.

NOTES

1. *The Table Talk of Martin Luther,* W. Hazlitt, trans., 2nd ed. (1968), p. 399.
2. C. H. M[ackintosh] , *Notes on Exodus* (New York, n.d.), p. 275.
3. *TDNT* 2, p. 50, n. 1, quoting from F. W. Sturz, *Lexicon Xenophonteum,* 1 (1801), p. 653.
4. E. Haenchen, *Die Apostelgeschichte.* Kritisch-exegetisch Kommentar ueber das Neue Testament, begr. von H. A. W. Meyer, 3 Abt.; 12th ed. (1959), p. 614.
5. *TDNT* 5, p. 116.
6. *TDNT* 1, p. 690.
7. K. Stendahl, "Biblical Theology," *IDB* 1(1962), p. 422.
8. S. Kierkegaard, *Concluding Unscientific Postscript,* D. F. Swenson, trans. (1944), p. 188.
9. Ibid., p. 189.
10. *TDNT* 6, p. 9.
11. Leon Morris, *The First Epistle of Paul to the Corinthians* (1958), p. 42.
12. Quoted by Will Durant, *The Story of Philosophy* (1954), p. 180.
13. H. Harrer, *The White Spider* (1960), p. 21.
14. It should be apparent to anyone that it is much more promising to depend on God than on ourselves, who are so finite as to be likened to a vapor that appears for only a short time (Jas 4:14).
15. Quoted by Erhard Peschke, "Zur Hermeneutik A. H. Francke," *ThLZ* 89 (February, 1964), p. 103.

14: The Judgment of the Gentiles in Matthew's Theology

GEORGE GAY

A review of studies done in recent times on Matt 25:31–46 shows clearly that its interpretation defies consensus.[1] Problems abound in identifying the judgment, the judged, and especially the "brethren" of the Son of Man. It just does not all come together. If one or two elements seem to fit, then others do not combine logically. The best solution would be that one that left the smallest residue of problems. A really integral solution has still not appeared. The following presentation is an attempt to come at the problem from another point of view with the hope that the suggestions made here may help us to find a better explanation of this most intriguing and important pericope.

In studying the various views held by scholars on this portion, one large difficulty seems to be present: they seldom base their presentations on Matthew's total theology. Redaction criticism has emphasized that the evangelists are theologians in their own right,[2] and therefore it only seems correct that the interpretation of Matt 25:31–46 should be thoroughly coordinated with the main points of Matthew's view of Jesus' teaching, especially his concept of the Kingdom of God.

This study then proposes to look at the judgment of the Gentiles in the context of Matthew's total theology. The main questions to be asked are the following: How is Matt 25:31–46 related to Matthew's theology? How is it seen in the immediate context of the Olivet Discourse? Who are the judged? Who are the brethren of the King? What judgment is this? All these questions are set against the background of the problem: Is the Kingdom of God continuous or discontinuous with history?[3]

199

1. The Context of the Judgment of the Gentiles

a. Brief Summary of Matthew's Theology

Modern discussion of the theology of the First Gospel revolves around such themes as ecclesiology,[4] Christology,[5] the law and righteousness,[6] discipleship,[7] particularism and universalism,[8] and history and eschatology.[9] Up to this point the very basic element in Matthew's theology, the Kingdom of Heaven, has not been given sufficient emphasis.[10] Trilling, more than others, refers to the Kingdom, but, understandably, only in relation to the Church, which is his main topic. However, as one studies the Gospel, it becomes increasingly clear that the Kingdom is the key concept around which all other themes should be grouped. Both John and Jesus announce its nearness (Matt 3:2; 4:17); the five discourses which form the backbone of the whole Gospel all deal with the Kingdom in various ways: its laws (5–7), its proclamation to others (10), its inestimable worth and total conception (13), its inner relationships (18), and its future denouement (24, 25). It is present in Jesus' exorcisms (12:28), it is mentioned in connection with the Son of Man (16:28), and it is the special subject of a majority of the parables. When the matter of the identity of Jesus in the minds of the disciples has reached a climax (16:16), then it is that Jesus begins to speak of the Church or people of God, which is composed of all those who presumably make the same confession that Peter made, that Jesus is the Christ, the Son of God.[11] But even here the Kingdom is prominent in that Peter is given the authority of the "keys of the kingdom" (16:19). Although a complete discussion of the importance of the theme of the Kingdom in Matthew cannot be presented here, yet it may be said that the vast majority of the material in this Gospel, either overtly or implicitly, is based on the concept of the Kingdom of Heaven. It seems to be Matthew's purpose to explain what God's total plan for his people is, how the Kingdom is related to Old Testament prophecies and really belongs to Israel, how it is to be taken from them and given to another people, how it appeared in the person of Jesus first of all as a spiritual power, and then later on how it is to have its eschatological denouement on the plane of history.

As far as this study is concerned, it is concluded that the Kingdom is Matthew's central topic and that the majority of the themes in Matthew are tied in to this key idea. This is especially true of the five principal discourses that make up the central core of his presentation. Since Matt 25:31–46 is found in this fifth discourse, the one on eschatology, it is taken for granted that the main burden of this pericope has to do with the manifestation of the Kingdom here on earth at the time of the parousia. In view of the foregoing, it is necessary to make a brief statement on Matthew's concept of the Kingdom.

b. Matthew's Conception of the Kingdom

Space forbids a thorough presentation here and the writer can only refer to the results of a longer study in this area.[12] Matthew skillfully builds his conception of the Kingdom on the basis of vertical and horizontal lines. It is a kingdom (= royal authority) that originates in heaven, whose head is not an oriental despot-king, but a compassionate Father who provides all necessities for his children (6:25–33). The royal authority comes down to earth in the person of Jesus, who has "the government . . . on his shoulder" (Isa 9:6). [13] The Father's will is done in heaven and it is the disciples' prayer that it be done on earth (6:10). It must be done in the disciples' lives or they will be excluded from the Kingdom (7:21–23). It is the Father who from heaven reveals to Peter that Jesus is the Christ, the Son of God, and presumably the head of the Kingdom (16:17). What is bound in heaven is bound on earth; what is loosed in heaven is loosed on earth (16:19; 18:18). The angels who behold the Father's face in heaven care for the despised little ones on earth (18:10). After the resurrection, the full authority of heaven and earth is given to Jesus (28:18). These are just a few of the vertical heaven-earth relationships that form a definite background to Matthew's theology.

Since the head of the Kingdom is not presented as a king (except by inference in one parable—22:1–10) but rather as a father, the character of the community is not that of subjects, but of sons who form a family. Besides, the sons are also called disciples, so they are part of a learning process directed by the Master himself. Thus the Kingdom creates a people of God that is both a family, a school of learners, and a church (only in this Gospel is *ekklēsia* used to refer to the people of God, 16:18; 18:17).

Besides the heaven-earth relationships, Matthew's theology has a horizontal line of thinking that is seen not only in his direct presentation of Jesus' teaching, but also in the parabolic approach.[14] The horizontal factor has its beginning in Jesus' command for a world mission, given after his death and resurrection. Although there are recognized problems as to the authenticity of this command, yet it is inherent in the nature of Jesus' teaching that it would have a universal application. If the announcement of Jesus' total authority over heaven and earth has any significance at all, it demands a universal proclamation (Matt 28:18–20). If there is a missionary command, this then calls for some satisfactory purpose and, consequently, climax to history. Jesus' eschatological teaching provides for this need by directly teaching his parousia; it is so firmly rooted in the gospels that it is impossible to excise it completely. Jesus' lordship requires not only a return but a reckoning with all his subjects.

This direct teaching is also supported in the parabolic approach. Despite the fact that many scholars do not find any time references in the parables,[15] yet as presented by Matthew they do teach certain basic principles of kingdom truth: the Kingdom has a beginning that is crucial for the whole story, a happening without which none of the rest of the parable would be understandable; then there is a period of development when a natural or human process must complete its cycle; and lastly there is a climax when the harvest occurs, a denouement to the whole development.[16] In Matthew's view this turns out to signify that the period of Jesus is a unique time-lapse, completely distinguished from all other periods of time, and absolutely crucial for the understanding of the whole Kingdom, whether in its initial phase, its development over the centuries, or its denouement. During the time of the preaching of the kingdom message in this world, hostile elements are introduced into the Kingdom which tend to disrupt and hinder the orderly development of the missionary cause. At the parousia the Son of Man is charged with the duty of cleansing the Kingdom of those inimical elements, so that there can be a truly righteous reign on earth.

c. Matt 25:31–46 in the Total Setting of Matthew's Theology

Having reviewed in a brief way both Matthew's theology and his presentation of the Kingdom, we shall proceed with a short study of the relationship of our passage to the total setting of the First Gospel, or perhaps we should say to the very structured way in which Matthew presents his theology, particularly as seen in the five large segments of teaching already mentioned. These are expertly fashioned by the Evangelist in order to present various facets of the meaning of the Kingdom.

The laws of the Kingdom (Matthew 5–7). This famous passage treats of the moral foundations on which the Kingdom rests. Jesus' approach here is to show what kingdom principles are by beginning where people are hurting; they are constantly battling poverty, death, injustice, cruelty, conflict, and persecution. The Kingdom, whether present or future, addresses itself to these problems. Although this is a new approach, it must be understood that Jesus has not come to abolish the "law and the prophets," but to fulfill them.

One of Matthew's purposes in combining all this material[17] is to show the difference between true and false piety. Jesus is dealing with a nation that is generally "religious" but far from pious, in the good sense. The righteous practice their piety one way, the hypocrites another. The latter are those who relax the law to their liking (5:19), despise their brethren (5:21–26), swear falsely (5:33–37), carry out their religious duties to be seen by men, whether it is praying, fasting, or tithing (6:1–18), are more anxious about this life (food, drink, clothing) than about God (6:25–33), are judgmental about others rather than about themselves (7:1–5), are false shepherds who bear no fruit (7:15–20). The truly righteous in the Kingdom do exactly the opposite.

This Sermon has an astounding conclusion: many who call Jesus Lord, and think that they are part of the Kingdom, since they prophesy, exorcise demons, and do wonderful works, are cast out as evildoers unknown to Jesus (7:21–23). The last section of the Sermon distinguishes those who hear the word and obey it from those who hear it but do not obey it (7:24–27). It is obvious that as Matthew presents Jesus' teaching of the principles of the Kingdom, he does it by contrasting the true and the false disciples. The whole Sermon deals almost exclusively with the people who would normally be considered part of the messianic Kingdom, at that moment, the Jews.[18] Unless their "piety" and "spirituality" accord with the moral stance of the Kingdom, at the end, on that day, they will not enter the Kingdom, they will be completely unknown to Jesus (7:23).

The proclamation of the Kingdom (Matthew 10). The second discourse takes up the theme of the proclamation of the kingdom message in the cities and towns of Israel, although Matthew has included here other sayings that speak of ministering among the Gentiles (Matt 10:18). The general tenor of the passage would give credence to the fact that the testimony is being given to those who know nothing of the message; and it must be taken into account that the messengers will suffer persecution and opposition (10:16–31, the major portion of the discourse). However, from 10:32 on, there is a distinguishing of two types of messengers: those who acknowledge Jesus before men, who love him more than their parents, who take up their cross, who lose their lives (10:32ff.), and those who do just the opposite in order to avoid persecution. But all messengers must realize that those who receive them are receiving Jesus and so will obtain either a prophet's reward or a righteous man's reward. Then there is special mention of a reward for those who receive and treat well "one of these little ones," even if it is just the offering of a cup of cold water because that one is a disciple (10:42). Thus it is that in this last part of the discourse we see three groups of disciples: the true, the false, and the "little ones"; this must be kept in mind as we study Matt 25:31–46.

The total conception of the Kingdom (Matthew 13). In this chapter we find a collection of parables that characterize the Kingdom in various ways: the inevitability of its development out of all proportion to the smallness of its beginning (13:31f.), its power to penetrate the evil environment in which it finds itself (13:33), its lasting value and reality for which those who find it are willing to sacrifice anything (13:44f.). But the parables of the sower, of the wheat and the tares, and of the drag-net attempt to present a picture of the total horizontal conception of the Kingdom in its widest aspect. It can be compared to the basic principles of agriculture or the art of fishing. The sower and the fisherman have all good intentions to sow good seed and fish good fish, but in the nature of things that is not what happens. So it is in the Kingdom. As the kingdom message is presented many are attracted, some true and some false. What is significant here is that the interpretation of the parable of the tares (13:36–43)[19] encompasses the whole time of the Christian enterprise, right from the beginning, with Jesus sowing the seed of the Kingdom during his lifetime, up to the denouement at the "end of the age" (13:39ff.). The first duty of the recently arrived Son of Man is to separate the false from the true in the Kingdom, which is up to that time a *corpus mixtum.* There can be no Kingdom of God on earth with that admixture of evildoers and righteous. Just as in the Sermon on the Mount and in the missionary discourse, there are those who think they form part of the Kingdom when in fact they have no legitimate stake in it.

The inner relationships in the Kingdom (Matthew 18). Tasker entitles this chapter, "Life in the Messianic Community."[20] The whole chapter has to do with the mutual treatment of those who form the community of the Messiah. The greatest one in that community is the humble, child-like person (18:1–4), also called the "little one" (18:6).[21] The topic of receiving "one of these little ones" seen at 10:42 surfaces again. Receiving such a little one is receiving Christ (18:5). The seriousness of the matter is based on the fact that the eternal destiny of a disciple rests on his attitude to and treatment of the little ones of the community (18:5, 6). It would be better if those who are over the little ones would cut off a hand or foot, or pluck out an eye, than offend them or cause them to stumble (18:7–9). Even if there is no overt act, yet just the despising of these little ones is a very grave offense since their angels have direct access to the Father in heaven (18:10). The parable of the ninety and nine reinforces this teaching—the one lost lamb is infinitely important to the Father in heaven (18:12–14).

The next section continues in the same vein: antipathies between fellow-members of the people of God are so serious that if a man will not make up with one whom he has offended he is to be considered an outsider—a Gentile and a publican (18:15–17). The importance of forgiveness between brothers is clinched in the parable that concludes the discourse (18:23–35). The unforgiving majordomo had been pardoned an enormous debt, but he could not bring himself to pardon a lesser important subject who owed him a comparatively insignificant sum of money; so he was severely punished.

It is crystal clear that this discourse teaches that those who have negative attitudes or an unforgiving spirit toward the "little ones," that is, the greatest in the Kingdom of Heaven, have forfeited the right to belong to that community; they are to be cast out and severely punished. They have mistreated or despised the greatest ones in the Kingdom, that is, those who hold a very special place in God's economy.

As we look back over the first four discourses, we see that one of the important elements is the question of the true and the false in the messianic community. Those who do not fulfill the Father's will are to be separated from the Kingdom as false disciples. Matthew 5–7 and 13 only mention the true and false, while Matthew 10 and 18 add a very special group, "the little ones," who really are the greatest in the Kingdom.

d. The Immediate Context of Matt 25:31–46

The judgment scene at the end of the discourse must not be wrenched, either from its relationship to the total context of Matthew's theology, or from its immediate context in the Olivet Discourse. This whole discourse has proved to be a most difficult passage to interpret.[22] The first section (24:4–14) seems to describe the character of the whole period from the time of the disciples to the end of the age when the gospel of the Kingdom will have been preached in all the world. The 24:15–28 section most likely reverts to the time before the destruction of Jerusalem, since it has such a Jewish flavor and context. But 24:27 uses language that could refer only to the parousia, the future coming of the Son of Man. Whether this section has a double reference to both the destruction of Jerusalem and the time before the parousia is difficult to decide.[23] But it appears quite evident that 24:29–31 does refer to the parousia and the gathering together of the elect from all nations of the world.

It is important to make note of the fact that in this presentation of the characteristics of the age of the Gentile mission we have various references to the false prophets within the group of disciples (24:4, 5, 11, 23–26) and to the possibility of even the elect falling away (24:10–13, 24).

After 24:29–31 the evangelist returns to the theme of exhortation: all disciples are to be watchful and faithful as the parousia of the Son of Man approaches, since no one except the Father knows the day and the hour of the coming (24:32–44). Then follow three parables that illustrate the need for watchfulness and faithfulness: the faithful and unfaithful servant (24:45–51); the ten maidens and the bridegroom (25:1–13); and finally, the parable of the talents or entrusted wealth (25:14–30).

At this point the exhortation through parables concludes and the theme of the parousia, broken off at 24:31, seems to be taken up again. The Son of Man has appeared on the clouds of heaven (Matt 24:30)[24] and he is given "dominion and glory and kingdom, that all people, nations, and languages should serve him; his dominion is an everlasting dominion which shall not pass away, and his kingdom one that shall not be destroyed" (Dan 7:14). But it is not for him alone—he comes to share it with his true followers: "But the saints of the Most High shall receive the kingdom and possess the kingdom for ever, for ever, and ever" (Dan 7:18). However, he must have a kingdom of righteousness and truth and justice; therefore, it is necessary that all elements that appear to form part of the Kingdom, but have not really carried out the Father's will, must be separated from the realm. This is the teaching that the three preceding parables are trying to show: at the return of the master, those who have not fulfilled the will of the Lord must be cast out or excluded.

These parables are distinguished from the Matthew 13 parables in that, instead of nature themes, we have presence-absence-return motifs, with the total scope of the Kingdom once again in mind. Whereas the Matthew 13 parables emphasize that the good and bad elements in the Kingdom are to be left together till the climax of the process, the presence-absence-return parables stress the separation procedure at the return of the master. This leads very naturally to the passage under study, where the Son of Man executes that separation judgment; however, here it is not under parabolic symbolism, but through direct description.

2. The Explanation of the Judgment of the Gentiles

Up to this point we have tried to show that Matthew's theology about the Kingdom is summarized very carefully in the five discourses. One of the general themes there clearly seems to be the discernment of the true and the false in the Kingdom: whether it has to do with the basic rules of kingdom piety (5–7), the dedicated or less dedicated messengers who proclaim the kingdom message in the world (10), the sons of the Kingdom or the sons of the evil one (13), the forgiving, loving disciple or the unforgiving, despising disciple (18), or the faithful or unfaithful servants (24:45–25:30).

Now it is time to take up the explanation of the judgment itself. First, it must be stated that 25:31–46 is placed at the end of a series of three parables and is vitally connected to them by the particle *de*. There is no phrase or explanation or introductory clause that would separate this section from the foregoing. It all flows together in such a way that it is imperative in Matthew's view to consider them together.[25]

In this pericope there are four main items that should be considered: (1) who is the judge? (2) who are the judged? (3) what is the basis of the judgment? and (4) what judgment is this?

a. Who is the Judge?

In the first century, general opinion among Jews attributed the "throne of glory" only to God and "the notion that anyone except God could sit on this throne is foreign to Jewish thought. . . ."[26] However, in the Similitudes of Enoch there are passages that indicate that the Elect One will sit on the throne and execute God's judgment.[27] The date of the Similitudes is still an open question, and it is difficult to say whether this writing actually precedes or follows Jesus' teaching.[28] But despite the references in this esoteric work, it was a new idea in those days that the Son of Man would occupy the throne of glory. It is interesting that in his general sayings on judgment earlier in the Gospel, Matthew makes no clear statement that God is the Judge, only that there would be a day of judgment. In the rest of the New Testament, both God (Heb 12:23; Jas 4:12; Rom 14:10 [his judgment seat]) and Christ (2 Tim 4:8; Acts 10:42; 2 Cor 5:10 [judgment seat of Christ]) are mentioned as judges. But these verses are neither contradictory nor mutually exclusive as Luke makes clear at Acts 17:31: "because he has fixed a day on which he will judge the world in righteousness by a man whom he has appointed, and of this he has given assurance to all men by raising him from the dead." Although God is the ultimate judge, he has granted to the Son as vicegerent the authority to execute judgment on the final day (cf. John 5:25–29). As mentioned above, it is not within the scope of this study to discuss the problem of the Son of Man; but as far as Matthew is concerned, the Son of Man as Judge is Jesus. He is the one who began the whole enterprise of the Kingdom (13:37), who sends out his angels to gather out of his Kingdom all causes of sin and all evildoers (13:41), and who at 25:31 sits on his throne to separate the "sheep" from the "goats."

b. Who are the Judged?

The question of the identity of the judged is a more complex problem. They are described as "all the nations" (*panta ta ethnē*, 25:32), who are divided into two large groups: (1) the "blessed of my Father" who enter the Kingdom prepared for them from the foundation of the world (25:34), and (2) the "cursed" who are condemned to the eternal fire prepared for the devil and his angels (25:41).[29] There seems to be little doubt about the identity of the blessed—they are the true disciples and subjects of the Kingdom. However, the interpretation of the cursed as all the unjust must be looked at very seriously.

Since all the "nations" are there, and since there is a division between good and bad with respective eternal destinies mentioned at the end (25:46), it seems evident that this is the final judgment. But the following questions disturb this picture: Why is it that the cursed call the Son of Man "Lord"?[30] and why is it that they seemed shocked that they were not included in the Kingdom since they thought they had done their duty? It is as if they had expected to enter into the Kingdom and as if they had expected to do those good works. Could these things be true of those who had never made any commitment to Jesus? Surely they are to be distinguished from those of Chorazin, Bethsaida, and Capernaum, who rejected Jesus totally (11:20–24), had never repented, and for whom a final judgment day awaited (11:22). If they are different, then *panta ta ethnē* must be qualified to mean those out of all nations who have made some sort of commitment, whether partial or total, to Jesus as Lord, being the results of the worldwide mission. *Ethnē* would then be better translated as "Gentiles" rather than "nations."[31]

c. What is the Basis of the Judgment?

If the identity of the judge is really not crucial, and if the identity of the judged, particularly the cursed, is not as clear as one could wish, the basis of the judgment may be more decisive. It is the attitude of mercy and love shown (evidently unconsciously) to the special group called the "brethren" of the king (*adelphoi*). The special love shown the "brethren" is in essence a demonstration of love of the Son of Man. The brethren then must be those who are already in the Kingdom since they sustain a special relationship to him. They thus form a third group within the judgment picture.

These acts of love are the responsibility of all those who belong to the Kingdom. As has been clearly shown above in the section on Matthew 18, Jesus has a special care for, and tenderness toward, the "little ones" of the community, and their angels give them special attention. Although the group as a whole is called *adelphoi,* yet once again the mention here is "one of the least of these my brethren," stressing the weaker ones of the group. They seem to be a special part of the larger group of the righteous ones. The three groups here are really the same groups found in Matthew 10 and 18: (1) the righteous as a whole; (2) the little ones or brethren, who may seem to be the lesser ones of the community, but are in reality the greatest in the Kingdom; and (3) the false disciples, who though a part of the community, do not live according to its principles.[32]

The interpretation that the brethren of the king are all Jesus' disciples[33] as they go out to preach the gospel in their mission to the world and that the "sheep" are the Gentiles who receive them with love and compassion in their need has the following difficulties: (1) it suggests that the thrust is toward the world outside, whereas the pericope itself gives the impression that both the "brethren" and the "sheep" are part of the Kingdom already. Technically, of course, these Gentiles have believed in the gospel and are new subjects of the Kingdom, and thus because of prior faith[34] treat the messengers with compassion. But this does not seem to fit the line of thinking so carefully presented by Matthew in the context, both total and immediate, of the five principal discourses. This context suggests that the judgment has to do with established interregnal relationships. What may be in mind here is well described in 1 John 3:17: "But if any one has the world's goods and sees his brother in need, yet closes his heart against him, how does God's love abide in him?" (cf. Jas 2:14–17). (2) No judgment of the kind envisioned here would be made on the basis of one or two occasions when the messengers of the gospel first preached to a Gentile person, who in the enthusiasm of the moment might treat them with compassion. As portrayed in the parables immediately preceding our passage, God's judgment is executed on the basis of the long haul, that is, the general attitude of the disciple over a long period during which true character and motivations can be tested by time. A judgment rendered as the result of an initial encounter with the preacher of the gospel is a very slim basis for a decision that will have eternal consequences. (3) If the "brethren" of the king are the same as the "child" or "little ones" of Matt 18:1–6, 10, it is illogical to conclude that all of them as preachers of the gospel would fulfil the conditions laid down, i.e. that they have humbled themselves and become as little children.

If the judgment is based on the treatment between two groups in the Kingdom,[35] how do we distinguish these "little ones"? According to Matthew 18, they do not form any certain group, whether preachers, missionaries, miracle-workers, or exorcists. The distinguishing is not by vocational gift, but by the inner condition of humility. This criterion cuts across all groupings—the humble could be from any of the groups within the Kingdom. However, it does set up another group that is held in the highest esteem by the king; he does everything to care for them, to search them out when lost, so much so that in Matt 18:5–9 mistreatment or despisement of them determines eternal destiny. So, yes, the brethren are disciples, but they are limited to those who are the greatest in the Kingdom, i.e., the "little ones" or those who have humbled themselves. Since they are the greatest in the Kingdom, it is only logical that they should receive special care and tender love from the king. The treatment these special ones receive from their fellow-disciples in the Kingdom really determines whether their faith is true or false, and thus what their eternal destiny is.

d. What Judgment is This?

If the preceding presentation holds any relevance for the understanding of this judgment, then it is highly unlikely that it is the final universal assize that includes all mankind. It would be unfair and illogical to judge the unrepentant who have never made any commitment to Jesus and know nothing of the demands of the Kingdom on the same basis as those who are within its sphere and know (or should know) something of its workings. What is conclusive is that those on the left thought that they would enter the Kingdom because as far as they were concerned they had fulfilled their duty; they would have ministered to the brethren if they only knew they were so personally related to Jesus (25:44). This surely follows Matthew's emphasis on the fact that the Kingdom is a *corpus mixtum* and that the Son of Man comes to separate from that Kingdom all causes of sin and all evildoers. But these evildoers must be clearly distinguished from total unbelievers. If not, then all mankind would have to be considered as within the sphere of the Kingdom, an opinion that Matthew does not seem to share.[36] Here the question of the continuity or discontinuity of the Kingdom with the world as a whole comes to the surface. If the Kingdom is continuous with the whole world, then there is no question; all the nations and all peoples would be present. But since Matthew evidently does not share that point of view, as we have already noted, then at least before the parousia there is a sense in which the Kingdom is discontinuous with the world. This leaves room for the fact that this is not the final judgment for all mankind.

Besides the interpretation of the pericope itself, the immediate context of the eschatological discourse cannot be ignored. The general topic is really judgment, first on Israel at the destruction of Jerusalem and of the temple, and secondly on the community of the Kingdom at the parousia. Old Israel, which is described by Matthew as the "sons of the kingdom" (8:12), the ones who should have inherited the Kingdom, is to be judged in a most severe manner since they have rejected the Messiah; their house is left desolate and forsaken (23:38)—all that remains for them is judgment. They are cast out, and a people producing the fruits of the Kingdom replaces them (21:43). The gospel is to be preached in all the world, and multitudes will be drawn into the sphere of the Kingdom from all nations. A new, or rather true, Israel is being formed,[37] but as in the case of old Israel, a judgment is to fall also on the new Israel for its mixed condition. For this reason, immediately after the announcement of the parousia (24:30f.), Jesus begins to warn the disciples that they must be careful, watchful, and ready for the coming of the Son of Man, because at that time there will be a judgment of those who form part of the Kingdom. The three parables that follow all emphasize this truth: all those who are within the sphere of the Kingdom must live up to its precepts and ethical principles, or else judgment will fall on them. These parables do not conceive of all the world being included, rather just those who profess to belong to the Kingdom. This is especially true of the parable of the ten maidens, which specifically declares that the Kingdom is to be compared to the maidens, all of whom had lamps and were waiting for the bridegroom.

The context seems to be this: old Israel, the entity that should have been the Kingdom, is judged for its failure to accept the person and message of Jesus; but even the new people of God, mainly Gentiles, will fall under the judgment of God if they fail to live up to the practices and principles of the Kingdom. In both cases the group is an entity with which God should have a direct and special relationship; neither group includes all mankind. At this point Matthew may well be saying to the Jews or Jewish Christians to whom he is writing to explain the universal character of the message, "Yes, Israel has to suffer for its disobedience and rejection of the Messiah, but never fear, the Gentiles who form the new Israel will also come to judgment if they fall into the same pattern." Therefore, the term "Gentiles" (*ethnē*) in Matthew's understanding is most likely not to be used as an indiscriminate word to describe all mankind, but rather the "Gentiles" as over against the "Jews," that is, two groups that have some relationship with the Kingdom, either past or present.

Matthew may have intended a chiasmus between the first and last discourses, both of which stress entry into the Kingdom.[38] The beatitudes of the Sermon on the Mount describe the character of those who will inherit the Kingdom: they are poor in spirit, the mourners, the meek, those who suffer hunger and thirst for righteousness, the merciful, the pure in heart, the peacemakers, the persecuted, and the reviled, that is, the needy, the lowly, the oppressed. These look very much like the "little ones" of Matthew 18, who are the greatest in the Kingdom and who enjoy a special relationship to their Lord. They also recall the "brethren" of the king in Matthew 25. If there is any correspondence between these two groups of needy ones, then they are crucial in both the first and last discourses.

But this is not all. Toward the end of the Sermon on the Mount there are three verses (7:21–23) that very accurately relate what is happening at the judgment of the Gentiles. Here Jesus describes those who will not enter the Kingdom, even though they are confessors of his lordship, prophets, exorcists, and miracle-workers, that is, very dedicated disciples. But they had this fault, they did not do the will of the Father in heaven; so Jesus solemnly declares to them: "I never knew you; depart from me, you evildoers."[39] If there is a chiasmus here, then it is clear that just as Matt 7:21–23 presents the separation of the true and the false in the Kingdom, so does Matt 25:31–46. It cannot then be the final judgment of all men.

The Sermon on the Mount concludes with the parable of the two men, one wise and one foolish (7:24–27). The wise man is the one who not only hears Jesus' words, but obeys them, and the foolish is just the opposite. The wise man's house remains solidly fixed on the rock, but the foolish man's construction falls because of its insecure foundation. This parable is an illustration of the preceding pericope and if the analysis so far given is accurate, it is also illustrative of the judgment at 25:31–46. All had the opportunity to hear Jesus' words; some heeded them, others disobeyed. The former inherited the Kingdom; the latter were cast out as unknown.

This approach has been described as a radicalization of the demand of God and of discipleship,[40] but it seems to fit Matthew's particular emphasis on the seriousness of following Jesus. The whole process comes to a climax at the parousia when the separation of true and false in the Kingdom takes place. It will be seen at that moment who really took Jesus' words seriously.

3. Conclusion

Both direct and parabolic teachings in the First Gospel clearly show that the Kingdom of God cannot remain in a pure state; in the very nature of things in an evil world it becomes a *corpus mixtum*. But before the Kingdom is publicly manifested on earth, the Son of Man must return to cleanse it of all causes of sin and all evildoers. The separation of the true and the false in the Kingdom is a crucial theme in Matthew's theology. It is seen in all the five principal discourses and in particular receives its major exposition at 25: 31–46. The catalyst in this whole equation is a group called the "brethren" whose treatment by kingdom subjects is the basis for separating true and false.

Since the five discourses are essentially concerned with the Kingdom of Heaven as a *corpus mixtum,* the judgment of the Gentiles cannot assuredly be the final judgment of all men. In Matthew's view it is rather the judgment of the subjects of the Kingdom gathered mainly from Gentile nations as a result of the world mission. Those with a total commitment both in word and deed enter the Kingdom; those with a partial or insincere dedication, despite oral protestations of loyalty, are condemned eternally. Therefore, the title "Judgment of the Gentiles" would refer to all those Gentiles who in one way or another belong to the sphere of the Kingdom. Matthew seems to place them over against the Jews to whom he is writing; if the latter suffer judgment for their rejection of the Messiah, so in their turn will the Gentiles for very similar reasons.

The uneasiness expressed in the first part of this study about the difficulties of interpretation of our passage still remains. We are very conscious of crucial unsolved problems that demand more research.[41] But if there is one firm conviction to be highlighted from our consideration, it is this: it is highly improbable that this is the final judgment of all mankind. Only if the pericope is wrenched from its setting in Matthew's total theological picture can it be made to support such a teaching.

A second and no less important conviction is the seriousness of Christian discipleship with all its concomitant responsibilities of true faith and social consciousness. If this study has done nothing else, it has shown that Jesus' kingdom message is irrevocably revolutionary.

NOTES

1. The present writer is indebted to Mr. Cecil Melvin Robeck, Jr., doctoral candidate at Fuller Theological Seminary, for the loan of his detailed research on this pericope.

2. Groundwork for this approach was laid many years ago by such scholars as A. Schlatter, B. W. Bacon, G. D. Kilpatrick, and K. Stendahl. More recently H. Conzelmann (Luke) and W. Marxsen (Mark) have used this method. But it is in the First Gospel where the most work has been done; cf. G. Bornkamm, G. Barth, and H. J. Held, *Tradition and Interpretation in Matthew* (1963), p. 57, as only one example among many. For other authors using this methodology see below under Trilling, Strecker, Rohde, and Kingsbury.

3. This question cannot be taken up in any detailed way in this short study.

4. W. Trilling, *Das Wahre Israel: Studien zur Theologie des Matthäusevangelium* (1964).

5. E. P. Blair, *Jesus in the Gospel of Matthew* (1960).

6. G. Barth, in *Tradition and Interpretation in Matthew*.

7. H. J. Held, in *Tradition and Interpretation in Matthew*; Trilling, *Das Wahre Israel*.

8. Cf. P. Nepper-Christensen, *Das Matthäusevangelium ein judenchristlichen Evangelium?* (1958); K. W. Clark, "The Gentile Bias in Matthew," *JBL* 66 (1947), pp. 165–172; C. F. D. Moule, "St. Matthew's Gospel: Some Neglected Features," *Texte und Untersuchungen der altchristlichen Literatur* 87 *Stud Ev* 2 (1964), pp. 91–99.

9. G. Strecker, *Der Weg der Gerechtigkeit: Untersuchung zur Theologie des Matthäus* (1962).

10. Even the latest edition of the W. G. Kümmel-Feine-Behm Introduction mentions the Kingdom only in a subsidiary way (*Introduction to the New Testament* [1975], pp. 105–119). F. V. Filson (*A Commentary on the Gospel According to St. Matthew* [1962], pp. 25–44) includes the topic of the Kingdom as one of six prominent themes in Matthew.

11. Cf. H. Ridderbos, *The Coming of the Kingdom* (1962), p. 351. Also J. D. Kingsbury, *Matthew: Structure, Christology, Kingdom* (1975), pp. 40–83, whose book stresses the fact that Matthew presents Jesus as the Son of God.

12. Dissertation done at the University of Manchester by the writer: *Matthew's Unique Presentation of the Kingdom*, 1971.

13. Matthew quotes Isa 9:1, 2 immediately before Jesus' first public announcement of the Kingdom at 4:17. Although Matthew does not quote Isa 9:6, anyone who knew that Old Testament passage would understand its relevance for what Jesus was doing at that point.

14. The principle used in this study is that parabolic teaching must be controlled by Jesus' direct teaching, so that there is an external canon by which one can judge parable exegesis. Cf. this methodology used in C. H. Dodd, *The Parables of the Kingdom* (1963).

15. R. Bultmann, *Theology of the New Testament* (1951–55), 1, p. 8; 99ff.; N. Perrin, *The Kingdom of God in the Teaching of Jesus* (1963), p. 160. G. R. Beasley-Murray (*Jesus and the Future* [1954], p. 183) thinks that it is a mistake to consider the parables of growth as proving that Jesus thought his Kingdom would develop over a long course of time; however, a few pages further on (p. 191) he allows for some lapse of time for development. C. J. Cadoux, *The Historic Mission of Jesus* (n.d.), p. 196, says: "But after all, growth is growth; and in the case of all these parables, the process culminates in some sort of a climax of completeness." W. G. Kümmel (*Promise and Fulfillment* [1957], p. 148) considers that "it is impossible to eliminate the concept of time and with it the 'futurist' eschatology from the eschatological message of Jesus. . . ."

16. It is recognized that growth or development referring to the Kingdom is limited to the subjects and their missionary outreach to all the world.

17. Matthew brings together in the Sermon on the Mount much material that Luke has placed in many different contexts in his Gospel. Matthew's thinking, of course, is guided by a different motif.

18. Matt 6:7 mentions the prayers of Gentiles; 6:32 their search for material things.

19. The general opinion concerning the explanation of the parable of the tares is against authenticity; see Jeremias, *The Parables of Jesus* (1963), pp. 81ff. However, N. A. Dahl, "The Parables of Growth," *StudTh* 5, Fasc I–II (1951), pp. 157f. and I. H. Marshall, *Eschatology and the Parables* (1963), p. 12, favor authenticity.

20. R. V. G. Tasker, *The Gospel According to St. Matthew: An Introduction and Commentary* (1961), p. 172.

21. Most commentators think the phrase *tōn mikrōn* refers to humble disciples alone (for example, Tasker, op. cit., p. 176); others refer it to both children and humble disciples (for example, Filson, op. cit., p. 200), there being a transition at 18:6 from *paidion* (four times

in 18:2–5) to *mikroi* (18:6, 10, 14). Matt 18:6a would tip the balance in favor of the latter view, i.e., adult believers who have nevertheless certain child-like characteristics.

22. It is not our purpose to enter into a discussion of the various approaches to the interpretation of the Olivet Discourse; for a detailed presentation see G. R. Beasley-Murray, op. cit.

23. Filson, op. cit., p. 255.

24. The appearance of the Son of Man is like that described in Dan 7:13f. See Filson, op. cit., p. 256. The scope of this study forbids any discussion of the perplexing problem of the Son of Man.

25. P. Bonnard, *L'Évangile selon saint Matthieu* (1963), p. 364.

26. T. W. Manson, *The Sayings of Jesus as Recorded in the Gospels according to St. Matthew and St. Luke Arranged with Introduction and Commentary* (1949), p. 217.

27. *Enoch* 45:3; 51:3; 55:4; 62:5; 69:27, 29.

28. No fragments of the Similitudes of Enoch (*1 Enoch* 37–71) have been found in the Qumran literature, although evidence of all the other sections is present. This has reopened the question of the date of the Similitudes. F. F. Bruce, *New Testament History* (1969), pp. 124ff., considers that the Similitudes are probably pre-Christian and that because of the identification of the Son of Man with Enoch they are not the work of a Christian author. Cf. G. E. Ladd, *The Presence of the Future* (1974), p. 89, n. 33.

29. The simile of the separation of sheep and goats was well understood in those days; it was based on the custom of Jewish shepherds of mixed flocks who had to separate them at night because the goats needed more warmth than the sheep. Mixed flocks can still be seen in Israel today.

30. It could rightly be assumed that if the cursed are really unbelievers, they would naturally use *kyrie* out of a sense of respect and awe on such an auspicious occasion without any theological significance. See below for the argument that these are similar to the false disciples of Matt 7:21ff.; the latter had made at least a minimal commitment to Jesus as Lord. The degree of theological meaning here at Matthew 25 is difficult to assess, but at least their intention in using *kyrie* was theological. The judge reveals the hollowness and hypocrisy of their "confession."

31. See above, pp. 211f., for the interpretation of *ethnē*.

32. Cf. Luke 13:22–30 (a passage partially parallel to Matt 7:21–23) where Jesus answers a question about the number of the saved. He indicates that many who think that they will be included in the Kingdom will be completely shut out. The sad words "I do not know where you come from" seal their fate.

33. G. E. Ladd, "The Parable of the Sheep and the Goats in Recent Interpretation," in *New Dimensions in New Testament Study*, eds. R. N. Longenecker and M. C. Tenney (1974), pp. 197–199; T. W. Manson, *Sayings*, pp. 249–252; J. R. Michaels, "Apostolic Hardships and Righteous Gentiles," *JBL* 84 (1965), pp. 27–38; Jean-Claude Ingelaere, "La 'Parabole' du jugement dernier (Matthieu 25/31–46)," *RHPR* 50 (1970), pp. 23–60.

34. Michaels, op. cit., p. 36; E. Schweizer, *The Good News According to Matthew* (1975), pp. 479f.

35. See Matt 10:42; 18:5–14, 15–20, 21–35; 24:45–51.

36. In Matt 10:14–31 the disciples are distinguished from the unbelievers who will not receive the message of the Kingdom; but from 10:32 on there is a distinguishing of two kinds of disciples, as over against the unbelievers. Matt 11:21f. certainly condemns those of Chorazin and Bethsaida for not receiving the mighty works done there, and because of their attitude a worse judgment than for Tyre and Sidon awaits them.

37. C. F. D. Moule, *The Birth of the New Testament* (1962), p. 39.

38. J. C. Fenton, *The Gospel of St. Matthew* (1964), pp. 14ff.

39. Cf. Matt 25:12: "Truly, I say to you, I do not know you"; and Luke 13:25, 27: "I do not know where you come from."

40. G. Barth, op. cit., p. 95.

41. The writer is especially conscious of the need of more research as to the identity of the "brethren" and of the "goats," the meaning of the word "Gentiles," and the interpretation of the particularly difficult verse, 25:46, for the reconstruction given in this study.

15: Christological Neglect by a Mission-Minded Church

CARL F. H. HENRY

1. Twentieth-Century Christological Discussion

American evangelical scholarship seems not to have been significantly engaged in the controversy over Christology that has characterized Western theology throughout much of the twentieth century. Amid concentration on Scripture as the watershed of theological affirmation and on global evangelism as the mission of the Church, Protestant evangelicals have at the same time been oddly neglectful of the very christological concerns which stand at the heart of Scripture and evangelistic commitment and which have been under relentless fire by non-evangelical critics.

In the aftermath of Albert Schweitzer's *Von Reimarus zu Wrede* (1906), translated as *The Quest of the Historical Jesus* (1910), one might indeed have expected a modern theology without christological priorities. Schweitzer not only held that a true history of Jesus could be written only from an eschatological perspective, but insisted also that Jesus was motivated by the mistaken eschatology of firm faith in the imminent emergence of the Kingdom of God. Jesus therefore died in vain, Schweitzer held; even his ethics lacks permanent validity since it was intended to have only interim significance.

Karl Barth's reaffirmation of Christology as the basic foundation of redemptive revelation put the modernist movement, which presumed to have demolished the absolute uniqueness of Jesus Christ, on the defensive. Like Bultmann, Barth had early roots in the *Religionsgeschichte* (History of Religions) school, which set christological discussion in the context of comparative religions and explained biblical realities without reference to special transcendent agency. But Barth held that the historical method cannot yield the truth of Jesus Christ; Christ's lordship is to be known only by

216

individual response to an inner work of personal divine grace.

Bultmann struck hard at the vulnerable point in Barthian Christology. Barth affirmed that the Jesus of history is irrelevant to faith; Bultmann emphatically underscored this emphasis: the Jesus of history has no essential relationship to the Christ of faith. But Bultmann additionally affirmed that the Christ of faith (i.e., of the New Testament) is a product of the early Church. Christology therefore has its roots not in the life of Jesus but in the teaching of the early Church. The essence of Christian proclamation, Bultmann insists, lies not in Christology—in the person and work of Jesus of Nazareth—but in God's radical call of beleaguered mankind to a personal decision of existential obedience and authentic being. In short, Bultmann held that, for apologetic purposes, the Christian community creatively attributed to the human Jesus certain titles (e.g., Son of Man, Messiah), powers, and perfections. Repudiating the view that the gospels give us an historically reliable account of Jesus, he appealed to form criticism as a literary discipline and method, and manipulated it on presuppositions inherited from the history-of-religions school and from existential philosophy. The resultant verdict was that we can assert little about Jesus of Nazareth other than the bare fact of his crucifixion, although Bultmann allowed the possibility that Jesus prophetically called people to repentance and announced salvation. "Though one may admit the fact that for no single word of Jesus is it possible to produce positive evidence of its authenticity, still one may point to a whole series of words found in the oldest stratum of tradition which do give a consistent representation of the historical message of Jesus."[1] But the early Church, Bultmann affirms, proclaimed the atonement and resurrection of Jesus as a preaching device that mythologically symbolizes new being to which man rises by faith-response to inner confrontation by God's Word.

Reacting to Bultmann's indifference to the historical Jesus, the "new quest" scholars sought to narrow the gap between the Jesus of history and the Christ of faith. Bultmann had no answer to the question, "What gave impetus to the Easter faith?" Günther Bornkamm presumed to find a bridge in the authority of Jesus: the Gospel accounts preserve a factual aspect of his life and ministry in reporting Jesus' readiness to forgive sins (*Jesus of Nazareth*, 1960). To escape the skepticism and the risk of Docetism implicit in Bultmann's attitude toward the Jesus of history, a stance which could easily dwarf Christianity into a Gnostic redeemer-myth, Ernst Käsemann found in the preaching of Jesus the desired link to the Christ of faith (*Essays on New Testament Themes*, 1964). By stressing Jesus' ministry to social outcasts, Ernst Fuchs also affirmed a continuity between Jesus' proclamation and the apostolic kerygma (*Studies of the Historical Jesus,* 1964). On the American side, James M. Robinson sought to correlate the existential selfhood of Jesus with the kerygmatic Christ (*A New Quest of the Historical Jesus,* 1959).

Yet Bultmann had insisted on the irrelevance of any connection between the Jesus of history and the kerygmatic Christ of faith. Not even the "new questers" on their premises succeeded in establishing that the two are basically and essentially related and intrinsically identical. H. E. Tödt contended, largely on Bultmannian assumptions, that the early Church identified Jesus with the title Son of Man, even if Jesus had earlier used the term (*Der Menschensohn in der synoptischen Überlieferung,* 1959; E. T. *The Son of Man in the Synoptic Tradition,* trans. D. M. Barton, 1965). Much the same position was taken by A. J. B. Higgins (*Jesus and the Son of Man,* 1964).

But other scholars insistently took more conservative ground. Oscar Cullmann insisted that Jesus intentionally called himself the Son of Man (*The Christology of the New Testament,* trans. S. C. Guthrie, 1959). Ferdinand Hahn, too, resists the Bultmannian approach (*Christologische Hoheitstitel,* 1963; E. T. *The Titles of Jesus in Christology,* trans. H. Knight and G. Ogg, 1969), and likewise W. Kramer (*Christ, Lord, Son of God,* trans. B. Hardy, 1966). Cullmann devoted his crowning years of scholarship to refuting Bultmann's speculative misuse of form criticism in support of existential theory and of *Religionsgeschichte* prejudices, and emphasized instead the indispensability of the Gospel history to the kerygma.

Many British New Testament scholars of divergent theological views voiced serious doubts about the one-sided German dialectical-existential reorientation of Christology. Continental trends nonetheless exerted mounting influence on British scholarship and even set the agenda for much of the christological debate there. For example, after publishing *The Doctrine of the Person of Christ* in 1925, Sidney Cave reflected in the preparation of the companion work on *The Doctrine of the Work of Christ* (1937) the shaping influence of the Swedish scholar Gustaf Aulén's *Christus Victor* (1931). Bultmannian theory found ardent support in commentaries by D. E. Nineham and others. Yet a vigorous cadre, evangelical scholars among them, posed a formidable challenge to Bultmann's views.

C. H. Dodd affirmed that antisupernaturalistic critics "deliberately neglected" in the gospels "those elements which in the eyes of their authors made them worth writing."[2] William Manson, refusing to be intimidated by claims made by Dibelius and Bultmann in their application of form criticism, in *Jesus the Messiah* (1946) drew much more constructive conclusions about New Testament Christology, later reflected also in his posthumously collected essays, *Jesus and the Christian* (1967). T. W. Manson wrote on *The Teaching of Jesus* (1945), *The Sayings of Jesus* (1949) and *The Servant Messiah* (1953); despite his emphasis on the fundamental historicity of the gospels, however, he avoided any chronological sketch of the life of Jesus. C. F. D. Moule also rejected radical form criticism (cf. *The Phenomenon of the New Testament*, 1967), and pointedly emphasized that had it not been for the resurrection of the crucified Jesus the early Church would not have arisen and the New Testament writings would not have appeared.

The only comprehensive work on Christology to emanate from evangelical circles since mid-century is the quite formidable two-volume effort by the Dutch theologian G. C. Berkouwer in his *Studies in Theology* series, translated as *The Person of Christ* (1954) and *The Work of Christ* (1965). Walter Künneth's *Theologie der Auferstehung* (1953; E.T. *The Theology of the Resurrection*, 1965) was a learned treatment of Jesus' resurrection by a German systematic theologian. Swedish conservative concern over questions of tradition, authority, and creativity in the gospels was represented by the New Testament scholars Birger Gerhardsson (*Memory and Manuscript,* 1961) and Harold Riesenfeld (*The Gospel Tradition and Its Beginnings,* 1961).

Apart from these volumes, English translations of continental treatises bearing centrally on Christology consisted predominantly of German neo-Protestant writings such as Emil Brunner's *Der Mittler* (1927; E.T. *The Mediator,* 1934); Rudolf Bultmann's *Jesus* (1926; E.T., *Jesus and the Word,* 1960); Karl Barth's *Die Kirchliche Dogmatik, IV: Die Lehre von der Versohnung* (1953 and 1955; E.T. Vol. 4, Parts 1 and 2 of his *Church Dogmatics: The Doctrine of Reconciliation,* 1956 and 1958); Wolfart Pannenberg's *Grundzüge der Christologie* (1964; E.T. *Jesus—God and Man,* 1968); and Jürgen Moltmann's *Der gekreutzigte Gott* (1973; E.T. *The Crucified God,* 1974). Cullmann was the most conservative scholar aggressively engaged in this continental conflict over Christology (*Die Christologie des Neuen Testaments,* 1957; E.T. *The Christology of the New Testament,* 1959, rev. 1963).

British scholarship in both evangelical and mediating camps had made an influential and impressive contribution to Christology from the late nineteenth and early part of the twentieth century. During the last half of our century, however, comparatively little has appeared in the succession of earlier works like James Orr's *The Virgin Birth of Christ* (1907) and *The Resurrection of Jesus* (1908), P. T.

Forsyth's *The Person and Place of Christ* (1909), and H. R. Mac-kintosh's comprehensive work on *The Doctrine of the Person of Christ* (1912), which in turn prepared the way for other books like T. R. Glover's *The Jesus of History* (1916) and A. C. Headlam's *The Life and Teaching of Jesus* (1923) and *Jesus Christ in History and Faith* (1925). To be sure, Forsyth, Mackintosh, and later writers like D. W. Forrest and R. C. Moberly leaned toward the *kenosis* theory espoused by German theologians. John S. Lawton surveys English theology from the publication in 1889 of *Lux Mundi* to the appear-ance in 1912 of *Foundations,* and indicates how the controlling premises that Jesus had a unitary personality and a human nature were formulated in a way that eroded confidence in the two-natures doctrine of Chalcedon (*Crisis in Christology,* 1947). Here and there after mid-century appeared readable works like Vincent Taylor's effort on the basis of the general historical trustworthiness of Mark to reconstruct *The Life and Ministry of Jesus* (1955), followed by *The Person of Christ in New Testament Teachings* (1958). L. W. Grensted's *The Person of Christ* (1933) should also be mentioned. It will be noted that in the earlier writings the person of Christ gained a centrality that is dwarfed in most later works by Western theologians writing on Christology.

Critical interaction with continental theology by a succession of British evangelical scholars was not extensively undertaken until more than a decade after the dialectical-existential view began mak-ing significant inroads into New Testament perspectives on the Brit-ish Isles. C. S. Lewis's *Miracles* (1947, rev. 1960) aimed at naturalism more than at the continental theologies which formed their views of nature and history to positivist theory, but Lewis nonetheless placed the high view of Jesus Christ once again in the center of the public arena. A. M. Hunter's *The Work and Words of Jesus* (1950) empha-sized the interpretative importance of presuppositions about world-view and about Jesus' person, and opted for supernatural theism.[3] F. F. Bruce reaffirmed the trustworthiness of the gospels in *The New Testament Documents: Are They Reliable?* (1960), and in numerous essays raised questions about the use to which existentialist writers deploy form criticism. Donald Guthrie's *New Testament Introduc-tion: The Gospels* (1965) championed the reliability of the writings against the tide of radical criticism. From England and then Austra-lia, Leon Morris contributed *The Apostolic Preaching of the Cross* (1956) and other volumes related to atonement theory. H. D. Mc-Donald wrote *Jesus—Human and Divine* (1968), which focused spe-cially on implications of the Nestorian controversy.

This material was solid scholarship, even if not all of it was in the league of classic christological works of earlier generations. Reasons for this were numerous. The frontiers of theological controversy seemed ever on the move and the time appeared right for the occupation of intermediary positions more than for all-out assault. Evangelical scholars found themselves, moreover, a conspicuous minority, and the many liberal Protestant university colleagues with whose views they contended were frequently at odds with each other in defending remarkably divergent positions. The British economy, moreover, increasingly discouraged book publication. The works of German critical scholars hurriedly translated and published in America gained influence through cheaply priced British reproductions, to the dismay of both evangelical and nonevangelical authors, whose original work publishers viewed as too costly to print. In these circumstances British evangelicals were more readily enlisted for cooperative commentary and symposium effort, and for essays in theological journals or more or less technical magazines like *The Evangelical Quarterly* or the erstwhile trans-Atlantic fortnightly *The Christian and Christianity Today*, or for encyclopedia effort. Encyclopedia essays ran the gamut from short contributions like those by Philip E. Hughes on "Myth" and Ronald S. Wallace on "Christology" in *Baker's Dictionary of Theology* (E. F. Harrison, ed., 1960) and similar works, to the noteworthy and extensive article by Donald Guthrie on "Jesus Christ" in *The Zondervan Pictorial Encyclopedia of the Bible.* Nor should we overlook the role of conservatively oriented British professors, particularly Bruce, Moule, and Hunter, in training young evangelical New Testament scholars who came from both sides of the Atlantic to pursue post-graduate studies.

While American evangelical scholars did not contribute to christological literature in the forepart of the century as notably as did their British peers, they nonetheless authored some significant texts. In the first quarter-century appeared B. B. Warfield's *The Lord of Glory* (1907), A. T. Robertson's *The Divinity of Christ in the Gospel of John* (1916), and E. Y. Mullin's *The Christian Religion in Its Doctrinal Expression* (1917). The second quarter-century began auspiciously with Geerhardus Vos's *The Self-Disclosure of Jesus* (1926) and ended with the mid-century collection of B. B. Warfield's earlier essays in the compilation *The Person and Work of Christ* (1950). Between these appeared J. Gresham Machen's closely reasoned *The Origin of Paul's Religion* (1928) and *The Virgin Birth of Christ* (1930), Warfield's *Christology and Criticism* (1929), William Childs Robinson's *Our Lord: An Affirmation of the Deity of Christ* (1937), Wilbur M. Smith's *The Supernaturalness of Christ* (1940), and Loraine Boettner's *The Person of Christ* (1943), some of these works clearly tagging far behind the European christological controversy.

These were years of increasing christological turmoil in American liberalism, marked by the growing capitulation of modernist Christology to humanist attack.[4] The liberal Protestant, as Machen was wont to say, had "great respect" for Jesus; but beneath his complimentary adjectives lurked the notion that Jesus was not the eternal *Logos* enfleshed, not born of a virgin, not raised bodily from the dead, not a redeemer who would personally return to judge all mankind.[5] Jesus was viewed as the best representation of a godlike humanity and our supreme moral example, but not the sinner's substitutionary and propitiatory substitute or the worker of external miracles. Machen refused to see in these half-truths a gratifying tribute which, even if it did not go far enough, nonetheless was to a confused culture a pointer in the right direction. Instead, he focused the alternatives clearly: "The Jesus thus reconstructed may be useful as investing modern programs with the sanctity of His hallowed name . . . but what ought to be clearly understood is that such a Jesus has nothing to do with history. He is a purely imaginary figure, a symbol and not a fact."[6] "The truth is that the life-purpose of Jesus discovered by modern liberalism is not the life purpose of the real Jesus, but merely represents those elements in the teaching of Jesus . . . which happen to agree with the modern process. It is not Jesus . . . then, who is the real authority, but the modern principle. . . ."[7] And it was indeed a fact of twentieth-century theology that neo-Protestantism, which hesitated to regard Jesus as the object of faith, would soon abandon him also as the example of faith: in Bultmannian existentialism Jesus was to become merely the evoker of faith. The call for a higher Christology came from within modernist ranks by spokesmen like Edwin Lewis (*A Philosophy of the Christian Revelation,* 1940) and Walter Marshall Horton (*Our Eternal Contemporary,* 1943).[8] For many chastened liberals the discussion of the doctrine of the two natures, of the virgin birth, of the bodily resurrection, and of much else christological remained an exercise in literary ambiguity.

While the mid-century does not wholly bring to an end American evangelical contribution on the theme of Christology, it nonetheless marks a significant divide. For the subject of Christology is notably dwarfed as an evangelical concern precisely at the time when the critical continental views ever more influentially pervade the Anglo-Saxon West. Moreover, Christology itself recedes further into the background as a center of evangelical interest; other themes, particularly scriptural revelation, eschatology, evangelism and missiology, counseling, and social ethics begin to overshadow Christology. While

Hugh Anderson's somewhat extensive selected bibliography of land-mark volumes in the recent "Jesus of history—Christ of faith debate" fails to mention some evangelical contributions worthy of inclusion, it nonetheless attests how sparse was American evangelical involve-ment in the controversy over how the primitive Church came to believe in Jesus of Nazareth.[9] Louis Berkhof's *Systematic Theology* (1946) in its list of forty-nine significant books on Christology reflects not a single volume on the christological debate reaching back to Barth and Bultmann and which was now at its height. Lewis Sperry Chafer's eight-volume *Systematic Theology* (1948) has no index reference to Barth, Brunner, Bultmann, or other neo-Protes-tants who were reviewing and revising christological doctrine. Even J. Oliver Buswell's two-volume *A Systematic Theology of the Christian Religion* (1963) virtually ignores the conflict in Christology posed by dialectical-existential theologians. Not from the whole gamut of evangelical seminaries or colleges or Bible schools on the American scene did there emerge a major technical work on Christology!

On the fringes of historic evangelicalism appeared William R. Cannon's *The Redeemer* (1951), which in line with recent neo-Prot-estant thought orients the discussion to the work more than to the person of Jesus and opts for paradox and mystery above rational revelation in affirming Christ's deity;[10] moreover, God is declared to be superpersonal. Also on the margin of traditional evangelical em-phases was Floyd V. Filson's *Jesus Christ the Risen Lord* (1956), which nonetheless takes Jesus' resurrection as the starting-point and illuminating center of New Testament theology and, in contrast to John Knox's kerygmatically oriented *Christ the Lord* (1945), keeps an eye on historical concerns as much as on faith.

Slowly but surely, however, a literature began to appear from mainstream evangelical sources in America, some of it stimulated by post-graduate studies under European scholars. Yet even Charles C. Anderson's *The Historical Jesus: a Continuing Quest* (1972), al-though more fully reflecting relevant evangelical literature than Hugh Anderson's *Jesus and Christian Origins*, does not impress the reader with any wide range of evangelical engagement at critical frontiers. Anderson himself repudiates modern mythologizing tendencies and considers Jesus' earthly life as history "of primary importance for the Christian faith,"[11] and he notes many of historic evangelicalism's strengths over against unorthodox alternatives. In this succession of American evangelical books belong George Eldon Ladd's *The Gospel of the Kingdom* (1959) and *Jesus and the Kingdom* (1964), Ned B. Stonehouse's *Origins of the Synoptic Gospels* (1963), Merrill C. Tenney's *The Reality of the Resurrection* (1963), Everett F. Harrison's *Introduction to the New Testament* (1964), and Daniel P. Fuller's *Faith and History* (1965), centering attention on the resurrection of Jesus.

The very possibility of writing a life of Jesus was thrown into doubt by the sharp conflict of viewpoints which had developed over the real person, teaching activity, and mission of Jesus. Refusing to yield to the resultant scholarly impasse, Harrison insisted that many of the influential views rested on ephemeral theories and were sponsored by imaginative critics. His *A Short Life of Christ* (1968) was produced, as he himself notes, "under the conviction that in spite of all obstacles in dealing with the text, there is still room for a treatment of the life of Christ that concerns itself with the leading events that carry us along on a fairly obvious sequence from the beginning to the end."[12] The Jesus of the gospels, he insisted, is not a product of the Church's imagination, nor were the gospels unhistorical accounts. Many who knew Jesus were still living when the gospels were written (1 Cor 15:6), and, moreover, converts were given systematic instruction from the very beginnings of the Church (Acts 2:42; 11:26).[13] The Church never knew any Jesus other than "the divine Savior, Son of Man and Son of God." No desupernaturalized Jesus could have made the impact the Nazarene made upon his generation, nor that his followers have made upon theirs.

In Harrison's view, therefore, there is no need to defer to the existentially oriented form critics and to dismiss the gospels as unreliable history. For him, Jesus is not simply the awakener of faith—though he is that incomparably—but also the object of faith; the gospels, moreover, are the trustworthy source of our knowledge of the days of his flesh. Harrison denies neither the objective historical factuality of divine revelation nor its rational intelligibility. He emphasizes rather that Jesus Christ is the supreme disclosure of the Creator-God who personally acts in nature and history and has communicated his truth verbally in prophetic-apostolic Scripture. He does not therefore see in the emphasis on divine revelation in the person of Christ a basis for moderating the historic evangelical assertion of rational, propositional disclosure. Here he stands not only over against the tide of German theology represented by Barth and Bultmann, but of English theology paced by Archbishop William Temple. Temple, for example, writes that "the whole reality of this revelation finds its perfect and local expression in Jesus Himself. It is of supreme importance that it should thus be given in a Person."[14] But Temple then moves to demolish a word-revelation by appealing to the so-called assured results of biblical criticism.[15] The biblical message is so inextricably human and divine in one, we are told, that "no single sentence can be quoted as having the authority of an authentic utterance of the All-Holy God."[16] Yet Temple seems unaware that the same argument, consistently applied, would demolish a person-revelation in Jesus of Nazareth. For he also remarks that "there is no single deed or saying of which we can be perfectly sure that He said or did precisely this or that."[17] Harrison, however, resists both Bultmann's notion that the gospels enshroud a myth and that history has no revelational significance and Barth's notion that revelation is not objectively given but is supernaturally communicated only internally in person-to-person encounters with the transcendent Christ known in faith. In an essay contributed to an evangelical symposium on the Founder of the Christian religion, Harrison labelled Bultmannian *Gemeindetheologie* "The bane of Gospel criticism."[18]

At the World Congress on Evangelism in Berlin during 1966, a major Bible study by George B. Duncan of Scotland was devoted to "An Apostolic Assessment of the Ministry of Jesus Christ"; but no main address was specially devoted to the person and work of the crucified and risen Jesus. But the position papers, and especially one by Johannes Schneider of West Berlin, vigorously engaged and confronted liberal German theology as imperiling the Christian faith at its christological center. At the International Congress on World Evangelization at Lausanne (1974) emphasis on the Holy Spirit far overshadowed that on Jesus Christ. No plenary paper or Bible study centered upon Christology, although the twenty-five papers on the theology of evangelization included one by Roger Nicole of the United States on "Jesus Christ, the Unique Son of God" and another by Rudy Budiman of Indonesia on "The Theology of the Cross and of the Resurrection in Our Unique Salvation."

Richard N. Longenecker's *The Christology of Early Jewish Christianity* stressed the inadequacy of both the Bultmannian and post-Bultmannian views:

> While Jesus made a decided personal impact upon his disciples during the course of his earthly ministry, it was the fact of his resurrection from the dead, as interpreted first by Jesus himself and then by the Spirit, which was the historical point of departure in their christological understanding. . . . The older theological debates regarding the centrality of either Jesus' teaching or his death in Christian faith, important as they were, have tended to obscure the point that in the earliest days of the apostolic period it was the resurrection of Jesus which was central. Both the teaching and the death were interpreted in the light of the resurrection, and both had significance for the early Christians only because Jesus had actually been raised from the dead.[19]

Christianity was from the first an historical faith rooted in the incarnation and resurrection of Jesus Christ; without those historical foundations it would neither have survived nor come into being. No chapter of Greek or Roman history rests upon consistent eyewitness accounts and written records more compelling than the biblical reports whose authors, in order to share its incomparable content with an avowedly unbelieving world, forsook all that common mortals cling to.

George Ladd's *A Theology of the New Testament* (1974) carried forward the American evangelical interaction with christological concerns to a still fuller wresting of the biblical data. Ladd further expounded the fundamental priority of the gospel history for apostolic preaching in his essay on "Revelation and Tradition in Paul."[20]

With an eye on the christological crisis, American evangelicals contributed in a noteworthy way to symposium and encyclopedia efforts. In an essay on "Jesus of Nazareth" Bastiaan Van Elderen insisted that "the historical Jesus is a basic constituent in the message of the early Church" both in the gospels and the epistles, and appealed to the many allusions to Jesus *of Nazareth* in support of his thesis.[21] In the same work, George Ladd asserted the priority and objectivity of Jesus' resurrection as an event in history, contrary to Bultmannian and post-Bultmannian emphases.[22] The trans-Atlantic symposium *Jesus of Nazareth: Saviour and Lord* (1966) set wide-angle focus on the contemporary christological crisis with essays by European and American scholars, reaffirming the strength of historic orthodoxy in contrast with novel contemporary theories.

2. Christology Question Today

While American evangelical scholarship is now slowly pulling out of its neglect of serious christological study, it is important to note how extensive has been the evasion of christological priorities earlier in the present generation. On the receiving end of thousands of articles hopefully submitted for publication, the writer, when editor of *Christianity Today* from 1956 to 1968, found that usable essays on Jesus Christ are almost as scarce as battleships in Zurich. Even evangelical Bible and preaching conferences, it is often said, will draw twice the audience for a message on anti-Christ than a message on the God-man. One can commute from church to church over a span of many months before he is likely to hear a sermon on the perfections of the incarnate and now glorified Son of God. In their studies many evangelical pastors work with books predating the modern crisis in Christology. Some evangelical publishers even reprint works from past generations with no flyleaf indication of when these volumes originated. Laymen can be rallied by the hundreds for polemical addresses on biblical inerrancy while an expository address on the heavenly ministry of the Redeemer will often beg for an audience. Even in personal devotional life the pressures of twentieth-century existence are such that Christian meditation most readily turns to other priorities than the incarnate and risen Christ—human physical need, international conflict, planetary pollution; if Jesus is in view, his redemptive work more than his divine person is central.

The temper of much Bible college study, and even of some seminaries, is that since the conjectural modern theories must sooner or later collapse, they can be ignored. But this removes evangelical study from pointed interaction with elements of stress posed by non-evangelical spokesmen and exempts conservative scholars from the burdens of an evangelical defense against modern theological assault. Even the so-called Jesus freaks who sought to pattern their lives after a hippie-like Jesus need to be steered through the factualities of the earthly life of Jesus in a time when historical skepticism and imaginative creativity pervade much Gospel interpretation. Nor are non-evangelicals any longer the only advocates of a revolutionary Jesus. Not only in the Third World but on the American scene a cadre of young evangelicals is enamored of supposedly radical implications of Jesus' ministry and runs the risk of subordinating emphases that do not fit well into the revolutionary motif. Again, evangelical preaching often fails to keep abreast of the best in biblical learning, let alone the transient critical views. It still echoes, for example, the long-entrenched notion that the term Son of Man refers to Jesus' humanity or that the conception of Jesus' lordship in the New Testament is exhausted by his role as Redeemer.

There can be no doubt that twentieth-century American evangelicals have maintained a superlative evangelistic and missionary witness in a theological climate in which many church leaders consider both activities dispensable. At the center of this global outreach has stood an uncompromising emphasis on the divine authority of the Bible and on the redemption that is in Christ Jesus. In their refusal to adjust Christian proclamation to anything but the scriptural centralities, the evangelical task force follows not only a sound instinct but a divine imperative. William Manson made the important point that "the foundation of our theology" is none other than Jesus himself— not Augustine, or Aquinas, or Luther, or Calvin, or Barth. "Jesus has the final word, the ultimatum, the word that will still ring, when the world's debate is done."[23] But evangelical theology just for that reason cannot afford to neglect the fullest possible concentration on

Jesus' life and teaching and work, important as other apologetic or polemical priorities may seem.

Even the study of comparative religions has been shadowed by the christological crisis, and competitive claims about religious reality invariably work themselves into para-evangelistic enterprises. When E. Washburn Hopkins wrote that "the religion of Christ stands to Christianity somewhat as that of Buddha to Buddhism,"[24] he covered by the adjective "somewhat" a multitude of misunderstandings spawned by "History of Religions" prejudices; repeatedly he explains Christian conceptions by supposed dependence on non-biblical religions. Much the same approach obtrudes in George Foot Moore's *History of Religions* (1947). That Jesus of Nazareth is related to the God of the Hebrew covenant by a category uniquely different from other great religious figures, in fulfillment of messianic promise and expectation, is here excluded in advance on alien conjectural principles. Points of external similarity between Christianity and other ancient faiths (the call for voluntary affiliation, the dying and rising savior motif, the prospect of a felicitous immortality for its followers) are made to diminish and cancel the staggering dissimilarities. What any religion would be like if it had nothing at all in common with other religions is nowhere considered, nor is the Christian view that all religions reflect in some ineradicable way an originally violated relationship to the incomparable God of Judeo-Christian revelation.

Hendrik Kraemer noted the way in which the Christian religion itself ongoingly treats with resilient diffidence all such reductionist attacks.

> Many efforts have been made and are still made to insert it in the great immanent process of human creativity in the field of religion; for it can safely be said that all investigations in the origins of Christianity, all endeavors to explain it as the outcome of religious development in the Jewish and Hellenistic world and to demonstrate its kinship to the mystery-religions, aim at making Christianity the result of the immanent process of history. It is one of the most fascinating things to notice that Christianity, the religion of revelation, constantly eludes these endeavours. Deepened investigation tends to reveal more and more not only its originality but also its refractoriness to this reducing treatment. The origins of Christianity are irreducible.[25]

Horace Shipp appropriately reminds us that agnosticism must work a greater miracle than any the New Testament depicts if it seeks persuasively to explain the ministry of Jesus as that merely of a man among men, the world mission of the disciples as the adventure of misguided enthusiasts, and the revolutionary redirection of the life

and work of Saul of Tarsus as a response to some grandiose halluci-
nation.[26]

Philip H. Ashby remarks pointedly that Christ is *"the* Person"
who from the beginnings of Christianity has always been centrally in
view.[27] The incarnation of the Living God in the historical life of
Jesus Christ stands indelibly as the central Christian emphasis. If it be
the case, as James Freeman Clarke once said of non-biblical religions,
that "in every instance we can touch with our finger the weak or
empty side,"[28] Jesus Christ towers ongoingly by contrast as the
unfaulty and unsurpassable center of the Christian religion.

On the surface it may seem incongruous to contend that in the
span of the thirty-three-year lifetime of the Nazarene the supreme
revelation of the Living God was given to mankind, indeed that the
revelation was conveyed in his three-year public ministry. Here is a
figure who at the age of twelve baffled learned doctors in the temple,
yet in two subsequent decades leaves us neither a scroll nor even a
written sentence by his own hand to pierce the obscurity, but who in
his ministry from the time of baptism by John the Baptist through
his crucifixion by Pilate and subsequent resurrection manifests the
Living God in word and deed and life as none before or after him. In
the hymn "Now to the Lord a Noble Song," Isaac Watts captures this
climactic claim in memorable lines:

> See where it shines in Jesus' face
> The brightest image of His grace;
> God, in the person of His Son,
> Has all his mightiest works outdone.

In some 150 weeks of the thousands of years of human history, and
in a single incomparable life in a particular place on this planet,
Christianity claims, the revelation of the God of the Ages was given
in Jesus of Nazareth. The Living God of Genesis, who through the
days of creation patiently shaped a universe in which *homo sapiens*
bears his divine image, in the day of redemption fashioned the
lifespan in which the incarnate Logos mirrored the perfections of
Godhead in the flesh, and moves even now toward that coming
moment of history when all the godly host of faithful men and
women will be conformed wholly to the likeness of Jesus Christ.

Of the ever-present Lord in his ongoing global ministry Marcus
Bach writes:

> Wherever man worships, there Christ is standing, seeking to save. . . . He
> stands beside the Hindu chanting his mantras and bowing his head at his
> shrine. He lingers beside the Jew reading the Torah or contemplating the
> Mezuzah on the doorpost of his home. He pauses beside the Parsi bowing to

the sacred fire in his secret temple. He watches the follower of Confucius who reverently beholds the tablets of the temple, the Taoist burning incense on his golden altars, the Buddhist spinning prayer wheels, and the Shintoist making his pilgrimages to the holy shrine. He keeps his vigil over the Moslem kneeling on his prayer rug in the Mosque, and hears the echo of the imam as he calls, "There is no God but Allah."[29]

Alongside the multiple forms of religion he challenges the Greek disposition dating from Xenophanes to regard these as a diverse but not contradictory expression of the many aspects of religious truth; instead, he bears the only name "whereby we must be saved" (Acts 4:12) as the apostles let it be known throughout the Graeco-Roman world and then in the regions beyond. While the Bible nowhere teaches that the realm of heathen worship falls outside "God's care and operation, or that all the heathen are devoid of any real knowledge of God," and does not equate Anti-Christ with heathenism, as E. C. Dewick properly reminds us,[30] nonetheless the New Testament verdict is that Christ will judge the world in righteousness and that Christianity is much more than merely the complement, fulfillment, or realization of the non-biblical faiths. Rather, it is the only religion proffering to human beings universally the eternal redemption found in Jesus Christ alone. To mesh that message with the modern mind at every level of learning and commitment, evangelical Christianity must put a swift end to any evasion of christological concerns.

The difference between Christianity and other world religions can never be decisively stated without central reference to Jesus Christ. Christianity affirms that God has definitively disclosed his nature and purposes in Jesus Christ—that Jesus Christ is the focal point where ultimate reality gives itself to man, the source of the norms to which we must orient our existence, the reference point by which the nature of ultimate reality, truth, and meaning must be defined and measured if we would not go astray. The reference in Heb 1:1-2 to "many and various ways" speaks, among other things, of the manifold forms and piecemeal character of the prophetic revelation in contrast to the full and final revelation in Christ. Christ as the complete revelation of God unites in his one person the whole spectrum of divine disclosure. In a broad sense, to be sure, God discloses something concerning his nature and will in all his deeds; even the prophetic-apostolic revelation of the meaning of the divine acts bears the structure of coherent personal communication. God's disclosure in nature, and external history, and to the mind and conscience of man universally, is self-revelation, since he discloses not only his eternal power but his Godhead or divinity (Rom 1:20). But only of Jesus Christ may it be said accurately that the very content of the revelation divinely given is God himself in the decisive meaning of self-revelation.

The difference between Christianity and Mohammedanism is not, as sometimes claimed, that Mohammedanism is the religion of a Book whereas Christianity is not; for the Christian religion has its own emphasis on a divinely inspired corpus of writings to which Mohammed was himself in a broken way indebted. But in Muslim religion, the Koran functions in place not simply of the Bible but of Jesus Christ also. The Koran is held to be the uncreated, eternal Word of God, the supreme form in which the Word of God is thought to be given, while both Jesus and Mohammed are viewed as prophets. The significance of the incarnate Logos is forfeited because the content of divine disclosure is regarded as channeled wholly into a sacred book and that book in turn manipulates the historical and theological data concerning Jesus.

Jesus Christ stands at the center of the Christian religion not simply as the founder of a religion but as God's supreme and final revelation. Buddha pointed not to himself, but away from himself, to Nirvana. It is true that, when asked how they can with consistency insist that Nirvana is a reality to be experienced here and now since Nirvana is asserted to be beyond description, Buddhists point to Buddha as having realized Nirvana, and to the testimony of other Buddhists who subsequently lay claim to the same experience. But Buddha said: "You must be your own lamps . . . your own refuges. . . . Do not look beyond yourselves." Each must enter Nirvana for himself and on his own. Emphasis on the permanent significance of Buddha would, in fact, be an embarrassment to the Buddhist doctrine of the transitoriness of the self.

Some other religions do speak of a divine revelation given to specially chosen persons or contained in sacred writings. But here too the nature of supernatural action is conceived very differently from the way it is in the Bible. What is important to these religions are certain presumably timeless truths or relationships which are in principle separable from the persons by or through whom these conceptions are said first to have been disclosed. But, as Pannenberg has written, "Jesus' person cannot be separated from God's essence if Jesus in person is God's self-revelation."[31] Pantheistic religions and philosophies view the world and man as externalizations of an Absolute Self. When everything that exists becomes personal, divine disclosure, the distinction between the revelational and non-revelational is nullified, and the contrast between special and general revelation is obscured. In affirming that Jesus Christ is the personal revelation of God, Christianity intends nothing in common with the

Hindu notion that there are many such divine incarnations, since biblical theism expressly repudiates the pantheistic premise of a hidden identity between God and all reality.

In the mood of German idealism, Hegel insisted on the importance and uniqueness of the historical person of Jesus because in the history of humanity he "first" (not "alone") brought to light the deepest knowledge (i.e., God-consciousness) and embodied it in his person. Much the same emphasis is found in Fichte's reference to "a prodigious miracle in view of which Jesus is the only-begotten and first-begotten Son." Here Christianity is not bound *essentially* to Jesus; he is the *way* to the Truth, but not himself *the Truth*. The distinction between the Christ-ideal or principle of God-manhood and the essential divinity of the historical Jesus and the person of Christ is here elaborated at the expense of historic, evangelical orthodoxy. While Bultmann and Reinhold Niebuhr are far removed from Hegelian rationalism, Niebuhr's emphasis on the Christ-ideal in distinction to the historical Jesus, and Bultmann's refusal to speak of the divine word and person of Christ in the dimension of the historical, share the Hegelian hostility to the emphasis that in the earthly life of Jesus of Nazareth God has given a full and final revelation of himself.

At the heart of the Christian revelation is, as Heinz Zahrnt writes,

what happened to a concrete historical person. One cannot separate Christian truth from this person, by bringing its message forward into the present, but leaving the person himself in the past. . . . The message itself consists of what happened to this person, his birth, life, teaching, death and resurrection. The validity of the revelation of God in Jesus Christ is final, conclusive, unsurpassable and universal. Although God may have revealed himself, and may still reveal himself in many other ways, in different places and at different times . . . he has revealed himself decisively through Jesus Christ. Consequently, theology treats the event of Christ as an "eschatological event." This word signifies that what took place through and in Christ was something "ultimate" in the history of the world, beyond which there can be nothing "more ultimate" or greater. In Him God "spoke" finally and once for all to the world: Jesus is the "Word of God" to the whole of mankind.[32]

NOTES

1. *Form Criticism: A New Method of New Testament Research*, F. C. Grant, ed. and trans. (1934), p. 61.
2. *History and the Gospel* (1938), p. 14.
3. Hunter, *Work and Words*, p. 59.
4. See Edwin A. Burtt, *Types of Religious Philosophy* (1939), pp. 359f.

5. Machen, *Christianity and Liberalism* (1923), pp. 85f.
6. Ibid., p. 34.
7. Ibid., p. 78
8. Many of these tensions between liberalism, realistic liberalism, and neo-orthodoxy are reflected in the chapter on "The Mid-Century View of Christ," in *The Protestant Dilemma* (1948) by the present writer.
9. *Jesus and Christian Origins* (1964), pp. 355–360.
10. Cannon, *Redeemer*, p. 206.
11. Anderson, *Origins*, p. 6.
12. Harrison, *Life*, p. 8.
13. Ibid., pp. 23f.
14. In *Revelation* by Gustaf Aulén, Baillie and Martin, eds. (1937), p. 114.
15. *Nature, Man and God* (1934), pp. 351f.
16. Ibid., p. 350.
17. *Revelation*, p. 114.
18. *Jesus of Nazareth: Saviour and Lord*, C. F. H. Henry, ed. (1966), p. 159.
19. Longenecker, *Christology of Early Jewish Christianity* (1970), pp. 148f.
20. In *Apostolic History and the Gospel*, W. W. Gasque and R. P. Martin, eds. (1970), pp. 223–230.
21. In *Christian Faith and Modern Theology*, C. F. H. Henry, ed. (1964), pp. 243–260.
22. Ibid., "The Resurrection of Jesus Christ," pp. 263–284.
23. *Jesus and the Christian* (1967), p. 134.
24. *History of Religions* (1918), p. 552.
25. *Christian Message in A Non-Christian World* (1938), p. 62.
26. *Faiths That Moved the World* (1946), p. 96.
27. *History and Future of Religious Thought* (1963), p. 27.
28. Quoted by David James Burrell, *The Religions of the World* (1934), p. 314.
29. *Major Religions of the World* (1959), pp. 13f.
30. *Gospel and Other Faiths* (1948), pp. 48f.
31. *Jesus—God and Man*, p. 158.
32. *Question of God* (1969), p. 203.

16: The Role of Women in the Church and Home: An Evangelical Testcase in Hermeneutics

ROBERT K. JOHNSTON

It is almost impossible for the interested individual to keep abreast of the burgeoning discussion on women's place in the Church and Christian home. Stirred by the steady stream of feminist literature which has caused a revolution in Western society, and prodded by the more liberal wing of the Church which opened up the discussion on the ordination of women twenty or more years ago, contemporary evangelicals have become increasingly interested in reevaluating the role of women.*

As the discussion has proceeded among evangelicals, sides have been drawn.[5] One faction is represented by supporters of the recently formed Evangelical Women's Caucus like Nancy Hardesty, Lucille Sider Dayton, and Virginia Mollenkott. The other, by such otherwise disparate individuals as George Knight, Elisabeth Elliot, and Larry Christenson. The one side argues that a Christian woman in today's society should be ordained to ministry if she possesses the gifts and has the training. It also holds that wives should join their husbands in egalitarian relationships characterized by *mutual* love and submission. The other side argues that a female in today's

---

*Books such as Marabel Morgan's *The Total Woman*, Helen Andelin's *Fascinating Womanhood*, Larry Christenson's *The Christian Family*, Gladys Hunt's *Ms. Means Myself*, Paul Jewett's *Man as Male and Female*, Letha Scanzoni's and Nancy Hardesty's *All We're Meant To Be* have taken varying positions and have been widely read and debated in evangelical circles.[1] Bill Gothard, through his Institute in Basic Youth Conflicts, has offered teaching on the subject of woman's rightful place to thousands, as have Francis Schaeffer, Howard Hendricks, and Tim LaHaye. Evangelical periodicals such as *The Other Side* (July-August, 1973), *Right On* (September, 1975), *Post American* (August/September, 1974), *Theology News and Notes* (June, 1975), and *The Wittenburg Door* (August-September, 1975) have devoted whole issues to the topic of women.[2] Other journals like *Christianity Today*, *Moody Monthly*, *Logos*, *The Reformed Journal*, *Eternity*, *Vanguard*, and *Sojourners* have published repeated articles on the issue.[3] *Daughters of Sarah* has come into being to provide for evangelical women who believe Christianity and feminism are inseparable.[4]

"liberated" society is still a "woman" and as such should fit into God's ordained and orderly creation, fulfilling her role of submission and dependence in Church and home without impatience on the one hand or servitude on the other.

From the earliest days of the current discussion, it has been recognized that the question regarding the role of women within the congregation and the home is largely a hermeneutical one. Krister Stendahl gave voice to this in his important essay *The Bible and The Role of Women: A Case Study in Hermeneutics,* written in 1958.[6] Donald Dayton expressed a similar position in his article in the *Post American:* ". . . the real question at least for most Christians [is] : Which of these views (the hierarchical or the egalitarian—or perhaps a synthesis of the two) has the clearer grounding in scripture?"[7]

Use of the Bible as a source of authority in the debate has brought mixed approaches and results. Feminists have tended to emphasize the broader affirmations of the gospel which stress oneness in Christ. Traditionalists have usually centered on specific passages of advice in Scripture such as Ephesians 5 and 1 Timothy 2. Moreover, in regard to specific biblical texts, differences of opinion have arisen at almost every conceivable place.† Both sides ground their positions in Scripture, and yet opposite conclusions are reached. Clearly, one's method of understanding Scripture is crucial

---

† Is the biblical picture normative (with its male predominance) or are there deeper principles implicit in the texture of the biblical fabric which make male authority a cultural, and thus relative, affair? Is the first-century lifestyle prepared or happenstance as it correlates with revelation, or perhaps some of each? Is it significant that Jesus was a male and appointed only male disciples? What is the significance of Jesus' "revolutionary" attitude and actions toward women? Does "subordination" imply inferiority? Such questions are basic to understanding a biblical position regarding women in the Church and home and are answered variously by each side in the debate.

Such questioning seems endless once begun. Is the order of creation normative, or has it been superseded by the fact of redemption? Can the Trinity serve as a model of submissiveness within a context of equality? Does man's "headship" as referred to by Paul relate to his rank in "authority" or to his role as "source"? Is Paul's use of Genesis in his discussion of woman's place illustrative or foundational? Does the fact that woman was made for man imply a hierarchy? Is the curse in Gen 3:16 descriptive or prescriptive? Is the use of masculine gender for God still significant for us today? Was the advice by Paul concerning women meant to be applied universally or was it a response to a localized need? Is it important that women in the Old Testament were prophets, but never priests? What is the meaning of words like *authentein* (1 Tim 2:12) and *exousia* (1 Cor 11:10)?

Are the arguments Paul uses in 1 Corinthians 11 meant to pertain to all men and women or only the husband/wife relationship? Does Gal 3:28 refer to a woman's "spiritual privilege" of being saved, or does it refer to her position and activity in the Church and Christian home as well? Are women more easily led astray than men? Does the fact that man was created first, according to Genesis, matter? When Paul speaks about women, is he referring to all women or only to wives (remembering that all women in those days married young)? Do all the details of Paul's advice to women apply equally today? If not, how do you decide what is normative?

at this point. Behind the apparent differences in approach and opinion are opposing principles for interpreting Scripture—i.e., different hermeneutics.

This essay will thus focus on the differing viewpoints toward women currently being argued by evangelicals today, in order that the underlying hermeneutical stances of those involved in the question might be evaluated. It will become apparent that what is at stake ultimately is the nature and authority of Scripture itself as reflected in this current theological debate. In order that readers can follow the hermeneutical issues as they relate to a biblical view of women, a brief overview of the contrasting positions—the egalitarian and the traditionalist—will first be presented. With this as background, certain inadequate methods of interpretation currently in use will be discussed and criticized. Finally, suggestions for a more adequate hermeneutic will be offered, together with indications of their helpfulness in the discussion of women's role in the Church and home.

1. An Egalitarian Position

What is the nature of woman? Gen 1:26, 27 recounts how God made man as male and female in his image. Man and woman were to be a fellowship of equals like the fellowship within the Godhead (i.e., the Trinity) and were given joint responsibilities (Gen 1:28). The second creation narrative (Gen 2:18–23) reinforces this basic point, portraying woman as being from God like man, as well as one with him, i.e., flesh of his flesh. With the Fall, the subordination of woman to man becomes a reality, the first example of mankind's exploitation of his neighbor. Now Adam names his wife "Eve" (Gen 3:20), and God describes her future relation with Adam as one of authority and submission (Gen 3:16). This "curse" is not applied to all women, but is sheathed in the context of husband and wife relationships. Moreover, it is clear that in Christ there is a new creation, superseding the conditions of the Fall (1 Cor 11:11–12; Gal 3:28). Through faith by grace, the equality of male and female in human relationships is restored.

This new creation was demonstrated in Jesus' life, as he broke with the existing hierarchical structuring of male-female relationships and treated women as equals (Luke 8:1–3; 10:38–42; 11:27–28; 13:10–17; 21:1–4; Mark 5:22–42; 16:9; John 8:3–11; 12:1–8). Within the Church, similarly, women, like men, were early converts, and the description of the first-century Church suggests that women were engaged in significant ministry within it (1 Cor 11:2–16; Rom 16:1–16; Col 4:15; Acts 2:17–21; 5:14; 8:12; 9:1–2; 9:36–42;

12:12; 16:12–15, 40; 17:4, 34; 18:2–3; 18:24–28; 21:9; Phil 4:2–3; 1 Tim 3:11; 5:1–16; 2 Tim 1:5–7; Tit 2:3). Moreover, the New Testament teaches that every Christian is to grow into maturity in Christ and to exercise fully the gifts he/she has been given. No sexual distinction is hinted at (2 Tim 1:6–7; Rom 12:6–8; 1 Pet 4:10; 1 Cor 12:4–31; Matt 25:14–30).

Those passages in Scripture which seem to speak against this fundamental position of equality between men and women (1 Cor 14:33–40; 1 Tim 2:8–15; 1 Cor 11:2–16; Eph 5:21–33; 1 Pet 3:1–7) must be understood as follows:

1. Our existing translations are often biased against women (e.g., in 1 Tim 2:11, "in silence [KJV] should rather be translated "quietly" [NEB] or archaic (e.g., an "help mate for him" does not mean a subordinate "helpmate," Gen 2:18).

2. Although the fact that man and woman are to be partners in fellowship was largely overlooked in patriarchal Israel, there is even there a depatriarchalizing tendency (cf. Song of Solomon, "honor thy father and mother," Judg 4–5). This is continued in the New Testament (Gal 3:28).

3. Christians shared the cultural attitudes of the first century A.D. regarding the position of women in a manner analogous to their attitude toward slavery (cf. Eph 5:21ff. where Paul expresses the reciprocity of marriage in terms acceptable to the Ephesians' cultural attitudes and the obligation of slaves and masters in a similar manner).

4. In Scripture, the understanding and application of revelation is an historical process (cf. Mark 10:2–5). We recognize this in relation to Christianity's influence on the emancipation of slaves. We must similarly apply this recognition to the issue of women's rightful role today.

5. Paul's letters are addressed to specific people with special problems which called for particular responses which were correct for that situation but must often be translated into underlying general principles if they are to be applicable to us today (e.g., 1 Cor 14:33–36, 40 probably refers to uneducated, married women disrupting the order of worship by asking questions; 1 Tim 2:8–15 may be a response to immature women believers teaching heresy in the Church).

6. Paul's advice regarding women in the Church must be correlated with his description of what women actually did in the early Church (see above for references).

7. We must beware of reading twentieth-century nuances into first-century advice (e.g., "head" in 1 Cor 11:3 is not meant to

designate a hierarchy but to suggest woman's "source" or "origin" as portrayed in Genesis 2).

8. Those who want to interpret Scripture "literalistically" must be consistent in their approach. If they are, they will see the inadequacy of their methodology (cf. 1 Cor 16:20; John 13:14; 1 Tim 5:23).

2. A Traditionalist's Position

In discussing the role of women in marriage and worship, we must begin by looking at where the Bible speaks specifically to the issue, not just at passages with more general import. Regarding women in ordained ministry, there are three such didactic passages which apply to the situation (1 Cor 11:2–16; 1 Tim 2:11–15; 1 Cor 14:33b–38). These passages transcend cultural relativity, for they are grounded in reasons always germane to man and woman, God's creative order and purposes for men and women, as well as the fall of Adam and Eve (1 Tim 2:13–14; 1 Cor 11:7–10; 1 Cor 14:34). These texts prohibit the Church from allowing a woman to hold a teaching/ruling office. In Eph 5:22–33 Paul uses a similar universalizing argument based in the creation order and its correlatives of headship and subjection to argue for a hierarchical relationship within the family. Peter similarly argues for the wife's submission to her husband, basing his advice on the example of Sarah. There is no hint that the hierarchical structuring of marriage is considered only an interim solution (1 Pet 3:1–7).

As for those passages which suggest that women can publicly pray and prophesy (1 Cor 11:5; Acts 2:17–32), it must be observed that these acts of worship are distinct from authoritative speaking, teaching, and ruling and are therefore to be allowed. Similarly, women may be involved in diaconal tasks and appropriate teaching functions (Rom 16:1; Tit 2:3, 4; Acts 18:26; 1 Tim 3:11; 5:9, 10).

Using as a guide these passages which deal explicitly with the question of women's rightful place, it is possible to avoid making erroneous deductions from other passages in Scripture which deal with more general concerns related to women. Gal 3:28 has become almost foundational to the cause of feminism because egalitarians have not followed this principle. If they would, they would recognize that the key to understanding this verse is "in Christ." Although there is spiritual unity and equality "in Christ" (i.e., *coram Deo*), among mankind in the Church and society there remains a necessary structuring of male and female relationships. This is symbolized by Paul's injunction concerning uncovered and covered heads (1 Cor

11). An analogous situation to woman's voluntary limitation of Christian freedom for the sake of order and stability is Paul's advice regarding the eating of meat (1 Cor 8:13; cf. 1 Cor 9:19). Receipt of Christ's full inheritance must await the second coming. The temporal order is not yet the baptismal order. That such an interim position of subjection implies inferiority does not follow. One has only to compare it with Christ's voluntary submission to, yet equality with, God the Father.

There are other considerations worth mentioning:

1. No one in biblical Christianity took feminism seriously until it became a dominant theme in our secular, humanistic culture.

2. Certainly males predominate in Scripture. The exceptions only prove the rule. Furthermore, Jesus chose only men as his disciples and therefore as the leaders of his Church. To argue for a biblically based "feminism" is inconsistent with the entire posture of Scripture.

3. The symbolism of the relationship of God to his people (Hosea) and of Christ to his Church (Ephesians 5) demands a male officeholder in the Church and a male authority in the home. Only in this way is divine authority, dominion, and supremacy adequately portrayed. We are not free to tamper with the biblical imagery without losing some of the mystery.

4. Culture is not happenstance, but prepared by God. Israel with its patriarchal system was peculiarly designed by God as his vehicle of divine truth. Moreover, in "the fulness of time" the gospel came. Thus, Christianity holds that biblical patterns are significant and normative. They reflect the mystery of the divine order. To man is confided the task of ruling; to woman the task of serving.

5. The virgin Mary examplifies the ideal woman in her voluntary submission and response to the will of God.

6. There is a hierarchy in the created order, each level being given its proper responsibility and privileges—God, archangels, angels, people, animals, etc. Within the human level woman has been given her place. She is made for man (1 Cor 11:9; Gen 2:18–23). Thus, woman is to be deferentially observant in marriage, and man, receptive and responsible. Because of the Fall, mankind has tragically revolted against this creation order.

7. The principles of obedience, submission, and authority are clear in both Old and New Testament. The teaching regarding male and female relationships is only one aspect of a larger and necessary ordering of reality that extends into the Godhead itself (cf. Christ's obedience and submission to the Father and the Holy Spirit's subordination to the Son).

3. Faulty Hermeneutical Assumptions Presently Surfacing

As these egalitarian and traditionalist positions are being argued, certain dangerous hermeneutical procedures are surfacing in both camps which threaten to undermine the full authority of the biblical record—a cardinal tenet of contemporary evangelicalism. In particular, problems are apparent in two areas: (a) the issue of "culture," and (b) the tendency toward inconsistency.

a. The Issue of "Culture"

In current discussions on women's place in the Church and home there is the danger among egalitarians of taking a dualistic approach to Scripture, isolating the time-bound from the universal, the human from the divine, the rabbinic from the Christian. There is among the traditionalists a parallel danger, that of spiritualizing Scripture by treating it ahistorically. Rather than viewing Scripture as being time-bound, it is now understood as timeless truth. Just as the dualist stumbles over the Bible's humanness, so the spiritualizer errs in his understanding of Scripture's "supernatural" nature. The former seems overcome by Scripture's time-relatedness; the later seeks to deny this time-relatedness any real significance. Neither approach Scripture as at one and the same time, fully and completely, God's Word as human words. Both seem unwilling to give themselves over to a fresh round of exacting, detailed research, for they are convinced that God's Word and/or man's words are clear.

Virginia Mollenkott, for example, states concerning Paul's advice to women: "My training as a literary critic simply will not permit me to indulge in interpretations which depend on evidence which is not yet available." Convinced that Paul treats women, at times, as inferior to men, she concludes that though she respects Paul greatly for his central affirmation about humanity, his words at other times fall away from that central vision. Something has interfered. "I have called the interference a distortion caused by the human limitations of the human channel." Unwilling to consider that Paul's writings on women might have been culturally (mis)interpreted for centuries, Mollenkott instead concludes that some of Paul's arguments reflect his "rabbinical training and human limitations."[8] "There are flat contradictions between some of his theological arguments and his own doctrines and behavior," she says.[9]

This position that there is a Pauline self-contradiction is also taken by Paul Jewett in his book *Man As Male and Female*. He believes that the inconsistency between Paul's arguments for female subordination and his fundamental awareness of Christian liberty (Gal 3:28) can only be resolved by recognizing "the human as well as the divine quality of Scripture." Paul's historical limitations, particularly his rabbinical background, affect his Christian insight. For example, Jewett argues that 1 Corinthians 11 commands women to cover their heads. He finds it a "curious idea" without foundation in text or context that this injunction was meant only for that time when prostitutes did not wear veils or long hair. Conflating Old Testament practice (Gen 38:15) with first-century Greek society, Jewett implies that, perhaps, prostitutes were veiled. He concludes that Paul considered the custom of head-covering part of the Apostolic tradition he had previously given the Corinthians (1 Cor 11:2). "Thus," concludes Jewett, "the apostle elevates the relativities of culture to the absolutes of Christian piety."[10]

There are exegetical difficulties in Jewett's interpretation.[11] The "traditions" referred to in verse 2 might better be taken as the central truths of the Christian faith given previously to the Corinthians by Paul in oral form. Verses 13 and 16 suggest that Paul did not consider his injunction one of the central tenets of the faith. The cultural situation in Corinth should not be so quickly ignored. Reevaluations of the meaning of *kephalē* (head) and *exousia* (authority) need to be considered. But what is more important than any particular exegetical mistake is the underlying hermeneutical principle it reflects. Jewett, like Mollenkott, would discard those portions of Scripture which reflect human limitation. Rather than struggle to understand the cultural background of the text and the alternate meanings possible which recent historico-grammatical exegesis has suggested, Jewett is content to judge the text as reflecting Paul's rabbinic chauvinism and to disregard it. Paul was a split-person, unable to resolve his conflicts of sexism and Christian liberty in a consistent manner.[12]

What is basic to both Mollenkott's and Jewett's positions is too facile an exegesis of key biblical passages. They have accepted traditional interpretations rather than reevaluating the evidence in search of an underlying consistency in Paul's position.[13] Behind this willingness to allow traditional interpretations to remain normative is the hermeneutical principle that the interpreter can separate that which is human from that which is divine in Scripture. Rather than seek to find a unity in Scripture as biblical texts mutually interpret each other, Jewett and Mollenkott take the Reformation principle that "Scripture interprets itself" (*Sacra Scriptura sui ipsius interpres*) to mean that Scriptures which seem to conflict with the central affirmations of the gospel and the example of Christ himself are to be discarded. This is, however, to set humanity over Scripture as the final arbiter of what is inspired and authoritative for Christian practice. Scripture is in danger of losing its normative nature.

Traditionalists, like Harold Lindsell, have been quick to challenge such an approach.[14] But feminists as well, like Nancy Hardesty, are aware of the implications of this position and have sought alternate approaches. In response to Lindsell's article which misrepresented her position, Hardesty replied in a letter to *Christianity Today*:

> Unlike some feminists, I do not rest my conclusions on any supposed contradictions within the writings of Paul, or between Paul and Jesus, on any alleged "rabbinic interpretations," or on the cultural relativity of any text. I see no difficulty in harmonizing feminism with the teaching of scripture. I do not disagree with any teaching of scripture on this issue. I disagree, rather, with the distorted *interpretations* based on patriarchal social patterns and neoplatonic philosophical systems which men have used to obscure the radical message of the Gospel and to oppress women.[15]

Whether a feminist position is as consistent with Scripture as Hardesty believes is open to further discussion. But she is certainly correct in rejecting a *dualistic* hermeneutic. The principle of "consistency" demands not the dismissal of seemingly contradictory texts, but the ongoing reevaluation of traditional interpretations in search of distortion.

Egalitarians are not the only ones who have difficulty understanding Scripture as time-related. Where some feminists reject what is time-bound, extrapolating "the essential, unconditional truths by discarding what [they consider] is nonessential," some traditionalists make Scripture's time-relatedness similarly of no account by claiming that "revelation is available in a pure and unambiguous form."[16] The gap between the centuries is conveniently minimized; the interpreter forgets "to what extent Paul's words belong to a certain situation."[17] Few traditionalists are consistent in this regard. For example, such advice as, it is "well for a man not to touch a woman" (1 Cor 7:1), or "use a little wine for the sake of your stomach" (1 Tim 5:23), is put into its rightful context by most hierarchicalists. But the context is ignored when discussing biblical passages which give women a subordinate role in worship and marriage.

Elisabeth Elliot Leitch, for example, believes that the biblical worldview and culture, with its patriarchal system, was "peculiarly designed and chosen by God as a vehicle of heavenly truth":

> Are we to assume that if first century Semite culture had allowed it Jesus would have appointed women apostles and addressed God as Mother? Or shall we find in God's choice of the Judaic framework of reference, in Old Testament times as well as in New Testament ones, the sovereignty of God?

For it was in "the fulness of time" that the Gospel came. It was the first century that is for the Christian Church normative.[18]

The first century is normative? By this is Elliot suggesting, for example, that the abolitionist movement was unchristian? Are Europeans correct to greet one another with kisses while Americans are guilty of acting non-biblically? Should we begin to wash one another's feet? Such positions follow, it would seem, from taking first-century practices as normative. But there is no evidence Elliot would adopt these procedures as universally normative. Moreover, if the patriarchal system in the Old Testament is understood as ordained by God to reflect his self-revelation, what of an absolute monarchy, or perhaps a theocracy, which biblical authors similarly considered to be God-ordained? Why are sexual politics timeless while national politics are relative to time and place? Again, if the biblical text is normative, are we to return to an agrarian lifestyle? Are we to support the punishment of whole families for the crimes of individuals? The list of contemporary cultural differences from biblical practices could go on and on.

Tom Howard, Betty Elliot's brother, takes a similar approach to his sister's. He sees the biblical picture of male predominance as normative:

> The burden of particular aspects of the splendor of the Divine Image, including authority and primacy, has been placed upon the shoulders of the man; whereas the answering burden has been placed upon woman—the echo, or antiphon, to the man's aspect, without which his authority and primacy are solitary and sterile. This pattern ... is implicit in the whole fabric of biblical narrative.

Exceptions to this ordering in Scripture are so embarrassingly few, Howard feels, that they only reinforce the basic fact:

> It was not just a random happenstance that Yahweh picked a patriarchal society to exhibit His Name in. He didn't take His cues from them: He prepared them, and ordered them, to exhibit, in the structure of their social and political and domestic and cultic life, the deepest mysteries of divinity and humanity.[19]

Howard looks at the overall picture and finds a pattern in biblical times that is meant for all times. Elliot, particularly in her latest book, *Let Me Be a Woman*, finds the key to woman's timeless place in marriage and worship, more particularly, in such specific references as "For man was not made from woman, but woman from man. Neither was man created for woman, but woman for man" (1 Cor 11:8–9). "Some texts," Elliot allows, "are susceptible of differing interpretations, but for the life of me I can't see any ambiguities in this one."[20] Biblical commentators who have struggled with the meaning of Paul's advice in 1 Corinthians 11 must wish the situation was as clear-cut as Elliot maintains. Only by taking Paul's words out of both their immediate text and their cultural context is such a stance possible. Elliot has spiritualized Paul's words, taking only their surface meaning, making them timeless and mysterious in their full intent. She finds them to reflect "a divinely inspired principle" and therefore "not negotiable."[21]

What lies, in part, behind Elliot's and Howard's common desire to maintain the "mystery" of God's hierarchical ordering is the ecclesiastical position they adhere to. With C. S. Lewis, whom they quote with respect on this point, they believe that women cannot be "priests," for the priest is to represent God to man. God, as they would have us know, consistently portrays himself to us as a male. Similarly, the Bible uses the Church's subjection to Christ as a symbol of marriage. Christians should not negate these symbols by allowing women to represent God's Word in the pulpit and sacrament or by proclaiming the validity of egalitarian relationships. To tamper with Christian imagery concerning God or his Church is to destroy the sense of the "mystical" which Christianity should contain. "The Church of England," Lewis asserts, and analogously the American Episcopal Church which is Howard's and Elliot's chosen home, "can remain a church only if she retains this opaque element."[22] The timeless is maintained out of a desire for the mystical, the mysterious, the opaque. Such a theological and ecclesiological position has a long cultural heritage in Christian tradition, but it must not imperialize on biblical interpretation by becoming the sole authoritative stance by which the entire biblical witness must be read. When this happens, Scripture loses its normative nature over Christian tradition and false conclusions soon follow.[23]

Jewett and Mollenkott arrive at their dualistic hermeneutic partly out of their cultural attachment to women's liberation. Howard and Elliot come to their "spiritualized" hermeneutic out of a need to buttress their High Church liturgical commitment. But to conclude that cultural and ecclesiological considerations are alone determinative of their approach to Scripture's cultural character would be untrue. G. C. Berkouwer, in his volume on *Holy Scripture*, rightly describes both the "dualist" and the "spiritualizer" and in the process offers a second and common motivation for both of these faulty approaches to Scripture's time-relatedness. He states:

> One may not . . . devise from the beginning a "method" that guarantees the safety of the road of faith. One such method is that of deduction [the "spiritualizers"], which seeks to prove as conclusively as possible that

scripture exceeds all time-relatedness. Another is that of induction [the "dualists"], which often runs the risk of bogging down in a "canon of interpretation," applying a critical yardstick to God's Word and preventing a true listening to the Spirit's voice to the churches. It is the abiding Word of God alone that tests and accompanies all study of scripture: it challenges and encourages us to continue on this road, critically weighing all human words about God's Word, with the expectation and certainty shared with the church of all ages that the "jewel" of the gospel will not be lost in a new and still unknown future.[24]

It is this fear of losing the "jewel" of the gospel which partially accounts for Jewett and Mollenkott becoming dualists, and Elliot and Howard becoming spiritualizers. Given society's growing recognition that men and women are equal, is the gospel to retain its power if it remains tied to a hierarchical structuring in which women are thought to be subservient and dependent? Given the mystery of the gospel proclaimed in the symbolism of Church and home, can Christians afford to dilute its strength in a time of increasing secularism out of a desire to accommodate to the latest cultural fad? Both dualist and spiritualizer believe they are protecting the gospel. But ironically, by undercutting Scripture's authority and culturally directed message, they end up diminishing its power.

The interpreter of Scripture must approach the biblical text critically and carefully, and with full confidence and certainty that its gospel message does not need defense, but rather proclamation. Christians must approach the text, willingly subjecting it to the literary-critical fate of all writing. They must admit that they do not know in advance what Scripture will say. We cannot lock ourselves in to what was formerly believed to be *the* correct interpretation of a passage. Instead, we must remain humble before Scripture as the Word of God and the words of men. At the same time, a Christian hermeneutic will also carry with it the predisposition of faith, both in the gospel *per se* and in its authoritative organ of communication, Scripture. Faithful as we approach the biblical record, we remain confident of its reliability, clarity, and sufficiency. To recognize that Scripture is culturally directed and time-related does not call into question its authoritative gospel message of faith and life. Rather, it is the necessary posture for those who stand reverently before the Word of God.[25]

b. The Tendency Toward Inconsistency

In addition to the improper handling of Scripture's cultural-directedness, there is a second area of hermeneutical concern in contemporary evangelical discussions of women's role in marriage and worship. This is the marked propensity among evangelicals to be inconsistent in their handling of the biblical sources. This inconsistency takes two major forms: (1) A selectivity in the texts considered germane to the issue, and (2) an unwillingness to apply uniformly the same hermeneutic to both the issue of women in the Church and the issue of women in the home.

Egalitarians and traditionalists accuse each other of manipulating the message of Scripture by picking and choosing which aspects of the biblical record they want to notice. And there often is truth in their assertions. Rather than a consistent, nonpartisan, thorough exegesis which seeks liberation from the pressures of "feminism" and "traditionalism," both sides tend to approach Scripture through a predetermined "interpretive filter."

Perhaps the most obvious example of such filtering is Billy Graham's discussion "Jesus and the Liberated Woman." In the article, Graham discusses the new prestige that Christ brought to women, but using two prooftexts, Gen 3:16 and Tit 2:4–5, he nevertheless concludes: "Wife, mother, homemaker—this is the appointed destiny of real womanhood."[26] Graham overlooks the fact that this is at best a half-truth of Scripture. He has turned the "curse" in Gen 3:16 into an eternal principle and has found the role of "homemaker" in the text from Titus, though it is not there. Moreover, what of other scriptural data? Mary, for example, is singled out appreciatively for her unwillingness to be just the homemaker (Luke 10:42). What of Paul's desire that the Corinthians remain single (1 Cor 7:8)? What, too, of the group of women who left home (and family!) to join Jesus' followers in traveling from town to town with him (Luke 8:2–3; Matt 27:55)? Again, how is a text like Luke 11:27–28 to be correlated with Graham's assertion that whatever else it describes, the New Testament declares that the "main job" for females is "the womanly assignment of wife and mother?"[27]

> While He [Jesus] was speaking thus, a woman in the crowd called out, "Happy the womb that carried you and the breasts that suckled you!" He rejoined, "No, happy are those who hear the word of God and keep it" (NEB).

Jesus was not belittling Mary; he was suggesting that real womanhood goes beyond being a wife and mother. Again, it is true that the Bible commands women to bear children. But both mother *and* father are given joint responsibility for the children (cf. Eph 6:4; Ps 103:13). Finally, Proverbs 31 describes the ideal wife, it is true. Yet how foreign is its description from Graham's ideal American homemaker—purchasing land, acting as a merchant, making "her arms strong." What is our traditional cultural pattern and what is biblical has been conflated by an editing of the biblical record.[28]

Such screening of Scripture is found among evangelical feminists as well. Kay Lindskoog, for example, concludes that "Paul's Bad News for Women" is in reality good news. "Surely," she says, "Paul was not endorsing the short-sightedness of his own culture any more than he would endorse the excesses of ours."[29] Unfortunately, when we look more closely at the basis for this conclusion, we find it is largely lacking. While purporting to ground her conclusions in a careful exegesis of 1 Tim 2:8–15 and 1 Cor 14:26–40, Lindskoog actually limits her discussion of 1 Timothy to pointing up the incongruity of traditional interpretations, concluding, "We must admit that Paul is not his clearest in this passage, to say the least."[30] Similarly, her selective analysis of Ephesians 5 points out the need to begin the discussion with verse 21 and then proceeds to concentrate on verses 25ff. What is conveniently ignored are verses 22 through 24, which deal with the wife's subjection to her husband.[31] The safest way to be sure Scripture supports your position is to ignore those passages you don't like.[32] Concentrate on "husbands loving your wives" and "doing all things decently and in order" and perhaps others will overlook the fact that you have bypassed injunctions to women to be silent in worship and subject at home.

A more sophisticated screening of Scripture is carried out by others who claim that we must look in Scripture for the *locus classicus* of a biblical doctrine and concentrate on its teaching, interpreting all else in light of its truth. Letha Scanzoni and Nancy Hardesty use this principle in their book *All We're Meant To Be:*

> The biblical theologian does not build on isolated proof texts but first seeks the *locus classicus,* the major biblical statement, on a given matter. . . . Passages which deal with an issue systematically are used to help understand incidental references elsewhere. Passages which are theological and doctrinal in content are used to interpret those where the writer is dealing with practical local cultural problems. (Except for Gal 3:28, all of the references to women in the New Testament are contained in passages dealing with practical concerns about personal relationships or behavior in worship services.)[33]

Here, and in other egalitarian literature, principle is given priority over application; admonition is given preference over description.[34] What is dangerous in such a procedure, though it admittedly works in many cases, is the implied epistemological claim in this procedure that objective, impersonal statements are of a somehow higher order of trustworthiness than the more personal and relational aspects of Scripture. Do we need systematic argument in order to be fully confident of the meaning of God's revelation? Is it not true that Paul's "purely" theological insights are, on closer inspection, responses to the cultural crises and life situations of young churches facing concrete problems, and that his practical advice has within it a theological dimension?[35] Paul neither "did theology" in an abstract, academic manner or "proffered advice" devoid of theological undergirding. Both his "systematic theology" and his "practical theology" are more accurately part of his one-and-the-same "church theology." Moreover, can we let Paul's church theology be equated with the full flowering of progressive revelation, when we now know that the theologian Luke, for example, wrote after Paul's death? Why is "epistle" superior to "gospel" as a medium of communicating God's truth?

The richness and variegation of the New Testament message must be maintained.[36] An evangelical biblical theology must listen equally to the theology of the Synoptics, of the epistles, of Acts, and even of Old Testament wisdom literature. The importance of recognizing the authority of multiple biblical theologies must be maintained if interpreters are to avoid twisting the biblical record to support outside aims.[37] Paul Holmer is correct in warning against evangelicals

> treating the Scripture as if it were a literary and metaphysical and causal gloss on a literal and systematic structure that it otherwise hides. The everlasting search among Evangelicals for that structure, that is literally true and that is interconnected, makes Scripture often look like an introduction into a better theological scheme that lurks within it.[38]

Such a danger is almost inevitable for those who search out the *locus classicus*.[39]

In the interpretation of biblical themes, selectivity in the texts considered is one danger. A more curious inconsistency is the unwillingness by some evangelicals to apply their hermeneutical method equally to the question of women in the Church and to the question of women in the home.

Harold Lindsell, for example, in his book *The World, The Flesh and The Devil,* finds the position of Paul regarding women exercising leadership and teaching/preaching functions in the Church to be an expression of the needs of his cultural situation. It is not to be considered as normative for the Church today. He states, furthermore:

> The Bible does speak rather specifically about male-female relationships for those who have been regenerated. Paul is the great advocate of Christian

freedom saying that in Jesus Christ, "There is . . . neither male nor female. . . ."

Lindsell concludes that women's roles in the Church should not be judged in terms of sexual classification but by "what a particular woman with certain talents, strengths and weaknesses can do."[40] When he discusses women's role in marriage, however, Lindsell asserts that the Pauline teaching for the Christian requires the husband to be the final authority in decision-making in the home. "The man was made head over the woman (1 Cor 11:3; Eph 5:23) . . . that teaching is very strong."[41]   On the one hand, Paul's teaching on women in worship is understood to be culturally directed and no longer binding on Christians today; on the other hand, Paul's teaching on women's place in the home is said to be timeless. Yet, the texts reveal that Pauline arguments are similarly based on an analogy with the creation accounts. George Knight is correct:

> This creation order and its correlatives of headship and subjection appear in each passage dealing with woman's ruling/teaching function in the church just as they provide the one and only foundation for the role relationships in marriage. To dismiss the role relationships in the church in regard to the teaching/ruling function as simply cultural would carry with it the dismissal of the analogous role relationship in marriage as also cultural. Lindsell is not that consistent; Scanzoni and Hardesty are.[42]

A second example of this same unwillingness to carry through on one's method of interpretation to include both facets of the woman question is Gladys Hunt's bestseller, *Ms. Means Myself.* She states her hermeneutical procedure in the preface:

> The rules of biblical interpretation require that we give any passage the obvious meaning the author intended in the context in which he writes. Secondly, scripture must interpret scripture.[43]

In chapter 2 which is tellingly titled "The Side Issue," Hunt takes up Paul's advice that women should be silent in the Church. She begins by painting redemptive history in which male and female were created equal, but in which sin also entered, allowing moral perversion and female discrimination. In Christ, however, woman is again treated as an equal, as Jesus' life, the early Church's ministry, and Paul's theology (Gal 3:28) declare. Furthermore, what inequality did exist in the biblical world must be contrasted with the stark situation for women among Israel's neighbors. With this biblical background, Hunt suggests, one can begin to understand Paul's words. But only as (1) the cultural situation Paul addressed, (2) the wider argument in the text, and (3) the other relevant statements by the same author are noted, can the interpreter do full justice to Paul's instruction.

Moreover, we cannot be slaves to a faulty church tradition. Doesn't common sense demand that women's gifts be used? Such is an outline of Hunt's argument, and her conclusion follows logically: "cultural adjustments" must be made if these texts are to remain meaningful today.[44]

However, when Hunt turns from "The Side Issue" (why is woman's service to God less basic than other of her activities?) to the real thing—the marriage relationship—she forsakes her hermeneutical procedure for a superficial reading of Gen 2:24 and Eph 5:21ff. She concludes that husbands are to lead, and wives are to follow. Because they are "one flesh," they can best operate as an entity in a hierarchical relationship.[45] Aside from the questionableness of her culturally based argument that two people must have a leader, Hunt fails to be convincing because she forsakes her quite adequate method of interpretation for a "literalistic" misunderstanding of the scriptural text.

4. Hermeneutics and the Role of Women

The current controversy over women's place in worship and marriage can be healthy for the evangelical church, for only as a position is argued passionately and under pressure are its possibilities fully explored. As long as both sides remain open to new insight, the discussion should spark a testing of tradition and current practice by the Word. As it does, the air can be cleared of accretions from the past and accommodations to the present. But such an optimistic assessment of the current debate is dependent on both sides taking their hermeneutical task seriously.

Given the present hermeneutical problems of many involved in the discussion, it is necessary, in conclusion, to sketch out some hermeneutical principles which might assist in answering questions about woman's place in the home and Church. An evangelical hermeneutic will accept the following principles (note: in each case, a short discussion of the application of the given interpretive guideline to the role of women will follow):

1. *A text must be treated within its full unit of meaning.* The reference to wives being subject to their husbands (Eph 5:22–24) can be adequately understood only in terms of the mutual subjection commanded in verse 21, the sacrificial love of the husband prescribed in verses 25–30, and the unity of the marriage partners, verses 31–33. Only by taking as one's pericope Eph 5:21–33, can the interpreter adequately understand the reference to the wife's submission in verses 22–24. Similarly, 1 Cor 14:34–35 is to be understood

as part of Paul's summary concerning public worship which begins with verse 26 and continues through verse 40. Seen in this context, Paul's specific advice concerning women not speaking within a worshipping congregation takes on the more primary meaning that all is to "be done decently and in order" (v. 40).

2. *Some translations must be corrected for their sexist bias.* "In the New Testament, masculine nouns and pronouns have often been substituted for the nouns and pronouns of common gender in the original Greek."[46] For example, 1 Tim 3:1 reads in the authorized version: "If a man desire the office of a bishop. . . ." It is better rendered, "If any one desires. . . ." There are other kinds of inconsistencies as well. Phoebe is labeled a "servant" (KJV) in Rom 16:1 and a "succorer" (KJV), a "helper" (RSV), in Rom 16:2, although the first word of description, *diakonos*, is elsewhere usually translated "minister," and the second, *prostatis* (a *hapax legomenon*), has a verb form which is translated "rule" or "be over" in other New Testament texts (Rom 12:8 [KJV]; 1 Thes 5:12; 1 Tim 3:4; 5: 17).[47]

3. *The literary form of a passage must be understood if it is to be adequately interpreted.* We must keep in mind that gospel and epistle are not sociological tract or disinterested treatise. The very nature of "letters" which were intended to answer specific questions about particular issues in the life of the churches in Corinth and Ephesus (the context of 1 Timothy) should make the reader extremely cautious in deducing universal principles from Paul's advice. Such deductions must stem from an appreciation of the intended meaning of the text which is mediated through specific literary forms. For example, that Paul's argument in I Corinthians 11 makes use of rabbinic methods of argument common in his day helps the interpreter focus upon Paul's real intent, while refraining from overinterpreting the supports Paul includes to buttress his point. Paul's rabbinic methodology does not lead to a dismissal of the text, but to a proper understanding of its meaning. A text is never "correct" in the abstract, but only as its literary genre and thus intent is first understood.

4. *The historical context of a passage helps the interpreter understand both the function and the meaning a text had in its own day.* Did the actions and words of Jesus and Paul *function* to reinforce the status quo in regard to women, or were they "liberating" even in their own day?[48] When we consider the evidently inferior status of women in biblical times, the meaning of the New Testament's advice to women changes drastically.[49] We must ask whether we are not being unfaithful to the biblical message if we use Scrip-

ture's liberating words to impede the leavening process they were meant to have. As to the *meaning* of a text, it is not proper to give a contemporary nuance to biblical language that was foreign in its day. Consider a word like "head" (*kephalē*, 1 Cor 11:3; Eph 5:23); if "head" did not have the current metaphorical sense of "decision-making" in Paul's day, we cannot assign to it that connotation. Again, the meaning of 1 Tim 2:8–15 depends not on our context, but on the double background of Paul's Judaism (where women were exempted from learning) and the situation at Ephesus (where un-trained women who had submitted to heretical teachers seem to have been seeking to spread their beliefs, perhaps like the *hierodules* in the service of the temple of Diana; cf. 2 Tim 3:5–7). Rabbinic law and Greek custom, as well as particular situations being addressed, add necessary background and coloring to a correct understanding of the 1 Timothy text.[50]

5. *The immediate context of a passage should be considered before one looks at other parallel texts.* Perhaps a negative example of this principle can be instructive. George Knight, in his discussion in *Christianity Today* on women's place, finds 1 Cor 11:8 and 9 to be of timeless significance.[51] He bases his conclusion on a correla-tion of that text with Gen 2:23, 24 and 1 Tim 2:13. What he fails to consider is the immediate context of these verses (1 Cor 11:11–12), where Paul qualifies them, lest this phase of his argument regarding women's head coverings be misunderstood. Similarly, in his discus-sion of 1 Cor 14:34 in the *Journal of the Evangelical Theological Society,* Knight chooses to turn to 1 Tim 2:11–14 for his interpre-tive key ("what is prohibited is teaching with particular reference to men"), rather than to 1 Cor 14:40, which summarizes the immediate discussion by commanding that "all be done decently and in order."[52] When he does consider the immediate context, Knight focuses on the preceding argument in verses 27 and 29, rather than on verse 35 which completes Paul's direct advice to women and sets the issue squarely in the context of "asking questions."

6. *The author's explicit intention, methodology, theology, and practice, as understood in other biblical texts, can provide helpful interpretative clues.* Paul's specific advice concerning women in the Church and home can be better understood if it is viewed as part of his larger *intention* to bring order to the Christian community. Only in this way could the Church's witness to the wider society avoid being compromised and its life together as a fellowship be strength-ened (cf. 1 Tim 5:14; Tit 2:5; 1 Cor 14:33). It is evident from Paul's advice concerning circumcision in 1 Cor 7:17–24 that Paul did not

see the maintenance of the status quo as a goal of the Church. However, it is also clear from his discussion of slavery in Philemon that Paul's *method* for social change was characterized by caution and orderliness. Perhaps Paul's *theological* statement of equality in Christ found in Gal 3:28 can help the interpreter focus on the particularity and time-relatedness of other of his advice (e.g., 1 Cor 14:34–35). Finally, the extensive description of Paul's *ministry* which is found in Acts, as well as the mention of current church *practice* within his epistles, shows Paul's attitude toward women through his action (cf. Acts 16:13; 17:4; Tit 2:3; 1 Cor 11:5; Rom 16:1–16).

7. *The Bible has an overarching consistency despite its multiple theological foci. Thus, all interpretations of given texts can be productively correlated with wider biblical attitudes, statements, themes, and descriptions.* If husbands are to duplicate Jesus' *attitude* toward leadership (Eph 5:24ff.; 1 Pet 3:1), they might consider Matt 20:25–28:

> You know that in the world, rulers lord it over their subjects, and their great men make them feel the weight of authority; but it shall not be so with you. Among you, whoever wants to be great must be your servant, and whoever wants to be first must be the willing slave of all—like the son of man; he did not come to be served, but to serve, and to give up his life as a ransom for many (NEB).

Anyone who finds Paul's advice regarding women to be straight-forward and clear might do well to recall the *statement* of 2 Peter that there are in Paul's epistles "some things . . . hard to understand" (2 Pet 3:16, RSV). In his study *Women in the Church*, Russell Prohl correctly places his discussion of the specific texts which relate to that issue within the larger biblical *themes* of creation and redemp-tion.[53] Other biblical themes, such as the doctrines of God and the Church, add further insight into the discussion of woman's rightful role. For example, though male imagery is predominantly used, nowhere does Scripture suggest (like texts from Israel's neighbors) that God is to be thought of literally as male. Again, if the Church as the body of Christ is ordered according to gift rather than gender (1 Corinthians 12), what is the significance of this fact for female members in our age with the apparent gift of preaching? Finally, the gospels *describe* women as being significantly involved in declaring the faith (John 4; Matt 28:9–10; John 20:15–17).

8. *Insight into texts which are obscure must be gained from those which are plain.* Here is a key hermeneutical principle for the

interpretation of women's place in the Church. Ordinarily, herme-neutical procedure would dictate that theologians seeking guidance on this topic should first turn to the three passages which speak directly about this area (1 Timothy 2; 1 Corinthians 14; and 1 Corinthians 11). But all of these texts are extremely difficult to interpret with crucial words remaining obscure (e.g., *authentein; exousia*), addressed situations being difficult to reconstruct, "surface meaning" proving contradictory with other Pauline material, and methods of argument reflecting cultural thought-forms no longer in use. Given these difficulties in interpretation in the texts which would seem most appropriate, the plain descriptions of Jesus' inter-action with women and the stylized but readily interpreted accounts of woman's creation in Genesis take on increased significance.

9. *Scripture should be read in faith for faith.* The goal of Scripture is to help its reader "put on Christ" (Rom 13:14; Eph 4:13). Any teaching regarding women must, therefore, square with the truth of the gospel and mankind's hope "in Christ." Christ's victory over sin and death has brought with it new possibilities for redeemed humanity. Gal 3:28 cannot be used reductively as a grounds for dismissing other texts, but neither can it be ignored. Redeemed humanity in the Church and Christian home should mir-ror creation's new order in Christ. Moreover, faith is not only the goal of biblical interpretation; it is also the means. For as Christians we come humbly and receptively to the text, believing in the Bible's authoritative message for us. A controlled subjectivity is our goal. Our predisposition of faith should allow us to let the text speak normatively in our lives.

10. *Interpreters of Scripture should seek the help of the Chris-tian community, past and present, in order that insights can be shared, humility fostered, and biases of culture and theological tradition overcome.* The Christian community can be wrong in its interpretation of Scripture, as the Church's former position on slav-ery indicates. Only the Church—past, present, and future—can cor-rect private presuppositions and cultural bias. Such a correctional process is currently attending the discussion of women in the Church and home. Augustine's definition of woman as man's helper in procreation has been rejected by most of the Church as sub-biblical. So, too, Aquinas's argument for female subordination based on the fact that she is the "weaker vessel," less rational, and misbegotten.[54] But to criticize the theology of past generations is relatively painless. To admit the possibility of similar cultural and ecclesiological limita-tions in ourselves is more difficult. But such seems to be the case presently where those in the Reformed (Knight) and Lutheran (Reu-

mann) traditions remain resistive to women being ordained, while those out of Holiness (Dayton) and Baptist (Lindsell) traditions do not.[55] Has personal background influenced exegesis on this point?[56]

11. *Scriptural interpretation must allow for continuing actualization as necessary implications are drawn out.* What is being claimed here is the fact of *progressive understanding,* not of ongoing revelation. Obvious examples of this need which have surfaced previously are the Church's doctrine of the Trinity and the Christian abolitionist movement. Both are rooted in the biblical text, though both go beyond it in their exact formulations. They are necessary implications which theological controversy and new cultural situations have brought to light. The changing role of women in the Church and home would seem to be another example of this principle. It is no longer a man's world in North America. E.R.A., birth control, Title IX, and the like, have brought a new consciousness of women's rights and possibilities to the contemporary Christian. Given this outside stimulus, the Church has begun to reevaluate its stance toward women. A key aspect in this is the hermeneutical task of setting forth Scripture's implications for women in *our day.* Those opposed to change claim that culture has determined the Church's interpretation of the biblical text. Although this is true in some cases, it need not follow from taking one's context seriously. Instead of being determinative of its interpretation, culture can serve the Church by being the occasion for renewed reflection and debate. A progressive understanding of Scripture should be continual as situations alter, allowing new implications of the text to come to light.

5. Conclusion

Does such a critical, yet faithful, approach as that outlined above imply that only the expert can arrive at an adequate biblical understanding of the role of women in the Church and home? It is true that evangelicals, following after the Reformers, confess the clarity (or "perspicuity") of Scripture. But by this they do not mean an "objective" clarity which demands no interpretation or translation. Rather they seek to emphasize by this credal stance that Scripture's purpose, its message of salvation, is accessible to all and is not limited to the clergy.

The need for ongoing exegetical reflection remains if Scripture is to be normative. Such reflection is necessiated not only because of our own faulty frames of reference but also because God's Word comes to us in the concrete form of historical language (which is not always self-evident). There is no substitute for receptive attention and faithful research. Thus, although Scripture is available to all and sufficient unto salvation for all who read attentively, an adequate hermeneutic demands that private interpretation seek correction and fresh stimulus from the ongoing collective insight of the Church. We need to listen to those who can teach us what Scripture is saying. This is true as we have seen regarding the subject of women's place in worship and marriage. Reverence for Scripture demands the best scholarship possible.

At present, division characterizes the discussion of woman's place. Teaching on the issue is hardly univocal. But perhaps greater attention to hermeneutical matters will hasten the convergence of lines. We, as evangelical Christians, have for too long taken an uncritical view toward our biblical understanding of women's role in the Church and home. Our contemporary culture provides the Church with an occasion for re-evaluating its exegesis. It is as the Church gives itself over to the continued and prayful reading, study, and discussion of Scripture that further clarity will be gained. It is the Spirit who provides insight, but his way is "through the Word (divine and human) in its historical form."[57]

NOTES

1. Marabel Morgan, *The Total Woman* (1973); Helen Andelin, *Fascinating Womanhood* (1973); Larry Christenson, *The Christian Family* (1970); Gladys Hunt, *Ms. Means Myself* (1972); Paul K. Jewett, *Man as Male and Female* (1975); Letha Scanzoni and Nancy Hardesty, *All We're Meant to Be* (1974). The discussion does not appear to be easing. Kathryn Lindskoog's *Up From Eden* (1976), Elisabeth Elliot's *Let Me Be a Woman* (1976), and Virginia Mollenkott's *Women, Men, and the Bible* (1976) should all prove to be bestsellers as well. Note: Although Helen Andelin is a Mormon, her book and workshops have been widely subscribed to by evangelicals; thus she is included here.

2. *New Wine* tried to counter what they felt was an unbiblical feminism be devoting a whole issue to "The Restoration of Manhood" (October, 1975).

3. E.g., George W. Knight III, "Male and Female Related He Them," *CT* 20 (April 9, 1976), pp. 13–17; Winnie Christenson, "What is a Woman's Role?" *MM* 7 (June, 1971), pp. 82–83; Charles Simpson, "The Home: Heaven or Earth?" *Log* 4 (September/October, 1974), pp. 13–15; Virginia Mollenkott, "Church Women, Theologians, and the Burden of Proof," *RefJ* 25 (July/August), 1975), pp. 18–20 and 25 (September, 1975), pp. 17–21; Nancy Hardesty, "Women: 2nd Class Citizens?" *Ety* 22 (January 1971), pp. 14–16, 24–29; David Scaer, "What Did St. Paul Want?" *His* 33 (May, 1976), pp. 12ff.; "Beyond the Barriers and the Stereotypes: All We're Meant to Be" (A *Vanguard* interview with Letha Scanzoni and Nancy Hardesty), *Vang* (March/April), 1975), pp. 13–16; Virginia Mollenkott, "A Challenge to Male Interpretation," *Soj* 5 (February, 1976), pp. 20–25.

4. *Daughters of Sarah* prints the following position statement in its pages: "We are Christians; we are also feminists. Some say we cannot be both, but Christianity and feminism for us are inseparable. *Daughters of Sarah* is our attempt to share our discoveries, our struggles, and our growth as Christian women. We are committed to scripture and we seek to find in it meaning for our lives. We are rooted in a historical tradition of women who have served God in innumerable ways and we seek guidance from their example. We are convinced that Christianity is relevant to all areas of women's lives today. We seek ways to act out our faith."

5. E.g., Thomas Howard and Donald W. Dayton, "A Dialogue on Women, Hierarchy and Equality," *PA* 4 (May, 1975), p. 10; Elisabeth Elliot Leitch, "Feminism or Feminity?" *CmbF* 5 (Winter, 1975–76), pp. 2, 6; Carl F. H. Henry, "The Battle of the Sexes," *CT* 19 (July 4, 1975), pp. 45–46; Nancy Hardesty, "Women and Evangelical Christianity," in *The Cross and the Flag*, eds. Robert Clouse, Robert Linder, and Richard Pierard (1972), p. 71.

6. Krister Stendahl, *The Bible and the Role of Women: A Case Study in Hermeneutics*, trans. Emile Sander (1966).

7. Dayton and Howard, "A Dialogue on Women," pp. 12–13.

8. Virginia Mollenkott, reply to Sharon Gallagher, *Soj* 5 (March, 1976), pp. 37–38; Mollenkott, "A Challenge to Male Interpretation," p. 22.

9. A Conversation with Virginia Mollenkott," *OthS* 12 (May-June, 1976), p. 22.

10. Jewett, *Man as Male and Female*, pp. 134, 138, 118.

11. Cf. Phyllis Alsdurf, "The Role of Women Within the Body of Christ" (March, 1976), pp. 6–8 (typewritten), for a helpful discussion of Jewett's exegesis.

12. Jewett, *Man as Male and Female*, pp. 112–113.

13. In this regard, Mollenkott acts at cross purposes with another of her basic hermeneutical principles—that consistency should be assumed if possible. She says, "One of the best guidelines is what theologians call the analogy of faith, or what I call assuming a book hangs together. In this connection I ought to be willing to give the Bible the same respect I give Homer or *The Divine Comedy* or Milton. So if I find a passage in *Paradise Lost*, I immediately suspect my reading and try to find a reading that is coherent with the rest of it." Unfortunately, Mollenkott then turns to a discussion of women in Scripture and says, "So when I see a few passages that seem to come down on certain members of the human race or seem to humiliate or reject them, I am going to be very slow to say that the vast majority of passages (which say the opposite) are wrong. When we find a passage, and a spirit which runs all the way through the Bible—at that point I know which one is for all time and which one for the hardness of our hearts." "A Conversation with Virginia Mollenkott," pp. 74–75. What escapes Mollenkott is the fact that the hermeneutical principle she enunciates in the preceding paragraph does not suggest dismissing a passage because of "the hardness of our hearts," but rather re-evaluating it with fresh, exacting, detailed research seeking a thread by which the "book hangs together."

14. Harold Lindsell, "Egalitarianism and Scriptural Infallibility," *CT* 20 (March 26, 1976), pp. 45–46.

15. Nancy Hardesty, letter in *CT* 20 (June 4, 1976), p. 25.

16. Stendahl, *The Bible and the Role of Women*, p. 14.

17. G. C. Berkouwer, *Holy Scripture* (1975), p. 188.

18. Leitch, "Feminism or Feminity?" p. 6.

19. Howard and Dayton, "A Dialogue on Women," pp. 8–9.

20. Elliot, *Let Me Be a Woman*, p. 22.

21. Ibid., p. 14. Elliot takes a similar uncritical view of Genesis 2, seeing its intent as being to describe more specifically the chronology of the creation of man and woman. Elisabeth Elliot, "Why I Oppose the Ordination of Women," *CT* 19 (June 6, 1975), p. 13. Elliot similarly views Paul's admonitions to women about praying and prophesying as "clearly exceptions to the rule of silence"(ibid., p. 14).

22. C. S. Lewis, "Priestesses in the Church," *God in the Dock* (1970), pp. 234–239.

23. E.g., Elisabeth Elliot's claim that "the pronouns referring to [God] in scripture are *without exception masculine*" (Elliot, "Why I Oppose the Ordination of Women," p. 16). Cf. Isa 49:15; Matt 23:37.

24. Berkouwer, *Holy Scripture*, p. 239.

25. Cf. ibid., pp. 213–239.

26. Billy Graham, "Jesus and the Liberated Woman," *Ladies Home Journal* 87 (December, 1970), p. 42.

27. Ibid., p. 114.

28. Graham's "cultural Christianity" finds a strong echo in his wife's comment concerning women's ordination in *Christianity Today*: ". . . . 'clergywomen'? I have serious reservations. I think if you study you will find that the finest cooks in the world are men (probably called chefs); the finest couturiers, by and large, are men; the finest musicians are men; the

greatest politicians are men; most of our greatest writers are men; most of our greatest athletes are men. You name it, men are superior in all but two areas: women make the best wives and women make the best mothers!" Ruth Graham, "Others Say . . . Women's Ordination," *CT* 19 (June 6, 1975), p. 32.

29. Kathryn Lindskoog, "Paul's Bad News for Women," *OthS* 9 (July-August, 1973), p. 11.

30. Ibid., p. 10. It is interesting to notice that one can almost predict a person's stance by his/her delimitation of the relevant text in both 1 Corinthians 14 and Ephesians 5. Is the text to be considered 1 Cor 14:34–38 or is the wider context of proper decorum and order necessary to its meaning? Does Eph 5:22 begin a new paragraph or must we begin with Eph 5:21, which discusses mutual submission? Cf. George W. Knight III, "The New Testament Teaching on the Role Relationship of Male and Female with Special Reference to the Teaching/Ruling Functions in the Church," *JETS* 18 (Spring, 1975), and Lindskoog, "Paul's Bad News for Women."

31. Cf. David and Eloise Fraser, "A Biblical View of Women: Demythologizing Sexegesis," *ThNN* 21 (June, 1975), p. 18. The Frasers similarly ignore Paul's advice to the wife in the discussion of Ephesians 5. On the other side, Gladys Hunt in her discussion of Ephesians 5, which is meant to support a hierarchical understanding of family authority, conveniently ignores Paul's advice to the husband (Hunt, *Ms. Means Myself*, pp. 97ff).

32. Cf. John Alexander, "Thinking Male: Or How to Hide Behind the Bible," *OthS* 9 (July-August, 1973), pp. 3–4, 43–47.

33. Scanzoni and Hardesty, *All We're Meant to Be*, pp. 18–19. Cf. "A Conversation with Virginia Mollenkott," p. 73; Howard and Dayton, "A Dialogue on Women, Hierarchy and Equality," p. 14; Jewett, *Man as Male and Female*, pp. 142–147.

34. This is faintly reminiscent of Edward Carnell's *The Case for Orthodox Theology*, which argued that some parts of Scripture must take priority over other parts. In particular, the New Testament is to interpret the Old Testament; the epistles are to interpret the gospels; systematic passages should interpret the incidental; universal, the local; and didactic, the symbolic (Edward J. Carnell, "Hermeneutics," *The Case for Orthodox Theology* [1959], pp. 51–65). It is interesting to note that Carnell found Romans and Galatians the supreme interpretations of the revelation of God in Christ. Several biblical feminists similarly find Gal 3:28 the "theological breakthrough" that is determinative of their interpretation of liberation in Christ. Cf. Jewett, *Man as Male and Female*, p. 144.

35. William L. Lane, "Task Theology: The Transcultural Character of the Gospel," paper presented at the southern sectional meeting of the ETS, Bowling Green, KY, February, 1976.

36. Cf. James W. Jones, "Task Theology and Dogmatic Theology," Spring, 1976 (typewritten).

37. A classical instance of this danger is Gerhard Von Rad's *Old Testament Theology*, which reduces the message of wisdom literature to that of a response to *Heilsgeschichte*. In *Wisdom in Israel*, a later volume, Von Rad tries to rectify this error.

38. Paul Holmer, "Contemporary Evangelical Faith," in *The Evangelicals*, eds. David F. Wells and John D. Woodbridge (1975), p. 77.

39. A variation on the *locus classicus* approach is the desire to judge Scripture by "what Jesus said and did ("A Conversation with Virginia Mollenkott," p. 75). What is not made explicit is the assumed identification of Jesus with a certain theological formulation of women's place. Aside from the fact that this merely shifts the problem from discerning what the "epistles" mean to finding what the "gospels" say, it also reflects the same propensity for a "canon within a canon." It is now Christology, rather than systematics, that is thought normative over the biblical witness. Cf. Scanzoni and Hardesty, *All We're Meant to Be*, pp. 85–87.

40. Harold Lindsell, *The World, The Flesh and The Devil* (1973), pp. 146–150.

41. Ibid., p. 132

42. Knight, "The Teaching/Ruling Functions in the Church," p. 89.

43. Hunt, *Ms. Means Myself*, p. 12.

44. Ibid., pp. 25–39.

45. Ibid., pp. 90–103.

46. Rey O'Day Mawson, "Why All the Fuss About Language?" *PA* 3 (August-September, 1974), p. 16.

47. J. Massyngberde Ford ("Biblical Material Relevant to the Ordination of Women," *JES*
10 [Fall, 1973], p. 677) notes that in the LXX the masculine form *prostatēs* (fem.
prostatis) is used of stewards (1 Chron 27:31), officers (1 Chron 29:6; 2 Chron 8:10),
governors (1 Esdr 2:12; 2 Macc 3:4). See Scanzoni and Hardesty, *All We're Meant to Be*, p.
217.
48. Donald Dayton, "A Dialogue on Women," p. 14.
49. Lucille Sider Dayton, "The Feminist Movement and Scripture," *PA* 3 (August-September, 1974), p. 10.
50. There is also a misuse of the cultural context of a given text which is possible. Hardesty
and Scanzoni, for example, conclude that the text in Ephesians 5 could not be teaching
support for a hierarchical marriage relationship, "because the dominant-husband submissive-
wife model of marriage was the norm in the societies of that time. There would have been
no reason to tell wives to submit to their husbands, or to tell husbands they were the heads"
(Scanzoni and Hardesty, *All We're Meant To Be*, p. 100). In order to be Pauline, it must be
"new," they feel. But surely Paul could as easily be arguing the need for a return to the
regnant pattern, after a false application of Christian freedom in the young Church, as he
could be proclaiming that which was at variance with his culture. To accept an interpretation of a text because it is new or distinct from dominant cultural patterns is a faulty
hermeneutical procedure.
51. George W. Knight III, "Male and Female Related He Them," *CT* 20 (April 9, 1976), p.
14.
52. Knight, "The Teaching/Ruling Functions in the Church," p. 89.
53. Russell Prohl, *Women in the Church* (1957), pp. 20–23.
54. Paul Jewett has an excellent, brief review of several classical theological statements
regarding women in his book *Man as Male and Female*, pp. 61–82.
55. Knight, "The Teaching/Ruling Functions in the Church"; John Reumann, "What in
Scripture Speaks to the Ordination of Women?" *CTM* 44 (January, 1973); Donald Dayton
and Lucille S. Dayton, "Women as Preachers: Evangelical Precedents," *CT* 19 (May 23,
1975); Lindsell, *The World, The Flesh and The Devil*.
56. Even with the sharing of insights through commentaries and books, biases remain. Thus,
to give one further example, Dorothy Pape provides us her 360-page personal journey
through the New Testament *In Search of God's Ideal Woman* (1976). She quotes commentators widely and provides strong evidence against a traditionalist position. But she nevertheless claims that her book is not meant as a brief for women ministers. Rather, it is simply a
defense of "great women missionaries [who] were not necessarily out of God's will" in their
teaching and preaching and evangelizing. It is hardly surprising to discover Pape is herself a
missionary out of a tradition in which women have historically been denied ordination.
Such an example, though more obvious than some, should remind us all of the need for a
basic humility in our claims to let Scripture speak authoritatively. We must be willing ever
to be corrected and then to act on what we hear.
57. Berkouwer, *Holy Scripture*, p. 297. Berkouwer's chapter on "Clarity" is excellent and
has influenced much of this discussion.

17: The *Sensus Plenior* and Biblical Interpretation

WILLIAM SANFORD LASOR

In presenting this token of my affection for and appreciation of my beloved colleague, it is fitting that I should deal with some subject that embraces our respective fields, the two Testaments. More and more, scholars have been devoting their attention to the relationship between the Old and the New Testaments—after a long and somewhat sterile period when the two disciplines were handled as having little or no organic relationship. More or less adhering to the position of R. Bultmann,[1] some scholars have found little reason for a New Testament scholar to study the Old Testament. A healthy reaction, sparked by such scholars as, *inter alia,* W. Eichrodt, G. von Rad, G. E. Wright, W. Zimmerli, P. Grelot, and C. Westermann, has set in against this dichotomy of the Christian Bible. R. E. Murphy[2] gives a very good survey of the development of the problem of the interrelationship of the Testaments in recent years up to the time of his writing. But the view that there is a discontinuity between the Testaments continues to attract many scholars. I suppose that the basic worldview of a scholar has something to do with this, for a theist who is a Christian would have relatively little difficulty in accepting a basic continuity in the redemptive and revelatory acts of God in the Old and the New Testaments. On the other hand, one who is basically nontheistic, or who sees the religions of the Hebrews and Christians as simply two of the man-made religions of the world, tends to look upon the concept of progressive revelation as something imposed by man and not originating in the activity of God. But even those of us who hold to the view that the authoritative Scriptures are both Old and New Testaments are not without our own set of problems. What, precisely, is the relationship of Old and New? How are we to perform objective, scholarly, and "scientific" exegesis, particularly on passages which are involved in this interrelation-

260

ship? In this essay, I shall attempt to come to grips with one small problem area in the larger discussion, namely, the validity or invalidity of the concept of *sensus plenior* in biblical hermeneutics.

But before entering into my subject, I cannot resist a little humor. Those of us who have known Everett Harrison over the years have come to recognize that his wit is keen and his ability to make a pun is delightful. Therefore, I suggest that to honor my colleague who has been at Fuller Theological Seminary for thirty years (during twenty-eight of which I have enjoyed collegiality with him), a paper on *sensus plenior,* "the fuller sense," is particularly apt.

1. Interpretation of Scripture

The art of preaching is the application of Scripture to the present situation. Of course, if Scripture has no application to the present, preaching is nonsense—as indeed it has become in all too many pulpits. For the preacher who believes that the Bible is the authoritative word of God in every generation, his task is to start with the text of Scripture and to derive from it a message that will be in effect the word of God to his audience.[3] But by what process is this done? What are the rules that must be followed, in order that the message will indeed be the word of God and not just the imaginations of a human speaker? There are certain well-recognized steps in the process. First, there is the study of the text itself (text criticism), in order to establish, as far as is humanly possible with the available means, the inspired text as it came from the biblical author. Then, there is exegesis, by which we attempt to understand as precisely as possible what the author intended to say and what his contemporary hearers or readers understood by his words.[4] Finally, there is the application of this message to our own day—but this is the most difficult, and seemingly the least controllable step of all. The believing community—whether the people of Israel, the Church in the New Testament, or the Jews and Christians of post-biblical times—has always attempted this last step, but the methods used have varied from place to place and from time to time. Our present study lies in this area.

The literal meaning. The basic meaning of any text, including the biblical text, is the literal meaning. This is universally admitted, but it is sometimes misunderstood or misinterpreted. In general, it is assumed that the literal meaning can be obtained by adding together the literal meanings of the words, taken in their syntax. Thus, for example, we read the account of Abram's migration from Haran to Canaan:

> Abram was seventy-five years old when he departed from Haran. And Abram took Sarai his wife, and Lot his brother's son, and all their possessions which they had gathered, and the persons that they had gotten in Haran; and they set forth to go to the land of Canaan (Gen 12:4b–5a).

This is perfectly clear. The words are familiar, the syntax is quite simple, and about all we need to do to get a clear understanding of the "literal" meaning is fill in definitions of the persons and places named.

But quite often the literal meaning cannot be obtained by this simple process. Take this brief statement:

> Yet it was I who taught Ephraim to walk . . . (Hos 11:3).

The simple sum of the words tells us that an unnamed speaker taught someone named "Ephraim" how to walk. But when we read the context, we discover that "Ephraim" is a figure of speech signifying the northern kingdom of Israel,[5] and "I taught Ephraim to walk" is intended to convey the meaning that Israel's religious and national existence was the result of the Lord's tutelage. In fact, "Israel" takes on the larger meaning, in the light of verse 1, and what is said of "Ephraim" is true of all Israel, northern and southern kingdoms. But this is still the literal sense. It is not an interpretation, subject to different viewpoints; it is precisely what the author intended and what his hearers would have understood. Common figures of speech must be understood as such, if we are to get the literal sense of the text.

Poetry not only makes extensive use of figures of speech, but it includes other features, and as a result, the literal meaning is often obscured and sometimes difficult to discover.[6] Take, for example, the following passage:

> Rebuke the beasts that dwell among the reeds,
> the herd of bulls with the calves of the peoples.
> Trample under foot those who lust after tribute;
> scatter the peoples who delight in war.
> Let bronze be brought from Egypt;
> let Ethiopia hasten to stretch out her hands to God (Ps 68:30–31).

This is a portion of a great psalm concerning the Lord God, his covenant people, and the nations of the world. Hence the figures of speech, "beasts" and "bulls," must signify the enemies of God's people. But it is not only a prayer that the enemies might be scattered; it is even a prayer that they might at last be brought to God. Allowing for certain details that may have been and probably were clearer to the people who first united in this song, which now escape us, we may take this as the literal meaning. The *Good News Bible,* which seeks to translate by giving the dynamic equivalent, renders this passage as follows:

> Rebuke Egypt, that wild animal in the reeds;
> > rebuke the nations, that herd of bulls with their calves,
> > until they all bow down and offer you their silver.
> Scatter those people who love to make war!
> Ambassadors will come from Egypt;
> > the Sudanese will raise their hands in prayer to God (Ps 68:30–31,
> > TEV).[7]

The literal meaning of the text, then, is the basic meaning and the basis for interpretation. When the literal meaning is ignored, all sorts of fanciful interpretations and applications result, as can be seen in the homilies of medieval Christians or in sectarian writings of modern times. Without the literal sense we have no control of any other sense.[8]

Grammatico-historical exegesis. Since the Reformation, biblical exegetes have generally applied a method that includes, among other things, the grammatical elements of the text and its historical setting. In the passages of Scripture which we have previously considered, we have seen the need for both of these elements. Now, let us take them up in a bit more detail.

In grammatical exegesis, the basic unit is generally taken to be the *word.* Students in the process of learning how to exegete usually begin with word studies. Unfortunately, they often stop there as well. It does not take much exegetical experience to recognize that words rarely exist alone. In some cases they cannot exist alone and convey any meaning. To study a word, the context is essential. The word "Sit!" conveys meaning, but only in the context of a person (or a pet dog) who is standing, whereas "through" is meaningful only when in the context of another word or word-group.[9] The study of the word is nevertheless of primary importance, for communication in written form (and usually in spoken form) is composed of words, and unless we know the meaning(s) of each word, the communication is nonsense.[10]

A few words of caution may be called for at this point. For one thing, any given word rarely has precisely the same meaning in every context. Therefore, if we are working from a Hebrew or Greek lexicon, we need to make use of one that gives contexts as well as meanings, and further, we need to study several of these contexts.[11] There simply is no such thing as a "word-for-word" translation. A second factor to be noted is the type of literature (or genre) in which the word occurs. We have already seen that poetry and other figurative language requires special study of words, but this same principle extends to other literary types. A third word of caution concerns the use of etymological word-studies.[12] While there is considerable value in tracing the cognates of a word in various related languages, it is undeniably true that each language has its own peculiar semantic development for the word under investigation.[13] A fourth caution concerns special usage of words, such as paronomasia, alliteration, assonance, and the like, where the author, in order to make a point, may make an unusual use of a word, use a word that is uncommon, or even coin a word for the occasion.

As we have already seen, meaning is conveyed by words in context, and the study of *syntax* is an essential part of obtaining the literal meaning. Since all grammatical study, and especially syntax, is in a sad state today, particularly in the United States of America, most students have a terrifying experience trying to learn Greek or Hebrew syntax. Students who have worked under Daniel Fuller or me know that we seek to get into the study of the text through the use of sentence diagrams. Diagramming is simply an attempt to visualize the rules of syntax. This deals with the "surface structure" of language. There is another approach through semantics, which goes beneath the surface structure. There are four basic semantic categories which "include exhaustively all the semantic subcategories of all languages."[14] These are:

(O) Object: things or entities which normally participate in events (i.e., nouns, pronouns, and other substantives);
(E) Event: actions, processes, happenings (i.e., verbs and verb phrases);
(A) Abstract: expressions which set forth qualities, quantities, and degrees of objects, events, and other abstracts (i.e., adjectives and adverbs);
(R) Relations: expressions of the meaningful connections between the other kinds of terms (i.e., prepositions, conjunctions, and the like).

It is possible to analyze any statement and restructure it in a way that is clear and unambiguous. This analytic process of reducing the surface structure to its underlying kernels is called back-transformation.[15] By whatever method we approach the problem, we must ultimately have a clear idea of how the words of the text are interrelated so as to convey the meaning.

It is well known that language undergoes changes as we move from place to place and from time to time. Therefore, if we would know precisely what the author meant and what his hearers/readers understood, we should know precisely where and when that text was composed. This is the *historical* element of grammatico-historical exegesis. History and geography are integral parts of the biblical Scriptures. The number of personal and place names in the Bible far exceeds that of any other religious literature. We of the believing community like to use expressions such as, "God is active in history." Especially when we turn to the Old Testament prophets we realize how much we need to know the historical situation in order to comprehend the basic message.[16] The historical context is as important as the textual context.

The failure of the grammatico-historical method. During the past century-and-a-half, exegetical scholars have refined grammatico-historical exegesis in many ways, creating in the process many tools of great value for understanding the Scriptures. But along the way, some scholars seemed to lose sight of the truth that the Scriptures are the word of God—of the living God whose word is alive and active. Exegesis was firmly anchored in history, but it was not the history of God's redemptive revelation; rather, it was the secular history of the past, and had only antiquarian interest for the present. The literal meaning of the biblical text is the basic meaning, but if it is the only meaning, then God is not speaking to us; he spoke to men of old—or so they believed—and that was that.

Part of the reason for this failure of the method must be traced to the dominance of the "scientific" worldview. The theistic system, according to which God is everywhere and always greater than the universe he created and active in the laws which he himself ordained, was replaced by a worldview that completely ruled out anything that could not be accounted for by the scientific process. The "god" of Israel was no different from the gods of the Canaanites or the Babylonians. When the prophet said, "Thus saith the Lord," he was simply expressing his own insights and attributing them to his particular deity. In fact, the god of Abraham, the god of Isaac, and the god of Jacob were different deities which the ancient figures worshipped. To talk of a "covenant," a "covenant people," a "progressive revelation," or indeed any kind of "revelation" is simply to impose upon the religious and mythological recollections of the people the concept of a later, but still prescientific, age. To discover the historical situation—which was now specified as the *Sitz im Leben*—was a circular process whereby it was first determined what the situation must have been at any particular time and then the scriptural data were reworked to fit that situation. The exegetical commentaries that resulted gave the preacher little if any help in his effort to discover what God wanted him to say to his congregation on the following Sunday.

It is not my intention to cast aside the grammatico-historical method. Quite the contrary, I use it and I try to teach it to my students. It is simply my purpose to show that this method brings us only to the end of the first stage of biblical preaching, namely, the literal meaning. B. L. Ramm has expressed it well: "Exegesis without application is academic; exposition that is not grounded in exegesis is either superficial or misleading or even both."[17]

The spiritual meaning(s). Starting from the premise that the Bible is the word of God to the people of his covenant, it follows that this word is applicable according to his will to all generations. Since he is a spiritual being and since his purpose is redemptive, it follows that his word is spiritual and redemptive. There is therefore a spiritual meaning—or possibly more than one spiritual meaning—implicit in his word. Discovering the spiritual message in, rather than imposing it on, the Scripture is a serious task; and the believing community has attempted various methods.

A full discussion of the history of interpretation can be found in the well-known work by Dean Farrar.[18] A useful summary is given by Ramm in his work on interpretation.[19] We need only take time here to remember some of the more striking methods. Jewish exegesis is often illustrated by the use of gematria, whereby the numerical values of the letters of a word unlock the secret of the meaning. Thus, "Shiloh shall come" in Gen 49:10 gives the value of 358, which is the number of "Messiah."[20] It is sometimes overlooked that the Jews also produced Philo of Alexandria (c. 20 B.C.–c. A.D. 54), and that his allegorical method largely influenced Origen (c. A.D. 185–254) and subsequent Christian exegetes. Using the trichotomous theory of the human being as a pattern, Origen held that all Scripture had three meanings, the sense of the words which was for the simple, the moral sense which is like the soul, and the spiritual sense which is the highest. John Cassian (died c. 435) held to a fourfold method of interpretation, the historical, the allegorical, the tropological, and the anagogical. His best-known illustration is the city of Jerusalem, historically a Jewish city, allegorically the church of Christ, tropologically the soul of man, and anagogically the heavenly city.[21] This fourfold method was adopted by Thomas Aquinas (c. 1225–1274) and used widely by Catholic exegetes.[22] Martin Luther started out using the allegorical method, and later claimed to have abandoned it—but a study of his commentaries, particularly those of the Old Testament, shows that he still reverted to it in order to find Christ everywhere in the Old Testament. Thus, for example, in his comments on Gen 28:12–14 (Jacob's ladder), he says: "The ladder is the wonderful union of the divinity with our flesh. On it the angels ascend and descend, and they can never wonder at this enough. This is the historical, simple, and literal sense." In the next paragraph, Luther gives the allegorical meaning of the ladder, "a union between us and Christ."[23] It is obvious that what Luther considered to be the "historical, simple, and literal sense" is rather the allegorical, and his "allegorical" is more like the tropological.

It was the Reformation, without doubt, that started the trend toward using the grammatico-historical exegetical method as the basis for developing the spiritual message from the text. In my opinion, John Calvin was the greatest of exegetes in this effort. If in some of his commentaries he seems to be a child of his day,[24] this does not greatly detract from his stature as an exegete. The test of the preacher is not whether he seems to relate the text overmuch to the situation of his own day, but whether indeed he draws this message from the text.

The spiritual meaning of a text, as I see it, is the timeless truth inherent in a passage of Scripture as it is applied to the preacher's day and its spiritual needs. This spiritual meaning may be drawn in different ways, by twisting or accommodating the text, by allegorizing it, by the use of typology (to be discussed below), or by strict application of the grammatico-historical method. We reject accommodation and most allegory as having no objective controls, thereby leaving the preacher free to find whatever message he will in any text that suits his fancy. The grammatico-historical method, we have seen, has sometimes failed to yield a spiritual meaning. Where does this leave us in our quest for meaning in the Word of God?

2. The Theory and Practice of *Sensus Plenior*

The spiritual meaning of a passage of Scripture, derived by using grammatico-historical exegesis, is completely valid and provides objective controls; but it often leaves us with a basic gap between the Old and the New Testaments. Take, for example, the account of the Davidic covenant in 2 Samuel 7:

> When your days are fulfilled and you lie down with your fathers, I will raise up your son after you, who shall come forth from your body, . . . and I will establish the throne of his kingdom forever (2 Sam 7:12–13).

The literal meaning is clear enough: The Lord is promising David, through the prophet Nathan (see v. 4), an eternal dynasty. Saul had been the first king of Israel, but he established no dynasty; David had supplanted Saul's son. The Lord was assuring David that his son would succeed him and the Davidic line would continue for future generations. We could add more details from the immediate context, such as the promise that David's son would build the "house" (temple) which David himself had longed to build for the Lord (7:13); that even though this son sinned, he would be chastened but not supplanted (vv. 14, 15); and that Israel would have a permanent and peaceful dwelling place (7:10). The spiritual truth is also clear: the Lord is faithful to keep the promises which he made to Abraham and the patriarchs concerning the people of his covenant in providing for them not only the land but also a dynastic succession that would give them rest from their enemies, hence we may trust him to keep other promises to us who are also people of his covenant.

But there are obvious flaws in a methodology that stops here. For one thing, the Davidic covenant, if we understand it only literally, was not kept; it was broken. Israel did not continue to live "in their own place, and be disturbed no more" (7:10); the Assyrians and the Babylonians uprooted them and demolished their holy temple. The throne of David was not "made sure for ever" (7:16); it vanished in 586 B.C. and no king of the Davidic line has ruled since then. A second fact must be faced, namely, the New Testament writers considered Jesus Christ to be the "son of David," and applied to Christ the promises that had been made to David. How can this be derived from the Old Testament text if we adhere strictly to the literal meaning and its spiritual truth? It becomes obvious that, for the New Testament writers (and for Jesus), at least, the Old Testament passage must have some deeper meaning.

Symbol, Allegory, and Type. There is a great deal of confusion in the terms that are used. According to some writers, "allegory" and "type" are the same, and others would even include *sensus plenior* in this category. Therefore, I shall first attempt to specify the terms that I shall use.

All language is symbolic, for words and clauses are merely symbolic ways of communicating. The proof of this can be seen when we translate, for the purpose of translation is to convert one set of symbols to another while conveying the same meaning. In a large sense, then, the entire Bible, like all spoken or written language, is symbolic. Obviously, this is too broad a definition to be useful. There are certain concepts which are capable of immediate visualization, for example, "chair," "red," "she smiled," etc. There are other concepts that cannot be visualized, such as "God," "transcendence," "the age to come," etc. To communicate such ideas, we use symbols, making use of some visualizable word or expression. The Bible is full of such symbols, and these must be recognized and treated as such in order to understand the message that is intended. For example, the account of the garden of Eden includes a tree identified as "the tree of the knowledge of good and evil" (Gen 2:17). We are not told what kind of tree it was—and that is unimportant. The symbolic meaning of the tree is most important, for it symbolized the right of the Creator to impose a sanction on the Adamic creature, to say, "This is a no-no," while at the same time it symbolized the free choice of Adam in his God-given ability to disobey the divine command. The serpent, likewise, is symbolic of the satanic. I use the word "satanic" here in its literal sense, to mean that which is adverse, specifically opposed, to God's will. The suggestion to disobey God's command did not originate in the Adamic pair; it came from outside. Therefore, Adam cannot blame God for making him satanic. At the same time, Adam and his wife are culpable, for they had a clear revelation of the will of God and they knowingly disobeyed. So far, we are dealing with the literal meaning by seeking to understand the significance of the symbols. This is clearly to be distinguished from allegory, as I use the word.

In some instances, the symbol is later replaced by a reality, or will be replaced by a reality in a future age. In this case, the symbol may properly be called a "type." The reality may be called the "antitype" of the symbol that it replaces. One of the best illustrations of this is the tabernacle which the Israelites constructed and carried with them during the wilderness period. The tabernacle was a portable building, an elaborate tent with decorations and furnishings. But it was more importantly a symbol, symbolizing the presence of the Lord. This is indicated by the names which it bore, namely, "tent of meeting," and *miškān*, "dwelling place." It was also indicated as such by another symbolic act, namely, the visible descent of the cloud upon the completed tabernacle (Exod 40:34–38). The tabernacle, however, was later replaced by the reality, when God became incarnate in the virgin-born child, Emmanuel (which means "God with us"). John puts this truth in clear language, "The word became flesh and tabernacled among us" (John 1:14, lit.).[25] It is even possible to carry the symbolism further, and see the Incarnation itself as a symbol of a greater reality; for in the Holy City of Revelation, the "tabernacle" of God is with men, and God himself, the ultimate reality, makes any further symbolic representation of himself unnecessary (Rev 21:2–3). Since the tabernacle was a symbol that was later replaced by the reality it symbolized, it is entirely proper to speak of the tabernacle as a *type* of Christ, and the earthly incarnation of Christ as a *type* of the presence of God himself in the new Jerusalem.

This use of the word "type" is clearly to be distinguished from allegory. An allegorical interpretation of the tabernacle goes into fanciful explanations of every color, every type of material, every piece of furniture, and sometimes results in a portrayal of Jesus Christ in such detail that the Incarnation would seem to be unnecessary. It is certainly true that some of the items used in the tabernacle cultus were in themselves symbolic of spiritual truth, and even types of realities to come. The sacrifices of bulls and goats, which (as the author of Hebrews reminds us) were not able to take away sin, were typical of the sacrifice of Christ which does take away sin. Other items may profitably be studied in similar fashion. As long as we begin with the reality that is symbolized in the text and proceed to the reality that replaces the symbol, we have controllable interpretation of the text. It avoids the criticism levelled against allegorizing the text, often deserved, and yields the spiritual meaning of the scriptural passage.

To speak of certain biblical persons as "types" (such as "David is a type of Christ") seems to me to be incorrect. David did symbolize something, but he was not a symbol. What he symbolized was later replaced by the reality when the Messiah appeared, but David himself was not replaced; and we believe that he shall continue to exist forever in the age to come. I would prefer to say that the Davidic office or throne was the type, and the messianic reign the antitype.[26]

Sensus plenior. The term *sensus plenior* ("the fuller meaning") is attributed to Andrea Fernández in an article written in 1925. The subject has been treated most fully by the Catholic scholar, Raymond E. Brown.[27] Brown defines *sensus plenior* as follows:

> The *sensus plenior* is that additional, deeper meaning, intended by God but not clearly intended by the human author, which is seen to exist in the words of a Biblical text (or group of texts, or even a whole book) when they are studied in the light of further revelation or development in the understanding of revelation.[28]

Brown's earlier presentations of the concept called forth considerable reaction, almost entirely limited to Catholic scholars, and a study of this material is most helpful—but it lies beyond our present purpose.[29] Some of the objections and clarifications will be considered here; those that deal principally with implications that concern Roman Catholic but not Protestant dogma we shall disregard.

The definition raises a particularly difficult problem by its statement "intended by God, but not clearly intended by the human author." This concept, it would seem at first glance, lies beyond grammatico-historical exegesis and therefore opens the door for subjective interpretation. In fact, it seems clear from the discussion that ensued that some Catholic scholars were making use of *sensus plenior* and the magisterial teaching of the Church to support certain Marian dogmas which Protestant scholars would disclaim as nonbiblical. At the same time, other Catholic scholars were raising the objection that if the biblical authors did not intend to teach something, it was not allowable to read that teaching into the passage.

There are a number of Old Testament passages which are used by New Testament authors in a way that seems to support the concept of *sensus plenior.* We may mention two that cause difficulty, namely, the "virgin shall conceive" passage in Isaiah (Isa 7:14), and the "out of Egypt" passage in Hosea (Hos 11:1). In neither case is there any indication that the author had some distant future event in mind, hence it is most difficult to conclude that the authors were speaking of Jesus Christ or even an unnamed Messiah. Isaiah 7 deals with Ahaz, king of Judah, and the Syro-Ephramite coalition of Rezin of Syria and Pekah of Israel. The point does not seem to be a virgin birth, but rather it lies in the sequence of events: a young woman is pregnant and will bear a son, and before this child is old enough to know good and evil, the Lord will deal with the enemy kings (Isa 7:1–17).[30] The prophecy is dated c. 735 B.C., and the fulfillment occurred in 732 and 722 B.C. Hos 11:1 ("out of Egypt I called my son") clearly deals with the deliverance of Israel from Egypt at the time of the exodus, and the words of verse 2 obviously cannot be applied to Jesus. The author is using the redeeming love of the Lord in contrast with the stubborn sinfulness of Israel to get across his lesson. Yet both of these passages are cited as "fulfilled" in Jesus Christ (see Matt 1:22–23 and 2:14–15). There are other passages in the New Testament that raise similar problems concerning the use of the Old Testament.

To say that "God intended" the Old Testament passages to refer to a later fulfillment in Christ raises as many problems as it solves. If God intended to foretell the virgin birth of Jesus, why did he do it in just this way? Until Matthew quoted Isa 7:14, would any Jew who carefully read Isaiah 7 have thought of the Messiah at all, much less have understood it to teach his virgin birth? It seems that it would have made more sense for God to have included the virgin-birth prophecy in Isaiah 9 or 11, both of which are more obviously passages dealing with a future period that could be associated with the Messiah. But any attempt to suggest what God should have done or what he intended to do is presumptuous, and I am reluctant to deal with his Word in such manner.

It is more common to find modern scholars suggesting that New Testament writers, notably Matthew and Paul, were simply using methods of their day, either "rabbinic exegesis," or simply searching for proof-texts. I find this effort no better solution, and so I return to *sensus plenior,* but with some concern that the definition may need to be reworded slightly.

There are passages of Scripture where there is indeed something "deeper" or "fuller" than the literal and the spiritual meanings as they appear on the surface. This has been obvious to the people of God through the centuries, and it occurs in the Old Testament, without the need of using New Testament illustrations. There is a deep sense of the organic nature of the elect people. The call of Abram was likewise a call to all of God's people to forsake everything and follow him (a spiritual sense), and the promise of blessing to all the nations of the earth through Abraham and his descendants was indeed to be fulfilled by those descendants. Yet, when Isaiah considered the glories of the future, he saw Israel (the descendants of Abraham through Isaac and Jacob) and himself as in need of redemption (cf. Isaiah 53).[31] Israel is portrayed in the Old Testament both as a redemptive agent (and hence a type of the Redeemer) and as a redeemed community (hence either a type of the Church or the earlier organic portion of which the Church is a later portion). At the same time, the completion of the redemptive activity of the Lord always lies beyond the Old Testament. Thus there is a *fullness* which is never achieved in the Old Testament but which is required. There is a *fuller* meaning of the promises of the Lord than is ever realized in the Old Testament.

Take, for example, the "protevangelium" of Gen 3:15. This is part of the curse which God pronounced on the serpent after the Adamic couple yielded to the temptation:

> I will put enmity between you and the woman,
>   and between your seed and her seed;
> he shall bruise your head,
>   and you shall bruise his heel (Gen 3:15).

To suggest that this story was first told to explain why women don't like snakes is ridiculous. But to suggest that the surface meaning, namely, that descendants (or some one descendant) of the woman would deal a mortal wound to one of the serpent's descendants, certainly does not exhaust the implicit purpose of the story. The entire account (Gen 3:14–19) contains two interwoven strands, one of which speaks of defeat, suffering, toil, and death, while the other speaks of future generations, provision of food and sustenance of life, and triumph over the satanic tempter. To suggest that the "seed" of the "woman" who would bruise the serpent's head is a prophecy of Mary, the Virgin Birth, and Jesus, is to get more from the text than can be gotten by grammatico-historical exegesis, spiritual interpretation, and the objective processes of scriptural scholarship. But to see a *fullness* in the story, in precisely the way it is told, that can be understood when (and only when) that fullness is revealed, seems to me to be reasonable. In the seed are all the elements that will ultimately develop into the tree, its leaves, and its fruit. Yet careful analysis of that seed, even under the highest-powered microscope, will not reveal those elements. So it is, I believe, with Scripture.

Or again, take the Davidic covenant, which we discussed previously (pp. 267–268, above). It is clearly implied that the Lord is speaking of something more than the successor of David on the throne, for the Lord declares a particular, personal relationship with the "son" of David: "I will be his father, and he shall be my son" (2 Sam 7:14). This, of course, was the same terminology used in Israel's relationship to the Lord, and we should not press it to mean that the successor is to be the "son of God"—but it can involve such a concept, and indeed this concept appears with reference to the king of Israel in the Psalms (e.g., Ps 2:7; 45:6). David wanted to build a "house" for the Lord, and in denying him this privilege, the Lord promised that David's "son" would make him a "house." But as we read the passage more carefully, we find that the term "house" means something more than a building (cf. 7:2, 6, 11, 13, 16). It is something that David's "son" would build (7:13), and something that the Lord himself would build (7:11). Like the throne, the house was to be permanent, and the Lord closed the promise with the words, "Your house and your kingdom shall be made sure for ever before me" (7:16). Certainly this demands a fuller meaning than Solomon, the Davidic dynasty, and Solomon's temple! It requires something more than a spiritual meaning. Even the people of the Old Testament came to realize that fact, for "son of David" came to be a term for the ruler who would inaugurate the age of justice and peace. They had more difficulty with the concept of the temple, but at least Jeremiah seems to have realized that the temple's continual existence was not guaranteed (cf. Jer 7:3–15). The early Church saw the fulfillment in Jesus Christ, the "son of David," in his kingship, even though he had been crucified (cf. Acts 2:22–36; 4:25–28), and in something other than Solomon's temple (cf. Acts 7:44–50).

To take one more example out of many that might be chosen,[32] let's look at Mic 5:2,

> But you, O Bethlehem Ephrathah,
>   who are little to be among the clans of Judah,
> from you shall come forth for me
>   one who is to be ruler in Israel,
> whose origin is from of old,
>   from ancient days (Mic 5:2, MT 5:1).

The prophecy was spoken prior to the Assyrian invasion (cf. 5:5). The scattering of Israel is in view (5:7). The people are filled with fear (4:9). The prophet not only deals with their sins, but he offers some promise of deliverance (4:10), and he offers assurance that the Davidic line will again rule Israel. Of course, he does not mention the Davidic dynasty, but the ruler comes from Bethlehem, David's ancestral home; and the "ruler" is one "whose origin is from of old, from ancient days" (5:2), not one from a new dynasty. Spiritually, this verse could be applied to any time of insecurity. But in the redemptive activity of God, an ultimate defeat of the enemies of God's people is required, along with a ruler who shall provide security and sufficiency for his people (5:3–4); and this *fullness* of meaning is present in the prophecy.

3. Conclusion and Implications

Something like a *fuller meaning,* a *sensus plenior,* is required by many portions of Scripture, possibly by all of Scripture. By the very nature of God's redemptive and revelatory activity, the ultimate purpose of God is contained in this process; and as the redemptive activity proceeds ever to its fullness, so the revelatory activity at last is complete—full. The concept of "fulfillment" is not to be looked upon as discrete events which "fulfill" discrete predictions. There are predictions of coming events in the Bible, to be sure; but the proper juxtaposition is not "prediction and fulfillment" but rather "purpose and fulfillment." Prediction is something that is associated with clairvoyants and wizards, who have no power to bring about the events that they predict. If one of their predictions is "fulfilled," it is a matter of chance, or at most of prescience. With God, fulfillment is the accomplishment of his purpose. What God revealed to the prophets and through them to his people, he fulfilled by his own power, for he is able to fulfill his own word.

The quest for a *sensus plenior* is part of the process of discovering the fullness of his purpose in his revelation. It is the recognition that at any moment in God's revelatory activity, he has the end in view and he has his people of future generations in mind. When he delivered the Israelites from Egypt, he was delivering all of his people from bondage—in a literal sense, for if Israel had not been delivered from Egypt there would have been no Israel; and in a fuller sense, for if there had been no Israel, there would have been no Davidic king, no prophets, no Scriptures, no Messiah, and no redemptive fulfillment. It was therefore true, in this fuller sense, that God did call his Son out of Egypt. In a similar manner we can trace the fullness of God's purpose in establishing the throne of David; for, as Isaiah saw so clearly (cf. Isa 9:1–7; 11:1–10, etc.), the ultimate hope of a world of peace and security was to be found in that throne.

There are guidelines to be observed. *Sensus plenior*, like typology, must always begin with the literal meaning of the text. It is not a substitute for grammatico-historical exegesis, but a development from such exegesis. It is not a reading into the text of theological doctrines and theories, but a reading from the text of the fullness of meaning required by God's complete revelation. The *sensus plenior* is derived from total context, usually including what has already been revealed of God's redemptive activity, and always including the ultimate purpose of that activity. In this sense, it is correct to say that the human author did not intend to say all that can be found in *sensus plenior*. On the other hand, it seems clear from our study of prophetic passages that the prophets were led by the Spirit, who inspired them to express their prophecies in such ways that the fuller meaning was not lost. In some cases, we can see in the words of the prophets only the general trend of God's redemptive work; but in other instances even the words are capable of conveying a fuller meaning. We must guard equally against reading into a text more than is there and failing to find the deepest meaning of the text.

Finally, we must reject any notion that the *sensus plenior* comes from any mystical, spiritual, or other source than the Scriptures. A person who is spiritually minded may find deeper meanings in the Bible, simply because he enjoys putting more effort into the task and because he is sensitive to the Spirit's leadings. But that does not mean that he has a special line of revelation direct from God. The Scriptures of the Old and New Testament are the *only* infallible rule of faith and practice. It is from the Word alone that we have this revelation, and from the word alone that we find any fuller meaning. The Scriptures are full of wonderful revelations from God. We admit that "we see through a glass darkly"—but that is no reason to shut our eyes. The concept of *sensus plenior* opens our eyes to see more of God's revealed truth.

NOTES

1. Cf. R. E. Murphy's comment, "Bultmann's position is one of radical denial of the true relevance of the OT to the Christian" ("The Relationship Between the Testaments," *CBQ* 26 [1964], p. 352).
2. Article cited in note 1.
3. What I say about the "preacher" applies equally well, *mutatis mutandis,* to the teacher or author, or to anyone who seeks to proclaim God's word to his or her own day.
4. Some would insert Introduction between Text Criticism and Application; I include it here as part of exegesis, for the problems of date and authorship are elementary parts of identifying the author and his day and place, which in turn are necessary (at least to some extent) for understanding his intention.
5. The capital of Israel was Samaria and it was located in the tribal territory of Ephraim.
6. The passage in Hosea 11, which we have just considered, appears to be in poetic structure. My reference here to "poetry," however, is to portions of the Scriptures that are entirely in poetic form, such as the Psalms.
7. Some may object that the TEV at times moves from dynamic translation to interpretation. This is a very fine line, and the TEV translators might reply that the original worshippers had *Egypt* in mind when they spoke of "the beasts that dwell among the reeds," and *ambassadors,* when they mentioned the bringing of bronze. In my mind, the TEV often adds interpretation, sometimes with great value, and sometimes with questionable result.
8. See further my remarks on "The Literal Interpretation," in my article on "Interpretation of Prophecy," *BDPT,* pp. 129–130. The encyclical *Divino afflante Spiritu* defines the literal meaning as follows: ". . . litteralem, ut aiunt, verborum significationem, quam hagiographus intenderit atque expresserit. . . ," i.e., what the hagiographer intended and expressed. Cf. *Enchiridion Biblicum* (2nd ed., 1954), p. 552.
9. With rising inflection in certain contexts, "Through?" may mean, "Are you finished (yet/already)?" and with falling inflection, "Through!" may mean, "I've finished." In any case, the context is required for the conveying of meaning, even if the context is a situation and not a text.
10. A splendid example is the poem "Jabberwocky" in Lewis Carroll's *Through the Looking Glass.* For a very clever analysis of the grammatical structure of this poem, see E. A. Nida and C. R. Taber, *The Theory and Practice of Translation* (1974), pp. 34–35. But though we may know from such a study that *toves* can *gyre and gimble* and that such activity takes place *in the wabe,* or that *borogroves* are *mimsy* whereas *raths* are *mome,* we haven't the foggiest idea of what is being said—because we don't know the meaning of the significant words.
11. The biblical student who cannot work in Hebrew or Greek can still accomplish such contextual study by the use of a good concordance, such as Young's or Strong's, where the Hebrew and Greek words are given and contexts using the same word can be examined.
12. The best-known of such works is Kittel's *Theological Dictionary of the New Testament,* 10 vols. (1964–76).
13. This was the strong point of criticism of Kittel's *TWNT* (the German original of *TDNT*) made by James Barr, *The Semantics of Biblical Language* (1961).
14. Nida and Taber, *The Theory and Practice of Translation,* pp. 37–38.
15. For a clear discussion with good illustrations, see Nida and Taber, *The Theory and Practice of Translation,* chapter 3, "Grammatical Analysis."

16. Failure to recognize the importance of this fact has led to two different results: on the one hand, there are those who see nothing significant in the prophets because they do not understand the situation that called forth the prophetic message; on the other hand, the prophetic messages have been cut up into predictions of things to come that have no relationship whatever to the basic prophetic message.

17. *BDPT*, p. 101.

18. F. W. Farrar, *The History of Interpretation* (1886; reprint 1961).

19. B. Ramm, *Protestant Biblical Interpretation* (rev. ed., 1956), chapters 2, 3.

20. The numerical value of the consonants YB'‿ŠYLH is 358 (10+2+1+300+10+30+5), which is the same as the value of the letters of MŠYH (40+300+10+8). This method is not entirely dead. Several years ago I attended a meeting where a learned Jewish scholar used gematria as the basis for deriving his message from a passage in the prophets.

21. *Collationes* xiv.8, in J. Migne, *Patrologia Latina* 49, 964A; cf. also Philip Schaff and Henry Wace, eds., *Nicene and Post-Nicene Fathers;* Second Series (1894), 11, pp. 437–438. The formula, *Littera gesta docet, quid credas allegoria, moralis quid agas, quo tendas anagogia,* attributed to Thomas (*Quaestiones quodlibetales duodecim* 7, Q.6, and *Summa Theologica* I.i.10), appears in a footnote to Cassian in *NPNF* 11, p. 438.

22. Thomas groups the allegorical, anagogical, and moral senses under the spiritual sense, and points out that all the senses are founded on the literal, insisting that only from the literal can any argument be drawn. *Summa* I.i.10; cf. Anton C. Pegis, *Basic Writings of St. Thomas Aquinas* (1945), 1, p. 17. See also *Commentary on Epistle to Galatians,* IV, 7, in Mary T. Clark, ed., *An Aquinas Reader* (1972), pp. 412–413.

23. *Luther's Works,* ed. Jaroslav Pelikan, Vol. 5, Lectures on Genesis, chaps. 26–30 (1968), p. 223.

24. On Jacob's Ladder, e.g., Calvin rejected the interpretation that "the ladder is a figure of Divine Providence," and says, "If, then, we say that the ladder is a figure of Christ, the exposition will not be forced." John Calvin, *Commentaries on . . . Genesis,* trans. John King (reprinted 1948), 2, pp. 112–113.

25. Even the verb in John, *skēnoō,* is reminiscent of the word for "tabernacle," which in Greek is *skēnē.*

26. I have dealt with this matter more fully in my article in *BDPT*, pp. 130–132.

27. Raymond E. Brown, "The History and Development of the Theory of a *Sensus Plenior*," *CBQ* 15 (1953), pp. 141–162; *The Sensus Plenior of Sacred Scripture* (S.T.D. dissertation; Baltimore: St. Mary's University, 1955), 161 pp.; "The *Sensus Plenior* in the Last Ten Years," *CBQ* 25 (1963), pp. 262–285. Fr. Brown gives extensive bibliography for further study, and his words deserve careful reading.

28. *The Sensus Plenior of Sacred Scripture,* p. 92.

29. Brown's article, "The *Sensus Plenior* in the Last Ten Years," *CBQ* 25 (1963), pp. 262–285, will refer the reader to the most significant reactions.

30. This is in no way to be taken as a denial of the virgin-birth of Jesus, which I cordially receive, believe, and teach, since it is clearly stated in Matt 1:18–20 and Luke 1:31, 34–35.

31. Cf. W. S. LaSor, *Israel, A Biblical View* (1976), pp. 26–28.

32. I have dealt with several others in my article in *BDPT*, pp. 133–135.

18: The Interpretation of the Parable of the Good Samaritan

ROBERT H. STEIN

Of all the parables of Jesus the most familiar and loved is the parable of the Good Samaritan. Probably no parable has had as long a history of interpretation and been so intensely investigated as this one. Yet seldom has a passage of Scripture been so frequently and continuously misunderstood. Even today we come across interpretations of the parable which seem to owe far less to established principles of exegesis than to creative imagination. The purpose of this article is to interpret this parable using the various insights that have been gained within the last century. In order to do this, however, we shall have to investigate how this parable has been interpreted in the past, to note the various errors that have been made, to list certain principles which should be followed in the interpretation of the parables, and then finally to apply these principles to the interpretation of this particular parable.

1. History of the Interpretation of the Parable

a. The Early Church Fathers (to A.D. 540)

Probably the earliest known reference to the parable of the God Samaritan is an allusion to this passage by Marcion (died 160) in which he interprets the parable as denying the incarnation. According to Marcion the Good Samaritan, i.e., Jesus, was not born of a woman but rather appeared for the first time between Jerusalem and Jericho as the Good Samaritan.[1] It is not important for us to know why or how Marcion interpreted this passage in accordance with his gnostic beliefs. What is important for us is to note that he interpreted the parable allegorically and christologically rather than literally and ethically. With Irenaeus (140–202) the allegorical-christological interpretation becomes more apparent and clear. For Irenaeus the Good Samaritan is Christ who had compassion and bound up the wounds of the man who fell among thieves, and the two denarii represent for him the "image and inscription of the Father and the Son."[2]

A contemporary of Irenaeus was Clement of Alexandria (150–215). Clement follows well the Alexandrian hermeneutical tradition and allegorizes the parable more fully than ever before. He gives the following interpretation:

> Good Samaritan = Neighbor = Christ
> Thieves = Rulers of Darkness
> Wounds = Fears, lusts, passions, pains, deceits, pleasures
> Wine = Blood of David's Vine
> Oil = Compassion of the Father
> Binding [of health and of salvation] = Love, faith, hope[3]

Although Origen (184–254) was the "successor" of Clement of Alexandria, it is not certain how much he may have been influenced by him. It is probably incorrect to think of him, however, as a pupil of Clement. Nevertheless, the same allegorical tendency which we find in Clement is also found in Origen. In fact, it would not be incorrect to say that with Origen the allegorical method of interpretation became a "science." Origen maintained that the Scriptures contained a threefold sense, for even as Paul in 1 Thes 5:23 spoke of the body, soul, and spirit of man, so Origen saw the Scriptures as consisting also of a "body" which was the *literal* sense of the text, a "soul" which was the *moral* or *tropological* sense of the text, and a "spirit" which was the *spiritual* sense of the text.[4] To arrive at the deeper spiritual sense of a text, Origen proceeded to allegorize the passage. Applying this methodology to the parable of the Good Samaritan the result was the following:

> The man going down to Jericho = Adam
> Jerusalem from which he was going = Paradise
> Jericho = This world
> Robbers = Hostile influences and enemies of man such as the thieves and murderers mentioned in John 10:8
> Wounds = Disobedience or sins
> Priest = Law
> Levite = Prophets
> Good Samaritan = Christ
> Beast = Body of Christ
> Inn = Church
> Two denarii = Knowledge of the Father and the Son

Innkeeper = Angels in charge of the Church
Return of the Good Samaritan = Second coming of Christ[5]

Two other church fathers can also be mentioned at this point. Ambrose of Milan (339–390) also interpreted the Good Samaritan as referring to Christ, but the man going down from Jerusalem to Jericho referred not to the fall of Adam but to the Christian shrinking back from a martyr's conflict to the pleasures of this life and the comforts of this world. As for the robbers, these were the persecutors of the Church, and being half alive (or half dead) refers to possessing a faith in which there still exists some breath of life in that God has not been totally cast out of the individual's life.[6] Far more complete, however, is the allegorical interpretation of Augustine, which surpasses even that of Origen. According to Augustine we have the following:

The man going down to Jericho = Adam
Jerusalem from which he was going = City of Heavenly Peace
Jericho = The moon which signifies our mortality (there is a play here on the Hebrew terms for moon and Jericho)
Robbers = Devil and his angels
Stripping him = Taking away his immortality
Beating him = Persuading him to sin
Leaving him half-dead = Due to sin he was dead spiritually but half alive due to his knowledge of God
Priest = Priesthood of the Old Testament (Law)
Levite = Ministry of the Old Testament (Prophets)
Good Samaritan = Christ
Binding of wounds = Restraint of sin
Oil = Comfort of good hope
Wine = Exhortation to spirited work
Beast = Body of Christ
Inn = Church
Two denarii = Two commandments of love
Innkeeper = Apostle Paul
Return of the Good Samaritan = Resurrection of Christ[7]

In summarizing the method of interpreting the parable of the Good Samaritan during this period, we can conclude that in general the parable was interpreted allegorically and that the main point of the parable was seen as a christological teaching involving the redemption of sinners by Christ rather than an ethical teaching such as love for one's neighbor. There were, of course, exceptions. Frequently a christological as well as an ethical meaning was found in the text. Clement of Alexandria is an excellent example of this.[8] It may even be that in the case of Chrysostom (349–407), Isidore of Pelusium (360–435), and Basil (329–379) an exclusively ethical and non-christological interpretation of this parable was propounded,[9] but at best these were voices crying in the wilderness. Clearly the allegorical method of interpretation dominated the scene, and this parable, as well as all the other parables and Scripture, were interpreted allegorically.

B. The Middle Ages (540–1500)

Whereas the main emphasis of the early church fathers lay in the area of biblical exegesis, the emphasis of the scholastics during the middle ages lay in the area of theology, and it was during this period that complex theological systems came into being. In general, the scholastics of this period relied rather heavily upon the exegetical work of the early church fathers. To Origen's threefold sense, however, they added still another—the *anagogical.* Now in addition to Origen's *literal, moral,* and *spiritual* (now generally called simply the *allegorical*) meanings there was added the *anagogical* meaning, which sought the heavenly or eschatological significance of a passage of Scripture. An example of this type of interpretation was the fourfold meaning contained in the term "Jerusalem." In the literal sense Jerusalem was understood as referring to a specific city in Judea; in the moral or tropological sense it referred to the human soul; in the spiritual sense it referred to the Church; and in the anagogical sense it referred to the heavenly abode of the saints!

In their interpretation of the parable of the Good Samaritan, medieval scholars were clearly debtors to the work of the early church fathers. When one, for instance, reads the Venerable Bede (673–735), it appears that he is reading Augustine once again, for he discovers the following:

The man going down to Jericho = Adam
Jerusalem from which he is going = City of Heavenly Peace
Jericho = Moon which signifies variation and change
Robbers = Devil and his angels
Stripping him = Stripping Adam of his glorious vestment of immortality and innocence
Wounds = Sins
Priest = Priesthood of the Old Testament
Levite = Ministry of the Old Testament
Samaritan = Christ
Oil = Repentance

Beast = The flesh in which the Lord came to us, i.e., the incarnation
Etc.[10]

Along with the Venerable Bede could also be mentioned Theophylactus (1050–1108), Bernard of Clairvaux (1090–1153), Bonaventura (1217–1274), and many others who continued to interpret the parable of the Good Samaritan along allegorical and christological lines; but we shall mention only one more since his commentary on the parable is essentially a compendium of scholastic and earlier allegorical interpretations.

Thomas Aquinas (1226–1274) in his commentary on Luke did little original work on the exegesis of the text. What he primarily did was to quote with approval the exegetical work of men like Augustine, Pseudo-Augustine, Basil, Chrysostom, Ambrose, Gregory the Great, Bede, Theophylactus, and others. The result is not unexpected, for his interpretation of such terms as man, Jericho, Jerusalem, robbers, wounds, priest, Levite, Samaritan, beast, etc. is essentially Augustinian. At times Aquinas even places side by side different opinions of what the allegorical significance of a term may be without commenting as to which opinion is more likely. An example of this is the significance of the terms "wine" and "oil" in the parable. After quoting Augustine who interprets them to mean the "comfort of good hope" and "exhortation to spirited work" respectively, he proceeds to quote Gregory the Great who interprets them as the "sharpness of constraint" and the "softness of mercy" as well as Theophylactus who interprets them as "intercourse with God" and "intercourse with man."[11]

c. The Reformation and Post-Reformation Period (1500–1888)

With the Reformation new insight was gained as to how to interpret the Scriptures. Luther (1483–1546) repudiated the fourfold sense of Scripture and thought of the allegorizers as "clerical jugglers performing monkey tricks (*Affenspiel*)." As for Origen's exegesis, he considered it "worth less than dirt," for the Scriptures should be treated literally and grammatically, not allegorically. Luther was sound in his theory, but his practice was not always consistent with his theory in that he tended to allegorize the parables and find everywhere in them examples of justification by faith. With regard to the parable of the Good Samaritan, Luther interpreted this parable in an allegorical manner on several occasions. In these instances he interpreted the parable as follows:

Samaritan = Christ
Oil = Grace

Man = Adam
Inn = Church
Wounds = Sins[12]

Of all the reformers, Calvin was clearly the best and most consistent exegete. His commentaries contain many lasting insights and still reward their readers. Like Luther, Calvin protested against the allegorical method of interpretation, and he referred to the allegorizing of the early Church as "idle fooleries." It is not surprising therefore to find in his commentary a complete rejection of the allegorical interpretation of the parable of the Good Samaritan. Calvin states,

> An allegorical interpretation devised by proponents of free-will is really too futile to deserve an answer. According to them, under the figure of a wounded man is described the condition of Adam after the fall. Whence they infer that the power to act well was not quite extinct, for he is only said to be half-dead. As if Christ would have intended to speak here about the corruption of human nature, and discuss whether the wound Satan struck on Adam was fatal or curable: as if He had not plainly declared, without any figurative talk, that all are dead unless He quickens them with His voice (John 5:25). I give as little respect for that other allegory which has won such regard that nearly everyone comes down in its favour like an oracle. In this, they make out the Samaritan to be Christ, because He is our protector: they say that wine mixed with oil was poured into the wound because Christ heals us with repentance and the promise of grace. And a third cunning story has been made up, that Christ does not immediately restore health but sends us to the Church, that is the inn-keeper, to be cured gradually. None of these strikes me as plausible: we should have more reverence for Scripture than to allow ourselves to transfigure its sense so freely. Anyone may see that these speculations have been cooked up by meddlers, quite divorced from the mind of Christ.[13]

In the passage just quoted we find the first explicit rejection of the christological interpretation of the parable of the Good Samaritan that had dominated the Church for centuries. For Calvin the parable should not be interpreted allegorically to teach Christology but rather literally to teach what it means to be a neighbor.

> But as I said, the chief aim [of the parable] is to show that neighbourliness which obliges us to do our duty by each other is not restricted to friends and relations, but open to the whole human race.[14]

Unfortunately, the successors of Calvin did not follow his wise hermeneutical insights, and the allegorical interpretation of this parable, and of the other parables of Jesus as well, continued to dominate. Melanchthon, for instance, continued to interpret the parable of the Good Samaritan much like Augustine, for he, too, interpreted

Jerusalem as Paradise, Jericho as the moon, the man as Adam, going down as the fall, the robbers as the devil, the Samaritan as Christ, the priest as the law and sacrifice, etc.[15]

Even in the nineteenth century the allegorical method of interpretation dominated. One of the most influential works of the last century was Archbishop R. C. Trench's *Notes on the Parables of Our Lord* (1841). After a careful exegetical analysis in which he interprets the parable in the context of the time and situation of Jesus and emphasizes the ethical dimension of the parable, Trench seeks to obtain "more" out of the parable and allegorizes the parable as follows:

The man going down to Jericho = Human nature or Adam

Jerusalem = Heavenly city

Jericho = Profane city, a city under a curse

Robbers = Devil and his angels

Stripping him = Stripping him of his original robe of righteousness

Leaving him half-dead = Covered with almost mortal strokes, every sinful passion and desire a gash from which the life-blood of his soul is streaming—yet still maintaining a divine spark which might be fanned into flame

Priest and Levite = Inability of the Law to save

Good Samaritan = Christ

Binding of wounds = Sacraments which heal the wounds of the soul

Oil = Christ in the human heart purifying the heart by faith—the anointing of the Holy Spirit

Wine = Blood of Christ's passion

Placing man on beast and walking alongside = Reminds us of him, who, though He was rich, yet for our sakes became poor

Inn = Church

Two denarii = All gifts and graces, sacraments, powers of healing, or remission of sins

Whatever more you spend = Reward for righteous service[16]

It is evident from the above that Trench owes far more in his exegesis to Origen and Augustine than to Calvin!

d. The Modern Period (1888 to present)

It is with Adolf Jülicher that the modern period of parabolic interpretation begins. The first volume of his *Die Gleichnisreden Jesu,* which was published in 1888, demonstrated once and for all that parables are not allegories. In an allegory each detail has meaning and significance. As a result of thinking that a parable was an allegory, men like Origen, Augustine, Bede, Aquinas, Trench, etc. saw significance in every detail in the parable of the Good Samaritan. Parables, Jülicher argued, are not allegories but similitudes and therefore have only one point of comparison or likeness. The details are insignificant. It is therefore unimportant that the man in this parable was going down from Jerusalem to Jericho. He could have been going up from Jericho to Jerusalem! This would not change the one point of the comparison. The "two denarii" has no particular meaning in the parable; it could just as well have been three or four! The wine and the oil have no independent significance. They simply add coloring to the story, for the wine served as an antiseptic and the oil would aid in keeping the wounds from forming scabs and thus help them to drain. The parable itself has only one point to make. It seeks to demonstrate "Who is my neighbor." Everything else is simply local coloring to aid in making that one point.

Jülicher's main contribution to the investigation of the parables was that he pointed out the difference between parables and allegories and in so doing laid to rest the allegorical method of interpreting the parables which had plagued the Church for centuries. Parables are not allegories, for a parable is an extended simile and thus has only one *tertium comparationis,* or point of comparison, whereas an allegory is a string of metaphors. The work of Jülicher was, of course, not without its own limitations,[17] but the student of the parables will always be in his debt for breaking the stranglehold that the allegorical method of interpretation held on parable research. Jülicher demonstrated that usually, if not always, the parables of Jesus tend to have only one point of comparison or *tertium comparationis.* As a result we can therefore formulate our first principle for the investigation of the parables:

> WHEN INVESTIGATING A PARABLE, ONE SHOULD CONTENT HIMSELF WITH SEEKING TO UNDERSTAND THE ONE MAIN POINT OF THE PARABLE. ONE SHOULD NOT SEEK ALLEGORICAL SIGNIFICANCE IN THE DETAILS OF A PARABLE UNLESS IT IS ABSOLUTELY NECESSARY.

It was C. H. Dodd who carried the work of interpreting the parables a step further. In his *The Parables of the Kingdom* (1935), Dodd pointed out that to understand the parables correctly one must seek to understand them in their original *Sitz im Leben,* i.e., in their original situation in life. By this he meant that the parables must be interpreted in the context of the ministry of Jesus and his message and not in the context of nineteenth-century liberalism or the present context of the reader. In other words, before one seeks to understand what the parable may be saying to the believer today, one must seek the original meaning and application of the parable that Jesus intended for his listeners in the first century. To put this in still another way, Dodd demonstrated that the question, "What does the parable mean to me today?" must be preceded by the question, "What did the parable mean to the original audience then?" To do this one must seek to understand:

(i) . . . such ideas as may be supposed to have been in the minds of the hearers of Jesus during His ministry. . . .
(ii) . . . the general orientation of the teaching of Jesus.[18]

Clearly Dodd is correct, for it is important to understand what Jesus assumed in the knowledge, experience, and situation of his listeners as well as to have a general idea of the main tenor of his teaching. This leads us to the second principle for interpreting the parables, which can be summed up succinctly as follows:

WHEN INVESTIGATING A PARABLE, ONE SHOULD SEEK TO UNDERSTAND THE *SITZ IM LEBEN* IN WHICH THE PARABLE WAS UTTERED.

When this is done, often the parables will breathe a new life and excitement.

With the rise of redaction criticism still another insight has been gained as to how to interpret the parables. Since the work of Hans Conzelmann[19] and Willi Marxsen[20] in the mid-fifties, there has resulted a great interest in the theological emphases and interpretations that the evangelists gave to the materials they incorporated into their gospels. It is now evident that the gospel writers were not merely editors who glued and pasted various traditions together but rather theologians who interpreted these traditions to meet the needs of their communities. As a result, it is important to understand and interpret the various parables in the light of the third *Sitz im Leben*, i.e., the life situation of the evangelists. Since at times a parable directed to a hostile audience such as the Pharisees and scribes in the first *Sitz im Leben* is directed in the third *Sitz im Leben* to the Church, it is important to investigate how the evangelists interpret and apply the parables to their own situations. This will prove most helpful when we seek to interpret what a parable teaches us with regard to our situation in life. We can therefore formulate a third principle for interpreting the parables:[21]

WHEN INVESTIGATING A PARABLE, ONE SHOULD SEEK TO UNDERSTAND THE *SITZ IM LEBEN* OF THE EVANGE-LIST.

The fourth principle for interpreting the parables is not in any way new but has been present since the very first proclamation of the parables. In the first *Sitz im Leben,* as well as the second and third, devout men and women have sought to understand exactly what God was saying to them through these parables. If the student of the parables ends his research after he has investigated the parables in the light of the three principles mentioned above, he has merely engaged in an intellectual exercise in historical research which "profiteth little." The first three principles are only significant if they serve as steps to the investigation of the fourth principle, which stated briefly is:

WHEN INVESTIGATING A PARABLE, ONE MUST SEEK TO ASCERTAIN WHAT GOD IS SAYING TO HIM TODAY THROUGH THIS PARABLE.

While it would be presumptuous for one person to tell another exactly what God is saying to him in a particular parable, it would be erroneous to think that there are no controls or guidelines for the application of the teaching of the parable to the life of the believer. In order to keep the fourth principle from degenerating into complete unbounded subjectivity, we must take care to see that our application of the meaning of the parable in our *Sitz im Leben* is in harmony with the main point of the parable in the first *Sitz im Leben* and its interpretation in the third. Stating this in another way, we can say that the fourth principle of parable interpretation must follow out of and be in harmony with the first three principles.

2. The Four Principles of Parable Interpretation Applied

a. *The Main Point of the Parable*

Clearly in its present context the allegorical interpretation of this parable is incorrect.[22] Far from charting a *heilsgeschichtlich* scheme of redemption or advancing a christological portrayal of Jesus, the parable both in its introduction and in its conclusion indicates that the main point of its teaching is "Who is my neighbor?" The parable is connected in Luke to Jesus' teaching concerning the great commandment (Luke 10:25–28) and is introduced as follows: "But he

desiring to justify himself, said to Jesus, 'And who is my neighbor?' "
(Luke 10:29); and concludes with: " 'Which of these three, do you
think, proved neighbor to the man who fell among the robbers?' He
said, 'The one who showed mercy on him' " (Luke 10:36–37a). It is
clear therefore that in its present context the main point of the
parable is "Who is my neighbor?"

While it is admitted today by almost all scholars that in its
present context the parable of the Good Samaritan seeks to answer
the question, "Who is my neighbor?" many scholars argue that the
present context is not original and therefore cannot be used to
interpret the original meaning of the parable. It is frequently argued
that Luke 10:25–29 and 10:37 could not have been joined to the
original parable for the following reasons: (1) Since Luke 10:25–29
is a parallel to Mark 12:28–31 and Matt 22:34–40 and since neither
Mark nor Matthew contain the parable, the insertion of the parable
of the Good Samaritan into the context of the pericope concerning
the greatest commandment is due to Luke and is therefore secondary. (2) There is a logical inconsistency between the meaning of
"neighbor" in Luke 10:27, 29 and in Luke 10:36; for in the former
passages the neighbor is the object of love, i.e., he is one who is to be
loved, whereas in the latter passage he is the subject of love, i.e., he is
one who is to love.[23]

These objections have been attacked from a number of directions. Jeremias, along with T. W. Manson and others, has argued
that Luke 10:25–28 is not simply a parallel to Mark 12:28–34, for
all these passages have in common is the double command to love,
and "it is quite probable that Jesus often uttered so important a
thought as that contained in the double command,"[24] for "great
teachers constantly repeat themselves."[25] Concerning the difference
between the meaning of the word "neighbor" in Luke 10:27, 29 and
Luke 10:36, Jeremias argues: "It is simply a formal inconsistency in
which there is nothing surprising when once the philological facts are
realized: the word *rea'* implies a reciprocal relation, like our word
'comrade'."[26] Nevertheless, it does appear that there is a difference
in the use of the term "neighbor" by the scribe and by Jesus that
must not be overlooked; but it is the very kind of difference which
one might expect to come from the lips of Jesus. Rather than seeing
here a conflict between the parable and the pericope of the great
commandment, we should see here a conflict between the lawyer's
concept of "What it means to be my neighbor" and Jesus' concept of
"What it means for me to be a neighbor." Elsewhere in a similar
manner Jesus demonstrates that the actions of his followers are not
to be in any way dependent upon any quality in the object of love.

We should not concern ourselves with what a person must do to qualify as an object of our love. We should concern ourselves only with loving. We are told to: "Love your enemies, do good to those who hate you, bless those who curse you, pray for those who abuse you" (Luke 6:27–28). Love is not dependent upon the object of love being able to qualify and meet certain requirements. The issue is not "Who is to be loved," i.e., "Who is my neighbor," but rather "What does it mean for me to love," i.e., "What does it mean for me to be a neighbor." We are to "lend, expecting nothing in return; and your reward will be great, and you will be sons of the Most High; for he is kind to the ungrateful and the selfish. Be merciful, even as your Father is merciful" (Luke 6:35–36). Our lending is to be totally independent of the ability to repay! In fact, we should lend especially to those who cannot repay (Luke 6:33–34). We are likewise to invite to our banquet those who cannot repay us with a return invitation (Luke 14:12–14). All this indicates that the "twist" we find in Jesus' use of the term "neighbor" is totally in accord with his teaching elsewhere. Whereas Judaism and the lawyer were concerned with the question, "What must a person do or be to qualify as my neighbor?" Jesus clearly rebukes this question with the parable and demonstrates that our concern is to be a neighbor! Far from seeing a logical inconsistency in the use of the term "neighbor" and concluding as a result that originally Luke 10:25–37 consisted as two separate traditions, we should note that this logical inconsistency exists due to the misconception of Jesus' contemporaries. The manner in which Jesus in Luke 10:25–37 rebuked this misconception is, however, perfectly consistent with his teaching elsewhere and argues strongly for the unity of the passage.[27]

Even if it is not possible to demonstrate the unity of Luke 10:25–37, however, it would appear that Luke 10:29 belongs to the parable and is not simply a Lukan editorial seam for the following reasons: (1) The way Luke 10:36 is worded seems to assume that the term "neighbor" has already been mentioned and apart from Luke 10:29 and (Luke 10:27) this term is not found in the account. (2) Luke would not have needed to create verse 29 to link the parable to Luke 10:25–28. All he would have needed would have been, "And he told them this parable" (cf. Luke 15:3); and something like this, according to this theory, must have already introduced the parable. (3) Whereas the question "Who is my neighbor?" was an important and much-debated issue in the Judaism of Jesus' day, it is less easy to discover a *Sitz im Leben* in the early Church where this was a debated issue.[28]

It would appear, then, that from the very beginning the parable of the Good Samaritan was associated with the question, "Who is (or What does it mean to be) a neighbor?"

b. The Meaning of the Parable in the First Sitz im Leben

One of the difficulties involved in seeking to understand the meaning of this parable in the first *Sitz im Leben* is that various terms used in the parable evoke attitudes and responses to the reader today which are quite different from and even antithetical to those of hearers in Jesus' day. The term "Samaritan" is an excellent example of this. To most Christians today the term tends to evoke a picture of a "Christ-like man of compassion" or "a good man who cares for others." Yet the term in Jesus' day was understood in a totally different way, for the Samaritans were despised by the Jews,[29] who avoided all contact with them.[30] In order to avoid such contact with Samaritans, Jews frequently in their travel between Judea and Galilee went to the extreme of proceeding eastward across the Jordan River and proceeding south (or north) and then recrossing the Jordan River, so that they would not tread upon Samaritan soil!

There were several causes for this animosity. (1) After the death of Solomon in 922 B.C., the ten northern tribes led by Jeroboam revolted against God's anointed king, the son of Solomon—Rehoboam—and divided the nation. This nation of "rebels," which destroyed the unity of God's people, was known at various times as Israel, Ephraim, and Samaria. The Samaritans were therefore the descendants of these rebels who destroyed the unity of God's people. (2) In 722 B.C. Samaria fell and went into exile. It was the policy of Assyria to scatter their defeated enemies throughout the world in order to prevent organized resistance from forming. As a result of this scattering, the ten northern tribes are frequently referred to as the "ten lost tribes of Israel." The Samaritans who remained in Samaria consisted of the common people, who gradually intermarried with the various foreigners scattered in their land by the Assyrians. As a result the Jews looked down upon the Samaritans as "half-breeds." (3) After the return from exile in Babylon, the Jews began to rebuild their temple in Jerusalem. The Samaritans offered to assist the Jews in the rebuilding of the temple, but for various reasons this offer was snubbed. (4) As a result of this snub, the Samaritans built their own temple on Mount Gerizim. This temple was destroyed in 128 B.C. by the Jews led by John Hyrcanus.[31] (5) Somewhere between A.D. 6 and 9 at midnight during the Passover, certain Samaritans scattered the bones of dead men throughout the court of the temple in Jerusalem and thus defiled it.[32] The result of all this was that Jewish-Samaritan relations were filled with much tension and great animosity.[33]

The question raised by the lawyer in Luke 10:29 must also be understood as a contemporary issue that was greatly debated. Generally it was agreed that under the term "neighbor" a Jew should reckon his fellow Jews and full proselytes,[34] but in certain circles the description of who was one's neighbor was drawn more narrowly. Pharisees tended to exclude all non-Pharisees; the Essenes tended to exclude all those who were not members of their sect and even required that a man should "hate all the sons of darkness,"[35] i.e., all those outside the sect whether they were Jews or Gentiles. Jesus quotes a popular attitude that prevailed in his day when he said, "You have heard that it was said, 'You shall love your neighbor and hate your enemy' " (Matt 5:43).

It is evident from the above that to see the parable of the Good Samaritan as a beautiful, lovely example of Christian love for one's neighbor is to lose sight of the context of the first *Sitz im Leben* in which it was uttered. On the contrary, "The parable is not a pleasant tale about the Traveler Who Did His Good Deed: it is a damning indictment of social, racial, and religious superiority."[36] In its original context the parable is a powerful attack against racial and religious bigotry as well as a new revelation of the limitless dimension of the command to love one's neighbor. In his command as well as in his parable, Jesus removes every limitation to the love command. No one can be excluded! The neighbor we are to love is anyone—publican, sinner, Samaritan, Gentile, or enemy!

c. The Understanding of the Parable in the Third Sitz im Leben

One of the first tasks in seeking to understand the way in which Luke used and interpreted the parable of the Good Samaritan is to ascertain his redaction of the tradition. If we assume with the more radical critics that Luke was the one who joined the parable to the pericope of the love command, then we shall interpret his theological emphasis in this passage somewhat differently than if we assume that his redactional work was minimal. Due to limitations of space it is, of course, impossible to do much more than to suggest how in general this parable fits and illustrates the evangelist's theological interests. Assuming a minimum rather than a maximum of redactional work in Luke 10:25–37, it would appear that Luke by selecting this parable for inclusion in his Gospel emphasizes two themes found throughout his work.

One emphasis of Luke in his Gospel is to demonstrate the love and grace of God toward the outcasts of society, or, as Cadbury refers to them, the "delinquent classes."[37] In Luke, more than in any other Gospel, we have described the loving concern of Jesus for tax-collectors,[38] sinners,[39] the poor,[40] enemies,[41] widows,[42] the poor-maimed-lame-blind,[43] Samaritans,[44] etc. It is clear that the parable and the entire pericope fits well with the Lukan theme that the time of salvation had come and that, whereas the religious elite (such as the priest and the Levite) have rejected their invitation, the outcasts of Israel (such as the Samaritan) have accepted and now share in the Messianic Banquet (Luke 14:15–24; cf. also Luke 7:29–30). In return, these outcasts love their neighbors and exhibit in miniature the love and mercy that their Heavenly Father has exhibited toward them (Luke 6:36). This love does not seek to limit its recipients in any way, for it is not concerned with whom to love but with loving (Luke 10:30–37 and 6:27–36).

A second theme found in Luke involves the generous use of possessions. Love is manifested by the wise use of possessions to perform acts of love.[45] The Samaritan manifests these qualities of self-giving love both in his care of the wounded man and in his use of his possessions, for without thought of himself he uses his oil and wire to treat the wounds, binds the wounds with his head-cloth or linen undergarment which he tore for this purpose,[46] pays the inn-keeper sufficient money to take care of the wounded man for some time,[47] and assures him that any additional debt which might be incurred would be paid for by him. Truly this Samaritan loved his enemies, did good, and lent, expecting nothing in return (Luke 6:35).

d. The Message of the Parable for Today

It is clear that the parable of the Good Samaritan teaches us to love our neighbor and that this love is to be unconditional and unqualified. The parable rejects all prejudice and discrimination whether it be racial, intellectual, financial, religious, nationalistic, or anything else that would restrict our doing acts of love.[48] The portrayal of the man who loved his neighbor as a Samaritan, indicates that not even enemies can be eliminated from this love. The Lukan understanding of God's loving concern for the outcasts of society and the needy reveals that we are especially to perform acts of love to the outcasts of our society today and to those in need.

The specific application of this love may vary according to our situation. In the racially tense South of the 1950s, we may seek to do acts of love especially for the black who was badly discriminated against.[49] In Germany in the 1940s, it might seek especially to help the persecuted Jew. In America in the early 1970s, it might especially seek to love the college activist demonstrating against the Viet Nam war or the bewildered policeman looking on. One thing is clear. We cannot choose whom we shall have as our neighbor. Rather, we must seek to be a neighbor and love all. But we must especially seek to love those who are most oppressed and in need. As the reader of this article reflects over the meaning of the parable, for whom should he especially prove to be a neighbor? Is it his cranky next-door neighbor? Is it the starving child in India whose name he does not know? Or is it . . .?

NOTES

1. See Werner Monselewski, *Der Barmherzige Samariter* (1967), pp. 18–21.
2. *Against Heresies* III.xvii.3.
3. *Who Is the Rich Man that Shall be Saved?*, XXIX.
4. Origen also used the Septuagint translation of Prov 22:20–21 to support this idea of a threefold meaning in Scripture. See *De Principiis* IV.i.11–13.
5. Commentary on Luke 10:30–35 (Homily 34).
6. *Concerning Repentance*, Book I, VII, 28 and Book I, XI, 51–52.
7. *Questiones Evangeliorum* ii.19.
8. *Who Is The Rich Man That Shall Be Saved?*, XXIX.
9. See Monselewski, *Der Barmherzige Samariter*, pp. 57–60. Although Chrysostom's interpretation is non-christological, this does not mean it was completely non-allegorical. See the references to Chrysostom in Aquinas's *Catena Aurea*. (See below, note 11.)
10. *Lucae Evangelium Expositio*, lib. III (*MPL* 92, 467–470).
11. *Catena Aurea: Commentary on the Four Gospels*, trans. J. H. Newman (1843).
12. The first two allegorizations are found in his Sermon on Ps 40:3 and the last three in his Sermon on Rom 12:3.
13. *A Harmony of the Gospels Matthew, Mark and Luke*, trans. A. W. Morrison (1972), 3, pp. 38–39.
14. Ibid., p. 38.
15. *Corpus Reformation*, 25, pp. 380–384, 389, 396, 410.
16. *Notes on the Parables of Our Lord* (1870), pp. 318–325.
17. Jülicher's work possesses two weaknesses. The first is an overreaction against the former emphasis on allegorical interpretation which caused him to deny the existence of any allegorical details in the parables of Jesus. The presence of such details is always attributed by him to the early Church or to the evangelists. This reaction against the presence of allegory in the parables of Jesus is also explained by the fact that Jülicher depended on Aristotle rather than the Old Testament for defining what a parable is. Today, it is evident that Jesus, as well as Paul and the early Church, has much more in common with the Old Testament and with contemporary Judaism than with the Greek classical writers. In the Old Testament the term *māshāl*, which is translated by *parabolē* in the Septuagint, can refer to a proverb, a taunt, a riddle, a story parable, or an allegory. We cannot therefore a priori eliminate the possibility that Jesus could have included allegorical elements in his parables. (For examples of allegorical details in rabbinic parables see Archibald M. Hunter, *Interpreting The Parables* [1960], pp. 113–116; and C. K. Barrett, *The New Testament Background: Selected Documents* [1961], pp. 148–151.) The second weakness of Jülicher was that the one point of comparison that he found in the parables of Jesus was always a good nineteenth-century general moral truth. Needless to say, Jülicher read into the parables his own liberal theology. This weakness Jülicher shared with many of the "Old Questers."
18. *The Parables of the Kingdom* (1935), p. 32. Dodd, too, had his limitations, his major

weakness being to eliminate entirely the futuristic eschatological dimension of the parables in favor of his own emphasis of "realized" eschatology.

19. *The Theology of Luke,* trans. Geoffrey Buswell (1960).
20. *Mark The Evangelist,* trans. James Boyce, Donald Juel, William Poehlmann with Roy A. Harrisville (1969).
21. We shall not formulate a separate principle for seeking to understand the interpretation of the parables in the second *Sitz im Leben* but shall assume that seeking to understand how the evangelist interpreted the parable demands in part at least understanding how the Church interpreted the parable.
22. For a recent attempt to defend the christological interpretation of the parable, see Birger Gerhardsson, *The Good Samaritan—The Good Shepherd?* (1958).
23. See John Dominic Crossan, *In Parables* (1973), pp. 58–59.
24. Joachim Jeremias, *The Parables of Jesus,* trans. S. H. Hooke (1963), p. 202.
25. T. W. Manson, *The Sayings of Jesus* (1954), p. 260.
26. Jeremias, *Parables,* p. 205. Jeremias bases his conclusion on the work of Gerhardsson, *The Good Samaritan,* p. 7. For a recent discussion involving this problem in which the author concludes that there is no discontinuity in the use of the term "neighbor" in Luke 10:25–37, see Gerhard Sellin, "Lukas als Gleichniserzähler: Die Erzählung vom barmherzigen Samariter (Lk 10:25–37)," *ZNTW* 66 (1975), pp. 23–52.
27. The form of Luke 10:25–37 resembles Luke 7:36–50 in many ways. Both parables are connected with an incident; in the former it is Jesus' teaching of the love command, in the latter it is the anointing of Jesus. In both the parable is preceded by a hostile question (Luke 10:29) or a hostile attitude (Luke 7:39). In both the parable is concluded with a question in which Jesus' opponent is forced to complete the parable (Luke 10:36 and 7:43), and in both there is a similar misconception. In the former it involves what it means to be a "neighbor"; in the latter it involves what it means to be a "prophet."
28. Eta Linnemann, *Parables of Jesus,* trans. John Sturdy (1966), p. 138.
29. Note how Jesus' opponents slander him by calling him a "Samaritan." "The Jews answered him, 'Are we not right in saying that you are a Samaritan and have a demon?' " (John 8:48).
30. "The Samaritan woman said to him, 'How is it that you, a Jew, ask a drink of me, a woman of Samaria?' For Jews have no dealing with Samaritans" (John 4:9).
31. Should John 4:20 be understood as a Samaritan rebuke of the Jewish destruction of their temple?
32. See Josephus XVIII ii.2 (or XVIII.30).
33. Linnemann, *Parables,* p. 54, states:
    Between the Jews and this heretical mixed people there reigned implacable hatred. On the Jewish side it went so far that they cursed the Samaritans publicly in the synagogues, and prayed God that they should have no share in eternal life; that they would not believe the testimony of a Samaritan nor accept a service from one. This hatred was fully reciprocated by the Samaritans.
34. The semi-convert or "God-fearer" was not included.
35. 1QS 1.10.
36. Geraint Vaughan Jones, *The Art and Truth of the Parables* (1964), p. 115.
37. Henry J. Cadbury, *The Making of Luke-Acts* (1927), p. 258.
38. Luke 3:12; 5:27–32; 7:29, 34; 15:1; 18:10–14; 19:2–10.
39. Luke 5:30–32; 7:34, 36–50; 15:1–2, 7, 10; 18:13; 19:7.
40. Luke 4:18; 6:20; 7:22; 14:13, 21; 16:19–31; 18:22; 19:8.
41. Luke 6:27–36 is far more extensive than its parallel in Matt 5:43–48.
42. Luke 2:37; 4:25–26; 7:11–17; 18:1–8; 20:46–47; 21:1–2.
43. Luke 7:22; 14:13, 21; cf. 4:18.
44. Luke 10:33; 17:16; cf. Acts 1:8; 8:1, 5, 9, 14; 9:31.
45. Luke 6:30, 34–35; 7:36–50; 12:13–21, 33–34, 41–48; 16:1–9, 10–12, 13, 19–31; 18:18–30; 19:1–10, 11–27; 21:1–4.
46. Jeremias, *Parables,* p. 204.
47. Ibid., p. 205.
48. To love one's neighbor or enemy does not refer primarily to an emotional feeling of

good will but rather to doing acts of love, as the synonymous parallelism of Luke 6:27–28 clearly reveals.

49. The translation of this parable by Clarence Jordan reveals how the teaching of this parable might be interpreted in such a situation. See his *The Cotton Patch Version of Luke and Acts* (1969), pp. 46–47.

19: Interpreting the Gospel of John

D. GEORGE VANDERLIP

The Gospel of John is at one and the same time the most beloved book of the Bible and the most elusive and inscrutable. It so touches the wellsprings of human spiritual aspiration that for centuries un-numbered Christians have quenched their innermost thirst at its supernal springs. Simultaneously it has thwarted all scholarly attempts to identify its primal setting and origin. It is benediction and enigma, blessing and puzzle in one. It has overcome its misuse by splinter groups of the Church, such as second-century Gnosticism, who exploited it to support alien dogmas. It has survived the attempts of form critics to disregard its portrayal of the life of Jesus as non-historical. It has refused to be confined to the narrow assessment of contemporary interpreters who deem it primarily an evangelistic tract. It continues to entice and to baffle. What is it about this Gospel which constitutes its mystique, its mysterious hold on the human spirit, its fascination to the scholar, on the one hand, and its warm appeal to the laity, on the other?

The Gospel of John combines a depth of theology with a unique degree of intimacy in its portrayal of the relationship of Christ with his disciples. The former quality of this Gospel led the early church fathers to refer to the author as "the theologian." His account of the life and person of Jesus was destined to play a major role in the formulation of the christological creeds of the early Church. Seeking to understand the origin and nature of John's theology continues to engage the best efforts of contemporary scholarship. Lay persons, on the other hand, are attracted to the warm, devotional character of this Gospel, especially present in the upper-room discourse. This section in John has an appeal for inspirational reading similar to that of the Psalms. Consequently, John attracts diverse readership for quite different reasons. Scholars and lay Christians would agree on one thing, namely, that John is one of the most important books in the biblical canon.

Nevertheless preaching from John presents certain problems. The high degree of interpretative material in John makes the knowledgeable pastor reluctant to say, "In John's Gospel Jesus says, etc." Form criticism has reminded us that we face the same problem in the Synoptic Gospels, but the issue is more prominent in the case of John, for the simple reason that the interpretative factor is present to a higher degree. We must neither ignore John for fear of utilizing it improperly, nor should we simply employ it uncritically, as if its distinctive character did not exist. We seek, therefore, a way to use it responsibly in our proclamation of the word of God.

In recent years Johannine studies have undergone significant changes. There is now a widespread recognition that John preserves an independent historical tradition which is to be distinguished from the sources drawn upon by the Synoptic Gospels. The discovery of the Dead Sea Scrolls has led to an acknowledgment that John is not primarily a Greek-oriented Gospel, but that it had its origin in a Palestinian milieu and that its thought-forms stem basically from the background of sectarian Judaism. The view that John is Gnostic has been sharply modified with the examination of the Nag Hammadi papyri, which show us Gnosticism and its thought at first hand. Attention is increasingly being focused on the probability that this Gospel reached its present form by passing through more than one stage. Oscar Cullmann[1] suggests that an early draft may have emerged in Syria or Transjordania prior to A.D. 70. An enlarged edition (namely, our present Gospel) was then published in Asia Minor toward the end of the first century.

It is clear that many issues are under review at this time in the area of Johannine research. In the meantime, each fresh discovery should make us feel somewhat more secure in our presentation of the gospel through the eyes of the fourth evangelist. Each new perception of John's background and theology gives to us a more sure footing in our task of presenting and interpreting its message. We do not need to wait until every critical issue is settled before we can preach with confidence from this Gospel.

1. Christian Realism: The Cosmic and the Particular as Light Encounters Darkness

It has been long noted that John has both a solicitude for the world and a special focus on those who are called Christ's "own" (13:1). John's perspective is simultaneously cosmic and particular.

Its concern for all of mankind is manifest. God's love is for the world (3:16). All who receive the Son become the children of God (1:12). As Jesus is "lifted up," he draws all persons to himself (12:32). Alongside this universal outlook there is reflected an "in-group" mentality, a sense of being a struggling, persecuted minority in a hostile and alien environment. This is illustrated by the command to love one another (13:34; 15:12), and the forewarning that the world will hate and persecute the followers of Jesus (15:18ff.; 16:1ff.). The disciples have been "chosen" out of the world (15:16, 19), and therefore the world hates them. These two vistas stand side by side.

The cosmic dimension represents the ideal, for it sets before the readers the eternal plan and will of God. This view portrays both what could be and what ought to be, namely, men and women united with God and with one another through faith and love. The flaw in this paradigm lies not in the intent or power of God but in the obstinacy and obduracy of humanity. Hence John realistically describes the dualism which marks the human scene. This ethical and spiritual division he delineates in terms of light versus darkness, truth against error, "from above" in opposition to "from below." Individuals must choose either to believe in Jesus as the Christ and thereby receive eternal life, or not to believe, and thus remain in darkness and in death, awaiting the judgment of the last days, when the words spoken by Jesus will judge those who are willfully blind and spiritually intractable.

John places the universal offer of salvation, as in 3:16, alongside the affirmation of Jesus' absolute choice of his followers (6:70; 13:18; 15:16, 19). Such election by Jesus poses a paradox to logical thought, but it is a tension that runs throughout Scripture. Experience points in both directions. We become believers because we exercise our wills to do so. At the same time we are cognizant of the fact that in a very significant way we are what we are only because the hand of God has reached down and made us his own. The thought expressed here may perhaps best be illustrated by the ancient words of Deuteronomy addressed to the people of Israel, "For you are a people holy to the Lord your God; the Lord your God has chosen you to be a people for his own possession, out of all the peoples that are on the face of the earth. . . . It is because the Lord loves you, . . . that the Lord has brought you out with a mighty hand" (Deut 7:6, 8). God chose, and yet those so chosen were called upon to respond in faith and obedience. Both emphases highlight fundamental spiritual realities, despite their seemingly contradictory assertions. Paradoxical as they seem, the proclaimer of the biblical word must hold the two in tension. In evangelism the offer of salvation needs to be freely presented to all. In Christian instruction there will always be the reminder that what we are, we are solely by the grace of a sovereign and eternal God. John will not allow us to focus on one emphasis to the neglect of the other. The nature and occasion of the proclamation will determine which of these two foci needs to be accentuated and given prominence. Both express divine truth, and both require proclamation.

Optimism and realism walk hand in hand in John's portrayal of the Good News. The new age has dawned in the person and work of Jesus Christ, who has manifested the Father and in whose ministry the majestic glory of God for a few years "tented" among men (1:14). That glory is still accessible, according to John, through the ministry of the Holy Spirit, the Paraclete, the Spirit of Truth, who continues the work of Jesus in the world. Those who respond to Jesus experience the blessings of the age to come, passing from death to life, and become even now the possessors of eternal life (5:24).

John's optimism is tempered by his authentic perception of the recalcitrant nature of sinful humanity. John accurately portrays the bondage in which mankind is held, an enslavement to sin which only God's grace and truth can conquer. In other words, John's sanguinary hope is moderated by the clarity of his understanding of the spiritual battle which rages for the souls and allegiances of men and women.

As we preach from this Gospel we, too, will wish to steer between the Scylla of utopianism and the Charybdis of despair. God remains sovereign in a world that threatens its own destruction by the nefarious abuse of scientific discoveries. Instead of working to create an Eden on earth, mankind rushes headlong from one enactment of Armageddon to the next, until there is wrestled from our despairing grasp the last vestiges of optimism and hope.

For times like these the Gospel of John provides needed reassurance. The author of the Fourth Gospel sees God working on the human scene according to his own plan and timetable. Christ's "hour" is also God's hour, and no ill or injury befalls the Son of Man apart from the permissive will of an all-powerful heavenly Father. This does not mean that believers will escape persecution or even death. Jesus did not shun these, and in John's Gospel Jesus predicts that such experiences will be the lot of those who follow him. John does affirm, however, that no matter what happens all is well. Why? The answer lies in the presence of God in the midst of the trials (14:23), and in the assurance that our future is safe in his hands (14:1ff). From John, then, we can preach a message of hope to counter the icy grip of despair.

2. Faith: John's Christocentric Perspective

John's Gospel centers totally in the person and teachings of Jesus. The miracles are viewed as "signs" which demonstrate who Jesus really is. The discourses elucidate the same truth. The Gospel is replete with personal testimonies which bear witness to the person and meaning of Jesus, and these include a number of remarkable self-affirmations of Jesus which are introduced with a formalized "I am" motif. The recognition of Jesus as Messiah is in John apparent from the first days of his public ministry, and reiterated throughout the three years of his preaching and service.

Much of the above stands in contrast to the portrayal given us by the first three Gospels. In these Jesus is seldom presented as making direct "I am" affirmations, although it must be noted that there is an undeniable stress on his personal authority. He who builds on his saying builds on a rock (Matt 7:24), and Jesus calls men to personal discipleship (Matt 11:28–30). Somewhat the same claims are implied, but what is implicit in the Synoptics is made explicit in John.

In regard to the testimonies of others to the Messiahship of Jesus, the Synoptics indicate that this insight came gradually and rather slowly during the time that Jesus instructed his disciples. Peter, near the close of Jesus' public ministry, comes to a clear statement of the Messiahship of Jesus (Matt 16:16). John appears, at first glance, to contradict this chronology. It is more likely that he does not at this point make chronology a primary factor. His purpose is didactic, and for this reason the *fact* that Jesus is the Christ is uppermost in his thinking. As to when this was recognized and acknowledged by Jesus' contemporaries is, in his judgment, incidental.

As is the case with John, Jesus Christ must ever be the heart of Christian proclamation. To lose this perspective is to be shipwrecked in our faith. In Christ is to be seen the clearest manifestation of the Father and of the Father's will. In him we find the call and the motivation for discipleship, and through him we find the strength to carry out the task which he has committed to his followers. When we draw near to Jesus in obedient discipleship, we draw near to the Father who sent him. This is John's message.

John's central theme leads to no distortion regarding the commandment to love God with the whole heart (Deut 6:5; Matt 22:37). For all its Christocentricity, John can never be accused of "Jesusolatry," that is, the undue worshipping of Jesus to the neglect of God the Father. In John, Jesus always points beyond himself to the Father who sent him (1:14; 14:6, 9). The Church's message needs always to be a Christ-centered one. At the same time its primary purpose is to manifest and make known the Father, since Jesus as the Son of Man came in order to be the link between heaven and earth (John 1:51). Jesus makes possible our fellowship with the Father, for when we proclaim the Son we present him as the Way to the Father, who sent him into the world. The first letter of John captures very well the heart of the message of the Gospel of John when it states, "Our fellowship is with the Father and with his Son Jesus Christ" (1 John 1:3).

John will permit us to place no wedge between the Father and the Son. He quotes Jesus as saying, "He who has seen me has seen the Father" (14:9). It is not an identity of persons that is affirmed by this statement, but rather a unity of purpose and of character. Jesus' task on earth was to accomplish the work which was assigned to him by the Father (17:4). Therefore when we proclaim the good news concerning the life and ministry of Jesus, we are simultaneously highlighting the love of God the Father for humanity.

3. Hope: The Present and the Future

John has what appears to be a felicitous balance between the present and the future, between the "now" and the "not yet." Eternal life is a present reality, as we have noted above; but it is also an inheritance, the full realization of which awaits the consummation of history in the return of Jesus Christ to "receive" his own (5:28, 29; 14:3; 17:24). John's perspective on eternal life is a significant shift from that portrayed in the Synoptic Gospels where this concept is exclusively a future promise. John's concern is focused as much (or perhaps more) on this life as it is on the life to come. He is concerned that the believers begin to appropriate what is already theirs and enjoy these benefits to the full, rather than having an undue other-worldly focus in their lives. It should be noted that the Synoptic Gospels obtain a balance between the present and the future by a twofold understanding of the Kingdom of God, which is viewed as inaugurated in the ministry of Jesus, but as yet to be consummated at the time of Christ's return in power.

Supportive of his stress on the present reality of eternal life is John's teaching that the Holy Spirit assures believers of the continuing presence of both the Father and the Son. There is no thought of an absentee Lord. He is a very present Master who indwells the believers and through the Spirit guides, empowers, and instructs them for ministry in the world. This is a wholesome life-affirming perspective which does not see Jesus as exclusively over against culture but as transforming culture as well. Both elements are genuine affirmations and emphases in Scripture. If either is highlighted without the other, an imbalance results which gives a false image of the biblical teaching and also ill prepares believers for accomplishing their ministry in the world. Too much underscoring of this life can result in disillusionment and despair. Life- and world-affirming perspectives need to be tempered by a realistic acknowledgment of human frailty and mortality, on the one hand, and human sinfulness and egoism, on the other. The hope for God's kingdom on earth needs to reckon seriously with these realities.

At the same time an undue stress on hope for a world to come faces the danger of regarding this life as unimportant, as under Satan's dominion, as alien territory for the believer, and as hopelessly beyond improvement or redemption. A strictly futuristic confidence may give the impression that life here and now is in some sense a secondary kind of existence in which the believer is primarily a bystander and an observer, rather than a creative agent and participant. Such a view tends to minimize the importance of the present in contrast to the life to come. The result is a distorted and nonbiblical viewpoint.

Scripture is concerned with both the present and the future, and a balanced biblical interpretation will keep these two foci in constant tension. John has done this remarkably well. He affirms both present (or "realized") eschatology and futuristic eschatology. Contemporary proclamation will do well to emulate the balance which he exemplifies.

4. Love: The Essence of Discipleship

For John, love is the distinguishing feature of Christian discipleship (13:34, 35; 15:12). This trait is to mark the relationship between believers, even as it describes most deeply the attitude and action of the Father for humankind. God so loved the world that he sent his Son. Christians are to love in order that the world may observe and know that the new age has dawned, and that Jesus is indeed the Savior of the world. Although the command to love is in John confined to love for those in the fellowship, the evangelistic and cosmic perspective of the Gospel implies the extension of that love into the wider circles of humanity. One illustration of this extension is the graphic portrayal of Jesus' acceptance of the Samaritan woman who was in so many ways an outcast in the eyes of her contemporaries. This incident becomes the occasion for urging the disciples to raise their eyes to see the fields around, which were "white for harvest" (4:35). As we read the story, it seems clear that the words addressed to the disciples are by the author intended also to be an exhortation for the Church. A concern for all persons is thereby enjoined.

In the call to a life guided by "love," the example for such love is none other than Jesus himself. "Love one another *as* I have loved you" (13:34). This is said in the context of a reference to Jesus' death on the cross. Not far in the background of John's experience, and that of his community, is the threat and probably the experience of hatred, persecution, excommunication from the synagogue, and martyrdom (15:18ff.; 16:1ff.; 16:33). In this portrayal of the cost of discipleship John can serve as a corrective to what has been appropriately termed the preaching of "cheap grace."

In the area of the ethical demands of the gospel, the First Epistle of John seems already to have become aware of the danger of an inadequate understanding of John's teaching regarding love. Real "love," says 1 John, demonstrates itself in more than verbal affirmation. It is revealed in concrete acts of helpfulness. The person who is in need of food and clothing should not be sent away with only words of encouragement, but with adequate provision for the necessities of life (1 John 3:17, 18).

5. Witnesses: The Disciples' Role in the World

Jesus says to the disciples, "And you also are witnesses, because you have been with me from the beginning" (15:27). The witness which his followers are to give concerning Jesus is not primarily related to factual data about his earthly life. It centers rather in declaring the nature and significance of his person. The crucial question is not, "What did Jesus do while he was here?" but, more importantly, "Who is Jesus and why did he come?" The Gospel of John was written to answer that question (20:30, 31), and when Jesus departed he committed to his followers the task of proclaiming the good news of his accomplished mission. Therefore he said to them, "As the Father has sent me, even so I send you" (20:21).

The author of the Gospel of John presents the scene of appointment to ministry as if it were like the passing of a baton in a race. That race continues, of course, and to each new generation there comes the challenge to carry the baton to the generation which follows. Not to bear witness "to what we have heard and seen" might be compared to dropping the baton, that is, to abandoning the responsibility with which we have been entrusted.

To each generation there comes the challenge to be Christ's witnesses in the world. That mission cannot be fulfilled in our own strength. In this Gospel Jesus says to the disciples, "Abide in me, and I in you. As the branch cannot bear fruit by itself, unless it abides in the vine, neither can you, unless you abide in me" (15:4). John sees the gift of the Spirit as the means by which the disciples will be empowered for the charge which has been assigned to them. For this reason, immediately following the commission of the disciples the statement is made that Jesus then breathed on them and said, "Receive the Holy Spirit" (20:22). To such an extent does John stress the Spirit that his account of the life of Jesus has fittingly been designated, "The Gospel of the Spirit." The Spirit bears witness to Christ (15:26), and by the gift of the Spirit the disciples, and those who follow in their footsteps, also bear witness. Herein lies the primary task of the Church.

6. The Holy Spirit: Guide and Strengthener

In John 16:12 we are told that Jesus had many things to share with his disciples but they were not ready. He then affirmed that after his departure the Spirit would guide them into all the truth. Presumably this would include instruction about those things which Jesus had to say to them, but for which at that point they were not ready. A number of interpreters have seen in this verse the author's defense of the new approach which we note in his portrayal of the life and teachings of Jesus. The Gospel of John embodies, in other words, tradition, reflection, and interpretation under the guidance of the Holy Spirit. This implies that John is much more than a mere verbal reporting of what Jesus said, but to a high degree an interpretation of his teachings. This exposition did not emerge in a vacuum, but is the result of seeking to apply the teachings of Jesus to the new circumstances faced by the Church at the time of writing. This situation would appear to have two major dimensions. The first would be the witness of the Church in its continuing encounter and dialogue with Judaism. Such an encounter is reflected in chapters 2 through 12 of John. The sharpness of Church-synagogue debates seems to be mirrored especially in chapters 7 and 8. The second dimension of John's message relates to the furthering and deepening of what we may call the distinctive lifestyle appropriate to a follower of Jesus. This involved, among other qualities, love, the gift of the Spirit, humble service, being witnesses in the world, a willingness to endure persecution in the name of Jesus, and a pursuit of a spirit of oneness through "abiding" in Christ. These concerns are highlighted in chapters 13 through 17, and some of them reemerge in chapters 20 and 21.

John's emphasis on the Spirit has far-reaching implications for twentieth-century Christians. It tells us that Jesus is even now in the midst of his Church. It asserts that in seeking truth and guidance for moral decision-making we have not only the written Word, and not only the tradition of the Church over almost twenty centuries, but we have a living witness in our midst who can take the things of Christ and declare them to us (16:15). We must always test such "guidance" by the written Word, and by the Christian community, for the Spirit is given not to us as individuals primarily, but to the community of faith. The Spirit will not lead contrary to the highest revelation which we have in Jesus of Nazareth, nor should we, as C. H. Spurgeon once so aptly put it, put such great value on what the Spirit reveals to us, but regard as of little worth what the Spirit reveals to others.

Certain moral trajectories are launched in the New Testament the full implications of which are never wholly articulated, or perhaps even envisioned and understood, within the confines of the New Testament canon. Who, for example, in the first century foresaw the full implications of Paul's exhortation to Philemon regarding his now converted runaway slave, Onesimus? Paul wrote to Philemon that he should receive him "no longer as a slave but more than a slave, as a beloved brother . . . in the Lord" (Philemon 16). It took a civil war in America to bring the whole issue of slavery under the full scrutiny of the Scriptures; and then by reflection, and I would argue by the guidance of the Holy Spirit, the Christian community came to an almost universal consensus on a proper Christian attitude to this centuries-old scandal of trafficking in "slaves, that is, human souls" (Rev 18:13). We have only begun to follow this particular trajectory, however, for much injustice remains entrenched in society.

When Paul wrote, "There is neither Jew nor Greek, there is neither slave nor free, there is neither male nor female; for you are all one in Christ Jesus" (Gal 3:28), he was declaring the Magna Charta of Christian freedom. This declaration of liberty is much more comprehensive than the matter of freedom from the necessity of observing circumcision. Paul is really saying that there are no second-class citizens in the Kingdom of God. All share equally. All have equal dignity. All must be given full freedom to serve and to lead as the Spirit apportions his gifts. By saying this, we are interpreting Paul's Spirit-given revelation and following his trajectory to its logical implications. We need not do so with apology or hesitancy. We need always to be concerned, however, that our interpretations are in keeping with the Spirit and with the mind of Christ. Surely the letter must be superseded by the Spirit. "The letter kills, but the Spirit gives life" (2 Cor 3:6).

There are those who will settle issues of debate among Christians by quoting a few scriptural texts. Can questions of capital punishment, participation in war, the right of women to roles of leadership in the Church, the matter of slavery, the problems of drugs, alcoholism, gambling, and marital infidelity be quickly disposed of by a list of Scripture verses? John would remind us that we must join to the Scriptures and to tradition the guidance of the Holy Spirit. The Spirit does not teach contrary to the written Word, but he does lead Christ's Church to a new sensitivity with respect to the implications of the message of Scripture. This will go beyond the letter to the intent. Jesus himself illustrated this in the Sermon on the Mount when he said repeatedly, "You have heard that it was said, . . . But I say to you. . . ." His concern was with motives as well as with external acts. Real sin dwells in the heart, and from within a person come those things which defile him. So we must press to discover, through the Spirit, what are the guiding moral principles of Scripture and then seek to apply them critically to the personal and social issues of our day. To do so is to read and interpret the Bible "responsibly."

The Gospel of John seems itself to illustrate this kind of listening to the Spirit, for it appears to be speaking incisively to the problems facing the Christian community at the time of writing. William Temple recognized the freedom displayed by John as he adapted the teachings of Jesus to the new concerns facing the Church. Archbishop Temple wrote, "Let the Synoptists repeat for us as closely as they can the very words He spoke; but let St. John tune our ears to hear them."[2]

The reality of the current guidance of the Spirit prevents the Church from fossilizing through a perpetual backward look. The Spirit, who is presented in John as an abiding presence (14:16, 17), is a contemporary teacher (14:25, 26), witness (15:26), convictor (16:7-11), and guide (16:13-15). John, therefore, accentuates God's contemporaneous and vital direction of his people. The Church looks forward as well as backward. Scripture, tradition, and the Spirit together provide enlightenment to the community of faith. Amos N. Wilder has spoken appreciatively of this insightful dimension of the Fourth Gospel's message. He wrote, "This Gospel can serve the renewal of Protestantism today both as a rebuke to sectarianism and as a norm of true catholicity. It assigns primacy to the present dynamic activity of God without forfeiting the significance of the saving historical events of the past."[3]

It should be noted concerning John's teaching about the Spirit that this Gospel makes no reference to special charismatic gifts or to unusual manifestations, such as speaking in tongues. Some persons in our day maintain that such occurrences are the primary evidences for the Spirit's presence and work. This is clearly not John's understanding of the function of the Spirit. His perspective can serve the Church today as a corrective to such misrepresentations of what is central in the Spirit's activity within the Christian community.

7. The Call For Decision

Opinions differ as to why the Gospel of John was written. Some have argued that it was penned primarily to win converts among educated Greeks. Others have regarded it to be an evangelistic work aimed at Diaspora Jews and at Gentiles who were attending their synagogues. More recently the tendency has been to conclude that a concern for Christian instruction, rather than evangelism, called forth this Gospel. This view appears to account best for the distinctive content of the Fourth Gospel. The intended readers are already confessing Christians. They need, however, to be strengthened in their faith. One way in which 20:31 can be properly rendered is: "These are written that you may *keep on believing* that Jesus is the Christ, the Son of God, and that believing you may have life in his name." The Gospel of John calls for firm commitment to Christ. The writer is anxious that his Christian readers not turn back from their profession of faith. It may well be that the words addressed to Peter were especially included with this concern in mind. Jesus asked, "Will you also go away?" (6:67). Peter's reply was, "Lord, to whom shall we go? You have the words of eternal life, and we have believed, and have come to know, that you are the Holy One of God" (6:68, 69).

Today John's Gospel lends itself for use both to present the claims of Jesus as Lord, and to deepen our understanding of the meaning of Christian discipleship. There is an urgency to its appeal which compels the reader to face seriously the challenge of personal commitment to the Lordship of Jesus Christ.

8. The Church: *E Pluribus Unum*

By symbolism and positive instruction the author of the Fourth Gospel makes it clear that there is a community that is gathered around the confession of Jesus as Lord. One of this Gospel's main concerns is that the Christian community be united (10:16; 17: 20–23). This involves a unity of faith, love, and witness. To read present ecumenical concerns into such passages would, of course, be anachronistic. Nonetheless the unity John describes would need to be visible enough that the outside world could take note of it.[4] Unity involves community. What binds believers together is their shared life in the vine, Jesus Christ (15:4, 5). John's Gospel gives little support to any effort which strives for organizational unity for the sake of structural union alone. It has much to say that is relevant, however, to existing divisions within Christendom which are characterized by lack of love, and by the absence of mutual respect. John's perspective opposes such fragmentation and division. We *are* one in Jesus Christ, says John. Christians are, therefore, urged to demonstrate their oneness to a world which has the Church under critical scrutiny. John's indicative becomes the Church's imperative. Make real in experience, he says, what God has in fact made a reality through the lifting up of his Son on the cross. Jesus died in order "to gather into one the children of God who are scattered abroad" (11:51, 52). Though many, we are yet one. God's love and power has made it so. This is a theme which in our day we can and should properly preach from the Gospel of John. In recent years a discussion has developed concerning the nature of John's concept of the Church. No hint of church organization, it is said, is contained within this Gospel. Consequently some have maintained that John stands in opposition to the institutional Church. This argument, however, is based largely on silence. It is true that John's perspective regarding faith, life, and salvation is personal, dynamic, and vibrant. Such realities do not in John's Gospel require a hierarchical institution to give them existence. They are made possible by the Spirit. Nevertheless the Spirit works through the community. Christians constitute a "flock" (10:16), and are joined to Christ and to one another in a "vine" (15:5). It is by faithful witness that this community continues to exist and to expand (15:27; 17:20–23). Furthermore, the well-being of the community depends on its being properly tended by spiritual leaders (21:15–17). All this suggests that while structure and authority are secondary to fellowship and the guidance of the Spirit, there is not in John a direct polemic against institutionalism. Other concerns were uppermost in John's mind.

John's primary focus on spiritual life through the Spirit can be for us a corrective whenever in our day institutional survival threatens to assume primacy in ecclesiastical discussions. We can be assured that where vital discipleship exists the institution will survive without too much difficulty. Where such discipleship is lacking, perhaps the institution does not deserve to endure.

9. Supplementing John's Focus

Up until now we have stressed the richness of the ore found in the Gospel of John. We must recognize, however, that John's perspective is geared to a specific time and to a localized situation. Consequently it neither contains everything that needs to be said concerning the Christian life, nor can all of its emphases be automatically transferred and repeated without modification in a new age. John gives a limited report, for example, of the teachings of Jesus. This Gospel has little to say in the area of practical Christian ethics. The imperatives of the Sermon on the Mount are conspicuously absent. Jesus as a great ethical prophet who came in the spirit of men like Amos and Micah is much more clearly depicted in the Synoptics than in John. Here the Synoptics can significantly supplement the Johannine picture.

In John's Gospel, Jesus moves with such majesty and control through the events described that his humanity is not as clearly visible as it is in Matthew, Mark, and Luke. There is also no "agony" in the garden. Jesus does not have to wrestle with an unknown or uncertain future. All is clear to him. The cross is the moment of "glory" (12:23, 24). Repeated stress on his pre-existence, his foreknowledge, and the divine timetable by which he moves through life, has led one interpreter to speak of John's "naive docetism."[5] While this is too harsh a judgment to make against John, nonetheless it aptly highlights the problem. John's rather one-sided emphasis on the deity of Christ needs to be read alongside the greater stress on his humanity and suffering as portrayed in the first three Gospels. A full picture of the biblical witness to Jesus demands a recognition of both dimensions.

In the Fourth Gospel the miracles performed by Jesus are never said to be done "out of compassion." This, however, is a frequent observation made by the Synoptic writers. In John the miracles are "signs." They prove who Jesus is. One of the most sensitive pictures of the humaneness of Jesus in this Gospel is that given in the story of the woman caught in adultery (7:53–8:11). This narrative is not, however, a part of John's original manuscript, but is a later scribal addition. Its portrayal of Jesus resembles in many ways that found in the Synoptic accounts of his ministry with people. It may very well be, therefore, that we have in this pericope an authentic piece of oral tradition. An exception to John's lack of focus on the compassion of Jesus seems to be the statement that on the occasion of the death of Lazarus he wept (11:35). Once again, then, the Synoptics in their stress on the empathy and tenderness of Jesus can enrich our understanding of what Jesus was like.

Another area in which we need to take into careful consideration the situation existing at the time of the writing of John relates to the attitude this Gospel displays toward those whom it calls "the Jews."

This term is used in John in a technical manner and refers almost without exception to the Jewish religious leaders who oppose Jesus and his followers. Of course, the disciples of Jesus and the common people who hear him preach are all Jews; but they are not so designated by John. "The Jews" epitomize "the world" which hates both Jesus and his followers. The Gospel of John emerged when Church and synagogue were in acrimonious debate. The polemics found in the Gospel mirror these hostile dialogues. In the midst of such arguments the Jews are called "the children of the devil" (8:44). In reflection we can understand how one group of Jews (i.e., those who confess that Jesus is the Christ) could say this of another group which rejects this doctrine, for such sharp language was not uncommon between rival sects in Judaism. We dare not, however, uncritically repeat such a charge. A passage such as this one should not be used as fuel to feed anti-Semitism. From the Jewish heritage has come the Christian faith (cf. 4:22), and we ought never to be unmindful of our great indebtedness to Jews and to Judaism. We can understand the bitterness which called forth an indictment like 8:44, but we cannot allow such an explosive counter-charge to become a normative judgment on contemporary Jews.[6]

10. Looking Ahead

John appears to have incorporated early sources and traditions, and then to have undergone a process of change through redaction and expansion as the Johannine community faced new challenges. There is a need, therefore, for further analysis of the different elements which went into the formation and subsequent modification of this Gospel. This involves both source and redaction criticism. Johannine studies are increasingly moving in this direction. The investigation needs to be based primarily on a careful inductive study of the Gospel of John as we now have it. Continued research in this area will hopefully shed additional light on the background and message of the Gospel of John, which remains for all of us one of the most captivating of all biblical books.

NOTES

1. Oscar Cullmann, *The Johannine Circle* (1975), pp. 95–99.
2. William Temple, *Readings in St. John's Gospel* (1959), p. xxxii.
3. Amos N. Wilder, *New Testament Faith for Today* (1955), p. 164.

4. See discussion in Raymond E. Brown, *The Gospel According to John,* xiii-xxi (1970), pp. 776, 777.

5. Ernst Käsemann, *The Testament of Jesus* (1966).

6. This issue is discussed briefly in my book, *Christianity According to John* (1975), pp. 139, 162, 163.

Bibliography

1934

"Have We a God of Destruction?," *Bibliotheca Sacra* 91 (January 1934), pp. 24–33.

1935

"A Study of Psalm 51," *Bibliotheca Sacra* 92 (January 1935), pp. 26–38.

Review of *An Introduction to the Books of the Old Testament,* by W. O. E. Oesterley and Theodore H. Robinson, *Bibliotheca Sacra* 92 (April–June 1935), pp. 244–247.

1936

"The Evidential Value of Paul's Conversion and Ministry," *Bibliotheca Sacra* 93 (April 1936), pp. 187–192.

"The Transfiguration," *Bibliotheca Sacra* 93 (July 1936), pp. 315–323.

1938

"The Ministry of Our Lord During the Forty Days," *Bibliotheca Sacra* 95 (January 1938), pp. 45–55.

"A Needed Apologetic," *Bibliotheca Sacra* 95 (October 1938), pp. 436–444.

"The Christian Doctrine of Resurrection," ThD. Dissertation, Dallas Theological Seminary, 1938.

1940

"Exegetical Studies in First Peter," *Bibliotheca Sacra* 97 (April 1940; July 1940; October 1940), pp. 200–210, 325–334, 448–455.

1941

"Exegetical Studies in First Peter," *Bibliotheca Sacra* 98 (January 1941; April 1941; July 1941; October 1941), pp. 69–77, 183–193, 307–319, 459–468.

"The Glories of Christ," *Moody Monthly* 41 (March 1941), pp. 389ff.

1946

Review of *The Revised Standard Version (New Testament)*, *Bibliotheca Sacra* 103 (April 1946), pp. 247–249.

1947

Review of *The Historic Mission of Jesus*, by C. J. Cadoux, *Bibliotheca Sacra* 104 (July 1947), pp. 378–383.

1949

The Son of God Among the Sons of Men. Boston: W. A. Wilde Company, 1949. [Reissued under the title *Meditations on the Gospel of John* by the same publisher in 1958. Reissued as *Jesus and His Contemporaries*. Grand Rapids: Baker Book House, 1970.]

Review of *The Religion of Maturity*, by J. W. Bowman, *Westminster Theological Journal* 12 (November 1949), pp. 53–59.

1950

"The Use of DOXA in Greek Literature with Special Reference to the New Testament," PhD. Dissertation, University of Pennsylvania, 1950.

Review of *An Introduction to New Testament Thought*, by F. C. Grant, *Westminster Theological Journal* 13 (November 1950), pp. 78–83.

1952

"The Teaching Ministry of the Church," *Moody Monthly* 52 (January 1952; February 1952; March 1952; April 1952), pp. 310, 393, 469, 545.

Review of *The Witness of Luke to Christ*, by Ned B. Stonehouse, *Westminster Theological Journal* 13 (November 1952), pp. 50–52.

1954

"A Key to the Understanding of First John," *Bibliotheca Sacra* 111 (January 1954), pp. 39–46.

"Germany's Spiritual Condition," *Bulletin of Fuller Theological Seminary* 4 (December 1954), p. 6.

1955

"Chief Theological Periodicals in German," *Fuller Library Bulletin* 27 (July–September 1955), p. 5.

"The Importance of the Septuagint for Biblical Studies," *Bibliotheca Sacra* 112 (October 1955), pp. 344–355.

1956

"The Attitude of the Primitive Church Toward Judaism," *Bibliotheca Sacra* 113 (April 1956), pp. 130–140.

"The Gospel of John" (The Bible Book of the Month), *Christianity Today* 1 (12 November 1956), pp. 14–15.

"The Importance of the Septuagint for Biblical Studies," *Bibliotheca Sacra* 113 (January 1956), pp. 37–45.

Review of *The Book of Acts in History*, by H. J. Cadbury, *Westminster Theological Journal* 19 (November 1956), pp. 53–57.

1957

"The New Testament," in *Contemporary Evangelical Thought*, edited by Carl F. H. Henry. Great Neck: Channel Press, 1957.

"Christian Fellowship," *Bulletin of Fuller Theological Seminary* 7 (Fall 1957), p. 6.

"The Holy Spirit in Acts and the Epistles," *Christianity Today* 1 (27 May 1957), pp. 3–5.

Review of *Paul Before the Areopagus and Other New Testament Studies*, by Ned B. Stonehouse, *Westminster Theological Journal* 20 (November 1957), pp. 112–114.

Review of *Studies in the Acts of the Apostles*, by Martin Dibelius, *Westminster Theological Journal* 19 (May 1957), pp. 215–220.

1958

Editor, Alford's *Greek Testament*, 2 vols. Chicago: Moody Press, 1958.

"The Phenomena of Scripture," in *Revelation and the Bible; Contemporary Evangelical Thought*, edited by Carl F. H. Henry. Grand Rapids: Baker Book House, 1958.

"Criteria of Biblical Inerrancy," *Christianity Today* 2 (20 January 1958), pp. 16–18.

1959

"The Christology of the Fourth Gospel in Relation to the Synoptics," *Bibliotheca Sacra* 116 (October–December 1959), pp. 303–309.

"The Gospel and the Gospels," *Bibliotheca Sacra* 116 (April–June 1959), pp. 109–116.

"Historical Problems in the Fourth Gospel," *Bibliotheca Sacra* 116 (July–September 1959), pp. 205–211.

"Must Christ Be Lord to Be Savior?," *Eternity* 10 (September 1959), p. 14.

1960

"Apostle," "Beelzebub," "Benediction," "Brother, Brethren," "Catholic," "Christianity," "Commission, the Great," "Compassion," "Concision," "Concursus," "Confession of Christ," "Death," "Descent into Hell," "Disciple," "Doctrine," "Egypt," "Exegesis," "Footstool," "Glory," "Hospitality," "Jesus," "Letter," "Merit," "Nazarene," "Only Begotten," "Paul and Paulinism," "Rapture," "Rebaptism," "Redeemer, Redemption," "Restoration of Israel," "Rock," "Saint," "Second Coming of Christ," "Separation," "Simplicity,"

"Soul Sleep," "Spirits in Prison," "Therapeutae," "Think, Thought," "Transfiguration," "Will," "World, Worldliness," "Worship," in *Baker's Dictionary of Theology*, edited by E. F. Harrison. Grand Rapids: Baker Book House, 1960.

"The Epistles," in *The Biblical Expositor*, edited by Carl F. H. Henry. Philadelphia: A. J. Holman Company, 1960.

"The Discourses of the Fourth Gospel," *Bibliotheca Sacra* 117 (January–March 1960), pp. 23–31.

1961

"Looking at John's Gospel, Part 1: Introductory Considerations," *The Sunday School World* (January 1961).

"Looking at John's Gospel, Part 2: The Person of Christ," *The Sunday School World* (February 1961).

"Looking at John's Gospel, Part 3: The Theological Thought of John's Gospel," *The Sunday School World* (April 1961).

"The New English Bible: A Seminary Professor's Appraisal," *The Sunday School Times* 103 (25 March 1961), p. 235.

Review of *Jesus of Nazareth*, by Gunther Bornkamm, *Christianity Today* 5 (13 March 1961), p. 41.

Review of *The Theology of St. Luke*, by Hans Conzelmann, *Christianity Today* 5 (3 July 1961), pp. 37–38.

1962

New Testament Editor, *Wycliffe Bible Commentary*. Chicago: Moody Press, 1962.

John: A Brief Commentary (Colportage Library 469). Chicago: Moody Press, 1962. [Reissued as *John: The Gospel of Faith*. Moody Press.]

"Galatians," "John," in *Wycliffe Bible Commentary*. Chicago: Moody Press, 1962.

"An Authentic Portrait of Christ," *The Collegiate Challenge* (March 1962).

"Some Patterns of the New Testament Didache," *Bibliotheca Sacra* 119 (April–June 1962), pp. 118–128.

Review of *The Interpreter's Dictionary of the Bible*, edited by George Arthur Buttrick, *Christianity Today* 7 (23 November 1962), p. 44.

Review of *The New Bible Dictionary*, edited by J. D. Douglas, *Christianity Today* 6 (28 September 1962), pp. 48–49.

1963

"The Atonement," in *Things Most Surely Believed*, edited by Clarence S. Roddy. Westwood, New Jersey: Fleming H. Revell Company, 1963.

1964

Introduction to the New Testament. Grand Rapids: Eerdmans, 1964. Revised edition, 1971.

"A Theologian Looks at the Gifts of the Spirit," *Christian Life* 25 (June 1964), pp. 24–26.

"The Theology of the Epistle to the Hebrews," *Bibliotheca Sacra* 21 (October–December 1964), pp. 333–340.

Review of *Dictionary of the Bible,* edited by James Hastings, revised edition F. C. Grant and H. H. Rowley, *Eternity* 15 (October 1964), p. 47.

Review of *Origins of the Synoptic Gospels,* by Ned B. Stonehouse, *Eternity* 15 (August 1964), p. 41.

1965

Study-Graph: The Life of Christ. Chicago: Moody Bible Institute, 1965.

Review of *The Central Message of the New Testament,* by Joachim Jeremias, *Christianity Today* 9 (16 July 1965), p. 27.

Review of *Interpreting the Bible,* by A. Berkeley Mickelsen, *Christianity Today* 9 (26 March 1965), p. 34.

Review of *Theological Dictionary of the New Testament,* Vol. 2, edited by Gerhard Kittel, translated by Geoffrey Bromiley, *Christianity Today* 9 (24 September 1965), pp. 22–24.

1966

"Gemeindetheologie–The Bane of Gospel Criticism," in *Jesus of Nazareth, Saviour and Lord,* edited by Carl F. H. Henry. Grand Rapids: Eerdmans, 1966.

"Are the Gospels Reliable?" *Moody Monthly* 66 (February 1966), p. 35.

Review of *New Testament Introduction,* by Donald Guthrie, *Eternity* 17 (May 1966), p. 41.

Review of *The Quest Through the Centuries,* by Harvey K. McArthur, *Christianity Today* 10 (24 June 1966), pp. 34–35.

1967

"Mark," in *The New Testament from 26 Translations.* Grand Rapids: Zondervan, 1967.

Review of *The Greek New Testament,* by Kurt Aland, Matthew Black, Bruce Metzger, and Allan Wikgren, *Christianity Today* 11 (6 January 1967), pp. 29–30.

1968

A Short Life of Christ. Grand Rapids: Eerdmans, 1968.

Review of *The Gospel According to John,* by George Turner and Julius Mantey, *Eternity* 19 (1968), p. 54.

Review of *The Gospel of Luke,* by G. B. Caird, *Eternity* 19 (1968), p. 50.

Review of *The Gospel of St. Mark,* by D. E. Nineham, *Eternity* 19 (1968), p. 50.

1969

Review of *God in the New World,* by Lloyd Geering, *Christianity Today* 13 (28 February 1969), p. 36.

Review of *Layman's Answer*, by E. M. Blaiklock, *Christianity Today* 13 (28 February 1969), pp. 36–37.

Review of *The New Testament Speaks*, by Glenn Barker, William Lane, and J. Ramsey Michaels, *Eternity* 20 (1969), p. 43.

1970

Review of *A New Testament Commentary*, edited by G. C. D. Howley, F. F. Bruce, and H. L. Ellison, *Christianity Today* 14 (3 July 1970), p. 24.

1971

Colossians: Christ All-Sufficient (Everyman's Bible Commentary). Chicago: Moody Press, 1971.

"The Tradition of the Sayings of Jesus," in *Toward a Theology for the Future*, edited by Clark Pinnock and David Wells. Carol Stream, Illinois: Creation House, 1971.

Review of *Witness and Revelation*, by James M. Boice, *Eternity* 22 (1971), pp. 43–44.

Review of *New Testament History*, by F. F. Bruce, *Eternity* 22 (1971), p. 51.

1972

"The Resurrection of Jesus Christ in the Book of Acts and in the Early Christian Literature," in *Understanding the Sacred Text*, edited by John Reumann. Valley Forge: Judson Press, 1972.

"A Modern Chapter in Church History," *Opinion* 12 (October 1972).

1973

"Antinomianism," "Chastening," "Contentment," "Forbearance," "Gentleness," "God," "Humility," "Kindness," "Longsuffering," "Patience," "Self-Control," "Temperance," "Tranquility," in *Baker's Dictionary of Christian Ethics*, edited by Carl F. H. Henry. Washington, D.C.: Canon Press; Grand Rapids: Baker Book House, 1973.

"Did Christ Command World Evangelism?" *Christianity Today* 18 (23 November 1973), pp. 6–10.

1974

"Acts 22:3—A Test Case for Luke's Reliability," in *New Dimensions in New Testament Study*, edited by Richard Longenecker and Merrill Tenney. Grand Rapids: Zondervan, 1974.

1975

Acts: The Expanding Church. Chicago: Moody Press, 1975.

"Jesus Christ," in *Zondervan's Pictorial Bible Dictionary*, edited by Merrill Tenney. Grand Rapids: Zondervan, 1975.

"1 and 2 Corinthians," "Galatia," "Herod," "Jesus Christ," "John, the Apostle," "John, the Gospel," "John, 1, 2, and 3, Epistles of," "Julius," "Lycia," "Pavement," "Philemon," "Philemon, Epistle to," "Romans, Epistle to," in *Wycliffe Bible Encyclopedia,* edited by Charles F. Pfeiffer, Howard F. Vos, and John Rea. Chicago: Moody Press, 1975.

"The One Ministry of Our Lord," *World Vision* (June 1975).

1976

"Romans," in *The Expositor's Bible Commentary,* edited by Frank E. Gabelein *et al.* Grand Rapids: Zondervan, 1976.

Forthcoming

The International Standard Bible Encyclopedia. Revised Edition. Edited by G. W. Bromiley *et al.* Grand Rapids: Eerdmans. Editor for the New Testament and author of many articles.

Index of Modern Authors

Index of Scripture References